Real Estate Finance
and Development

Casebook in Real Estate Finance and Development

J. Miller Blew
Harvard University

edited by
A.E. Washburn

Scott, Foresman and Company
Glenview, Illinois   Boston   London

Library of Congress Cataloging-in-Publication Data

Blew, J. Miller.
    Casebook in real estate finance and development / by J. Miller
Blew ; edited by A.E. Washburn.
        p.   cm.
    ISBN 0-673-38348-2
    1. Real estate development—Finance—Case studies.   I. Washburn,
A. E. II. Title.
HD1390.B64 1989
333.7'2—dc19   88-24996
                                                       CIP

To Carol,

"O Loyal to the royal in thyself,
And loyal to thy land, as this to thee --"

TENNYSON

ACKNOWLEDGMENTS

Acknowledgments

This casebook has been helped immeasurably by many people over the course of more than a decade. Both institutions and individuals have contributed, and Editor A.E. Washburn and I thank all sincerely. While we cannot possibly include everyone, we must specifically thank the following.

Dean Gerald McCue of the Harvard Graduate School of Design played a major leadership role. Dean McCue's consistent support for curriculum development in real estate, as well as financial support, provided the inspiration and institutional base for *Real Estate Finance and Development*. Dean Maurice Kilbridge of the Graduate School of Design and Dean Burton Malkiel of the Yale School of Management also contributed significantly. The Urban Land Institute made an important early financial contribution to real estate studies at the Graduate School of Design, as well as to case research and teaching nationally.

Professor Peter Walker, former Chairman of the Department of Landscape Architecture at the Graduate School of Design, gave me the opportunity to teach. His enthusiasm for real estate and land development education are unsurpassed. Professor Howard Stevenson, the Sarofim-Rock Professor of Business Administration at the Harvard Business School, inspired me to teach and provided many of the conceptual underpinnings of this work. He demonstrated the importance of reaching out to all the professions involved in real estate. Dr. C. Roland Christensen, Robert Walmsley University Professor of Harvard, showed me how to teach. And last, but certainly not least, Professor Philip David of M.I.T. and Harvard, who wrote the first casebook, and Professor William Poorvu, Harvard Business School, pioneered and developed to a high art case research and teaching in this field. Two of Bill Poorvu's cases (Savannah West and Costa Mesa) are included here, but no case course in real estate can possibly be complete without others of these gentlemen's classic cases.

40 High Street and Masonic Hall were written by Geoffrey Smyth who is my partner in one office development and is now Vice President at Cabot, Cabot and Forbes. Joey Kaempfer was funded, as was Parcel 1B, in part by the Urban Land Institute of Washington, D.C. Mr. Washburn and I would also like to thank Mr. J.W. Kaempfer, Jr. and members of his firm for their help and commitment to education. Savannah West was written by John Vogel, who was research associate at the time, under the direction of William Poorvu. John Vogel is President of the Neighborhood Development Corporation of Jamaica Plain, a non-profit developer, and he teaches Real Estate Finance and Development at the Graduate School of Design.

The introduction to Part II, Capital for Real Estate, was influenced by research done by Peter Aldrich and Richard Kopcke. Park Place was written with the assistance of research associate Michael Spies. Financial Accounting in Real Estate and Organization and Taxation were reviewed by a number of generous professionals, most recently Dennis Fusco of Seidman & Seidman, Boston. Zayre Headquarters Tract was enriched by the work of several students, especially research associate Michael Brooks. We would like to thank Dick Reynolds and Jack Griefen for their consistent support and many classroom appearances.

Brea Specialty Center is by John McMahan, Lecturer in Business Administration at the Stanford University Graduate School of Business. He is President of John McMahan Associates, Inc. of San Francisco. Location, Design and Market Analysis was written with the assistance of research associate Paul Mehlman. Dean Gerald McCue, Professor Jonathan Lane of the Harvard Graduate School of Design, and Professor McMahan all contributed to this note. Chadwick Lead Works would not have been possible without the contributions of Bob Yelton and Harry Standel, principals of The Bay Group. Mr. Washburn and I wrote The Warner Theatre Project.

In addition I would like to thank Sally Baer, Tom Berkenkamp, Michael Bryant, Robert Gifford, Richard Graf, Glen Koorhan, Marianna Knottenbelt, and Ken Wong for their past case research, and Paul Mehlman and teaching assistant David Sun for their work in assembling and presenting the graphic material. For

her help through the years, we give sincere thanks to Francesca Shakespeare.

All of the above contributions would not have resulted in publication of this work. What was needed was the energy, enthusiasm and dedication of editor A.E. Washburn. We got it done, and I am grateful.

Before closing, one further acknowledgment is necessary. These cases and notes have been refined and proven over the course of several years' teaching, and therefore, I owe a debt of gratitude my students.

J.M.B.

PREFACE

Preface

This book attempts an impossible task. In a collection of 23 text sections and case examples, it will try to teach the art of real estate development -- what it takes to get started, to succeed, and, perhaps most difficult, to stay successful in a fantastically challenging and rewarding profession.

Written by a teacher who is also a successful developer of office buildings, the book is aimed at students at graduate professional schools as well as working professionals who want to be real estate developers. These people will often be starting or advancing careers as principals, general managers, project managers, or development planners. Others who will read this book will be individuals in business, the design professions, law, public administration, engineering, construction, and other related fields, who want to learn how their special knowledge and skills can contribute to the developer's success.

This book takes a comprehensive approach to real estate development. In addition to notes covering many technical subjects, it features a number of case studies on developers and their projects. Nearly all of the cases represent actual real estate development situations that occurred since 1978, a period of rapid and dramatic change in real estate practice. Reading and thinking about the problems faced by these real developers leads to a broad, non-technical perspective, well suited for today's complex and evolving real estate environment. The technical notes provide a base of fundamentals and technical background necessary to understanding the developer's art. But most of the lessons to be learned are in the cases.

The author, J. Miller Blew, is Adjunct Professor of Real Estate Development at the Harvard University Graduate School of Design. At Harvard, he developed a course, Real Estate Finance and Development, on which this volume is based. Mr. Blew also founded the Real Estate course at the Yale University School of Manage-

ment, where he was a visiting faculty member. He has given numerous short courses for professional audiences and for educators.

Mr. Blew's academic work draws heavily on his experience as a private real estate developer. He is President of Bulfinch Development Corporation of Boston, a commercial real estate development and property management firm. Under his leadership, the firm has built a substantial reputation through a series of downtown office developments in New England.

While it does stress practical applications and successful examples, this book is not intended to be a catalog of unchanging truths. The fundamental tenet of this book is that real estate today is a world of constant change. Indeed, a format for a successful project may become a format for a very unsuccessful project in just a few years time.

More than anything else, this book is based on faith in the *individual*. It is a casebook, full of real-life examples, developments guided by real people. The rules of real estate development can and will change; the leadership provided by the developer will be the constant. However much research and analysis may be done, however much marketing, design and financial sophistication may be involved, after all is said and done, the process requires leadership and judgment.

That leadership and judgment are provided by the individual developer drawn to this dynamic field. The goal of this book is to lend experience through the cases and thereby show the determined individual the possibilities. For some, the drive will be for wealth; for others, artistic satisfaction. But for all, this field offers the satisfaction of a life of hard work, where that work results in a different and better environment.

A.E.W.

CONTENTS

Contents

PART I
THE REAL ESTATE DEVELOPER

In this Part I, we will become acquainted with the real estate industry and its participants. We will introduce income property and property held or developed for sale. We will examine closely the role of the entrepreneur and the basics of financial analysis. Cases will feature a variety of land uses -- high and low density housing, as well as office -- and both new and rehabilitation construction.

THE CHANGING WORLD OF THE REAL ESTATE DEVELOPER

Risk and reward set the real estate developer apart from the rest of American industry. By the nature of what they do, developers operate at the margin, conceiving unbuilt realities and venturing their capital and energy toward an uncertain future. For taking these risks, successful real estate developers have made great fortunes and great reputations.

Yet the rules of the game are changing. What worked for James Rouse or Gerald Hines in the 1960s and 1970s cannot simply be repeated today. New rules govern how the next generation of real estate developers will operate and, to a great extent, who will succeed and who will fail over the next twenty years. In this brief introduction, we will look at both the developer and the changing world.

The Real Estate Developer

Most of the people employed in the real estate industry are concerned with the ordinary operations and maintenance of existing real property or with its orderly transfer to new ownership. These aspects of real estate are not unlike other industries. Employees engaged in these activities enjoy job security, solid compensation, and regular opportunities for advancement.

But that is only part of the story. Real estate also means building, and building, by its nature, is entrepreneurial. Any new building or rehabilitation, no matter how conservative in design or situation, represents an entrepreneurial risk. It is a change in the physical environment and depends for its success on a complex economic and regulatory environment. In real estate, the agent of change is the developer.

The real estate developer's primary role is to give a project a sense of strategic purpose. He or she must serve as the focus of the development. Much like the conductor of an orchestra, the developer must be prepared to take responsibility for the entire enterprise, while at the same time guiding and shaping the many different elements of the development process.

Development Decisions. In essence, the developer's role is to relate the *people* and the *property* involved in a project to an appropriate *financial structure* over time. This process involves a great number of decisions, large and small, which must be made over time. A conceptual framework[1] for these decisions may be visualized in the accompanying table.

Decisions about people, property, and financial structure are, of course, interrelated, and their successful resolution demands a centralization of purpose. The skilled developer has a sense of vision about property, the ability to ignore the present and to see instead the potential future. This sense of vision provides the unifying element on which the many decisions may be based.

When property is to be developed, decisions are focused in eight broad areas which often overlap in time:

Acquisition, the choice and control of a piece of land, is the first step, although other activities and decisions may precede this.

Organization of the human resources necessary for the project is, in the minds of many developers, the most important step.

Design decisions follow. The developer not only selects the

---

[1] The author is indebted to Professors Howard Stevenson and William Poorvu of Harvard Business School for their teaching and encouragement over the past fifteen years and for their contribution to the basic ideas contained in this framework.

appropriate architects and engineers for the job, but also guides carefully the design process.

Approvals are sought and obtained, often from multiple regulatory agencies.

Financing involves preparing budgets and establishing a working relationship with a set of lenders or investors.

Construction decisions center on the choice of contractor and the contractual relationship entered into, as well as the myriad technical issues to be resolved.

Marketing decisions must be made regarding brokers, incentives, and promotional tactics.

Property management includes decisions about the many services

Conceptual Framework for Real Estate Decisions

PEOPLE	FINANCIAL STRUCTURE	PROPERTY
Who are the people involved and affected?	What are the sources of funds? - Venture capital (seed money) - Construction Debt - Permanent Debt - Equity - Operating income	What is the present use and ownership of the property?
What are their objectives and time horizons?		What are the potential uses considering: - Location - Physical condition - Market demand - Regulatory controls - Encumbrances
What are their resources and limitations: - Personal skills - Education - Professional qualifications - Capital - Time and energy	Are these funds adequate and appropriate for the project?	
	What is the form of ownership and how does this determine: - Allocation of risks - Control	What are the capital costs? - Acquisition - Construction - Indirect
What organizations do they represent?		What is the timing of capital expenditures?
How are they organized with each other? - Organizational form - Personal relationships	What are the financial benefits for whom and when are they realized: - Cash flow - Tax savings - Capital appreciation	What are the cash income projections over time?
What commitments are they prepared to make?		How does the capitalized value of the income stream relate to the capital costs?

DEVELOPMENT PROCESS			
-Acquisition	-Organization	-Design	-Approvals
-Financing	-Construction	-Marketing	-Property Management

which may be provided to users of the completed property.

We will look more fully at the development process in Part IV, but the brief listing here should underscore an important point -- the developer must be a "Renaissance" person. The developer's position at the center of decision making demands expertise in all the fields relating to the project. Though the developer is not a designer, he or she must have both vision and the ability to communicate it. The developer is not a financier, but must stay a step ahead of financing brokers, investors, and mortgage lenders. The developer is not a construction manager, but must be able to judge how something should be built. The developer is responsible for everything, and responsibility means risk. He or she must have the confidence to face that risk.

The *sine qua non* of any developer is confidence, and with it, the willingness to take the lead. There is simply too much risk involving too many decisions for the self-doubter to operate in a timely fashion. "Lead, follow, or get out of the way!" is an appropriate motto for many. The developer's confidence is inevitably tied to an optimism about himself or herself and the world at large. He or she must deal daily with a constantly changing set of obstacles and must relish negotiating them. Development does not discriminate on the basis of race, sex, creed, or color; it does, however, discriminate on the basis of confidence, ability, and willingness to take risks.

But the developer, though a risk-taker, cannot afford to be cavalier. Because he or she has ultimate responsibility for a project, anything left undone, unresearched, unanalyzed or unresolved, may result in a mistake. A mistake could mean anything from a cost overrun to a failed project, and in the end it is the developer and his or her career that pays. It is in the developer's interest to be thorough.

The Developer's World

The world in which the developer competes consists of a complex and diverse industry -- really a great many separate industries. Real estate in the United States is very different, however, from other industries. Important to developers are a number of special characteristics.

Real estate is big business and represents a major form of wealth. To comprehend the magnitudes involved, consider this:

> The population of the United States, some 241 million people, occupies more than 91 million housing units. The average value of those units is $55,000 today. The value of residential real estate alone is therefore on the order of $5 *trillion*. (Source: U.S. Census Bureau)

The sums are enormous, yet the scale of enterprise may be exceedingly small. Barriers to entry are minimal at the smallest scale of the real estate business.

The real estate industry is *diverse* in its business enterprises. It involves hundreds of thousands of small business entities, which employ millions of people. But every large corporation must also of necessity participate in real estate, if only as a tenant in rented facilities. Every family and individual must also participate, of course, and the goal of home ownership is ubiquitous in this country.

The organizational forms are often quite *complex*. Real estate organizations include partnerships and joint ventures, as well as corporations, trusts, and proprietorships. Public or private, large or small, real estate enterprises depend on *individuals*. The track record of an entrepreneur is often of much more importance than the organization's holdings. Will the Rouse Company, a large, publicly-owned corporation, or Gerald D. Hines Interests, a large proprietorship, be the same after their founders' eventual retirements?

Real estate is a *risky* business. The industry is highly *cyclical* and reacts quickly, often dramatically, to changes in the prospects of the national economy. The industry relies heavily on *borrowed money*, which presents the risks of volatile interest rates and possible unavailability of new funds.

These risks of financial leverage are compounded by those of cyclicality. Companies engaged in selling real estate or in holding property for income often find widely fluctuating markets for their products. Financial results will also vary widely.

At the same time, the real estate industry is *regulated* in many ways. Local, state, and national laws regulate the use of land, parking provisions, density of development, standards for construction, access and safety features, energy systems, and many other aspects. Rents and sales prices are sometimes controlled.

Products of the industry are varied and have a *long production cycle* compared with typical industrial enterprises. Yet, the product lasts a very long time and is *fixed* in its *location*. Large capital investment transactions are the norm in real estate; these are the exception in the manufacturing enterprise.

The Changing World

Because each new development faces an uncertain future, the industry has always been highly exposed to external economic and environmental changes. In the United States, the period since 1978 has produced substantial changes at a very rapid rate. As a result, the practice of real estate development today is radically different from that of the post-World War II period. Two of the most important areas

of change are *interest rates* and the emergence of *new products and markets*. These changes are structural and very likely permanent. For the remainder of this century real estate developers and their organizations will be adapting to these new realities.

Interest Rates. Interest rates in the 1980s have generally been higher than in previous years, and they continue to be so. The accompanying graph shows the movement of representative interest rates since 1967. The residential mortgage rate roughly approximates the cost of capital for prime real estate development ventures. As can clearly be seen in the graph, 1978 marked the end of an era of generally lower and relatively stable interest rates. This was what was termed the "Golden Era" of lending, where bankers lent by the "3-6-3" rule (corporate loans at 3%, home loans at 6%, golf at three o'clock).

Why did this era end? The most commonly accepted reason is that interest rates had to be higher in order to offset the rate of inflation. Inflation is not a new idea, of course. What is new is the apparent vulnerability of the U.S. economy to inflation -- even inflation caused by external events, such as the Middle East oil shock -- and the difficulty of controlling inflation for any extended period of time in a free enterprise economy. Our expectations about the likelihood of *future* inflation have changed.

Inflation may well remain at modest levels for a time. With this have come lower interest rates, or at least lower *short-term* interest rates. The problem is that real estate depends on *long-term* financing and long-term interest rates, once comfortably low and stable, today remain stubbornly high. The change to which the real estate developer must adapt is the likely continuation of this. Once the *possibility* of high inflation has been accepted, the expectation is unlikely to be reversed. Lenders have learned their lessons and are no longer willing to provide the kind of low fixed-rate long-term financing that used to get everyone to the golf course by three o'clock.

Developers must now choose from many differing types of financing. If they want to avoid high rates for long-term financing, they have to be content with short-term or variable interest rate financing, or long-term financing with equity participation features of various kinds, or they will have to put more of their own equity funds into their projects. Furthermore, the simple relationship between borrower and lender, prevalent until 1979, is gone forever. What was once usually a very simple agreement specifying an interest rate, a schedule of repayments, and sometimes a small penalty for prepayment, is now a complex legal document covering numerous business issues and contingencies.

New Products and Markets. As the interest rate environment has changed, so have the real estate products being developed. One major economic effect of high interest rates generally is to reduce long-term investments -- such as real estate -- relative to shorter-term investments and consumption expenditures. Thus, the real estate projects that can be postponed often are. This means that older facilities remain in service longer. Rehabilitation and

Prime Rate, Treasury Bill Yield, and Residential Mortgage Rates

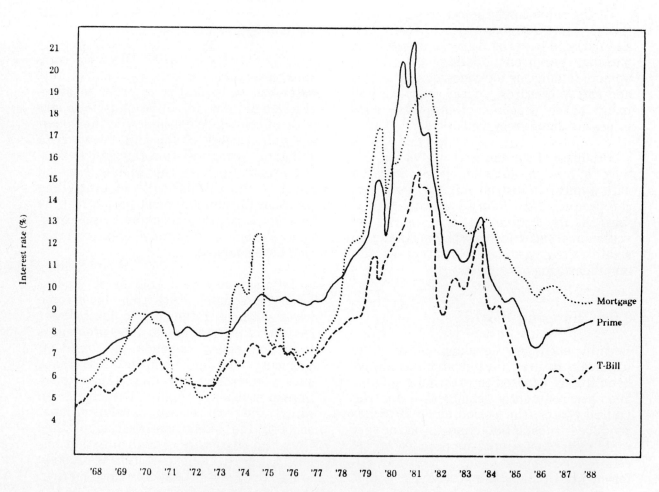

more intensive use of existing properties are therefore encouraged.

Major differences have been felt among the various sectors of real estate. Housing, for example, has experienced, and is continuing to experience, reduced levels of investment relative to the past and to the general economy. The general tendency among the population is to consume less housing, although housing is nevertheless costing more. It is also likely that new housing being developed will become physically more efficient.

These trends are dramatically affecting the housing development industry. In the last few years, inflation has caused a big runup in prices of existing housing stock, especially in coastal regions. This has enriched many who are homeowners relative to those who are renters. Combined with the high cost of financing and the concurrent slackening of new construction, this phenomenon caused sharply-reduced housing mobility in the population generally. For rich or poor, owner or tenant, it is now almost always easier -- and often essential -- to stay put, rather than move. Many new housing investments are thus being postponed.

Housing developers are therefore targeting those who cannot postpone their investments -- the young working people, primarily -- and those who will invest anyway -- the upper income population. Hence are emerging new housing products aimed at these markets. Some examples are condominium conversion of existing apartments with widely varying amounts of physical rehabilitation, new houses with much reduced floor areas, cluster and multiplex condominium designs, amenity-based planned unit developments, etc. The luxury market is continuing to attract investment.

It is the lower-income groups for whom no new investments are being made. These people must therefore remain as tenants in the lower quality existing

housing stock. The likelihood of government assistance significantly offsetting this trend has been much reduced. Governmental housing programs are seen to suffer from the same problems of escalating costs, in the face of scarce financial resources, which affect the private housing investment picture. What little government assistance there is is becoming the responsibility of local governments and will be sporadic at best.

Although the picture for low- and middle-income housing development is gloomy, opposite tendencies may be observed in other real estate sectors. If a business enterprise is prospering in the current environment, its real estate needs *must* be met, regardless of cost. Accompanying the high costs, there is a tendency towards greater concern for design and construction quality. For example, the typical high technology firm must compete for highly skilled technical personnel. To retain these people, this kind of firm must provide a high quality, efficient and attractive work environment. Such a firm often decides to invest in exercise facilities, a cafeteria, and works of art for the common areas, rather than build the cheapest type of industrial or office space. There are many more examples of this trend. One need only tour some suburban business parks to see the sharply higher general level of quality compared with that of the 1960s and early 1970s.

Other Areas of Change. The two areas considered above are closely related. High costs of capital for long-term investment will be with us for the rest of the century. Real estate products and markets are adapting. But during the same brief period since 1978, many other important structural elements of real estate development have also changed:

Financial institutions have become predominant sources of capital for development. As economic uncertainty has increased, larger pools of capital have been attracted to real estate for its inflation-hedging characteristics. A national effort aimed at providing retirement income through pension funds has led to dramatic growth in investments by them in real estate. Large pools of foreign capital also invest in U.S real estate in hopes of preserving asset values. Real estate-based investment products are being offered to the world capital markets.

Regulation has greatly increased. Environmental protection has become a national priority. New laws have given federal, state, and local agencies the responsibility to protect clean air, water, coastal resources, historic resources, and open space, and to regulate extractive industries, hazardous waste disposal, and other aspects of real estate development. Other areas of regulation, including consumer protection, banking regulation (and de-regulation), and securities law each have their consequences for real estate.

Taxation of real estate investment has become an area of considerable volatility and future change. Once thought to be subject only to very infrequent change, the federal tax code has been altered radically and frequently since 1976. These efforts for a time had the general purpose of encouraging long-term investment in an inflationary period through the use of tax incentives. However, the 1986 tax re-

form seems to have completely reversed many tax policies, some of them in effect for only a few years. What the future holds is unknown, of course, but it now seems likely that a process of annual revisions to the code will continue as legislators try to keep up with the economy and the unforeseen effects of previous tax changes.

The changes discussed in this Part all directly impact the practice of real estate development today. Many other areas of change, seemingly at the periphery of real estate, are having their own impacts as well. For example, the microcomputer revolution -- the dispersal of small, powerful computers to ever lower levels of business organization -- has an important effect. Building operations -- cost control, energy and security, in particular -- are being computerized. Financial decisions are evaluated by computers, and market data is becoming more widely shared.

CONCLUSION

Change has become the norm in the developer's world. Adapting to change presents enormous opportunities to the young developers who are prepared to undertake the challenge. New real estate products must be invented and marketed. New financing techniques must be found. New building technologies must be proven, and new organizations must be formed with the skills to develop responsible projects in this changing world.

Case 1

40 High Street

Jeff and Mary Benington were concerned. A week previously they had for the third time signed a Purchase and Sale agreement on 40 High Street, a Victorian rooming house in Charlestown, Massachusetts. This time they had paid a non-refundable deposit of $10,000 against the purchase price. They were due to close in one week and were now unsure if it were wise to do so. By now, January 1982, Jeff and Mary had been involved with the property for six months and wondered whether it would ever result in a good personal and business deal.

OBJECTIVES

Having lived for several years in rental apartments, Jeff and Mary had concluded that paying rent was not building them any capital. Nor was it providing any tax benefit (mortgage interest payments, unlike rental payments, would be tax-deductible). Jeff was a graduate of a well known eastern business school who had been working for three years in the real estate industry. Mary was an architect with experience in rehabilitation projects. With their joint income of $80,000 they now wanted to own their own home.

Jeff also hoped that their financial objectives might be met as part of a larger real estate development. Perhaps a property could be acquired and converted into several smaller units either for sale as condominiums, or as rental units additional to their own. He thought this would be good experience and improve his personal track record in real estate. He thought that there were many ways he and his wife could add value to a project -- they had experience with design and construction, and both felt willing to undertake part of any work themselves. Further, they had savings of $40,000 available, which they thought should be ample equity for their purposes.

Jeff and Mary had chosen Charlestown as a location after extensive discussion and research on the alternatives. Both of them worked in downtown Boston and wanted to avoid a long commute. They believed Boston's urban revitalization would continue and would provide increased appreciation in real estate values in the inner urban areas. Jeff felt that the pressure of demand would inflate values in urban areas more rapidly than in suburban locations.

LOCATION

There were several neighborhoods close to downtown Boston which Jeff and Mary had examined. They toured the districts both during the day and at night. They researched the characteristics of the population, using the most recent census data available. They bought the local papers for each district, talked to friends who lived there and studied the public transportation and available parking in each area.

Beacon Hill was the most prestigious area, closest to downtown, but it was very densely developed and expensive. The Back Bay was another very desirable residential area, but here the properties were large, often six stories or more, and most had already been rehabilitated for rental or sale. In both Beacon Hill and Back Bay, condominium developers had caused significant escalation in prices of buildings for residential rehabilitations. Jeff did not believe he had sufficient resources to compete in these locations.

The South End was adjacent to Back Bay and seemed to offer greater possibilities. As a residential area, the South End had early been surpassed by the Back Bay and had a multi-ethnic population with typically lower family incomes. Recently, however, the district had experienced a degree of "gentrification" with buildings and even entire blocks being rehabilitated into higher rent apartments. Although the housing stock available was less expensive and on a smaller scale than Back Bay or Beacon Hill, Mary was concerned about getting to and from downtown, and Jeff was not sure about the potential for escalation in values compared with other districts.

The last district which Jeff and Mary examined and rejected was the North End, a predominantly Italian community sandwiched between downtown and Boston Harbor. Although the area had great charm and an excellent location, it was very densely built and had severe parking problems. Furthermore there were very few buildings on the market, since buildings tended to pass from one owner to another without ever becoming available to the public.

CHARLESTOWN

Finally, Jeff and Mary considered Charlestown, a community just across the Charles River from downtown Boston. Although it was part of the city, it retained its own distinctive community identity. The identity derived from its stable, traditional Irish lower and middle income population, its architecture, and from the physical barriers of the water and expressway ramps which separated it from its neighbors. The settlement of Charlestown actually pre-dates Boston, and its dominant landmark is the Bunker Hill Memorial, which celebrates the British victory over the rebels in 1775. The hilly topography and the lengthy evolution of the town fostered a great variety in the area's residential buildings, a mix of brick and timber houses from one to six stories in height. Many of the houses were extremely well built, since Charlestown had been a wealthy residential area in the 19th century.

Although there had not been the same degree of recent investment in Charlestown as had occurred in Beacon Hill and Back Bay, Jeff thought that this might favor achieving their objectives. There appeared to be ample housing stock available in a variety of states of repair. The area closest to Bunker Hill had enjoyed the greatest degree of investment, although not always with the support of the indigenous community. In that area, there were many examples of modernized single family houses, rental apartments, and, very recently, condominiums.

Jeff and Mary investigated the district thoroughly. It was served with excellent public transportation, with two bus routes providing five minute travel to Boston, in addition to a newly modernized subway stop connecting to downtown. Although the elevated expressways were an eyesore, they provided excellent auto access. While run down and shabby in parts, Charlestown had received considerable investment from government funds in the 1970's. As a result, there were new sidewalks and numerous trees. Though in some streets parking was tight, the relatively low population density, compared with the Back Bay, made parking relatively easy.

Main Street, which ran along the west side of the town was the principal retail street. Jeff was concerned that many of the retail units were vacant, even those in a new mall which had been constructed a few years earlier. On the other side of town were the "projects" -- subsidized housing developments which had a bad reputation in the community. Jeff realized that they should carefully scrutinize the immediate location of any property they might buy. Some streets, while having beautiful houses, backed onto the expressway, and therefore these properties were offered at a discount. One fine house they were shown was opposite a liquor store. When Mary complained that drunks hung around outside the store, the broker explained that they only had that problem for half the day since the drunks moved to the other side of the store when the sun moved around in the afternoon!

THE SEARCH

The *Boston Sunday Globe* was the principal vehicle for advertising residential real estate. Jeff found that there were four brokerage firms who regularly advertised properties for sale, sometimes on an exclusive listing basis. He contacted all four brokers to find what they had for sale and what advice they had to give him. Since Jeff and Mary did not know exactly what they wanted or how much they could afford, the brokers were not always very helpful, and wished to show them properties all over town, not just in desirable locations. They were surprised at how unsystematic the brokers typically were. One broker, Joel Gibson, appeared to have more property listed than the others and provided them with information on recent sales.

One problem was the diversity of building types, which made objective comparisons among properties difficult. Jeff compiled a list of what he thought were key variables: location, size, price, brick or timber, size of yard, off-street parking potential, multi or single-family zoning, views, state of repair. Mary went to Boston City Hall and bought a 1:100 map of the town. As they became familiar with each street, they could identify properties in which brokers were trying to interest them and build up information additional to that supplied by the brokers, such as asking price per square foot.

One thing quickly became clear: it was going to be difficult for Jeff and Mary to buy an already operational apartment property. The reasons for this were that the apartment layouts generally did not satisfy their personal requirements, and the prices were generally too high for them. A four-unit apartment building, for example, grossed perhaps $2,000 per month or $24,000 per year in rental income. From this were deducted such expenses as heating, electricity, common area cleaning, insurance, maintenance, replacement reserve and real estate taxes. These might total $10,000, leaving a net income after vacancy and collection losses of about $12,000 per year. But the asking price for the building would be $150,000 or more. This would mean a cash return on asset cost of only 8%. Jeff thought this a low return and wouldn't come close to covering his interest costs.

It appeared to Jeff that the market values reflected other factors than rental cash flow and were being inflated by owner occupants and the potential for condominium conversion. If the example building were 4,000 square feet at $150,000, its price would be $37.50 per square foot. A condominium developer would then spend $20 to $25 per square foot to modernize and market the space as condominiums and then sell at $75 per square foot, which was about the current market price for condominium sales. If successful, this would yield the developer a reasonable profit margin on the transaction.

Jeff and Mary were shown apartment buildings which could be converted into condominiums, but none had what they considered a suitable unit for themselves. They concluded that they could not readily add value to a property that was already operating efficiently. They could best create value in a project by being patient and buying from an anxious seller at a discount price or seeing physical potential in a property where others could not. They could also contribute "sweat" equity by participating in the design, construction and management of the project and by carefully controlling costs during development.

40 HIGH STREET

One day in July 1981, Joel called wishing to show them 40 High Street. He said that Jeff and Mary shouldn't expect too much, since it was an old Victorian rooming house, and was still occupied. As they edged around the piles of clothes and picked their way past decaying food, they both began to feel that the property had potential. They thought they could hardly fail to add value here.

40 High Street had been built as a family home in the mid 19th century. Most of the original detail was intact, including marble fireplaces, gilt mirrors and some elaborate ceiling mouldings. The floors, underneath linoleum, were oak. The home was a four-story detached brick structure, and its lot had a vehicular access to a yard at the rear. Because the ground fell away to the rear, the ground floor was partly below grade at the front. The main entrance was at the first floor level, a few steps up from the street. The property was superficially very run down and cluttered with debris. The house did have storm sashes, however, and the roof areas, according to the owner, had been replaced and insulated six years before. There were two small run down kitchens and one bathroom on the second floor. At some stage, the owners had installed a bathroom on the ground floor (existing floor plans are shown in Exhibit 1).

There were two new 150 amp electrical services to the property, as well as gas, but the wiring in the house was quite old. The boiler was oil fired, and the oil bill for the preceding year had been $5,000. According to the neighbors, with whom Jeff and Mary spoke, 40 High Street was the only house on the block that never had to sweep snow off the sidewalk -- the excess boiler heat simply melted it off! There was one soil stack in the building, which connected through the front of the house to the sewer in the street.

As Jeff and Mary continued their inspection, they concluded that 40 High Street was structurally sound. Many of the windows had even been replaced a few years previously. The joists on all floors ran from side wall to side wall. The base-

ment was dry, and there appeared to be no sign of termites or rot. There was one feature which Jeff and Mary had seen in other Charlestown houses -- the main staircase ran from the front door at the first floor up to the third (top) floor, but there was a second staircase, back to back with the main stair, connecting the second floor to the ground floor. In addition, an external fire stair had been installed at the rear of the building. Jeff thought that these various staircases offered the opportunity to subdivide the building for a multi-unit rehabilitation. The roof areas of the second floor rear and the third floor front were flat and could be turned into roof decks with fine views of the Boston skyline.

The asking price was $95,000 for some 4,200 square feet. Jeff and Mary were definitely interested, but wanted some time to think it over. Although they were still not sure what approach to take in rehabilitating the property, they called Joel two days later and said they would take it. They were too late, though, Joel told them. The property was already under agreement to a local developer, Sean O'Sullivan, who was planning to convert the property into four condominiums.

Jeff and Mary were disappointed, but continued looking for properties over the next two months, finding nothing as well-suited to their needs as 40 High Street. Driving regularly past the property, they were somewhat surprised that there was no evidence of construction to be seen. Mary called up Joel to ask him what was going on. Joel called back excitedly to report that Sean was thinking of canceling the project and might be willing to re-sell it to them for $110,000. Jeff and Mary, although shocked that their two days of indecision had cost them $15,000, agreed to the price and asked Joel to prepare a Purchase and Sale agreement within the week.

PLANNING THE PROJECT

The next few days were hectic. Jeff and Mary realized that there were several alternative strategies they could follow, providing four, three, or two units. Four units would be one per floor, three units might be the top and ground floor as apartments with the first and second as an owner's duplex. They could also have a two unit configuration -- a triplex and a flat.

There were alternative investment strategies as well. They could sell extra units as condominiums, thereby reducing their investment, or they could rent them out. After due consideration, they decided on a rental strategy. This appeared to be simpler and had the advantage of providing them with additional tax deductions from interest on a larger mortgage and from depreciation deductions on the rental units. They would also be able to retain full control over the property, rather than have to depend on other unit owners to agree on and carry out maintenance expenditures.

Since the house was presently zoned as a rooming house, and had potential for parking in the rear yard, they foresaw no problem in having it down-zoned to rental apartments. However, they were unsure of how long a zoning change might take and how it would impact their financing. Jeff thought that maybe the Purchase and Sale agreement should be made subject to a change in zoning.

It was clear that all the period features in the house should be retained, since the recent interest in historic preservation had caused such elements as marble fireplaces and wood mouldings to be highly valued. Although Mary believed that they were seldom used, working fireplaces were also appreciated by tenants, and she asked Jeff to determine which of the flues were still functioning. Sound isolation between the units would be important, especially

since Jeff and Mary intended to live in the building. Lastly, new mechanical and electrical systems would permit equitable apportionment of the utility costs as well as energy efficiency. They thought that apartments which had these characteristics would not only rent up faster, but would achieve premium rents. Jeff discussed these alternatives with Joel, who provided useful comparables for the rents which might be achieved for each unit. Joel was enthusiastic about the alternatives, and seemed eager to find tenants.

FINANCING

It was important for Jeff and Mary to ascertain how much financing they could obtain on a project. Jeff phoned several banks to ask about the availability and terms of mortgage financing. Some banks had no money to lend on a long-term basis at any price. Others were not prepared to lend money against a rehabilitation project and pointed out to him that before the property would qualify for a long-term mortgage loan, it would first have to be rehabilitated using an interim construction loan. Jeff and Mary were rather disillusioned about all this. They had not realized that financing the project would be so complicated and that banks were wary of lending to anyone without either a track record or an established relationship with them. Finally they found that the First National Mortgage Corporation (FNMC) was prepared in principle to lend both interim and permanent financing. The interim financing would cost 2.5% over the prime rate, and a fee of 1% of the loan amount would be charged. The prime rate was at 20.5%.

On the permanent loan, FNMC was able to commit to a loan, but only at the interest rate prevailing on the actual day of the loan closing. At present, their rate was 17.5%, but there was no certainty of what the rate would be when they actually closed the loan. The loan term would be

30 years. The maximum amount that FNMC would provide could be calculated by adding Jeff and Mary's personal income to the income they planned to receive from rentals, then allocating 28% of that against the total of mortgage debt service payments, real estate taxes and real estate insurance. Furthermore, the bank's appraiser would have to examine the property and satisfy himself that the combined value of the property and any renovations proposed would be 125% of the loan amount. These criteria were quite firm, since most mortgage notes were re-sold by the lender in a secondary market or to "Fannie Mae," the Federal National Mortgage Association. These secondary buyers could not, obviously, ascertain the soundness of the notes they bought in bulk unless the primary lender applied a stringent and consistent screening to each individual note.

Given that they had $40,000 of their own to put into the project, the required value to loan ratio of 125% meant that they could afford a project costing up to $200,000. The 28% rule would then need to be applied. This would determine what their mortgage payments could be and therefore the mortgage amount for any given interest rate.

CONSTRUCTION

Meanwhile, Jeff had been trying to determine how to build the project and how much it would cost. He asked several friends who had had work done on their houses how they had gone about it and how much the various items had cost. There were alternative ways of running a construction job, from being your own general contractor and hiring all the subcontractors and direct labor, to contracting for a fixed price from a general contractor (G.C.). Many people urged Jeff to do the job himself, thereby saving the G.C.'s profit and overhead. But Jeff wondered whether he would really have time for this or be able to find competent subcontractors. He also realized that there was a close relationship between some of the trades -- if the electricians did a messy job of re-wiring, it might double the work of re-plastering. He saw that a G.C. providing constant supervision would have an incentive to minimize the work. Of all the trades, the heating, plumbing, and electrical would be the most important, with plastering and painting next. In addition, the project would need floor finishers, carpet layers, and various other specialized trades.

After much deliberation, Jeff and Mary decided on a building program of three units. The top floor would be a one bedroom unit of 800 square feet with the living room opening onto a roof deck. They would occupy the next two floors themselves in a large duplex of 2,000 square feet with two baths, two bedrooms and a study on the second floor, and living room, dining room, kitchen, and a half bathroom on the first floor. Because the main staircase served the top floor rental unit, it could not effectively be used by them too, so they developed a plan retaining the rear staircase for their own use and making a new passage down the middle bedroom to comply with building codes. The ground level unit was to be a one-bedroom-plus-study unit with its own side entrance. The new heating and electrical equipment would be installed in the unlit portion of the ground floor. They also thought that if they could not afford to finance the ground floor unit now, they could defer the work and finance it later out of savings.

Jeff had found two builders, one of whom had been referred to him by Joel and the other by the consultants whom he had retained to design the heating and plumbing system. He had met both of them, and shown them around the building, along with their plumbing subcontractors. After these discussions, and his earlier research into construction costs, he prepared his construction budget (see

Exhibit 2). The major line items were the plumbing and heating and the electrical, which would be subcontracted by the G.C., and the work which the G.C. would do himself, in which he included the G.C.'s profit and overhead allowance at 10%. He felt that other specialized trades he could bid and organize himself, thereby avoiding the G.C.'s markup. He allowed a contingency of 5%.

Jeff continued developing a capital budget (see Exhibit 3) by tabulating his estimates of the indirect costs which would be associated with the project. Legal fees were estimated by the bank and by his attorney. Boston City Hall told them how much the building permit fee was likely to be. Real estate taxes on the property were presently $2,400 a year and would be unlikely to increase. They therefore allowed a budget for taxes for the five months it would take to construct.

They knew that with the prime rate at 20.5%, their interim financing would be at 23% (interest only), carried for the five months until it was replaced by the permanent loan. The average amount borrowed during that period was estimated at 50% of the total loan, which looked to be around $139,000. When all the costs including buying the property were added together, the total came to almost $180,000.

Next Jeff and Mary worked out the impact of financing on the proposed development. They calculated their expected gross incomes, including the rental of the apartments, (see Exhibit 4). Joel had given them an estimate of the rent they could charge for the apartments, together with estimates of the operating expenses, such as heating, electricity, cleaning and maintenance for which he had comparables from other buildings. They were dismayed to find that the bank's formula expenses were greater than 28% of their gross income. This meant that although they were investing $40,000 of their own

money into a total project costing about $180,000, and therefore qualified under the 125% value to loan ratio requirement, they could still not qualify for the loan under the bank's present criteria. Not only that, the mortgage payments--principal and interest--would total over $2,038 per month, and would have to be paid even if the apartments were not rented.

Jeff and Mary decided that the project was not feasible and reluctantly called Joel to tell him that they were unable to proceed with signing the Purchase and Sale agreement.

ROUND TWO

Over the next two and a half months, Jeff and Mary continued searching for a property. Since the per unit price of 40 High Street was comparable to the market, they wondered how anyone could make a development work. In October they were surprised to receive another call from Joel, who told them that Sean was still interested in selling the house, and that they could have it for $95,000. They were both excited and set about re-working the budgets and pro formas. They decided to also consider a lower cost program with a rental on the top floor and the basement vacant.

When the other financial analyses were complete, the deal looked feasible, but tight. Jeff asked his attorney to draw up a P & S for signing on Friday. The P & S provided for a 30-day closing with a financing contingency. But as closing approached, they had still not received their loan commitment. FNMC said there was some problem in including Jeff's bonus in their calculations, but that it would be satisfactorily resolved.

After several more false starts, they finally realized that FNMC was not going to make a loan. Jeff called his lawyer and, rather embarrassed, told him that they couldn't proceed with the purchase.

THE FINAL ROUND

Several weeks went by, but Jeff and Mary could not stop thinking about the project. Deciding to try again, Jeff went to see the Bank of New England to see whether they would finance the project. The construction loan officer there had been a branch manager in Charlestown and knew the district well, and liked both the property and the location. He also knew Jeff's company well since they had been banking with the Bank of New England for years. Jeff presented the same information to them as he had to the FNMC, only by now so much time had passed that he and Mary had saved a further $10,000. Furthermore, the prime rate had dropped to 18%, and the bank's mortgage department would offer a permanent mortgage commitment at 17.25% rather than the 18% expected from FNMC. This would mean annual payments of 17.40% of the loan amount for principal and interest.

Mary had found out that Sean's other condo projects were not selling and that he was anxious. She had also found out that he originally purchased 40 High Street for $93,500. Although he thought it was a long shot, given their history with 40 High Street, Jeff called Joel to say that he had received a verbal financing commitment from the Bank of New England and could close the deal in two weeks if the price were dropped to $90,000. Sean and his attorney were wary, but had still been unable to sell the building. Clearly, Jeff and Mary were committed to it since they had been pursuing it for so long. Sean agreed to sign a P & S, but only on condition that a non-refundable deposit were given, of $10,000.

A written commitment for a construction loan had been received, but Jeff and Mary still had only verbal assurances that they could get a permanent loan. However, since the total development cost had now been reduced to $150,000, and they only needed a loan of $100,000 for the two units, they decided to go ahead. Within three days, they had all their financing commitments in place and had signed the P & S and parted with their $10,000. Mary then pursued the zoning variance through City Hall and the Fire Department, and Jeff started chasing contractors for their formal prices.

It was ten days before closing. Jeff had been working closely with two contractors over the past four months, but they had become a little confused with the change from three to two units, leaving the ground level unconverted, and they also found the drawings rather complicated. On Sunday night, Jeff went to the local builder and was shattered to be told that the job would cost over $80,000. Panic struck, he called the other builder, who confirmed that the price for his work was $67,000 which when added to the owner's subcontracts totaled $73,000. Jeff and Mary's budget was $52,000.

Jeff offered to pour Mary and himself a stiff drink, but in a state of some emotion she declined. Half in tears and half in joy, she told him that she was pregnant! Jeff reached for the bottle.

EXHIBITS

1.   Existing conditions plans.

2.   Construction cost estimate.

3.   Project capital budget.

4.   Bank financing formula.

QUESTIONS FOR DISCUSSION

1.   Should Jeff and Mary complete their purchase of this property?

2.   Does the property fit their personal needs?

3.   How would you evaluate their search process and their planning of the project?

4.   Why is the seller selling?

5.   Who are the other participants in the process, and what are their roles?

Exhibit 1

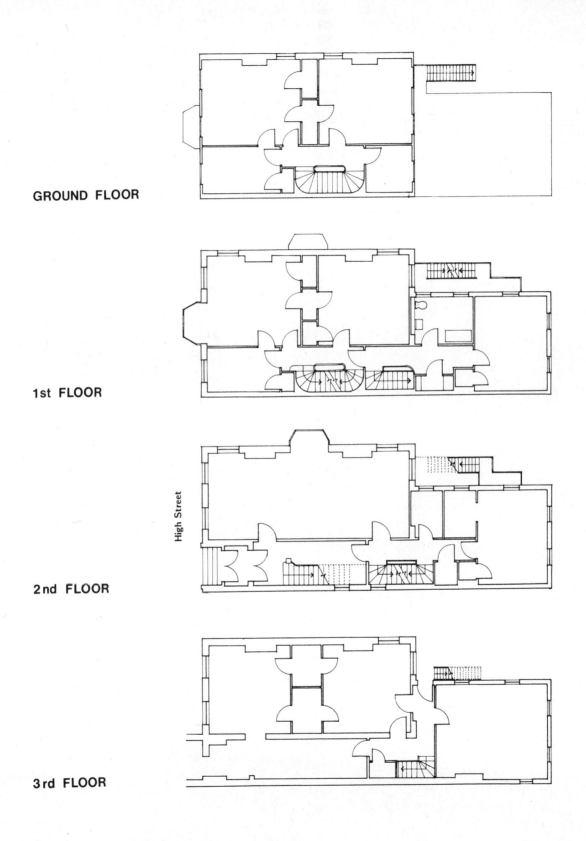

GROUND FLOOR

1st FLOOR

2nd FLOOR

3rd FLOOR

High Street

Exhibit 2

CONSTRUCTION COST ESTIMATE

Program: Rehabilitation into three units

Subcontracts let by G.C.:
Heating and plumbing	$17,000	
Electrical/Lighting	8,000	

		25,000

General Construction:
Demolition	2,000	
Plastering after subcontracts	3,500	
Carpentry/floor repairs	2,500	
Drywall	2,500	
Door overhaul	1,250	
New Thermopane doors: 1A	1,000	
3B	1,200	
Install kitchens: Grd	400	
1st	500	
3rd	400	
Roof deck	750	
Window overhaul	250	
Concrete	500	
Gutters/downspouts/roof repair	400	
Bathroom finishes: Grd	600	
1st	400	
3rd	600	

		18,750

Subcontracts let by Owners:
Lead paint removal	300	
Extermination	100	
Kitchen unit supply: Grd	600	
1st	800	
3rd	600	
Carpet: 156 sq. yd. @ $16	2,500	
Exterior painting	2,500	
Interior painting	2,500	
Chimney cleaning	100	
Floor sanding and sealing 1666 sf @ $.60	1,000	

		11,000

Subtotal	54,750
Contingency @ 5%	2,738

Total construction cost	$57,488

Exhibit 3

PROJECT CAPITAL BUDGET

Acquisition	$105,000
Total Construction Cost	57,488

Total Direct Cost	162,488
Indirect Costs:	
Architectural and Engineering fees	1,600
Legal fees	1,600
Loan application fee (Permanent)	350
Building permit	1,230
Real Estate taxes during construction (5 months)	1,000
Interim loan interest (139K estimated @ 23%, 50% average balance for 5 months)	6,660
Interim loan fee (1% of estimated $139k)	1,390
Permanent loan fee (2.5% of estimated $139k)	3,475

Total Development Cost	$179,793

Exhibit 4

BANK FINANCING FORMULA

Gross Revenue:

Personal Income	$80,000
Gross Rent from 3rd Floor Unit	8,400
Gross Rent from Grd Floor Unit	6,600

	95,000
x 28% (Bank Formula)	$26,600

Formula Expense Budget:

Debt Service ($139K, 35 yrs, 17.5%)	24,381
Insurance	1,500
Real Estate Taxes	2,400

	$28,281

This note is the first in a series on real estate financial topics. In it we will introduce the basics of Static Financial Analysis.

Nearly all real estate development and investment decisions are made in reliance on relatively simple and straightforward approaches to financial analysis. These are generally based on static or present day conditions and do not consider explicitly the effects of changes over time. Students of financial analysis should master these basics first, before considering more complex approaches. Once the static financial analysis is complete, it may then be useful to consider financial projections over time. The ubiquitous microcomputer has made this very popular in recent years, and this type of analysis is examined in a subsequent note, *Discounted Cash Flow Analysis*. For now, as is the practice of most developers, we will stress the basics -- *numbers that can be worked on the back of an envelope*. This note contains three sections:

Section I presents the basics of capital budgeting for the real estate development or investment. The **capital budget** is used to determine the required investment for a project and as a baseline for measuring the value added by the developer.

Section II presents the basics of income analysis for rental property. The **setup** or pro forma statement of pretax cash flow is the basic real estate financial statement. The Setup is used to assess the value of income property investments and the effects of their financial structures.

Section III presents a series of **valuation and return measures** commonly used in the real estate industry. These measures are used to determine the value of real property, assess the feasibility of projects and measure the results of particular investments.

I. THE CAPITAL BUDGET

To be successful, the real estate developer must control the capital costs of the project. Even in the case of a simple cash purchase of a piece of property, there will always be costs over and above the nominal purchase price of the transaction. Developers and their financiers must be able to estimate the total investment that will be required. Such an estimate, called a capital budget or project cost budget, will typically be drawn up at the early stages of a project and updated frequently as time goes by. The major categories of the capital budget include **land and acquisition costs**, **building construction costs**, and **indirect development costs**.

Land and Acquisition Costs

To the real estate developer, land is a commodity. Land is one of many raw materials which, together with labor, are used to produce the finished real estate product. In some situations, land is itself the product -- mobile home parks, parking lots, agricultural land, etc. -- but in most urban settings, the raw land must be developed before it can be used. The value of land thus depends on both the value of its eventual use and the cost of development for that use.

Land may be carried in the capital budget either at its cost or at its market value. For most purposes, the value of the land is the more relevant figure. If a developer can sell land for a profit above costs and instead chooses to develop the land, the foregone profit should clearly be considered a part of the developer's investment. Hence, the full value of the land should be included in the capital budget.

Value of land is often increased during the early stages of a project. Approvals may be obtained, such as rezoning or subdivision approval, which increase or make certain the development rights of the land, thus increasing its market value. Land value will sometimes increase merely by the passage of time or by the effect of increased demand or reduced supply in the relevant market. Land value may also be increased by physical improvements -- the installation of roads and utility systems, for example.

Accordingly, the capital budget may reflect the cost of all of the components of final land value. These might include the costs of obtaining approvals; carrying costs, such as interest and operating expenses, property taxes, landscape maintenance costs, etc.; and land development costs. Land development costs must sometimes be allocated between the costs of developing a particular site and those attributable to a larger project. For example, in a large scale Planned Unit Development (PUD) or New Town, land development costs may include townwide costs, sector costs and subdivision costs, in addition to those attributable to a particular lot. In addition to roads and utilities, the cost of amenities and common facilities may be included as land development costs.

No matter how elaborate the cost-based analysis may be, developers should also consider the value of the land. At times, the value of a finished lot may turn out to be less than the cost of producing it. This is an unfortunate fact which many residential developers learn each time there is a cyclical decline in the residential market. Normally, of course, the finished lot should be worth more than it costs.

Acquisition costs will normally include the land, but will often also include improvements such as buildings and related site improvements. Normally, the price in any transaction has been negotiated between buyer and seller to reflect the aggregate of all components of value. Often the buyer will need to make an allocation of the cost between components. This may be done variously by estimating the cost of the components or appraising their market value. Property tax assessments may also provide a basis for allocation.

Other acquisition costs are often included in the capital budget. These might variously include real estate brokerage commissions, legal fees, the costs of an engineering inspection, and the costs of obtaining a loan, title insurance and other "closing" costs. The cost of insurance policies and property taxes, prorated between buyer and seller, may be included, as may the estimated costs to carry and/or operate the acquired property for some period of time.

As noted above, the land and acquisition cost budgets may include both actual historic costs and proposed future costs. Additional land parcels or buildings may be acquired; land development costs may be needed; and substantial carrying costs may be incurred. Each of these should be included in the capital budget.

Building Construction Costs

Control of building construction costs is often the most central problem facing the real estate developer. Estimates of probable construction cost must be drawn up at the very beginning of a project. Costs must be monitored continuously over time as designs are developed and construction contracts let and administered.

The initial cost estimate for the project is a simple budget allowance based on the scope of the project. This will usually be a cost per square foot of building, or in the case of a residential project, a cost per dwelling unit. Most architects, contractors and developers are able to put a rough cost on a project based on construction type, number of stories, urban or suburban location, and the timing of the project. Naturally, these initial costs are only approximations, accurate within perhaps 10-15% one way or the other.

The next level of cost estimation involves considerably more research. Techniques of professional estimators vary widely, but a common frame of reference is useful. The Uniform Construction Index (UCI) provides a standard trade breakdown, in effect, a chart of accounts for construction. The UCI system is used by the American Institute of Architects, the Associated General Contractors of America, and the Construction Specifications Institute. The table below lists the major standard categories of construction.

UCI Work Classifications

1. General Requirements
2. Site Work
3. Concrete
4. Masonry
5. Metals
6. Wood and Plastics
7. Moisture-Thermal Control
8. Doors, Windows & Glass
9. Finishes
10. Specialties
11. Equipment
12. Furnishings
13. Special Construction
14. Conveying Systems
15. Mechanical
16. Electrical

The construction contractor normally will base his estimates on the areas of trade or subcontract specialization. Some subcontracts will cover more than one of the UCI classifications; other classifications will be further subdivided according to the specifics of a particular job. Hence the contractor will often modify the standard captions as the estimate is developed.

Published sources are available to provide guidance in developing cost budgets. One of the best known sources is the Robert S. Means Company, which publishes annually updated cost information from computerized files. Means' prototype cost model for a typical suburban office building is presented for illustration.

COMMERCIAL/INDUSTRIAL INSTITUTIONAL	2.460	Office, 2-4 Story

Model costs calculated for a 3 story building with 10 foot story height and 58,000 square feet of floor area

NO.	SYSTEM/COMPONENT	SPECIFICATIONS		UNIT	UNIT COST	COST PER S.F.
1.0 FOUNDATIONS						
.1	Footings & Foundations	Poured concrete; strip and spread footings and 4' foundation wall		S.F. Ground	2.79	.93
.4	Piles & Caissons	N/A		—	—	—
.9	Excavation & Backfill	Site preparation for slab and trench for foundation wall and footing		S.F. Ground	.69	.23
2.0 SUBSTRUCTURE						
.1	Slab on Grade	4" reinforced concrete with vapor barrier and granular base		S.F. Slab	2.42	.81
.2	Special Substructures	N/A		—	—	—
3.0 SUPERSTRUCTURE						
.1	Columns & Beams	Fireproofing; interior columns included in 3.5 and 3.7		L.F. Floor	17.40	.47
.4	Structural Walls	N/A		—	—	—
.5	Elevated Floors	Open web steel joists, slab form, concrete, columns		S.F. Floor	5.59	3.73
.7	Roof	Metal deck, open web steel joists, columns		S.F. Roof	2.64	.87
.9	Stairs	Concrete filled metal pan		Flight	3915	.47
4.0 EXTERIOR CLOSURE						
.1	Walls	Face brick with concrete block backup	80% of wall	S.F. Wall	17.64	4.10
.5	Exterior Wall Finishes	N/A		—	—	—
.6	Doors	Aluminum and glass, hollow metal		Each	1840	.19
.7	Windows & Glazed Walls	Steel outward projecting	20% of wall	Each	360	.91
5.0 ROOFING						
.1	Roof Coverings	Built-up tar and gravel with flashing		S.F. Roof	1.62	.54
.7	Insulation	Perlite/urethane composite		S.F. Roof	1.08	.36
.8	Openings & Specialties	N/A		—	—	—
6.0 INTERIOR CONSTRUCTION						
.1	Partitions	Gypsum board on metal studs, toilet partitions	20 S.F. Floor/L.F. Partition	S.F. Partition	2.50	1.21
.4	Interior Doors	Single leaf hollow metal	200 S.F. Floor/Door	Each	445	2.23
.5	Wall Finishes	60% vinyl wall covering, 40% paint		S.F. Surface	.83	.66
.6	Floor Finishes	60% carpet, 30% vinyl composition tile, 10% ceramic tile		S.F. Floor	2.68	2.68
.7	Ceiling Finishes	Mineral fiber tile on concealed zee bars		S.F. Ceiling	3.38	3.38
.9	Interior Surface/Exterior Wall	Painted gypsum board on furring	80% of wall	S.F. Wall	2.62	.61
7.0 CONVEYING						
.1	Elevators	Two passenger elevators		Each	57130	1.97
.2	Special Conveyors	N/A		—	—	—
8.0 MECHANICAL						
.1	Plumbing	Toilet and service fixtures, supply and drainage	1 Fixture/1320 S.F. Floor	Each	1067	.81
.2	Fire Protection	Standpipes and hose systems		S.F. Floor	.15	.15
.3	Heating	Included in 8.4		—	—	—
.4	Cooling	Multizone unit gas heating, electric cooling		S.F. Floor	7.44	7.44
.5	Special Systems	N/A		—	—	—
9.0 ELECTRICAL						
.1	Service & Distribution	1000 ampere service, panel board and feeders		S.F. Floor	.59	.59
.2	Lighting & Power	Fluorescent fixtures, receptacles, switches and misc. power		S.F. Floor	4.95	4.95
.4	Special Electrical	Alarm systems and emergency lighting		S.F. Floor	.14	.14
11.0 SPECIAL CONSTRUCTION						
.1	Specialties	N/A		—	—	—
12.0 SITEWORK						
.1	Earthwork	N/A		—	—	—
.3	Utilities	N/A		—	—	—
.5	Roads & Parking	N/A		—	—	—
.7	Site Improvements	N/A		—	—	—
			SUB-TOTAL			40.43
	GENERAL CONDITIONS (Overhead and Profit)				15%	6.06
	ARCHITECT FEES				7%	3.26
				TOTAL BUILDING COST		49.75

BUILDING TYPES

Source: R.S. Means Co., 1987

Note that this cost model is broken down on the basis of building systems, rather than trades, another common approach to estimating.

Cost estimates focus primarily on quantities and unit costs. The construction contract incorporates these two variables, plus a third very important variable -- quality. Without an understanding of quality, of course, no cost estimate or budget can be of much value. Quantities generally are spelled out in drawings prepared by an architect; qualities are specified in written construction specifications, also normally prepared by the architect. Price, as well as schedule, terms of payment, and other details are specified in the contract text itself. All three items -- the contract, the drawings, and the specifications -- are needed. These are referred to collectively as the "contract documents."

Not all costs can be specified at the outset of construction. Construction contracts will usually distinguish between "core and shell" or "base building" costs and "tenant finish" costs, which are not finally determined until later in the process. In speculative commercial projects, the final configuration of spaces and selections of finish materials must await decisions by the actual tenants. The construction contract will normally provide "unit prices" for standard finish materials and a budget allowance, but tenants and landlords will often modify these substantially to meet particular tenant needs. In some markets, landlords will use generous tenant finish allowances as incentives to attract tenants.

In retailing, particularly, tenant requirements vary widely. For this reason, retail space is often leased on a "shell" basis, that is, the tenants will invest in their own internal construction. In office development, above-standard tenant work is quite normal among the higher-rent types of tenants. Cost-sensitive tenants are more likely to remain within the standard cost allowance, but will, of course, configure the space to their own requirements. In hotel development, substantial allowances for furniture, fixtures, equip-ment and decoration must be included in the capital budget, as well as the usual construction costs.

Indirect Costs

The third major area of the capital budget is that of indirect development costs, the so-called "soft" costs of the project. These costs are no "softer" than any others, of course, but this term is sometimes used to distinguish them from the "hard" costs of acquisition and construction. Five types of indirect costs are encountered: professional services; financing costs; carrying costs; general and administrative costs; and profit centers.

Professional Services. These costs include the fees and associated expenses of various categories of professionals -- design professionals, including architects, landscape architects, space planners, mechanical, electrical, structural and civil engineers; lawyers, typically required to prepare purchase and loan transactions, contracts and lease documentation; accountants and appraisers, if required; and real estate brokers or leasing agents.

Financing Costs. These costs include fees to lenders, investors and brokers for providing financing. Costs related to the financing transaction usually include legal and other "closing" costs similar to those incurred in an acquisition transaction. Lenders and investors often require independent appraisals and engineering inspection services during construction as well. Multiple loans and fees may be involved. Where the construction loan is to be replaced by a permanent loan from another source, two sets of fees and closing costs will be required. Costs related to other forms of financing, such as equity investment, may also be budgeted.

Carrying Costs. These costs include costs incurred during the development period to operate and finance the property. Operating expenses include those charges for real estate taxes, insurance, security and utilities during the construction period. Interest on project financing is usually a major cost factor. An important consideration is the carrying cost *after* construction is complete. Developers should allow for the cost of operating expenses, real estate taxes and debt service during the period of rent-up, when the building is finished, but not fully occupied. These costs may be offset by early rental income. Many capital budgets will carry an item called "rent-up deficit" or "deficit to breakeven." Others will simply calculate an overall interest budget on the basis of a longer time period. (Note: see Part II: "The Setup" for a more complete discussion of mortgage and debt service payments.)

Example: Mr. Holliday's office building renovation project is to be financed with a $1 million construction loan, which he can extend to a five year term. Interest will be at 2% above the prime rate. Mr. Holliday expects the project will take eight months to complete construction and will rent up to breakeven occupancy in twelve additional months. Ignoring the effects of any operating expenses, his calculations of carrying costs would thus include two components:

1. Construction Period Interest: If the initial loan advance were $200,000 for acquisition, and if the remainder is advanced at a steady pace, the average loan balance during the construction period would be approximately $600,000; if the prime rate remained constant at 10%, interest would be 8 / 12 x .12 x $600,000 = $48,000.

2. Rentup Deficit: If rent payments began immediately upon completion and increased at a steady pace, the income would offset 50% of the interest cost for the rentup period. Thus, if the prime interest rate continued at a constant 10%, the net carrying cost would be .5 x 12/12 x .12 x $1,000,000 = $60,000.

Since interest rates are not likely to be so steady, Mr. Holliday might also want to include a safety factor in his capital budget. He could attempt to make precise forecasts of exactly how the interest rates might vary and when various tenants would begin to pay rents. (If he were very good at this, of course, he should consider speculating in money market futures contracts.)

Note that the effect of allowing a longer time period would be roughly equivalent to allowing a higher average interest rate. Mr. Holliday would avoid making *both* estimates "conservative," however, because this would produce an unrealistically high budget.

General and Administrative Costs. So called "G&A" costs or developer's overhead costs are often contentious items in the project budget. Many lenders and investors take the view that projects should not budget for such costs or should provide only minimal allowances. Nevertheless, these costs are real. For larger projects, developers must provide a project manager and staff support over an extended period of time. The salaries, fringe benefits and office overhead costs may be quite substantial. For the principals of even a small development firm, the value of alternative uses of their own and their staff's time should be considered part of the project cost.

Profit Centers. A final area of the capital budget may be treated in a wide variety of ways. The individual preparing the budget must decide whether or not to include profit margins in various components. Depending on what capabilities a particular developer may have "in-house," he or she may reasonably expect to make a profit from construction, design, brokerage and financing services, as well as allowances for G&A and possibly a gain in the value of the land. Developers may also profit from annual fees for property management functions. Each of these sources of profit might be in addition to the profit attributable to the development itself.

Whether these items should be considered as "costs" or not depends on the type of project and the purposes to which the capital budget will be put. For example, in a very small project, it would be unusual for more than one source of profit to be available. Small residential developers often construct their own projects, making a single profit for their combined roles as builder and developer. For a major project, however, the developer could certainly hire a third-party general contractor, and the capital budget would thus be expected to carry a normal profit for the value of this service, regardless of who does the work.

In any event, every project capital budget should either provide an entrepreneurial profit directly, or alternatively the project must produce a significant annual income. Projects that fail to do either are unlikely to attract sufficient financing from lenders or investors to be built.

II. THE SETUP

The "setup" is the standard real estate income statement. The setup is a pro forma statement of annual pre-tax cash flow. For income-producing real property, as distinct from property held or developed for sale, the setup provides a standard for determining value and for relating value to the associated capital costs. The setup normally includes the following major elements.

Gross Potential Income
- Vacancy Allowance

= Effective Gross Income (EGI)
- Operating Expenses
- Real Estate Taxes

= Free and Clear (Net Operating Income)
- Debt Service

= Cash Flow After Financing (CFAF)

The setup is a **pro forma** statement. That is, it is prepared for a typical future or "stabilized" year, usually the first or second full year of operations. The setup does *not* normally reflect "actual" results. The setup may contain elements of actual cost experience for a property, but is normally drawn up to show expected (or hoped-for) results.

A developer's setup, like his or her capital budget, is a planning tool. Thus it may be updated frequently during the development period. A developer's setup may also be a selling tool, drawn up to accentuate the positive elements of a particular development.

The setup is generally calculated on a pre-tax basis. Tax consequences are important to real estate owners, so the tax effects in the pro forma year may be presented as a supplement to the setup. Since tax laws change and change frequently, however, *pre-tax* cash flow remains the industry standard for measuring the value of the income stream. Elements of the setup listed above are discussed in the following sections.

Gross Potential Income

The setup begins with the rent schedule. Rentals are generally quoted on a per square foot or per dwelling unit basis. Rents are paid according to terms of a **lease**, a contract which provides the tenant (lessee) the right to use property owned by another (lessor). Under a long-term lease, rents may be contractually fixed and bear no relationship to the present market. For shorter-term leases or new space being rented up, rent levels will depend on the market.

Rent levels in the market generally will depend on supply and demand for various types of property. Whether for office or retail space, hotel rooms or rental apartments, an over-supply of space in the market will lead to downward pressure on rents; conversely, low vacancy rates in existing space will generally lead to increases in rent levels and eventually to new development projects being built.

When vacancies are low and rent levels high, new development becomes economically feasible. The newest project in any market will generally require the highest rents. As development costs have escalated in recent years, further upward pressure on rents has been experienced. Although owners may blame the need for higher rents on increased costs, rental levels depend ultimately on the market. When demand for space is great relative to supply, rent levels tend to increase, offsetting fully any normal level of costs. On the other hand, when demand is slack, rentals may not increase at all and may even decline, no matter what the costs of producing new space may be.

Both research and judgment are required to determine appropriate pro forma rent levels for new space. The best information to seek is detailed data on comparable and competitive properties within a market area. Data on comparables can be generated from newspapers, real estate brokers, and trade publications, or by asking owners and tenants in the market. Considerable research effort may be needed to obtain a complete picture of market conditions. From this base, one must judge whether the rents are likely to increase, to remain at the historic levels experienced by the comparable properties, or possibly to decline. Although they may be buttressed by elaborate market studies, these judgments are made typically on the basis of experience in the market.

Under favorable circumstances, a developer's setup may carry a pro forma rent level which is higher than that observed currently in the market. The most likely circumstances are:

1.   continuation of a trend, as rental increases continue under tight market conditions; and

2.   the result of superior quality or location or an underserved market niche, as compared with other properties.

The more unusual situation, but one with considerable profit potential for real estate investment, is the anticipation of a major change or discontinuity in the market. Examples are investments made in anticipation of rapid suburban growth, neighborhoods becoming fashionable, a major public investment, such as a highway, or a major new employer entering a market. Negative discontinuities are also possible, however, and markets may spiral into decline.

Rental income is not always the sole source of income in the setup. In the hotel business, for example, food and beverage income represents a major portion of the income stream. In urban areas, parking is often an important source of revenue. In residential developments, income from laundry and vending machines may be significant, as may income from amenities such as golf and tennis facilities. Income from services provided to tenants of office buildings, shopping centers and industrial parks may also be significant, although it is unusual for these services to contribute a substantial profit. Whenever revenues of this type are included in the setup, care must be taken to include all associated costs.

Vacancy Allowance

The building owner does not normally expect to receive 100% of the Gross Potential Income. The amount actually received is the Effective Gross Income (EGI). The difference between scheduled and effective incomes reflects rentals *not* collected due to periods of vacancy, losses due to bad debts, and possible collection costs, as well as rebates and rental concessions for tenants. The standard method for reflecting such losses in the setup is the vacancy factor or allowance. Most commonly, a percentage allowance is used.

In speculative multi-tenant office, retail and residential setups, vacancy allowances normally range from 3% to 8%, with the most commonly used figure being 5%. A vacancy allowance below 3% should be considered suspect. Even in the case of a ten-year lease, a four month vacancy period to find a new tenant and renovate the space results in a 3% overall vacancy experience.

There is only a very limited relationship between the appropriate vacancy allowance in the setup and the overall vacancy in the market. Generally, when market vacancy levels are high, the vacancy in any particular building would also tend to be high; the reverse is also true. However, there is no reason at all for the two figures to be identical. A 14% market vacancy rate usually means several buildings are standing empty for a time. Most buildings therefore are experiencing lower than a 14% vacancy, while a few have a much higher rate. Conversely, if the overall vacancy is a very low 1%, most individual buildings will have no vacancy.

Where high vacancy levels are being experienced, they may reflect special market circumstances, such as seasonal, short-term or high-turnover occupancy, for example. Occasionally this may also reflect serious problems -- poor quality or overbuilt markets, etc. Where low vacancies are being experienced, of course, landlords will normally raise the rents, which will tend immediately to increase turnover and vacancy losses. The setup should reflect this long-term reality, rather than the temporary low vacancy allowance.

As noted above, overall market vacancy data is not a direct indicator for selecting a vacancy allowance for a setup. However, market vacancy data is very useful in estimating future trends in rent levels. Trends in vacancy rates over time are also useful in gauging the relationship of supply and demand within the market.

Many published sources may be consulted for vacancy and rent level information in local market areas. Surveys are often published by trade associations, local Chambers of Commerce, and by brokerage firms interested in particular markets. Among the national sources, *National Real Estate Investor* magazine provides frequent local area reviews and *Real Estate Analyst* provides historical data series for many markets.

Operating Expenses and Real Estate Taxes

Once a building is constructed and occupied, the owner's attention shifts to property management and control of operating expenses. Operating expenses and real estate taxes vary quite widely according to property type, tenancy, age and design of structures, climate, and regional and local fiscal policies. In the setup, operating expenses are often lumped together on the basis of a per square foot or per unit allowance. However, as in the case of construction cost estimation, research into the component costs will always be fruitful. Building operating expense categories are as follows:

Marketing Expenses. Marketing expenses are those associated with rerenting spaces on an on-going basis as leases expire. Initial rentup is normally considered part of the capital budget. On-going operating expenses for marketing will include subsequent advertising and promotion costs, staff costs for the owner's employees, and commissions paid to outside real estate brokers. Also important to a successful marketing program is an appropriate program of physical maintenance. For residential properties, property management firms will often include the marketing function in their services.

Property Management. Property management expenses are those associated with day-to-day operations -- rent collection, coordination of maintenance and marketing activities, coordination of services to tenants, and reporting to regulatory authorities and the property owners. These services may be provided by the owner's staff or may be contracted out, normally to a property management firm which has a number of properties under management. Property management fees are normally calculated as a percentage of property income. Other services, including marketing, security and maintenance staff costs may also be included in this category.

Tenant Services. Tenant services will include a variety of services, most prominently cleaning and security. Cleaning service normally includes at least the common areas and exterior facilities. In Class A office space and in the hotel industry, management will also be responsible for cleaning tenant spaces. Security may involve off-hours staffing, electronic off-site surveillance, and other contracted inspection and guard services. The amount of services to be provided by the landlord will vary widely with the type of occupancy. An industrial firm in a single-user building will require none, for example, where luxury office and residential tenants will demand a high level of service.

Utilities. Utilities expense will depend on building type and design, climate, and on the form of lease. Categories of cost include energy costs -- electricity, natural gas and fuel oil -- as well as service and consumption charges for water, sewer, and fire protection which may be customary in the locality. Historically, tenants have been expected to pay their own electric bills, but increasingly in recent years, heating, ventilation and air conditioning (HVAC) systems are being designed also to permit direct charges to tenants. In older buildings, the systems may be fully centralized. Since tenants tend to resist allocations based on arbitrary measures, this puts the owners of older buildings at a disadvantage, compared with newer properties. In older buildings, too, insulation may be inadequate, and mechanical equipment may be inefficient.

Insurance. Insurance expense includes typically a package of fire insurance and owner's liability insurance. The fire insurance will permit damage to be repaired or an entire building to be rebuilt in the event of a loss. Fire insurance can be a major expense, depending on occupancy, construction type, fire safety and sprinkler systems, and location. Owner's liability insurance protects the owner in the event someone is injured in or near the property. The owner's employees will normally be covered by Workman's Compensation Insurance. Other types of insurance coverage may be important in specific situations, including title insurance, mortgage insurance, and insurance for flood and storm damage, loss of rents, theft by employees, death of key employees, and others.

Maintenance and Repair. Maintenance and repair expense includes staff and contract costs for a wide variety of tasks. These costs may include routine painting and redecorating; snow removal, gardening and landscape services; maintenance of mechanical systems, including periodic cleaning, adjustment and repairs of elevators and HVAC systems; repairing roof leaks, drains and plumbing; and relamping. Many other items may be included as well. Maintenance costs depend a great deal on the relative quality and age of the original construction.

Replacement Reserves. Replacement reserves are the only operating expenses in the setup which are calculated on a **non-cash** basis. Instead, an amount is set aside in the setup to reflect the cost of eventually replacing building systems which have a shorter useful life than the building as a whole. Building systems such as roofing, HVAC, carpet and appliances normally have to be replaced every 5-10 years. Expenditures to do this are capital costs and are made irregularly as needed. To offset these irregular expenditures, the setup should carry an annual replacement reserve charge, often calculated as a percentage of rental income. When buildings are offered for sale, maintenance and replacement may have been deferred. Thus the buyer should be careful to adjust the price downward and plan on making the necessary improvements after completing the transaction.

Real Estate Taxes. Real estate taxes, especially in the East and Midwest, are the largest element of the expense budget and are usually listed separately in the setup. Real estate taxes are an annual charge, generally based on the value of property, which is made by units of local government. Value may be determined arbitrarily by local assessment customs or may be based on the market. Knowledge of both nominal tax rates and of local assessment practice is therefore required to estimate the likely tax expense. Local governments may allow below-normal taxes to encourage certain types of real estate investment. These concessions may be specifically permitted under local law or may be the result of informal agreements. Property taxes vary quite dramatically among different localities, depending on the need for government services, availability of other revenue sources, and local traditions.

Examined above are the various items which constitute the operating budget for a property. While these are usually paid by the building owner, both operating expenses and real estate taxes may sometimes be charged to tenants. In a **net** lease, tenants are billed directly for some or all of these costs. In a **gross** lease, the owner is responsible for many or all of them. Many leases now provide **escalation** clauses which specify a base level of expenses and/or taxes which the owner will pay. When costs increase through the term of the lease, the tenant will be billed for the increase. Alternatively, a lease may specify contractual increases in rent or increases tied to inflation as a means of recovering increased operating costs.

Published sources may be useful in establishing operating expense budgets in the setup. Various industry groups provide pooled historical income and expense data, as listed in the table below.

Debt Service

In the setup for income producing property, the net operating income is called **Free and Clear income**. This is defined as gross potential income less vacancy allowance, operating expenses, real estate taxes, and replacement reserves. The income-generating potential of a particular

Sources of Real Estate Operating Experience Data

Property Types	Publications
Residential Apartments	*Journal of Property Management,* Institute of Real Estate Management
Office Buildings	*Office Building Exchange Report,* Building Owners and Managers Association
Retail	*Dollars and Cents of Shopping Centers,* Urban Land Institute
Hotel	*U.S. Lodging Industry,* Lavanthol and Horwath

property depends on the type of property, its location, age and physical quality, market conditions and government fiscal policies in the area, and on the skill of its management. This income will generally *not* depend on who owns the property or how it is financed.

The next step in preparing the setup is to take explicitly into account the method of financing and associated annual costs. Debt service payments may include annual payments on a variety of debt instruments, including mortgage loans, ground leases, master leases, leasehold mortgages, and deeds of trust. Subtracting these debt service payments from the Free and Clear income yields the net cash available for the property owners, called **Cash Flow After Financing (CFAF)**.

The most common form of real estate financing is the mortgage loan. This is a loan to the owner of a property secured by a **mortgage** on the property. The mortgage is a legal instrument which creates a "security interest," a legal claim on the property for the benefit of a lender. The owner "gives" a mortgage to the lender as security for a loan. Hence the lender is the "mortgagee," the property owner the "mortgagor." A mortgage is normally recorded with the deed to the property in the public records of the locality.

A "first" mortgage is a security interest second only to the right of the government to assess taxes, which is called the right of "eminent domain." A "second" mortgage is subordinate also to the interest of the first mortgagee. A subordinate claim takes effect only after the senior claim is fully satisfied. Third and fourth mortgages, etc., will also be encountered. Mortgage loans may be personally guaranteed by the borrower, or they may be **non-recourse** loans. Under a non-recourse loan, the lender has a claim only on the property mortgaged and *not* on other assets held by the borrower. Normally, residential loans are personally guaranteed, while commercial loans will often be non-recourse.

Other forms of security for real estate debt are also encountered. The property owner's legal interest in the property is called the **fee** or "fee-simple interest." Through the mechanism of a long-term lease of the property, such as a "ground lease" or "master lease," the fee interest may be assigned to a lender to provide security for indebtedness. The owner of a leasehold interest may in turn give a mortgage on that interest -- a "leasehold mortgage" -- to another lender. In some states, a loan may also be secured by a "deed of trust." In this situation, title to the property (the legal document evidencing fee ownership) is given to a trustee during the term of the loan in accordance with a trust agreement. Title is automatically returned to the borrower when the loan is retired.

The mortgage loan may have a short or long **maturity** (or "due-date") -- as short as a "demand" note, which is due upon demand of the lender, or as long as forty years or more. Long-term loans are now very common in the United States, but until the government established its programs of loan guarantees following World War II (the Federal Housing Administration and Veterans Administration loans), mortgage loans were rarely made for longer than five years. With the government guarantees in place, twenty, twenty-five, and thirty-year terms became the norm. Today, long-term loans are also insured by private mortgage insurance companies. Long-term loans are still relatively uncommon in the rest of the world.

The most usual provision for repayment of long-term loans is the **constant payment** or "direct reduction" method. Under this type of loan, the borrower pays a fixed amount each year, usually in the form of monthly payments at the end of each month. The payments include interest on the outstanding balance plus sufficient principal to "amortize," that is, pay off, the loan amount over its term. The mathematics of this are complex, requiring a series of approximations. Until about 1980, most practitioners relied on mortgage loan payment tables, but today a financial calculator is normally used.

Given the following variables:

---

i = interest rate per time period
n = number of periodic payments
pv = loan amount

One may calculate the required payment per period (*Pmt* or *K*). (The above abbreviations are standard on most financial calculators.) As time goes by, the outstanding loan balance will decline. As a result, the interest portion of the payment declines. The graph below illustrates this.

For constant payment mortgage loans, interest is not the only factor affecting debt service outlays. For any given interest rate, the longer the term of the loan, the lower will be the required constant payment. Thus the effect of the government guarantee of home mortgages after World War II was to allow lenders at no risk to stretch out the term of the typical mortgage loan. Home-buyers could then buy more expensive houses for the same monthly payments. The table on page 35 illustrates the point.

(Note: This table will serve as a reference for those times the reader is temporarily away from a calculator. Most, but not all, real estate loans require monthly payments. As an exercise to check understanding, you are invited to determine whether the payments in the table are made monthly, quarterly or annually, and at the beginning or end of each period. How significant are these differences? Refer to your calculator handbook and examples for further guidance on this point.)

Increasingly in recent years, commercial loans have reverted to shorter terms. The lender may permit a long amortization schedule to keep the payments as low as possible, but the loan will be due in only five or ten years. These so-called "bullet" loans must be refinanced by the property owner to pay off the still large outstanding balance. Some loans are written with interest payments only. Sometimes payments may be lower than the interest rate; this results in so-called "negative amortization," and the loan balance will slowly increase over time.

Another recent trend is toward **variable** interest rates. These have been popular with borrowers because, for at least an initial period, the required payments are lower than would be those for a fixed-rate loan. Lenders like the fact that rates

Constant Payment Loans: Interest Payment and Amortization

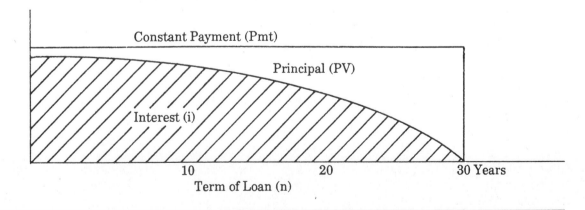

may be adjusted periodically in the event of a run-up of interest rates, so the lender may better be able to cover its underlying cost of new funds. Borrowers are betting their incomes will rise in future years to cover any escalation in rates.

Tax Consequences

So far, we have calculated the property cash flow before financing (the "Free and Clear") and after financing ("CFAF"). This is sufficient for most purposes, but as a final step, investors will sometimes calculate the effect of income taxes on the typical year's return.

In real estate, the difference between cash flow and taxable income is quite substantial and comes from two sources:

1. cash payments which must be made, but which cannot be deducted; and

2. expenses which are permitted for tax purposes, but which do not involve the expenditure of cash.

In the setup so far, we have discussed two items of the first type. Replacement reserves are not deductible as expenses against income. These reserves should be

added back to the cash flow. To the extent replacements have been made, the expenditure should be considered a capital investment, and the costs recovered as depreciation expense (see below). Mortgage principal payments (also called "amor-tization") are also not deductible and should be added back to the cash flow in calculating taxable income.

The second source of tax consequences -- non-cash charges -- is the most important in real estate. **Depreciation expense** represents the consumption of a "wasting" asset over its useful life. Thus, a capital asset (such as a building) will normally have only a limited useful life, and where the asset is held for business or investment, the tax code allows the cost to be recovered as an expense deducted from income. Land is not a wasting asset and is, therefore, not depreciable.

The simplest method of calculating depreciation expense is to divide the cost of the asset by its useful life -- the "straight line" method. Before 1986, the tax code permitted owners, in some situations, to take larger deductions in early years -- the "accelerated" method. Before 1981, there was a wide range of available methods for calculating depreciation. Useful lives could be as short as five years or as long as forty-five years, and several accelerated

Constant Payments (calculated as %)

| Interest Rate | Term of Loan (Years) | | | | |
	15	20	25	30	35
5%	9.49%	7.92%	7.02%	6.44%	6.06%
6%	10.13%	8.60%	7.73%	7.19%	6.84%
7%	10.79%	9.30%	8.48%	7.98%	7.67%
8%	11.47%	10.04%	9.26%	8.81%	8.52%
9%	12.17%	10.80%	10.07%	9.66%	9.41%
10%	12.90%	11.58%	10.90%	10.53%	10.32%
11%	13.64%	12.39%	11.76%	11.43%	11.24%
12%	14.40%	13.21%	12.64%	12.34%	12.19%
13%	15.18%	14.06%	13.53%	13.27%	13.14%
14%	15.98%	14.92%	14.44%	14.22%	14.11%
15%	16.80%	15.80%	15.37%	15.17%	15.08%
16%	17.62%	16.70%	16.31%	16.14%	16.06%
17%	18.47%	17.60%	17.25%	17.11%	17.05%

methods were used. Enterprising owners could also choose to allocate their costs into building "components," to take advantage of shorter allowable useful lives for various building systems.

In 1981, all depreciable real estate was given an arbitrary 15-year cost-recovery period. In 1984, this was increased to 18 years, and in 1985 to 19 years. Only two methods were then available to calculate depreciation. Under the straight-line method, 1 / 19th of the cost of the property was deducted each year. Under the accelerated method, 175% of the straight-line percentage was applied to the then-remaining balance of the cost to calculate each year's deduction. The Tax Reform Act of 1986, however, allows only one method, the straight-line method, and mandates a 27.5-year cost-recovery period for residential-rental real estate and a 30.5-year period for all other rental or business real estate.

Other costs of a real estate development project may be classified as "amortizable" expenses. The concept of **amortization** is similar to that of depreciation, but is applicable to intangible assets. Like depreciation, amortization is a non-cash expense, matching a cost to production of income. For example, brokerage commissions may be amortized over the term of a lease. The costs of forming an organization are amortized over five years. This use of the term amortization should not be confused with the payments of principal on the mortgage.

In summary, calculating taxable income requires the following steps:

     Cash Flow After Financing
 + Reserves
 + Mortgage Principal Payments
 - Depreciation Expense
 - <u>Amortization Expense</u>

 = **Taxable Income**

The alternative approach begins with the Free and Clear:

     Free and Clear
 + Reserves
 - Interest Expense
 - Depreciation Expense
 - <u>Amortization Expense</u>

 = **Taxable Income**

From taxable income, the impact of taxes on a particular owner may be estimated. For individuals, the Federal income tax is calculated as a percentage of income after certain adjustments and deductions. The maximum marginal tax rate is 33% under present law. Local and state income taxes may add to the effective tax rate. Before 1986, an important benefit to owners of real estate was the ability to offset losses from income-producing or business property against income from other sources. Current law has limited the categories of income which real estate losses may offset, however, so any assumptions used in calculating tax effects should be carefully considered.

Once the tax rate assumption is made, the final step is to deduct from Cash Flow After Financing the taxes payable or to add back savings from taxes otherwise payable. The result is the **After Tax Cash Flow** for the property (ATCF).

Tax consequences are rarely presented in a setup unless the intent is to increase the apparent returns. This happens when the property produces negative taxable income and hence positive tax savings from other income. This happens frequently in real estate, but usually only when the property is financed with a high proportion of mortgage debt, which entails high interest costs. Pre-tax cash flow may therefore be relatively poor. Of course, tax savings can be found for any property, regardless of its fundamental quality. Good decisions should not be based on taxes alone.

III.   VALUATION AND RETURN MEASURES

Part I of this note examined the capital budget for real estate development projects and investments. Part II examined the setup, the pro forma income statement for rental property. This final section will review the measures of valuation and return which are commonly used in the real estate industry. Each of the measures will rely on either the capital budget or the setup or both. The measures are used for assessing the feasibility of development projects and for measuring the results of investments in real estate.

Profit Margin

The most straightforward measure of return in real estate is the same as in most other commercial enterprises -- "can I sell it for more than it costs?" In the case of property developed or held for sale, the formula for examining this question is a simple one:

          Revenue from Sales
    -    Selling Costs

    =   Net Revenues
    -    Development Costs

    =   **Profit**

As simple as this formula is, there are some subtleties. Selling costs are often treated separately, as above, because they are largely paid from sales proceeds, rather than from the capital at risk during the development period. Otherwise, development costs contain all the costs discussed in Part I -- land and acquisition costs, building construction and indirect costs.

Revenue from sales will ultimately be determined by the market. Pro forma estimates should be based on careful research and judgment. As in the case of rental property, the best information to seek is detailed data on comparable and competitive properties within a market area. Comparable data on sales transactions can be generated from newspapers, real estate brokers, and from published records of completed transactions. Considerable research effort may be needed to obtain a complete picture of present market conditions. Even with complete research, experienced judgment will also be necessary to estimate the results of a sales program.

Given a reliable estimate of potential revenue from sales, selling costs and other development costs, the potential profit may be estimated. The question then becomes "is it enough?" This question is often addressed by computing the **profit margin**, the estimated profit as a percentage of costs or as a percentage of sales revenues. Thus the profit potential of the development may be assessed in relation to the capital to be committed (costs) or in relation to the value of the completed product (sales revenues).

The minimum acceptable profit margin for a particular development will depend on the property type, scale of the project, length of time required, the level of uncertainty about sellout revenues, construction costs, overall economic conditions, and on the developer's attitude toward the project. Profit margins in the range from 15%-25% of costs would be considered normal for conventional competitive sales properties, such as townhomes and condominiums. Profits below this range are insufficient to offset the risks of construction and marketing and to attract capital. For a project with any material marketing and development risks, probably the lowest profit margin any developer would consider feasible would be 10% on sales revenues.

Profit margins higher than about 25% are only achieved in unusual situations or where additional risks are involved. Retail land sales programs commonly project very high profits in relation to costs. Such programs also may involve selling costs higher than direct development costs. Conversion of existing buildings to condominium ownership may also produce a high profit margin. In both examples, the effort required for direct marketing is substantial and may be seen to be a major source of profit. These examples may also involve high risk to the sponsor.

Capitalized Value

For developers of income-producing property, the most straightforward question to be asked is "will it be worth more than it costs?"

Real estate appraisers base their valuations on three approaches to value. One is the **market value** approach, which bases the estimate on sales of comparable properties. A second is the **replacement value** approach, which bases the estimate on the cost to produce a similar property. The third approach -- and the one we consider here -- is to judge value based on the **capitalization of income**. A simple formula is used:

$$\text{Value} = \frac{\text{Free and Clear Income}}{\text{Capitalization Rate}}$$

In this formula, the Free and Clear Income is the income for the property to be valued. Typically, this will be a pro forma figure calculated as discussed in Part II. Note that the Free and Clear Income depends on characteristics of the property alone, and not on how it is financed.

Value is then determined by selecting a "**capitalization rate**" for the above equation. Capitalization rates (often called

"cap" rates) reflect overall rates of return. These rates are selected judgmentally in relation to the property type and quality and the returns available for alternative investments at the time. Cap rates may also be adjusted for specific characteristics of the property, relative levels of risk, the attitude of the individual making the appraisal, and numerous other factors. Basically, however, the cap rate should be selected to answer the question: "How much would this particular income stream (i.e., the income from this particular property) be worth to a willing buyer at this time?"

Guidance on capitalization rates may be obtained from the market. From data on sales prices and income for recently sold properties, the capitalization rate judged acceptable to the buyers and sellers may be calculated. Most developers and practitioners are alert for representative transactions and cap rates over time and thus build up a base of experience from which to make judgments. Although many books have been written to provide a scientific rationale and methodology for selecting capitalization rates, a few actual transactions -- willing buyers and willing sellers agreeing -- provide the most reliable basis. Most developers take a judgmental and highly unscientific approach to selecting capitalization rates.

A common benchmark for selecting cap rates is the interest rate charged for long-term real estate mortgage loans for similar types of property. This rate would be adjusted downward typically for prime real estate, because the inflation protection and tax benefits of ownership serve to add value which more than offsets the risks of equity ownership. The degree of inflation protection makes an important difference. In recent years, regional shopping centers, for example, have been valued very highly in relation to their current income (i.e., a low capitalization rate is applied), because their Free and Clear Income is expected to increase very rapidly with inflation.

At times when commercial mortgage loan rates have ranged from 12% to 14%, many prime commercial properties have sold at prices which suggest cap rates as low as 7% to 9%. For low-quality property, prices reflecting much higher cap rates are required to attract capital. Capitalization rates will vary over time as yields on alternative investments vary and as the attractiveness of particular classes of real estate varies.

Return on Total Assets

For proposed investments in income property, the most basic measure of return is the Return on Total Assets. This return measure is calculated as follows:

Return on Total Assets (ROTA)

$$= \frac{\text{Free and Clear Income}}{\text{Asset Cost}}$$

This equation is very similar to that for the determination of value by capitalization of income. Asset cost may simply be the proposed purchase price or, in the case of a proposed development, the total investment required in the project capital budget. Asset cost may be estimated as discussed in Part I above.

Return on Total Assets (ROTA) is the industry benchmark for judging the relative merits of proposed development projects. Lenders expect to see pro forma returns comparable to other proposed development ventures in a market. At the same time, this return measure gives an indication of overall return relative to alternative investments.

Residual Analysis

Analysts often combine the approaches of capitalization of income and capital budgeting in the form of residual analysis. In this type of analysis, the final value of a completed property is compared to its costs. Naturally, the completed value should be higher than costs, and the difference will reflect the value created by the developer. This margin of value should be comparable to the profit margin in sales property.

A variation of this is called a **land residual appraisal**, which is calculated as follows:

Value of Completed Property
- Development Costs

= **Value of Land**

This type of analysis should be used only with caution, because the calculation is quite sensitive to the choice of capitalization rate. In a land residual appraisal, a developer's profit should be included as a development cost if there are risks involved. One often-heard rule of thumb is that the land value and the developer's profit should be roughly equal.

Return on Equity

Up to this point, all of the valuation and return measures have been entirely independent of how a project may be financed. These are called **unleveraged returns**. The next measure of investment performance, Return on Equity, takes borrowing into account, relating the net cash income to the net equity investment required:

Return on Equity (ROE)

$$= \frac{\text{Cash Flow After Financing}}{\text{Equity Investment}}$$

Cash Flow After Financing is the Free and Clear Income less debt service payments; Equity Investment is the Asset Cost less the amount borrowed. The Return on Equity is also called the "Cash-on-Cash" return. Because it measures a return on actual net cash invested, many developers and investors regard this as the most important return measure. This measure should be used with caution, however, because the returns are leveraged.

Financial leverage in real estate investments results from the use of borrowed money. Borrowing has the effect of leveraging (or amplifying) the consequences to the equity owner of any change in income or expense. Small changes to the Free and Clear Income or the Asset Cost, either positive or negative, will produce a major change in the Return on Equity percentage figures. Thus the ROE measure is considered relatively volatile.

The leverage effect of the borrowing for any particular investment may be positive or it may be negative in relation to the earning power of the real estate asset. Where the borrowed funds cost more than the Return on Total Assets, the leverage is called negative; where the asset earns more than the effective cost of the debt, an immediate profit will be earned on the borrowed funds, hence positive leverage. Most typically, the Return on Total Assets (ROTA) is compared with the debt constant (principal and interest), although occasionally the analyst may refer to the interest rate as a base for comparison.

> Example: A rental apartment development is proposed, which will cost $1.25 million, of which $1 million will be borrowed. The Equity Investment will be $250,000. The completed development will return a pro forma Free and Clear Income of $155,000 per year. Thus the ROTA will be 12.4%. The available debt may involve a constant payment anywhere from 9%, in the case

of a government-assisted loan, to 15%. The following table computes the effect of the cost of the debt on ROE.

Financial Constant	Payment	CFAF	ROE
9%	$90,000	$65,000	26.0%
11%	110,000	45,000	18.0%
13%	130,000	25,000	10.0%
15%	150,000	5,000	2.0%

Where the cost of the debt is high (negative leverage), return on equity is sharply lower than the ROTA; in the cases of positive leverage (ROTA higher than the debt constant), equity returns are enhanced, relative to the overall return. Once considered unusual, negative leverage is very common today, especially during the early years of a project. Investors in prime property are more willing to wait for inflationary increases in income to catch up with the cost of borrowing.

After-Tax Return on Equity

As noted in Part II, some investors may wish to focus on after-tax returns. After-Tax ROE is defined as follows:

After-Tax ROE

$$= \frac{\text{After-Tax Cash Flow (ATCF)}}{\text{Equity Investment}}$$

This measure of return may be useful in relating a real estate investment to alternative tax-exempt investment opportunities which may be available to the investor. In the case of highly leveraged real estate investments, inclusion of the tax consequences in the return calculation will always have the effect of increasing the apparent returns. This happens because the property produces negative taxable income and thus positive tax savings from other income.

For example, in the apartment development considered above, assuming $125,000 non-depreciable cost of land, and ignoring the effects of reserves and principal payments, tax savings will be approximately as follows:

Cash Flow After Financing	$5,000
Depreciation Expense (27.5-year Straight Line)	(40,909)
Taxable Income	($35,909)
Tax Rate Assumption	x 30%
Tax Savings	$10,772

After Tax Cash Flow will thus be $15,772, and the After Tax ROE would be 6.3%, rather than the 2% cash-on-cash return actually generated by the property. It is important to note that similar tax savings will be found for *any* property, regardless of its fundamental quality. This calculation provides no additional information about the property or its financing, and should be considered as subordinate to other return measures.

Two other approaches are sometimes encountered in measuring equity returns. One approach defines the return as "cash flow plus equity build-up." Thus, the mortgage principal payments, sometimes an average over the first five years, are added to the cash flow. This return measure attempts to measure total annual pretax returns, which may be compared with the equity investment.

Another approach to returns is called the "payback" period. This calculation indicates how much time it will take to provide the equity investor with benefits (usually defined to include tax benefits)

equal to the investment amount. These approaches may occasionally be useful.

Break-even Analysis

In leveraged real estate investments, **break-even analysis** can be a very useful technique. Break-even analysis is usually aimed at answering a particular question about a proposed development.

For income property, a frequently used break-even calculation is to determine what percentage occupancy will be required to cover base levels of operating expenses and debt service. This is calculated as follows:

Break-even Occupancy (%)

$$= \frac{\text{Total Required Income}}{\text{Gross Potential Income}}$$

In this equation, Total Required Income is the sum of operating expenses, real estate taxes, and debt service payments. Break-even calculations are particularly useful in assessing the likelihood of achieving certain milestones and relating the investment to possible consequences of failure. For example, in the rental apartment development discussed above, an increase in debt service constant payments will also increase the break-even occupancy, and therefore the risk of operating at a deficit. Thus, in the case of the highest interest rates, the owner must not only accept a lower cash return on equity, but also must accept increased risk.

For sales property, a similar form of break-even analysis would address such questions as: "How many units do we have to sell to cover our costs?" or "What average price will cover our costs?" Many other uses of break-even analysis will be encountered.

Case 2

Masonic Hall

The future of the Masonic Hall Building in downtown Providence, Rhode Island, was uncertain. Ms. Prudence Rashleigh was well aware of this, and it made her efforts as Director of the Providence Historic Rehabilitation Society even more important. She was, in August 1979, in the process of preparing and evaluating a proposal for an adaptive re-use development, which she hoped would avoid demolition of the building.

The Masonic Hall was a five-story plus basement building, constructed in 1897 as the ceremonial home of the Providence Freemasons. It was a handsomely proportioned and well built steel and brick structure on a land parcel of 8,500 square feet, with approximately 6,200 net square feet per floor (see Exhibit 1). The building had been vacant and disused for several years. A local businessman, Mr. Meaney, was presently the owner of the Hall, and he intended to demolish the building to provide additional parking for his nearby retail business.

Although the Masonic Hall was not on the Historic Register, the various preservation groups in Providence felt that the Hall made an important contribution to the architectural and historical quality of downtown Providence, and as such ought to be preserved. Under pressure from prominent citizens, particularly Mr. Bright, who was a member of the Society and a friend of the Hall's owner, Mr. Meaney had agreed that the Hall could be purchased from him for $250,000 cash before the end of the present year. Prudence, who had just completed a continuing-education real estate development program at a well known eastern design school, had elected to investigate courses of action which would preserve the building. Although the Society's budget was not large, her board felt that the opportunity to save the Hall was not to be missed, and voted $7,500 for carrying out a feasibility study on the preservation of this fine building.

VALUING THE PROPERTY

Prudence wondered first of all whether the asking price of $250,000 was reasonable: what were the building and land worth, either to the present or to another owner? She decided to review her knowledge of the Hall and its location in the economic context of the city.

Pulling out a map of downtown Providence (see Exhibit 2) she saw that the Hall was near the edge of the Central Business District at the corner of Dorrance and Pine Streets. The Hall was a detached, freestanding structure and occupied just under half of the small city block on which it sat. The remainder parcel was in different ownership and was presently used for parking. There was therefore access on three sides of the building. The main frontage was on Dorrance Street, which was generally a good address, with most of its buildings fully occupied. Dorrance Street led to the center of the city, and City Hall was three blocks north. Across Pine Street to the north was the new Broadcast House building, which included offices and radio/ television facilities. To the south there was a large vacant parcel, also used for parking, but designated as the site for a new State Courthouse which was scheduled to break ground in mid-1980. To the west was the Outlet Company parking garage, which connects to the city's leading downtown department store. Across Dorrance Street to the east was a vacant four-story building which Prudence considered also to be of historic significance, but which at present was not under threat of demolition.

The economy of Providence and Rhode Island had suffered over the previous few decades as their traditional manufacturing industries had declined. Local and federal government policies and a re-orientation of private industry were combining, however, to reverse the decline. The establishment of an Industrial Development Corporation had recently been announced to encourage new industry in the city. The Biltmore Hotel had just been remodelled into a first-class hotel and conference center. Various plans were afoot to remodel the railroad station and Kennedy Plaza. The economic climate seemed to be improving for the city, and this meant increasing demand for space in a variety of categories. Prudence knew that the service sector, representing office and retail demand, was an increasing part of the U.S. economy as a whole.

How was she to value the Masonic Hall? She remembered that there are three common approaches. One is to value the income a building produces; another is to estimate what it would cost to replace the building; finally she knew that recent sales of buildings comparable in size and location would give a guide to the Hall's worth on the market. The "replacement cost" approach did not seem relevant, since there was clearly no demand for another Masonic Hall in downtown Providence. She found out, however, that a new office building of approximately the same size as the Masonic Hall would cost approximately $65 a square foot to build and develop, excluding the land on which it sat. Prudence decided to find out whether any useful comparable sales had occurred. In her official capacity, but not letting on the specific reason for her inquiry, she called several prominent brokers in Providence to ask whether any recent sales had occurred and, if so, what the buildings were like and what condition and location they were in. She also noticed that a four-story empty warehouse building nearby was advertised for sale in the Sunday paper and made inquiries about that, too.

The owners of that property were asking $10 a square foot. The building, from what Prudence could see from the outside, was not in such good structural condition as the Masonic Hall, and had good light and exposure on only two sides. From the brokers she ascertained that two vacant, older buildings had changed hands recently. Although they were unable to tell

her the terms of the transactions, which she knew to be an important factor, they informed her that one, a large industrial building on the outer edge of the CBD, had sold for $3 per square foot and another partially empty building in the center for $15 per square foot. Another downtown building had been swapped for a suburban retail property in a tax-free exchange, but no further details were available.

It occurred to Prudence that an important issue in valuing the property was what Mr. Meaney might do with it should he not sell. At present the Hall probably represented a liability in that the owner was presumably paying taxes and incurring some maintenance and security expenses on the property. On the other hand, Providence had no ordinance requiring approval for new parking lots. Mr. Meaney could therefore demolish the Hall at a cost of, say, $60,000, deducting this from his taxable income, and then generate income from parking. Although the lot would be too small to warrant its own attendant, and would need about $10,000 spent on it for curbs and paving, the operator of the adjacent lot might be able to run both together. Parking spaces were currently costing $2.25 a day in this area of Providence. With some jockey parking, the land would accommodate 30 cars, representing a potential income of about $20,000 per year. Since Mr. Meaney might impute additional value for having convenient parking for his own business, his asking price of $250,000 did not seem unreasonable.

Mr. Meaney had called for a cash purchase, but Prudence knew that the terms of a sale were often as important as the price. She knew that if the building were conveyed to a charitable non-profit entity at a below-market price, then the present owner could take a tax deduction of the difference between the appraised value and conveyed price. This might be to both the buyer's and seller's advantage. Prudence decided to ask Mr. Bright to try to find out more about the circumstances and expectations of the owner insofar as they affected the price and possible terms of sale. Meantime she proceeded with other avenues of research.

ADAPTIVE RE-USE STRATEGY

One possibility suggested by the board to preserve the building was to quickly process an application to include the Hall on the National Register of Historic Places. This alone might achieve their goal without need for further involvement. There were three factors against such a ploy, however. First, Mr. Meaney had indicated he would demolish the building before the designation were approved; second, since he wanted the site for car parking, the tax disincentives for erecting a new building on the site would carry no weight; thirdly, she was aware that mysterious fires were prone to break out in buildings whose demolition or redevelopment were obstructed through legislative or legal actions. Prudence decided that a more positive and constructive approach might provide better chances of success.

It was clear that the Masonic Hall could not simply be preserved in its present state. If it weren't occupied, who would pay to maintain it? The Masons clearly didn't want it. There were parts of the interior which Prudence thought had character and history, but they did not seem of critical historic value. She recognized that an effective historic rehabilitation program involved many tradeoffs and concluded that, in this case, the paramount purpose of any rehabilitation of the Masonic Hall was to preserve the exterior massing of the building as an important part of the urban streetscape of the city. But what would be the proper use?

The possibility of renovating the building for subsidized elderly housing occurred to her, but the zoning was commercial, and even if a variance were obtained it was unlikely that any development could be processed sufficiently fast to place the property under contract by the end of the year. Furthermore, there was the probability that people would prefer to live outside the center of the city, and that policy-makers would prefer to locate subsidized projects closer to neighborhood services. A hotel development was clearly impossible since the building was too small, and the recent renovation of the Biltmore would represent insurmountable competition. One attractive idea was to adapt the building as a preservation headquarters center, or for some other special user. But she was not aware of any organizations needing this amount of space in this location, and she knew that such users were often unable to pay for rehabilitating the building. Furthermore, institutions were reluctant to loan money against real estate developments which were supported by tenants who might not continue in business for more than a few years.

This diagnosis left the choice of rehabilitation for good-quality professional offices, with commercial or retail uses on the ground floor, as the most suitable program. This strategic decision still left many questions unanswered. What rents might various tenants pay? What kind of tenants might want the space, and therefore what design approach should the rehabilitation involve? What competition in other buildings would the Masonic Hall eventually face, should its redevelopment occur. Prudence decided to call in Gladstone Bagges, Inc., a consulting firm who specialized in market studies for real estate development.

Mr. Bagges said that his firm would be prepared to do a market survey for the project. He showed Prudence several voluminous studies for other projects, and told her that a study would cost the Society approximately $10,000. Prudence was horrified. She explained that she had a budget for the entire project of only $7,500. After some discussion, Mr. Bagges agreed that his firm would do a study for $4,500, but that it would not be of their usual depth and thoroughness. He explained that should the project proceed, a lending institution would probably require a more comprehensive survey of supply and demand, which could be adapted from the first version. Prudence accepted this, and asked him to proceed at once, investigating both office and retail segments of the market. Mr. Bagges concurred with Prudence's opinion that these two segments of demand probably represented the highest and best use for the Hall, that is, the property would be worth the most for development for those uses.

Happy that her judgment had been corroborated by an independent professional, Prudence called an architect friend, Frank L. Wrong, to ask whether he could help her with the feasibility study for the proposed rehabilitation. Frank was delighted to help, and said that he could finish design drawings within six weeks and construction drawings within three months. Prudence felt that this might be a little premature and explained that what was needed at this stage was a quick design scheme, an appraisal of any potential uncertainties and reasonably accurate construction costs and a completion date for the scheme. She explained that any design proposal must comply with the Secretary of the Interior's Standards for Historic Rehabilitation and felt that Frank should be able to do the work for $1,500. Frank expostulated that to survey the building alone would take several days for two people and cost at least that. Prudence explained that she had reduced scale copies of the Hall's original construction drawings and pulled them out for Frank's inspection. (Exhibit 3 contains selected drawings from the set.)

He was pleased with what he saw and said that having drawings of the building would save several days. But he pointed out that he would have to retain a structural engineer for a few hours to advise on alterations to the structure, and any pos-

sible foundation problems with new elevators. Also, he did not feel happy with giving contract cost estimates on building conversions. He suggested that he evolve a contract cost estimate in conjunction with a contractor who was experienced with rehab work. Prudence was satisfied with this approach, and she and Frank agreed that he would work on an hourly basis with an upper limit of $1,750, including any engineering fees. Frank wanted to get started and asked whether he could see the building right away. Prudence had been loaned a set of keys, and she and Frank set off to inspect the property.

THE MASONIC HALL

The exterior of the Hall was indeed in excellent condition. External fire stairs had been incorporated in the building over the years, and Prudence and Frank agreed that these should be replaced, if possible, by internal stairs complying with the building codes. The drawings showed clearly the masonry and steel framed structure to the Hall. The floors were solidly constructed of timber joists and boards with lath and plaster ceilings. Frank explained that the availability of original detailed construction information would make any engineering appraisal of structural alterations easy and accurate and avoided the necessity of opening up the structure for specific investigations. Although there were no details of the foundations available, the original design loadings of the Hall, for Masonic gatherings, were likely to be in excess of those required for contemporary office and retail use. No settlement of the structure was in evidence, so further examination of the foundations would wait until the project proceeded.

As Frank expected from the asymmetrical elevations, the floor plans were not entirely regular or repetitive. There were three staircases in the Hall: the central stair ran only between the basement, first and second floors. The corner enclosed stair, on Eddy street, ran the full height of the building from basement to roof. The central stair on Eddy Street connected the second through fifth floors. The main meeting room for the Masons was twenty-eight feet high and located on the third floor. There were galleries in this hall and these obtained access from a fourth floor which occupied only the Pine and Eddy Street sides of the building. On the fifth floor, roof leaks were clearly visible. Frank thought that the damage was only superficial, though he intended to check later whether any dry or wet rot had resulted. Up on the roof, which was virtually flat and unencumbered with any mechanical equipment installations, Frank observed that replacing the roof finish would be relatively simple. Furthermore, the parapets, which often deteriorated quickly, were in excellent condition and a tribute to their Masonic builders. Frank and Prudence lastly went down to look at the basement. Prudence had been put off by what she found. There were low ceiling heights, with many masonry walls and service pipes threaded around the place. She was not sure whether the existing oil-fired steam boilers worked or were capable of being retained in any rehabilitation.

Frank explained that he would have to consider these many issues in due course. There were five major issues, however, which had occurred to him as important. First was how to locate a new core of elevators, stairs, service risers and lobbies in the building so as to maximize rentable area and flexibility in renting subdivided floors. Second, was the extent to which masonry walls might be demolished to open up the floors. He knew that in adaptive use a golden rule for economy and avoiding construction problems was to touch as little as possible. Third, Frank felt that the structure would easily carry a new sixth floor on top of the roof and that such a floor would command fine views over the city. He also told Prudence that he could not imagine many tenants wanting space with a twenty-eight foot high ceiling and that the Mason's Hall itself might accommodate another floor. Fourth, although the basement was in poor condition now, it could easily be linked to the ground floor through independent staircases, and the brick and beam construction might make an attractive bar or restaurant. Lastly, he wondered whether there would be any advantage in incorporating a new core or building on the adjacent parcel, and adjoining the Hall's windowless wall, where the new Courthouse was shortly to start construction.

Prudence was somewhat taken aback by all these suggestions and promised Frank that she would consider them all and let him know shortly what her conclusions were. Frank reminded her also to consider what level of finishes and services would be required. Prudence explained that the market study she had commissioned might help arrive at decisions on these points, but that this would not be ready for another two weeks. Frank explained that he could wait on these issues and would meantime proceed with a preliminary design evaluation. He left her with the observation that good professionals sometime earned their fee in five minutes, through identifying broad strategic issues and benefits in the development process. Prudence laughed and asked whether Frank would therefore settle for a fee of $100.

Prudence called Mr. Bagges to find out how his researches were proceeding and whether he could include restaurants in the survey. He confirmed that the report would be ready in a few days, but that evaluating the demand for restaurant use was a more difficult problem than offices, although he would offer his opinions when they met.

Prudence decided to use the time before her meeting with Mr. Bagges to prepare the documentation necessary for nomination to the Register. She reasoned that if rehabilitation were infeasible then at least inclusion on the Register might dissuade Mr. Meaney from immediate demolition. She also decided to ask her friends on the Rhode Island Historical Commission for an official preliminary opinion of eligibility for the Register.

THE MARKET STUDY

The market report (see Exhibit 2) from Gladstone Bagges, Inc., eventually arrived, and Mr. Bagges followed it a day later. Prudence understood the difference between Class A and B office space, but was not sure what significance there was in the differentiation between new and rehabilitated space and why their rent levels differed. Mr. Bagges explained that new space tended to be more efficiently planned than rehabilitated space with a higher ratio of net-to-gross area. Tenants tended to prefer brand new space, and it often was available in larger units of floor space. She expressed concern over the availability, now or in the immediate future, of approximately 164,000 square feet of offices, when the Providence market could absorb 80,000 to 100,000 square feet a year. Mr. Bagges agreed that this was a valid concern and that Prudence should study the report to see how she could position and promote the rehabilitated Masonic Hall to fill gaps in the market or how to make it superior in quality and therefore more desirable to users than alternative property.

They agreed that proximity to the new Courthouse was a distinct advantage, since Dorrance Street would be a main connector between it and the CBD. If the Courthouse were not being built, the Masonic Hall would be very much on the periphery of downtown. The Hall had no parking, but there was an abundance of public parking facilities close by. Prudence and Mr. Bagges agreed that the most appropriate market sector to attract would be the professional and law firms who would find the floor areas of the Hall and its location very appropriate to their business. If the rehabilitation were to the highest standard, they could position the rent levels at the top of the rehabilitation scale but below new Class A space.

Mr. Bagges observed that the costs of a sensible rehabilitation would usually be less than new construction and would therefore need lower rent levels than new construction to support the investment. Mr. Bagges felt that rents between $9 and $10 per net square foot might be asked for the upper floors if they were efficiently planned. As far as the ground floor was concerned, he had ascertained that there were no branch banking or restaurant facilities as close to the Courthouse building as this, and there might well be strong demand for these uses as a result, although he was unable to give an opinion as to the likelihood of obtaining such users. He explained that restaurants tended to generate high rents, but were often unstable long-term tenants. Any restaurant/bar tenant would have to be of high quality if it were not to detract from the image of the professional office tenants. Rent levels of $11 might be expected for the ground floor and anything from $2 to $9 for the basement, depending on how ground floor tenants could utilize the space.

Prudence asked about adding another floor on the roof. Mr. Bagges liked the idea and said that such space, if it had good views, would command the highest rents in the building. Allaying Prudence's fears about the number of announced rehabilitation projects which might provide even more competition to the Masonic Hall, Mr. Bagges explained that many such proposals were infeasible for one reason or another and that their announcement was often "preemptive." Prudence might well play the same game, once she had the Hall under agreement, to dissuade other developers from entering the market.

Prudence called Frank after the meeting and explained her conclusions. They agreed that Frank would provide an either/or cost for a new sixth floor. Prudence asked him to consider the implications of lifecycle costing on the building mechanical systems, a concept which she had read was becoming increasingly important, and also to allow for separate floor-by-floor metering of all utilities. Mr. Bagges had explained that changes had been noticed in his survey regarding commercial lease agreements; they were increasingly being negotiated with escalators for real estate taxes, utilities, and other operating costs, and sometimes even for the base rents themselves. Frank said that he had finished his first cut at design, and was meeting Mr. Gil Bane, his local contractor friend, the following day.

COSTING THE REHABILITATION

Mr. Bane, who was working on another rehabilitation project nearby, was enthusiastic about the Hall, noting that you couldn't get workmanship like that anymore. Frank said that he wasn't expecting fine craftsmanship or lavish restoration, but rather intelligent and good quality refurbishing of the interior. He explained that he wanted budget prices within around 7% either way. Mr. Bane said that this was just as well, since his estimator would need several days to do a detailed takeoff of the outline specifications and drawings and was too busy at the moment to do so.

Frank asked how else they could price the work? Mr. Bane pointed out that he had recently finished two rehabilitations which had elements in common with the proposed Masonic Hall development and that they could adjust these prices for physical differences in the jobs and for inflation over time. Maybe Frank had some other costings which could serve as comparables? They went back to the contractor's office and while he was digging out his files, Frank called a couple of architect friends to get some figures. The cost breakdowns they both had were based on different elemental analyses, which made the problem rather tricky, but after a couple of hours, and with some reference to R.S. Means' Cost Data, they produced a cost estimate (see Exhibit 4). Frank was concerned with having only 5% contingencies on such an approximate costing and was not sure whether he should have made an allowance for "bonding" any eventual contractor. He suspected, however, that Mr. Bane's input might have pushed the price up, and that this would reveal itself in eventual bids on the work. He knew that if a contract were negotiated on the Masonic Hall, it would be more expensive than a bid contract. On the other hand, negotiating with a builder experienced with renovation would have certain other advantages. After returning to his office, he arranged to meet Prudence the following day to review his initial data.

Exhibit 5 contains the drawings that Frank prepared. In addition to the cost estimate, Frank had sketch plans for a typical upper floor, ground and basement. He also had prepared a layout plan of a typical upper floor in use to show how it might work for a tenant. Lastly he had sketched a section through the building showing the additional optional floors, at the fourth floor in the Masons' hall, and at the sixth floor. His structural engineer had explained that there should be no problem in supporting a new light steel structure and floor within the Masons' hall. It was clear that neither the new 4th nor the 3rd floor would be pleasant for office use without alterations to the glazing. Providing adequate windows to these levels necessitated breaking through the spandrel panels below the lattice glazing to the Dorrance Street elevation. He had redrawn the main elevation to show how plain glazing would appear, but he was not sure how Prudence or the Department of the Interior would react to these changes. The following day, when they met again,

Prudence was delighted with the scheme and cost plan; it was just at the level of detail she wanted. She asked Frank about code compliance, the pro-rated cost of the new sixth floor, and any damp-proofing or other problems connected with using the basement. She and Frank drew up a summary of net rentable areas.

Level	Use	Net Rentable Area
6(optional)	Office	5,500 SF
2-5	Office	24,800 SF
Ground	Retail	6,000 SF
Basement	Retail	2,000 SF
Basement	Storage	2,000 SF
Total		40,300 SF
Total (less level 6)		34,800 SF

Having satisfied herself on these points, she thanked Frank and said that she would come back to him in due course.

She was also pleased to know that Frank had only spent $1,500 of his budget. She felt that she might need some additional advice from a lawyer before the project was through, and that would require some budget allowance.

FINANCIAL ANALYSIS

At last Prudence had sufficient information to undertake a first cut at a financial analysis. The Historical Commission had unofficially told her that the Hall certainly complied with the requirements for inclusion on the Register. Prudence had ascertained from the city what the probable tax burden on the rehabilitated building would be, and had obtained an estimate of operating expenses from the management department of one of the brokers to whom she had spoken. She plugged in her new programmable financial calculator and worked through a stabilized pro forma income and expense statement for the

Stabilized Pro Forma Cash Flow (Setup)

Scheduled Gross Rent:		
Office (24,800 SF @ $9.50 average)		$235,600
Retail (8,000 SF @ $11.00)		88,000
Storage (2,000 SF @ $2.00)		4,000
Gross Potential Rent		327,600
Vacancy Allowance @ 5%		(16,380)
Effective Gross Income		311,220
Operating Expenses:		
Cleaning (@ .65/SF)	$21,320	
Energy (@ 1.00/SF)	32,800	
Management (@ 6%)	18,670	
Maintenance (@ 5%)	15,560	
Insurance (@ .08/SF)	2,780	
Replacement Reserve (@ 2%)	6,220	
Subtotal		(97,350)
Real Estate Taxes (@ 16%)		(49,795)
Free and Clear Income		$164,075.

Hall. She knew that this "setup" was the most critical of the pro formas.

Prudence decided not to allow for constructing a sixth floor at first. She priced the office space at a level above most other rehabilitation comparables, but well below the cost of new office space. Mr. Bagges had suggested a rent level of $11 per square foot for any ground floor retail or commercial space, with part of the basement allocated at the same rent, and part as low-cost storage. Prudence allowed a vacancy factor as was normal in the industry, and having then deducted all the anticipated operating expenses, arrived at a "free and clear" income or cash flow before financing of $164,000.

Next, Prudence calculated all the development costs. She assumed an acquisition price of $250,000 and added in the contract sum which Frank had provided, and then computed the indirect costs. Frank had given her an estimate of the architectural and engineering fees. Mr. Bright had put her in touch with a local law firm who had suggested figures for the legal work involved and who had explained

that accountants must be retained, particularly if investors were to become involved in owning the building. Insurance seemed important during the course of the development to protect the owners from liability or loss. Prudence had thought that Frank's cost estimates might be rather tight at around $31 per square foot and decided to build in a further contingency figure.

Lastly, it was clear that construction financing would be needed during the project until a permanent mortgage could be placed on the property. A call to a local bank had produced quotations of 11.5% interest for such a loan, plus a one-point fee for processing it. Prudence thought that this was rather a high figure, but the banker had explained that the construction and rent-up phase of a development was always the riskiest part and required close supervision, and high rates were charged accordingly. He also noted that credit worthiness of the borrower was important to the bank because construction loans are normally guaranteed by the owner. No guarantees would be required once the project was fully rented.

Masonic Hall Development Cost

Acquisition of land and shell		$250,000
Building construction		1,078,250
Indirect Costs:		
Architectural (@ 5% construction)	53,910	
Engineering (@ 1.5% construction)	16,170	
Legal fees (@ 2% total)	26,570	
Syndication/Acct (@ 1.5% total)	19,920	
Insurance (@ 2% total)	26,570	
Contingencies (@ 5% construction)	53,910	
Finance charge (@ 1% total)	13,280	
Construction interest (1 year; $1.5 million x 45% x 11.5%)	77,630	
Subtotal		287,960
Total development cost		$1,616,210

Next Prudence wondered what assumptions she should make about permanent financing for the project. She knew that anyone who developed the building would need long-term mortgage financing in addition to any cash equity invested in the property. She had heard that institutions sometimes used a rule of thumb that 75% to 80% of the free and clear cash flow was considered appropriate as interest and amortization on a loan. Mr. Bright had told her that commercial loans had recently been obtained at 10.5% interest over a 30-year period. This worked out to a constant annual payment rate of 10.98% if payments were made monthly at the end of each month. By this rule of thumb, Prudence calculated, a mortgage of no more than $1.2 million would be supported. This would leave her needing to raise over $400,000 in cash equity for the project.

Mr. Bright had pointed out that recently a number of industrial and, in a few cases, commercial projects had been financed using state tax-exempt revenue bonds. These were not guaranteed or subsidized by the government, but were essentially a state authorized way for a

lending institution to lend money to a desirable project with the interest being exempt from Federal income tax. This had the effect of reducing the interest rate by several points, or to around 8%. Prudence returned to her setup, punched her calculator again in an optimistic frame of mind, and calculated a constant of 8.81%. After all, she had been told that most other parties to a real estate deal will take a pessimistic view of the proposer's projections so she might as well be positive. She knew that obtaining tax-exempt financing would take time, but might be possible for a rehabilitation of the Masonic Hall. Prudence also hoped she could justify a larger loan, perhaps $1.5 million, which would reduce the need to raise other funds. If tax-exempt, the debt service on this loan would be $132,077.62 per year. She continued with her cash flow to compute a stabilized cash flow after financing.

Prudence looked hard at her figures: the return on total assets showed 10.15%, which did not seem very high given the risks of development. But she recalled that there are three components to return in real estate: cash flow, tax effects and future appreciation in value. She knew

After Tax Cash Flow

Effective gross income	$311,220
Expenses and real estate taxes	(147,145)
Free and Clear	164,075
Debt Service (80%)	(132,078)
Cash flow after financing	31,997
Add: Mortgage amortization	12,530
Less: Depreciation:	
Shell (note 1)	(6,667)
Improvements (note 2)	(273,242)
Taxable income	(235,382)
Tax savings (50% tax bracket)	117,691
After tax cash flow	$149,688

Notes:
(1) Shell cost depreciated on straight line basis over 30 years; land cost of $50,000 not depreciable.
(2) Improvements depreciated on straight line basis over 5 years.

that the 1976 Tax Reform Act had provided for a 60-month straight-line depreciation of rehabilitation costs for buildings rehabilitated in accordance with the legislated guidelines. If the owner of the Masonic Hall were in a high tax bracket from other income, the non-cash losses from depreciation would provide a valuable "tax shelter" for the owner in the first five years. Prudence decided to calculate taxable income and tax savings assuming this were the case.

STRUCTURE OF OWNERSHIP

Prudence supposed that although the cash flow after financing showed a good cash return on equity, this was very sensitive to her assumptions on operations and financing. The value of the tax shelter would be an important part of the return if suitable investors could be found to use the losses. The ownership structure of the development seemed very important, so Prudence arranged a meeting with a local law firm, Sue, Grabbit and Runn, P.C.

Mr. Runn was only too pleased to meet with Prudence. After reviewing the plans and financial documents for the project, Mr. Runn explained that his firm had had several involvements with subsidized housing projects, but that although they were interested in historic-rehabilitation commercial developments, there had been very few completed so far. Mr. Runn explained that real estate ownership could be structured in many ways, but that partnerships were a common form, particularly where tax shelter played a significant part in the returns. High tax bracket individuals join as "limited partners," absorbing the negative taxable income, while other partners, "general partners," have responsibility for instigating and managing the development during its life. General partners usually receive only limited cash returns in the early years, and a higher percentage of the "futures" from cash flow,

refinancing, or sales proceeds of the property.

Mr. Runn stressed to Prudence that even with the valuable tax shelter, the fundamental quality of the rehabilitated property was of critical importance. If the property were in a poor location or had doubtful financial expectations, no one would invest in it, however much tax shelter were involved. Cash flow to the owners of the property was the acid test. Prudence thought that this was a salutary observation and asked Mr. Runn what he would suggest as a next step. Mr. Runn pointed out the need to formalize the Society's option to purchase the Hall. His firm would be pleased to be retained as counsel for the project and if she liked would begin to draw up the necessary papers. Mr. Runn then asked Prudence what resources the Society and its backers were committing to the venture. Prudence explained that her board wished to limit its investment in order to assist other meritorious historical projects.

Mr. Runn thought for a few moments and then asked if he might discuss the case in confidence with some of his clients and partners. They were all in high tax brackets, had significant cash resources and were well connected with the local financial and development community. It might be good from both a community and financial viewpoint for them to get involved. Prudence told Mr. Runn that his idea was interesting. Perhaps Mr. Runn would outline a proposal for the Society to consider?

NEXT STEPS

Prudence left the meeting with mixed feelings. Shouldn't she be suggesting terms to Mr. Runn, not the other way around? But how could she suggest terms when the Society didn't even control the property? How could they raise $250,000 to buy the building? Maybe they shouldn't even do this with so much uncertainty surrounding the project. She decided to call Mr. Bright, whom she felt she could trust completely, and ask him to help her commence negotiations with Mr. Meaney to attempt to secure an option on the Hall. She knew that the balance of her initial budget would be insufficient for this but wondered how much Mr. Meaney would require for an option. If Mr. Runn was as keen on the project as he seemed, she should move fast.

She pondered her next step.

EXHIBITS

1. Masonic Hall, exterior view

2. Location plan and market study

3. Drawings of existing building

4. Construction cost estimate

5. Proposed designs

QUESTIONS FOR DISCUSSION

1. What are the implications of not receiving tax-exempt financing and relying on current commercial financing?

2. Is the market survey useful? Might it have been carried out better?

3. What alternative designs for the Hall might be appropriate?

4. Should a new sixth floor be included in the development?

5. What alternative next moves should Prudence consider?

Exhibit 1

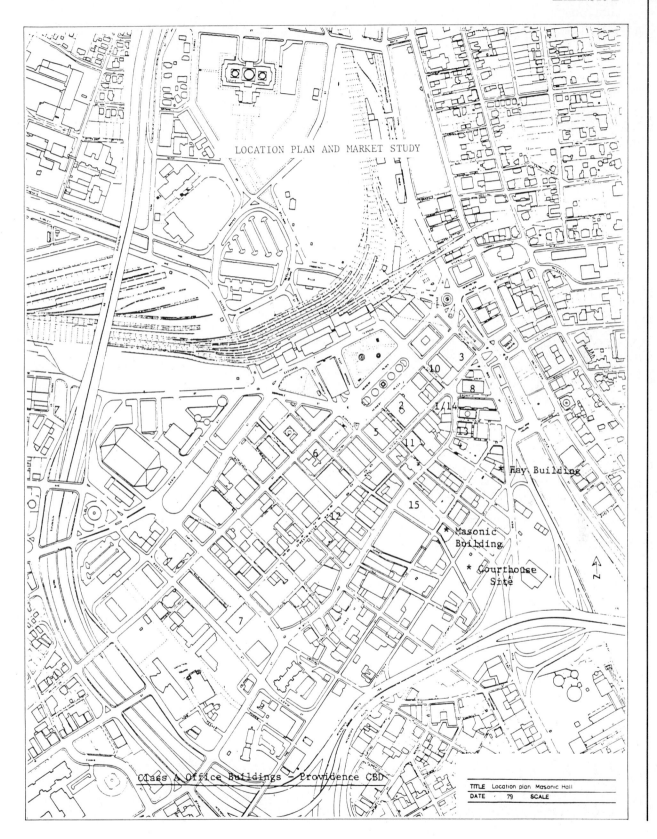

LOCATION PLAN AND MARKET STUDY

Class A Office Buildings — Providence CBD

| TITLE | Location plan Masonic Hall |
| DATE | 79 SCALE |

Exhibit 2
continued

PROVIDENCE OFFICE MARKET SURVEY: GLADSTONE BAGGES INC.

Market Overview

The Providence office market is essentially a two tier market. Class B
and lower space rents for around $5 per square foot per year, and is
generally composed of older, poorly maintained stock. Class A space, either
new construction or rehabilitated, is currently commanding $9 if available.
Class B space is plentiful, while the current Class A market is extremely
tight. A brief historical review of the Providence office market is helpful,
focusing on the competitive Class A market.

A thorough inventory of Providence office space was completed in
December 1968 as part of the planning for the Hospital Trust Tower, the
city's largest office building, which opened in 1973. In that inventory,
downtown space comprised the following:

1969 Office Data

	Gross Bldg. Area (SF)	Net Rentable Area (SF)	Vacant Space	%
Government Office Space	1,015,400	754,255	13,011	1.7%
Total Commercial Office Space	3,735,063	2,970,045	235,553	7.9%
Class A Commercial	1,512,030	1,202,200	14,856	1.2%
All Other Commercial	2,223,033	1,765,845	218,697	12.4%

Unlike many other major metropolitan areas, little suburban office
development activity has occurred. Other than two corporate headquarters
developments in suburban industrial parks, all of Providence's office
activity is within the city proper.

The above Class A office space inventory of 1.5 million SF included 11
buildings in the city of Providence. Of these, four buildings comprising
277,400 square feet were located on South Main Street, to the east of the
downtown core area. The seven downtown Class A office properties were
developed as follows:

Exhibit 2
continued

1969 Inventory of Class A Properties in Downtown Core

Key Map#	Name	Address	Date	Gross Bldg. Area (SF)
1.	Turk's Head	76 Westminster St.	1913	161,280
2.	Industrial Nat'l Bank	115 Westminster St.	1927	388,250
3.	R.I. Hospital Trust Co.	15 Westminster St.	pre-1925	260,000
4.	Old Colony Bank	58 Weybosset St.	1940's	60,000
5.	Howard Bldg.	10 Dorrance St.	1958 1968 add.	134,000 90,000
6.	Providence – Washington	1 Washington St.	1949	70,000
7.	Blue Cross Bldg.	444 Westminster Mall	1968	71,100
TOTAL				1,234,630

Since the time of the above inventory, significant new investments have been made in office space in the downtown core area. Eight such investments have been completed as follows:

1969-1979 Office Investments in Downtown Core

Key Map#	Name	Address	Date	Gross Bldg. Area (SF)
8.	Amica Insurance	40 Westminster St.	1971	260,000
9.	One Weybosset Hill		1972	103,000
10.	Hospital Trust Tower		1973	320,000
11.	Lauderdale Bldg.*	144 Westminster St.	1976	42,000
12.	Kinsley Bldg.*	260 Westminster St.	1977	30,000
13.	Wilcox Bldg.*	42 Weybosset St.	1979	30,790
14.	Turk's Head Bldg.*	76 Westminster St.	1979	161,280
15.	Broadcast House	Dorrance St.	1979	100,000+

TOTAL space added/rehabilitated   947,070+

11-year average new investment space (SF/yr)   86,097

*indicates rehabilitation investment

Exhibit 2
continued

Three additional small investments were made along North and South Main Street during this period totaling about 145,000 square feet. The Providence Class A vacancy rate is today again quite low for the first time since the construction of the major buildings of 1971-73. Hence the net overall occupancy of Class A space increased overall in pace with the inventory approximately as follows:

Class A Inventory

	1969	1979	11 Year Average Absorption
Downtown Core Area	1,234,630	2,020,420	71,435
Main Street Area	277,400	422,400	13,182
TOTAL	1,512,030	2,442,820	84,617

The eleven year period covered in the above analysis contained two major national recessions. It is reasonable to conclude that in years of good economic conditions generally, as is the case today, the Providence office market can sustain in excess of 100,000 square feet of new investment per year. A more conservative view shows apparently successful investments in the downtown area, including rehabilitation of older property, averaging 86,000 square feet over the eleven year period.

These gross figures are somewhat deceptive, and have three components: new business, existing firms trading up, and internal expansion of existing Class A office users. Estimates are that approximately 50% of total Class A space absorption is generated by new businesses. Vacancies created by firms trading up have generally been filled by Class C and D tenants, creating systematic vacancies only in the poorest quality buildings.

Comparable Properties

By either measure, it would appear that the Providence downtown market would support several office developments of the scale of the Masonic Building each year. A more detailed review of the market will be useful to compare this property to its current competition. The following table compares Masonic to other competitive space currently available in recently constructed buildings, and in rehabilitated structures.

Exhibit 2
continued

The most significant recent comparable developments are the Wilcox Building and 10 Orms Street. Wilcox is a high-quality rehabilitation of a fire-damaged historic building in the financial district. The basement, first and second floor space has been leased as follows:

Level	User	Net Area (SF)	Lease Terms
1	Auto Club	1800	$10.15/net usable SF
B,1	Restaurant	3300	$8.50 average ($10, 1st floor; $7.50, basement), with expense stops.
2	Office	1100	5-year lease starts at $8.00, increases .25 per year to $9.00 in year 5, with expense stops.
2	Office	1100	Same
2	Office	Remainder	Under option at above rates.

The Wilcox Building has been slow to lease because construction completion has been delayed. Elevators and lobby are not yet finished. The space is 'L' shaped, subdivided rather poorly, and lacks a view.

10 Orms Street is a new suburban-type office building of 50,000 square feet on an urban renewal site north of the CBD. This project is said to be 85% leased at rents of $10.90 per net usable square foot. The building is located across the street from the new Marriott Hotel, and provides parking for tenants.

A condominium office rehabilitation project, The Hay Block, recently began construction along Dyer Street. This is a three story brick and frame structure which will be partially owner occupied. Of the other projects, only the Owen Building provides comparable quality space and location. Of the total current inventory of Class A space, including those projects under construction, only a small portion are in competitive locations, or possess the amenity and character of the Masonic Building. The current and "under construction" inventory of Class A space will be absorbed at existing rates within 2 years, yet there are no Class A planned rehabilitation projects to meet future needs. We believe the potential oversupply which would be created by the INB bank building (600,000 s.f.) to be beyond a 4 year horizon. The Masonic Building will meet the interim needs in a tight Class A market. Rents during the initial occupancy can be reasonably projected in the $10-11 range.

Exhibit 2
continued

COMPETITIVE OFFICE SPACE: LEASING SURVEY

Name/Location	Map Code	Leasable Area	Vacancy %	Rent P.S.F.	Comments
1. NEWER STRUCTURES					
40 Westminster		260,000	0	$8.25	Absorbed slowly after 1971 construction.
One Weybosset Hill		103,000	0	$8.00	
Hospital Trust Tower		320,000	0	$9.25	Rapidly absorbed in 1974
10 Orms Street		50,000	15%	$10.90	Built in 1979, with parking provided outside C.B.D.
Howard Bldg. 10 Dorrance St.	NA	224,000	NA	$6-8.00	Class B office space
2. REHABILITATED STRUCTURES: Completed					
Lauderdale Bldg. 144 Westminster St.	229-11	40,000	0	$8-9.00	Substantially owner occupied.
Turk's Head* 76 Westminster St.	229-1	152,000	0	$8.00	Only 13,000 s.f. were rehabilitated.
104 Eddy	225-1,21	40,000	2%	$7.00	Started 1975. Ground floor retail at $10.00.
Mason Building 165 Weybosset	224-3	46,300	17%	$7.50	
Rite-Aid* 217 Westminster St.	261-1	13,500	NA	NA	Class B+ on retail mall.
20 Westminster	238-1	21,000	0	NA	Owner occupied.
Owen Building*	250-2	40,000	0	$7.00	Class A mill rehabilitation. Net rent.
Wilcox Building* 42 Weybosset St.		30,800	50%	$8.50	2 years on market. Botched construction.
260 Westminster*	311-2	40,000	0	$5.00	Class B rehabilitation.
71-87 Washington *	135-2	36,000	22%	$7.00	Converted movie theater with government tenants paying net rents.

Exhibit 2
continued

3. REHABILITATED STRUCTURES: Current Projects

Fletcher Building
3 Charles St.	NA	12,500	75%	NA	Outside CBD location. Only ground floor retail has been preleased at $10 p.s.f.
51-55 Eddy*	217-2	22,200	0	$6.50	Class B+. 1/3 owner occupied remainder 100% preleased to city.
Slade Building
40 Washington St.	227-1	35,000	NA	$5.50	40% preleased to xerox and owner-occupant.
Canal Furniture
189 Canal St.	NA	28,800	NA	$7-10.00	Currently building Class A office space, parking to be provided.
Misch Building
398 Westminster St.	310-4	37,800	85%	NA	Class B space, poor building configuration.
20 Westminster*	238-1	21,000	NA	NA	50% owner occupancy planned.
Hay Building*
117 Dyer	250-2	41,200	NA	NA	Class A condominium project, 10% owner occupied. Building started.
122 N. Main	NA	50,000	NA	NA	Class B+, outside of CBD.
100-110 N. Main		36,500	NA	$5	Class B+, outside CBD.

4. REHABILITATION CANDIDATES

Ballor Johnson-Nichols*	264-2,3	42,000			$500,000 asking price.
70 Pine Street	264-1	32,600	80%	NA	Will be 100% vacant when city lease expires.
Studley Building*
86 Weybosset St.	254-1	50,000	NA	NA	Last building in Custom House district. New Owner plans "B" rehabilitation.
Remington Building	261-1	15,000	NA	NA	
La Salle Square	126	100,000	NA	NA	Jewelry trade convention center and merchandise mart.
Union Trust*
170 Westminster St.	227-1	80,000	0	$5	Currently full at these rates but poor quality space. Rehabilitation considered.

Exhibit 2
continued

5. NEW STRUCTURES: Current Projects

Gilbane Building Weybosset Hill	NA	100,000	NA	NA	Reynolds metals and Gilbane occupancy +30,000 s.f. open market.
Randall Square Charles St.	NA	100,000	NA	$13	IBM owner occupied with 13,000 s.f. open market short-term sublet.
Industrial Nat'l Bank	209	600,000	NA	$13	Financing has been obtained.

6. SUMMARY Unabsorbed space in CBD – Class A Space

New Construction	50,500
Existing rehabilitated projects	31,200
Committed rehabilitation projects not yet complete	83,000
Total:	164,700

*1976 Tax Act involvement.

Plans for
FREE MASONS' HALL
Providence R.I.

PINE ST. ELEVATION
Scale ⅛ inch=1 Foot

Fred E. Field Architect,
28 Custom House Street,
Providence R.I.

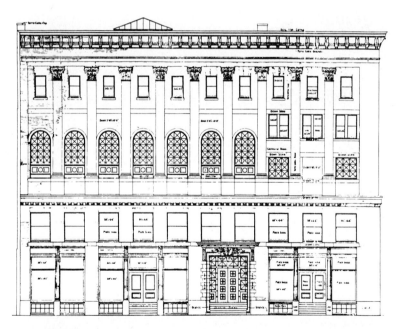

Plans for
FREE MASONS' HALL
Providence R.I.

DORRANCE ST. ELEVATION
Scale ⅛ inch=1 Foot

Fred E. Field Architect,
28 Custom House Street,
Providence R.I.

Exhibit 3
continued

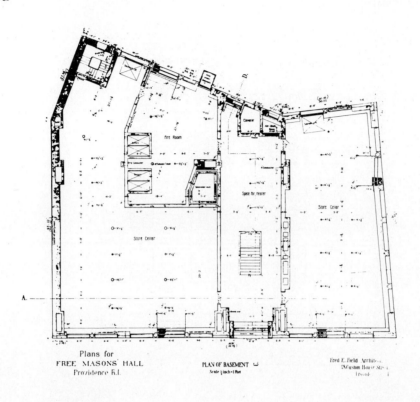

Plans for
FREE MASONS' HALL
Providence R.I.

PLAN OF BASEMENT
Scale ⅜ inch = 1 Foot

Fred E. Field Architect
28 Custom House Street
Providence R.I.

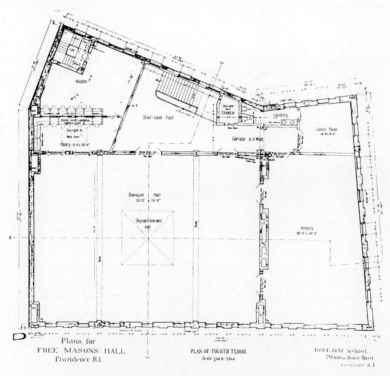

Plans for
FREE MASONS' HALL
Providence R.I.

PLAN OF FOURTH FLOOR
Scale ⅜ inch = 1 Foot

Fred E. Field Architect
28 Custom House Street
Providence R.I.

Exhibit 4

Masonic Hall: Construction Cost Estimate

Item	Units	Unit Price	Total
Demolition	35,000 SF	$1.25	$43,750
Superstructure			
New 4th floor	3,000 SF	6.00	18,000
Framing		Allow	25,000
Stairs		Allow	35,000
Core construction	5,000 SF	30.00	150,000
Foundations		Allow	15,000
Wall repairs		Allow	2,100
New windows	7 ea.	300	2,100
New windows	14 ea.	175	2,450
Internal doors	35,000 SF	.18	6,300
External doors	3 ea.	200	600
Floor repairs	35,000 SF	.20	600
New roof	6,000 SF	2.00	12,000
Services			
Elevators	2 ea.	40,000	80,000
Plumbing	35,000 SF	1.15	40,250
HVAC	35,000 SF	5.50	192,500
Electrical	35,000 SF	4.80	168,000
Drainage		Allow	2,000
Finishes			
Flooring	24,800 SF	1.00	24,800
Decorating	24,800 SF	.63	15,650
Ceiling	24,800 SF	.95	23,550
Lobby		Allow	13,000
Total Direct			891,100
Contingencies		5%	44,550
General requirements & overhead		10%	89,100
Contractor's profit		6%	53,500
Total contract cost			$1,078,250
Extra for new 6th floor			
Construction	5,500	42.00	231,000
Contingency, overhead & profit		21%	48,500
Total extra			279,500

Exhibit 5

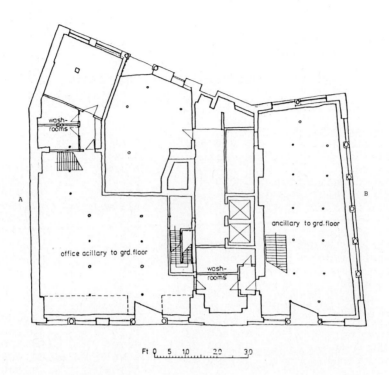

BASEMENT PLAN

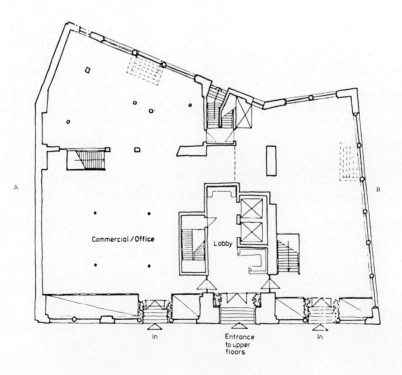

FIRST FLOOR PLAN

Exhibit 5
continued

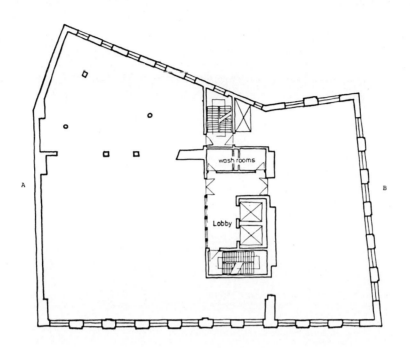

TYPICAL UPPER FLOOR PLAN AFTER REHABILITATION

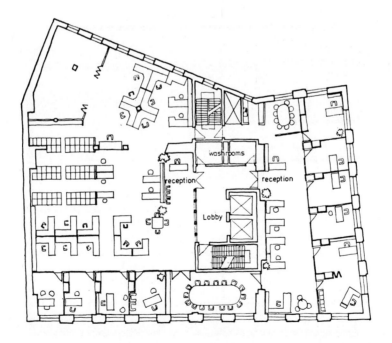

TYPICAL UPPER OFFICE FLOOR IN USE

Exhibit 5
continued

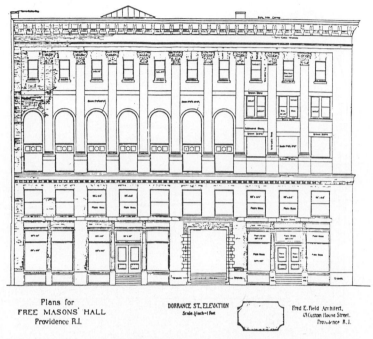

Plans for
FREE MASONS' HALL
Providence R.I.

DORRANCE ST. ELEVATION
Scale ⅛ Inch = 1 Foot

Fred E. Field Architect.
49 Custom House Street.
Providence R.I.

DORRANCE STREET ELEVATION

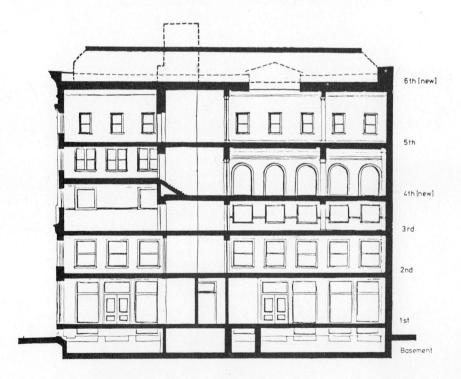

6th [new]

5th

4th [new]

3rd

2nd

1st

Basement

PROPOSED SECTION   A–B

Case 3

Joey Kaempfer

In November 1978, J.W. Kaempfer, Jr., President of the Great Northwest Land Company, Inc., was preparing himself for a meeting with his limited partners. These were the investors who had backed him in the several deals he had put together since forming the company in 1977.

The Great Northwest Land Company, Inc., was a small development and building company which specialized in higher-priced urban residential development. Its projects were located in the Northwest region of Washington, D.C. (Georgetown, Foggy Bottom), as well as in the nearby areas of Alexandria, Arlington, and Fairfax Counties in Virginia, and Montgomery County in Maryland. Typically, the company's projects involved new townhouse construction on bypassed or under-utilized parcels, rehabilitation/conversion of existing apartment complexes into townhouse units for sale, and renovation of older apartment projects for increased rentals.

Joey Kaempfer made it a policy to meet two or three times a year with his regular limited partners. He liked to review with them informally the overall direction of the firm, as well as the specific projects in which they were participating as investors. As general partner, he had no obligation to hold these meetings, but he did so because he valued the partners' input. Three of them were former employers or senior partners of his other projects; one headed one of the country's giant residential building companies; and one was President of one of Washington's largest banks. Their years of experience reached back to the post-Korean war recession of the Eisenhower era. Joey considered these meetings important, "I feel comfortable that when there's a decision involving throwing dice, I can ask their opinion. It's incredible to have that kind of experience on my side."

This meeting would be no different from the others. Joey wanted to go over the two renovation projects he was just now completing, the Union Street new townhouse development that was getting under way in Alexandria, Virginia, and the four new projects that were in varying stages of preparation. Joey also wanted to share his concerns about the future state of the economy.

As he sorted through the documents on these various projects, Joey reviewed with the casewriter his background and the history of the Great Northwest Land Company.

BACKGROUND

As an undergraduate, Joey Kaempfer had little idea he would end up where he was now. He had originally intended to go to law school. In fact, while a senior at New York University in 1967, he had applied to and been accepted by several law schools. A friend of the family, whom he much admired, took him aside and suggested he would be more satisfied with a career in business, rather than law. The man was a very successful businessman in Europe, South America, and in the United States. He told Joey he would be willing to discuss with him the possibility of Joey becoming involved in his organization, once he completed his business school training. Joey applied to Harvard Business School and was admitted at the last possible moment.

Late in his first year in the MBA program, Joey's plans for summer employment fell through. While passing through Baker Library, he noticed a sign announcing that Cartwright and Sons, a housing "giant," (then a subsidiary of an international conglomerate) was coming to interview. When he checked with the placement office, he learned the interviews were being held that very day, and all appointments had been booked for weeks. At that moment, someone rushed into the office and asked to cancel his interview because he had just accepted another job. The employment office director said, "That's perfect. Mr. Kaempfer, you will take the next appointment." Joey responded, "Great, let me just run back to my apartment and throw on some clothes and shave (I was dressed in shorts, an old shirt and had a three day growth. You always wore a suit to a B-school interview)." She said, "Oh well, no, here's the gentleman now." Out from the interview room came the Director of Corporate Planning and Special Assistant to the President. "It was too late, I went in and had my interview."

"He and I had a fairly heated argument about the merits of Co-op City in New York. He came down on the side of how spectacular it was. I expressed how unfortunate I thought it was. After the interview, I went home and decided there was no way he would hire me. I wrote him a nice letter and apologized for not being better prepared to meet with him, and I told him how much I wanted the job. Out of the ten candidates he interviewed, he hired me. He told me later that summer he had decided early on that he liked me best, but that he wasn't going to hire me because he was sure that the interview was a put-up, that I was probably number one in my class (not even close), that I had already been offered a job by everyone for the summer, and that my friends had encouraged me to see what lengths I could go to and still be accepted for the job. I think he credited Harvard Business School students with more imagination and mischievousness than they actually have."

During that summer, Joey spent three weeks each with the Assistant to the President, who had hired him, the President, the Vice President of Real Estate, and the head of marketing at the giant housing firm. He performed marketing studies, "cranked numbers," such as discounted cash flows, and made an inventory of commercial properties they owned in the East. In this latter assignment, he determined which of their shopping centers were in the best position to sell and pro-

jected returns that could be anticipated. He met everyone at the top level of Cartwright and Sons headquarters and made several lasting friendships as a result. The man who hired him remains one of his best friends today.

In the spring of 1969, after graduating from Harvard, Joey went to work full time for Cartwright and Sons. His first position was Assistant to the President, with responsibility for writing and editing the yearly business projections for submittal to the parent company. This document was a lengthy analysis of the previous year's corporate activities ($200+ million volume in housing), a comprehensive plan for the next 12 months, and a forecast for two, three, and five years in the future. Later, he ran the New England operation for the multi-housing development and construction arm of the company.

After three years at Cartwright and Sons, Joey joined a smaller company, Douglas, Inc. of Washington, D.C. His duties there included managing numerous rezonings, some syndications, and the analysis and purchase of new real estate investments for the Douglas family members.

In 1974, he went to work for the Hendricks Corporation as Vice President of New Project Development. Hendricks was a large building and development corporation in Washington, D.C., with a volume of $25-$35 million per year. He came to the organization when it purchased from Douglas a half interest in "Restful House in Westchester." Restful House was a specialized elderly housing project in Westchester County, New York, which Joey had been managing for Douglas at the time.

"Restful House is perhaps the least successful deal I've done." It was designed for well-to-do elderly residents. It provided small, luxurious apartments and a variety of common spaces, including greenhouses, recreation rooms, game rooms, dining rooms, etc. It required detailed management beyond that normally encountered in the development business. The project was originally conceived with the participation of a man who specialized in this type of facility. He subsequently dropped out of the deal, leaving Douglas, Inc., and Joey with the problem of completing the project. Restful House failed to yield a return in proportion to the investment that was required. Douglas had hoped to earn $150,000 per year on an investment of $300,000. Instead, Restful House probably returned $50,000 per year on an investment of $500,000, and considerable management effort was required to earn even that amount. Joey learned from this project that it was best to stay in one's own field.

SHERWOOD FOREST

Later at Hendricks, Joey developed his most successful project, "Sherwood Forest." Located in Chevy Chase, Maryland, this was a renovation project involving conversion of 600 older government financed (Section 608 program) apartment units, in a series of two-story buildings, into 340 condominium townhouses. Joey spoke with great satisfaction of Sherwood Forest.

"It is the project of which I am, hands-down, the proudest. It is the most remarkable project I ever conceived. It had been passed in front of every buyer in the marketplace and had even been offered to the company (Hendricks) and turned down. I was sitting around one evening having a beer with the senior partner's son, who worked for the company, and who had been shown the apartment property. He said there was no way to make the numbers work, which was too bad because it was brilliantly located in Chevy Chase (one of the really spectacular near-in suburban markets in the metropolitan area). I said, let's go take another look, and we took a drive over there.

"What I saw when I arrived was an extensive two-story project. It occurred to me that if you ignored what it was, you could slice it up like baloney and make townhouses out of it. And that's what we did. We sliced it up like baloney and made 340 townhouse units that sold from $77,990 to $129,500. We bought the project in rolling segments for a total of $9 million and the final sales volume was in the mid-30's. Quite a lot of work went into it (about $35,000 for each townhouse), but there was just one hell of a lot of profit in that deal. Location, location, location!

"It would have been cheaper and more profitable if we had had raw land in that location. But the closest raw land was ten miles further out. Even if there had been raw land available, we would not have been able to achieve anywhere near the density with townhouses. 'Sherwood' is essentially an urban project in a suburban location. We took the project to Montgomery County, told them we were not expanding the square footage but were cutting the number of units and parking to 60% of what they had been. The County loved it. When it was all finished, the assessed value had increased seven-fold.

"There was opposition by the tenants, however. Though we had a legal right to do the project, we had a full-time employee for two years who found people places to live. We scheduled moveouts and gave all the tenants first right of refusal. There is no doubt that we put lower income people out so that the well-to-do could move in. Nobody was ever evicted, and everyone found a place to live, but we displaced a lot of people. We did our best, short of not having done the project at all. This always presents something of a quandary for me."

While with Hendricks, Joey did a lot of subdivision work and rezonings involving large, 1,000 unit projects characteristic of the type of development Hendricks was doing at the time. He considered this to be the least exciting aspect of development work. He recognized its importance to the overall success of a project but found it to be fairly dull for him personally and to require a considerable amount of effort.

GREAT NORTHWEST LAND COMPANY

Joey made the decision to start his own business in the immediate aftermath of the success of Sherwood Forest. "The truth is, I had reached a point where I just did not want to work for someone else. I woke up one morning with a book I had been reading the night before, and it was more appealing to me to just sit in bed and read that book than to go to work. I knew then that I needed to be on my own."

It cost Joey ten months of effort and a great deal of money to set up his own business. While at Hendricks, part of his compensation had been a percentage interest in each of the deals in which he had a significant involvement. A consequence of his leaving was loss of value of his interest in ongoing projects. He sold his interest in one deal for $30,000 (a fraction of the actual value of his share) so he would have money to live on his first year. In addition, each of his partners put up $25,000 in working capital for furniture, a car for his construction manager, deposits on land, etc.

By November 1978, Joey estimated that Great Northwest Land Company was operating at a level of $5 million in annual gross revenues. The primary thrust of this was in new construction ranging from ten to sixty dwelling units. At the time of the case, the company had one large project about to begin construction and had nearly completed two others. Sales had been brisk, Great Northwest had only sixteen units available for sale in November,

but these couldn't be delivered until February to April of 1979.

"Guilford Green," patterned on Sherwood Forest, was the first project begun by Great Northwest. It was located in Old Town Alexandria, and consisted of thirty-two sale units. Four 1,800 square foot units were new construction, and twenty-eight were 1,500 square foot renovated units. The latter were constructed out of four-unit apartment buildings, partitioned in the middle to form townhouses. This project had been on the market for nine months and had sold approximately 67% of the units at prices from $103,500 to $139,500.

Another renovation, "MacArthur Mews," was just being completed. Located right outside of Georgetown, MacArthur Mews consisted of six older apartment buildings, previously containing thirty-four units, which were reconfigured and rebuilt into forty-one apartment units and subsequently re-rented. Behind these were two smaller buildings which were being reconfigured into twelve sales townhouses. The four smaller of these were sold from $92,500 to $106,500. The eight larger units, consisting of approximately 1,200 to 1,800 square feet, some with basements, were being brought to the market at prices from $125,500 to $155,000.

Joey hoped to begin construction shortly on "Union Street Townhouses," the newest and largest of the three major projects by Great Northwest. This was to be its first all-new construction project. The Union Street Townhouses had an excellent location in the center of the Old Town historic area of Alexandria, Virginia, on land purchased from the Washington Post Company. A total of forty-two luxury townhouse units, ranging from 1,425 to 2,875 square feet, were to be built and sold at prices estimated between $145,000 and $225,000. Joey expected an average sales price of $185,000.

The Union Street Townhouses each had at least one garage plus guest parking totaling 2+ spaces per unit. The buildings were of colonial design, as prescribed by the city's Board of Architectural Review. Materials were masonry with multipaned windows, slate or tin roofs and brick entry walks and driveways. All units had private fenced brick patios off dens or living rooms. Complete kitchens and bathrooms, strip-oak floors, wood trim and crown moldings, and twelve-foot ceilings in living rooms were special features intended to enhance the market appeal of these units. Joey estimated a project cost of $5,097,000, or $121,000 per townhouse.

He was expecting to complete his financing at 9.25%, interest only for up to a 24-month term. The loan would be guaranteed by himself and his partners. He planned to phase the project in three stages of 15, 15, and 12 townhouses each, and he would not begin phase two without selling at least 8 of the first 15 townhouses; phase three wouldn't begin without selling all of phase one. Joey was also hoping to arrange commitments for permanent financing for his potential buyers with a 30-year term and 9.25% interest rate.

ORGANIZATION

Each of the projects was organized as a separate partnership or S corporation. Joey owns 100% of Great Northwest; however, his net worth is substantially invested in real estate projects in which he has been involved (see Exhibit 1). Hence, Great Northwest could not operate without financial backers. The limited partners were brought in on a varying basis for each project. Generally, they included the big builder and Joey's three former employers. On two of the deals, he involved the banker as an investor, although he made it a practice not to loan Great Northwest money. His name lent considerable credibility to the deals, however.

When Joey was asked who would guarantee his loans, it helped to see the signature of a man who heads a large and well-known lending institution.

Joey operates as general partner, and his agreements all contain a "Caesar" clause giving him complete control. Once the limited partners have signed an agreement, they cannot object to his policy decisions, and they remain responsible for their share of indebtedness, regardless of the success of the project. Joey makes it a practice, however, to check with them before making decisions of serious consequence.

While Joey obviously enjoys owning his own company, he acknowledges that it takes an incredible amount of time. "Nobody ever accomplished anything substantial without a hell of a lot of work. I have fun making deals that are exclusively mine. Before, I was always a part of a joint effort, even when the idea was mine in the beginning. The negative for me is having to spend time running a company: I'm not having any fun with the day-to-day necessities of writing checks and buying stamps."

As his organization has grown, Joey has had to delegate certain internal operating responsibilities. His staff now includes John Nicolosi, construction manager, a full time bookkeeper, a full time secretary, several construction superintendents, and twenty to sixty carpenters, masons, and laborers.

John Nicolosi oversees the construction superintendents. He was thirty-three years old. The son of a drywall contractor, he grew up in the building industry working for a number of general contractors before Joey asked him to join Great Northwest. He visits every job on a day-to-day basis and negotiates the greater part of every subcontract that is required for each job. Joey assumes responsibility for negotiating the last 30% of the subcontracts. He functions with John in a good guy-bad guy strategy, ramming home the price he wants after John has done most of the bargaining. John is compensated for his services with a $36,000 annual salary plus the use of the company car and a small equity position in every deal in which he is directly involved.

There was one full time construction superintendent on each of the jobs under construction. They averaged about forty-five years of age, had extensive building experience in the field, and earn from $25,000 to $35,000 per year.

Joey acted as his own general contractor and tried to subcontract out everything possible. However, he found it difficult to obtain fixed-price subcontracts on masonry and carpentry for his renovation jobs. Consequently, he was forced to put carpenters and masons on his payroll for these projects. They ranged in numbers from twenty to thirty during the off season, and up to sixty when building was at its peak.

Every construction project was visited by Joey on an almost daily basis. He insists on being current on the progress of his jobs, and he maintains close control over all other aspects of his business. Joey takes a project all the way from conception through construction and marketing. Much of his personal time was taken up with work needed to "package" a project. He spends considerable time on site acquisition, obtaining rezonings, building permits and other governmental approvals, and preparing applications for financing. Over the last sixty days, he has been reviewing applicants for a position with his firm as an assistant to aid him in coordinating the various approval processes.

Joey explained what he thought he needed and the difficulty he was having finding the right person. "Time happens to be my most valuable asset and my only depletable resource. Money is relatively easy; you can get it. People are dying to put some money behind anybody who can make a reasonable buck. But time is where I'm short. I've been trying to hire an assistant for the last sixty days, and I've had no luck. I've been trying to find someone who could put the kind of package (loan application) together and also be a good sounding board for me. It's someone very hard to find. I could go to the Harvard Business School and find someone for $25,000, but within three years they'd want to be earning $100,000.

"I need someone who is a little less ambitious than I have been. I went through things too quickly; that is, I think my employers never got as much out of me as they should have. They were always satisfied, and at the same time I certainly don't think I was taking from them. In retrospect, however, I could have given them more by not being 60% concerned with where I was going and only 40% concerned with the job. Rather, perhaps, I should have been 95% concerned with doing my job and hope that that would get me where I wanted to go. I was always concerned with positioning myself which is, I think, why I'm now an entrepreneur."

PIPELINE PROJECTS

The upcoming meeting with his partners would probably involve three or four hours of discussion going over every aspect of the business. Progress of present projects, the profits that were being made and the details of new ventures Joey was putting together would be covered. This last topic was very important for the future of his company. Joey needed their continued support if he was to be able to maintain his present volume.

He had already received their backing for "Wilkes Street Townhouses," another new townhouse project in Old Town Alexandria, Virginia. His loan application had been successful in getting construction financing for the proposed twenty-five units. Joey had excerpted portions of the loan application package for the partners' review (see Exhibit 2).

Recently, he had received an offer to sell the Wilkes Street property. Joey had assembled two parcels for the project at a total contract cost of $387,000 and had invested $12,000 of front end money going after financing. The offer amounted to $485,000. The buyer would make the purchase directly from the landowner, and Great Northwest would receive all cash at closing. This offer would certainly be a matter of interest to his partners.

Three other deals were presently under purchase agreement subject to rezoning. In Fairfax County, Virginia, he had arranged to buy a 9.8 acre portion of a country club. The contract runs for four years and contains escalator clauses. Joey anticipated he could obtain rezoning for eighty-eight units and that each unit would sell for $125,000 to $150,000. He pegged the chance of success with this project at 60%. He expected little problem getting the rezoning. The neighbors and the county government were both in favor of development of the property; the state, however, wished to build a road through the property.

In McLean, Virginia, Joey was buying a thirteen-acre farm. He planned to joint venture with the family who owned it for development of approximately sixty townhouses in the $150,000 to $200,000 range. McLean was one of the most prestigious locations in the region. The project was brought to his attention by his consulting engineer. The members of the family had been looking for a way to sell the property on the most advantageous basis and had asked the engineer to send anyone reputable their way, as they did not wish to deal with real estate brokers. Joey ended up in a bidding contest with several other developers. The owners liked his proposal best and gave him a five-year contract. Joey estimated a 75% chance of success for this project, with the rezoning being the only question. If the rezoning failed, he had the right to buy the ground at a lower price for a single family development.

The project that had his greatest confidence (90% chance of success) involved another property in Fairfax County - the 5.2 acre Lucas property near Falls Church. The site was located within a fast developing area and, once rezoned in accordance with the county plan, would yield approximately fifty townhouse units in the $90,000 to $110,000 range or eighty "piggy-back" condominiums at approximately $65,000 or, alternatively, 115 apartments which could be rented or sold as condominiums now or in the future.

MARKET

Joey knew that his development plans for the three new properties he had under purchase agreement would require considerable refinement before he would be in a position to make specific zoning requests and before he could begin packaging for financing. One of his first needs would be to do a detailed review of existing market conditions as he had for the Wilkes Street Townhouse project. He was sufficiently confident with his judgment call for each site, however, to go ahead with commitments to purchase. After all, he had been doing business in this area for several years with his own firm and with Hendricks and Douglas.

With this experience, Joey believed he knew how to build to meet market demand. He was very careful to avoid putting too much of his own personal preferences and tastes into his residential units, yet he builds the type of housing in which he has confidence. Joey watches the cost of his housing units very carefully. He tries to get the maximum price he can squeeze out of his market, but at the same time, while he watches the cost end carefully, he is not afraid to build in solid value. He doesn't skimp when he selects materials, furnishings and fixtures.

He was not afraid to take extra steps to enhance the sales appeal of his units. In his renovation projects, for example, he chose to do some site work and exterior improvements prematurely. He would risk the necessity of making some repairs on elements that were damaged during subsequent construction phases, but he did it for the sake of creating an image that would stimulate buyer interest and early sales contracts.

Joey chose to operate in the middle income ranges. His units were aimed at single professional people earning $35,000 to $75,000 or to two-income families earning an equivalent combined income. Regardless, his buyers must earn at least an income sufficient to obtain a mortgage loan of no more than 2.7 times gross income, the ratio banks and lending institutions used to qualify a borrower.

The cost of housing had risen 10% per year consistently over the past several years in the Washington, D.C. area. This was a source of concern to Joey. He knew a house worth $100,000 today will be selling at $110,000 tomorrow, but where there were 15 people who could buy his $100,000 house today, there will be only 14 who can afford $110,000 tomorrow. He believed the system was rapidly pricing people out of his market. Over the last seven years, income in constant dollars had gone up significantly, but the average price of a single family house rose 75%.

Despite these pressures, Joey was reluctant to change his product. He was not interested in building in the $50,000 range. He always delivered a decent unit; he didn't cut to the bone and wasn't sure he'd know how.

FUTURE

Of greatest concern to Joey, during the coming meeting, was the discussion of his strategy for the future. His plan for the next five years was to increase profits from Great Northwest's projects by 10% in constant dollars each year. He expected his share of the profits to increase likewise. He was unsure how best to safeguard this future, given the present state of the economy.

Joey was concerned by the current national trends. The increase in the prime rate and the weakness of the stock market and other indicators did not alarm him as much as the effect they had on people's moods. As happened in 1974, he saw a general malaise spreading caused by a reaction to all of the bad news one reads in the papers. People constantly read about such issues as an outrageous rate of inflation and devaluation of the dollar, the risk of oil price rises and other problems, capped off by the prediction of an imminent recession or worse.

Joey believed that much of his market was made up of people trading up from their $65,000 to $100,000 houses or condominiums to his $95,000 to $150,000 townhouses. He thought they would not be willing to do this if they didn't feel confident of the country's economic well-being. "Those in the $150,000 to $200,000 market do not seem to be as affected as those at the lower end. They still continue to buy houses. And the most incredible thing of all is the phenomenon that occurs once the malaise is over: When the sun returns and the people find out they haven't lost their jobs, they run out and gorge themselves, buying everything in sight."

Joey wanted to be in the best possible position to take advantage of the period of prosperity that was bound to follow the coming economic downturn. He knew he must prepare carefully in order to weather the immediate storm unscathed. He hoped his partners would be able to assist him with his planning.

EXHIBITS

1. Real estate and partnership interests.

2. Loan summary, Wilkes Street Townhouses.

QUESTIONS FOR DISCUSSION

1. What are the key decisions leading to a career in development?

2. Has Joey been "lucky" so far?

3. How can he make Great Northwest a more permanent organization?

4. How do the current and proposed projects fit with the company strategy?

Exhibit 1

REAL ESTATE AND PARTNERSHIP INTERESTS (June 30, 1978)

1. RESTFUL HOUSE IN WESTCHESTER is a general partnership that operates an 86-unit retirement home in Westchester County, New York. The facility was opened in January, 1976, and is now full. It is now making money and should produce $50,000 per year cash flow in 1979. J.W. Kaempfer, Jr. owns 10% of the equity.

2. WASHINGTON HOUSE ASSOCIATES is a limited partnership that owns and operates a 103-unit retirement home at 5420 Connecticut Avenue, N.W., Washington, D.C. Starting in 1976, the facility is now full. This project will have a cash flow of $250,000 for the year 1978. J.W. Kaempfer owns 7.5% of the equity.

3. SHERWOOD FOREST ASSOCIATES is a limited partnership that is renovating 116 townhouses for sale in Bethesda, Maryland. The project has been completely sold out at prices from $70-115,000. J.W. Kaempfer, Jr. owns 5.0% of the equity.

4. RESIDENTIAL BUILDING LOTS, WASHINGTON, D.C., is land for three single family houses on Chain Bridge Road in northwest Washington, D.C., with a mortgage of $73,000.

5. LAUREL ASSOCIATES is a limited partnership that owns a 224-unit apartment project near Laurel, Maryland. It was completed in May of 1977, and is now fully rented. Permanent financing of $3,575,000 at 9.25% interest was provided by the Travelers Life Insurance Company. Projected cash flow of $110,000 per annum should be reached by late 1978. J.W. Kaempfer, Jr. owns 3% of the equity.

6. 4508 MACARTHUR BOULEVARD, N.W., WASHINGTON, D.C. is a four-unit apartment building that has a gross income of approximately $16,000 yearly. There is a $70,000 mortgage on the property. A value of $55,000 above the mortgage has been assigned to this equity based upon a 12.5% return on equity and $125,000 comparable selling prices for four-unit buildings in this area.

7. MACARTHUR AND V STREET ASSOCIATES is owner of the Shady Brook apartments on MacArthur Boulevard, N.W., Washington, D.C. The project is now being renovated into 12 fee simple townhouses for sale between $95-155,000 (six have already been sold) and 12 apartments which are rented at rates of $345-385/month. While an estimated combined project pretax profit on the townhouses and value for the apartments will exceed $450,000, $250,000 has been used as the value of the equity.

8. ALEXANDRIA INVESTORS owns 28 townhouses presently being renovated for sale and four townhouse lots upon which new units are being constructed in Alexandria, Virginia. Seventeen of the 32 units have been sold and the project is projected to make $500,000. A value of $250,000 has been placed on this equity at this time.

Exhibit 1
continued

9.   UNION STREET ASSOCIATES, ALEXANDRIA, VIRGINIA is a parcel of property
     for the development of 40 luxury townhouse residences in a prime
     location in Old Town Alexandria, Virginia. This property is presently
     being rezoned and construction is projected to begin in December of
     1978. The owning entity, Union Street Associates, Inc., has been
     offered and has rejected a bonafide offer to purchase the land for
     $200,000, more than the present total investment. Half this figure has
     been used as a measure of value. J.W. Kaempfer, Jr. owns 34% of Union
     Street Associates, Inc.

10. PRINCE STREET is a limited partnership that owns land for 10 townhouse
     units in Alexandria, Virginia. The value of this project is placed at
     the amount of equity invested in it. J.W. Kaempfer, Jr. owns 20% of
     this project.

11. DUKE STREET PARTNERS purchased 10 small houses in Alexandria, Virginia
     for $27,500 apiece in early 1978. Two of these have been resold for
     $34,000 and the remaining eight are now being marketed. A value of
     $25,000 has been placed on this project. J.W. Kaempfer, Jr. owns 10%
     of this project.

12. J.W. Kaempfer, Jr. owns a fully renovated period house in northwest
     Washington, D.C. The house has a $120,000, 75% mortgage. Value above
     mortgage is $40,000.

NOTE: On items 7, 8, 9, 10 and 11, J.W. Kaempfer, Jr. has signed on
        acquisition, construction and operating loans as one of a number
        of guarantors.

Exhibit 2

WILKES STREET TOWNHOUSES

Loan Summary

The developers wish to arrange a comprehensive acquisition and development loan and a permanent financing package for a 25-unit townhouse project in the colonial style located in Old Town Alexandria, Virginia.

ACQUISITION/DEVELOPMENT:

Purchase Price (land)	$ 300,000
Development Costs	1,750,625
Total Project Cost	$ 2,005,625

Requested at Acquisition: $ 300,000 x 80% = $ 240,000

Requested Over
24 Month Term of Loan: $1,705,625 x 80% = $1,364,500

Total Acquisition/
Development Loan Request: $1,604,500

Phasing Plan: The developers anticipate closing will take place in the late part of November or early part of December of 1978. Construction is planned for two phases. The first phase will be 15 units. The second phase, which will not begin until binding contracts have been received on 5 of the first 15 units, will be 10 more units.

Acquisition/Development
Loan as a Percent
of Sales Price: 67.9%

Projected Schedule:
Acquisition:	December 1, 1978
Phase I (15 units):	March 1, 1979
Phase II (10 units):	June 1, 1979
Job Completion:	January, 1980

Security: A first mortgage on the land (54,000 SF) and improvements (25 units) located on Wilkes, Patrick and Henry Streets in Alexandria, Virginia.

Borrower: A Subchapter S corporation with J. W. Kaempfer, Jr. as president and other stockholders.

Exhibit 2
continued

Loan Summary (continued)

Term: 24 months

Fee: 1% payable at closing.

Rate: 10.50%

Extensions: One automatic six month extension for 1/2 of 1% of balance at the end of the original term.

Release: 80% of sales price or 110% of pro rata loan amount whichever is greater.

Guarantee: All of the above mentioned stockholders.

Closing: Projected for December, 1979.

Draw Schedule: Monthly draws in accordance with approved cost breakdown; initial draw of $ 240,000 at closing.

PERMANENT LOANS:

Amount of Loans: An aggregate sum of $ 1,850,000 composed of as many as 25 individual loans with an average mortgage amount of $ 74,000.

Commitment Fee: One point paid at closing of construction loan.

Commitment Term: 24 months

Extension: One automatic six month extension for a fee of one half percent of unused portion.

Loan Term: 30 years

Loan Rate: Local market at time of individual closings.

Buy Down Right: Developer shall have the right to buy loans down to a lower rate at the generally accepted price.

Exhibit 2
continued

WILKES STREET TOWNHOUSES

Development Proposal

SUMMARY: Wilkes Street Associates proposes to acquire a 54,000 sq.
            ft. parcel of land in Old Town, Alexandria, Virginia on
            which it will erect Twenty-five (25) moderately priced [1]
            townhouse units for sale to the public on a fee simple
            basis.

THE PROPERTY: The property (54,000 sq. ft.) is bounded on the East by
                Patrick Street (223 feet) on the West by Henry Street (237
                feet) on the South side by Wilkes Street (242 feet) and on
                the North by private owners (192 feet). At this time
                Southern Railway Corporation owns the property. It is
                vacant and the property is zoned RB (Residential) and the
                City Fathers are anxious to see this developed as
                townhouses, an allowed use under RB.

THE CITY: Old Town Alexandria is a quaint, historic seaport city
            with a very special colonial charm. Originally a thriving
            port for Northern Virginia and the District of Columbia (4
            miles to the North), it was a favorite of George
            Washington and the place where he drilled his first
            provincial troops in 1754. Today, Alexandria is a busy
            commercial and residential city; one of the three free
            cities in the Unites States. Many government and
            industrial executives reside in Alexandria because of its
            beautiful residential areas (of which Old Town is the
            premier one) its convenience to Washington and surrounding
            business areas and its quality shopping and dining
            facilities.

            Old Town, itself the center of the city's quality shopping
            and the seat of government, is older and larger than
            Washington's famed Georgetown. Its many cobble stone
            streets and beautifully preserved colonial buildings
            create an ambience that is unequaled anywhere in the
            country.

LOCATION: The subject site is on the edge of Old Town's presitgious
            residential area. It is three blocks from King Street,
            the quaint but busy commercial street that leads down to
            the water and houses elegant shops, restaurants and
            professional offices.

[1] In the Old Town market where new reproductions of federal style town-
     houses can cost up to $225,000, units priced in the $85-95,000 range can
     only be called moderately priced.

Exhibit 2
continued

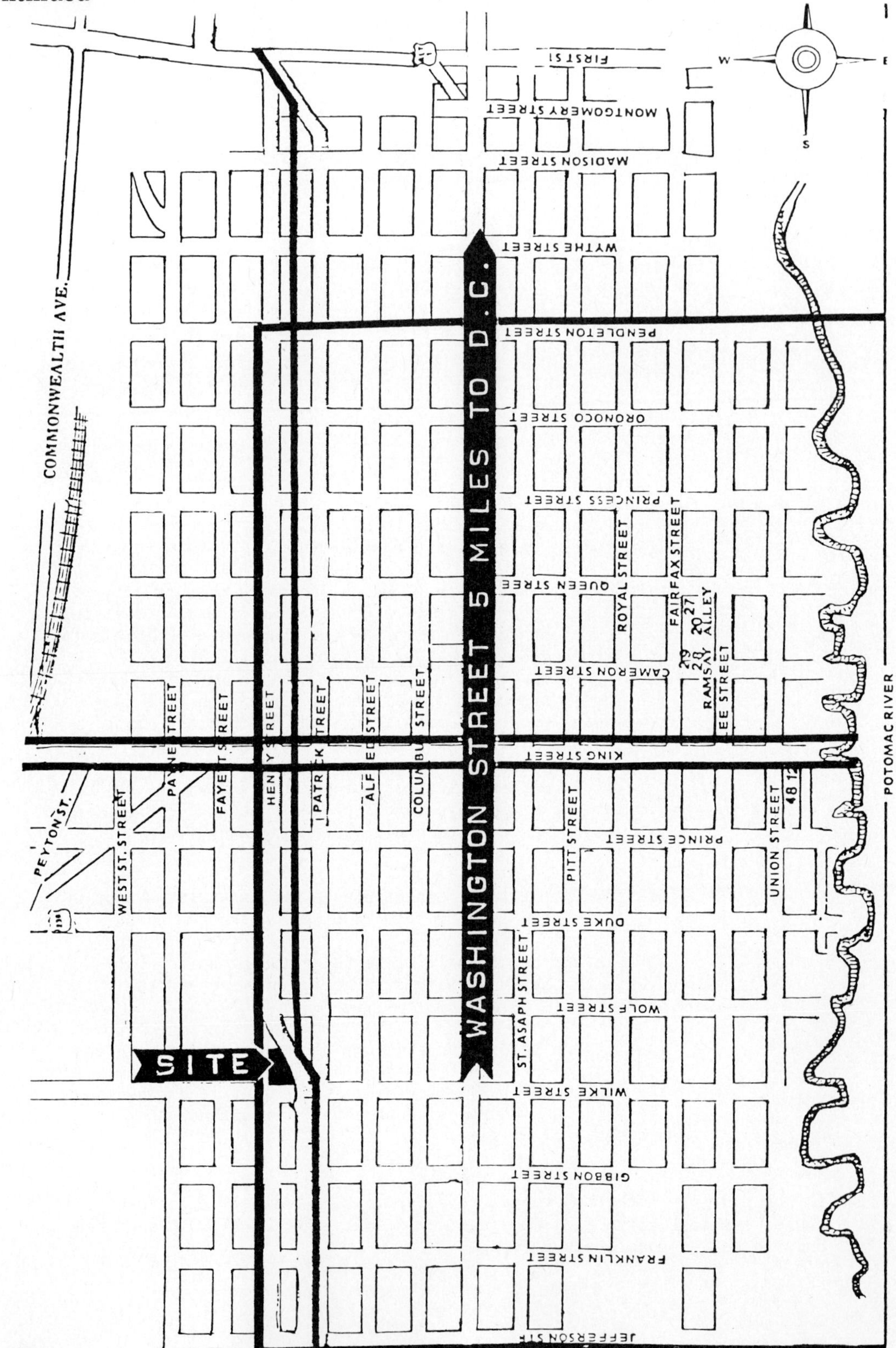

Exhibit 2
continued

LOCATION (con't)   While the site is in an area that has been moving rapidly
                     from commercial/industrial to residential use in recent
                     years, there was intense competition to buy it for a
                     number of reasons. First, the site is one of the few of
                     this size remaining in even close proximity to Old Town.
                     Second, the price is quite low (see land comparables)
                     which enables the developer to build houses in the "magic
                     under $100,000" category; and finally, unlike many
                     properties in Old Town there is nothing to demolish, no
                     historic buildings to worry about - just plain straight
                     forward new construction.

THE MARKET: Old Town Alexandria is one of Washington's most sought
                     after residential areas. Many new townhouses in the
                     $100,000 to $150,000 range are absorbed yearly. The
                     developers of Wilkes Street Townhouses have a 32 unit
                     project priced from $103,500 to $131,500 that has sold one
                     unit every 10 days for the six months it has been open.
                     This is only one of the many examples that could be made.
                     Critical to understand , however, is that Wilkes Street
                     will be available to all those people who have aspired to
                     Old Town, but found the available houses out of their
                     price range.

                     Price will be the developers strongest asset along with
                     the great value of a location in Old Town Alexandria. The
                     price alone should assure the project a strong, welcome
                     market reaction. When the price, location and quality
                     design are combined the Wilkes Street project will have a
                     great market appeal. It should be noted that most of the
                     existing comparable projects will have been sold out when
                     the Wilkes Street Townhouses reach the market, and that,
                     in fact, not much is available in Old Town in this under
                     $100,000 price range.

RENDERING: The architects' elevation on the next page attempts to
                     depict the feeling the finished units will have. The
                     rendering is, of course, missing the warmth the real
                     project will have with its brick walkways, landscaping,
                     brass hardware and other authentic colonial touches.

Exhibit 2
continued

Lewis/Wisnewski & Associates Ltd.

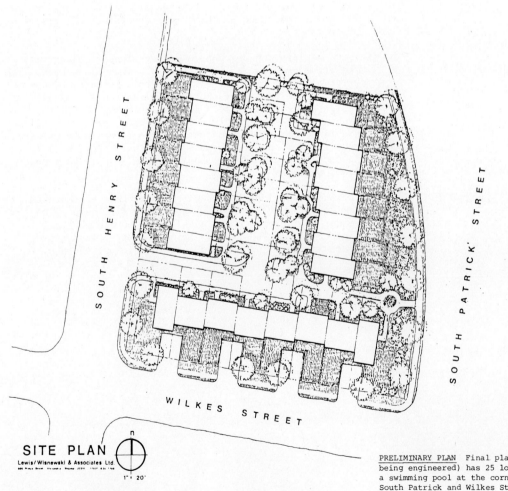

SITE PLAN
Lewis/Wisnewski & Associates Ltd.

1" = 20'

PRELIMINARY PLAN Final plan (now
being engineered) has 25 lots and
a swimming pool at the corner of
South Patrick and Wilkes Streets.

Exhibit 2
continued

WILKES STREET TOWNHOUSES

The Product

The developers plan to offer two (2) basic unit types. These are:

      A 16 foot wide 38 deep unit with 1,216 square feet
      of finished space plus an expandable attic for an
      extra bedroom and bath or den. This unit will have
      two bedrooms and 2 full and 1 half baths. There will
      be eight (8) of these units.

      An 18 foot wide 37 deep unit with 1,332 square feet
      of finished space plus an expandable attic that can
      be used for two extra bedrooms and a bath. This
      unit will have two bedrooms and a den, 2 full baths
      and 1 half bath. There will be seventeen (17) of
      these units.

All attics will be expandable into additional living space by the addition of
insulation and drywall. This is a feature much sought after and not generally
offered by the competition. The developer is considering offering a fixed
price package to purchasers for the optional completion of this attic space.

The units will, of course, be of colonial design as prescribed by the city's
Board of Architectural Review and demanded by buyers in Old Town. Each house
will have 1.5 parking spaces, .5 more than the city requires. In addition,
the project will preserve enough additional street frontage for guest parking
of 25 spaces. Parking in this neighborhood is not now difficult, but offering
2.5 spaces per unit can only serve to enhance the marketing effort.

The buildings will be all masonry with multipaned windows, steeply pitched
roofs and brick entry walks. All units will have private fenced patios off
the living rooms.

Each unit will have luxury kitchens including frost free, ice maker
refridgerators, double oven, self-cleaning ranges, dishwashers, disposals,
quality oak cabinets, formica countertops and ceramic tile floors (a very good
marketing feature).

Bath and powder rooms will be of ceramic tile. There will be complete two
coat paint jobs throughout with enamel on all wood trim. Dining rooms will
have chair rail and both dining and living rooms will have rich crown
moldings. All rails and spindles will be wood instead of the cheaper metal
railings so often seen on the inside of new units in the under $100,000
category.

All floors that are not ceramic tile will be select oak, finished to the
purchasers choice of stains. The ceiling heights will be 8 feet with the
exception of all living rooms which will be 11 feet high. The developers are
known throughout the Old Town and Metropolitan market as being sticklers for
detail. While this kind of attention is costly, it insures that even these
moderately priced homes will offer solid, long-lasting value.

Exhibit 2
continued

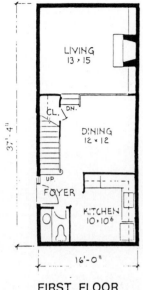
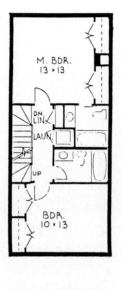
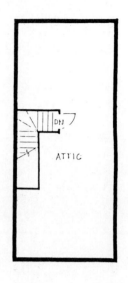

FIRST FLOOR   SECOND FLOOR   ATTIC

FLOOR PLAN TYPE A   1/8" = 1'- 0"

Lewis/Wisnewski & Associates Ltd.
605 Prince Street Alexandria, Virginia 22314   (703) 836-7766

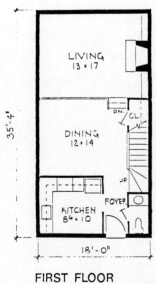
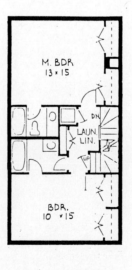
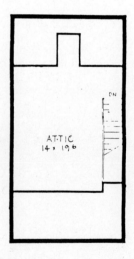

FIRST FLOOR   SECOND FLOOR   ATTIC

FLOOR PLAN TYPE B   1/8" = 1'- 0"

Lewis/Wisnewski & Associates Ltd.
605 Prince Street Alexandria, Virginia 22314   (703) 836-7766

Exhibit 2
continued

WILKES STREET TOWNHOUSES

MARKET DATA

Townhouse Comparables

In this section an effort has been made to show the market segment against which the proposed project will compete.

The section includes the following:

A Comparable Map showing location of the competition in relationship to the proposed site.

A chart showing # of units, size, prices, square footage prices, speed of sellout when first on the market, and whether the project is a fee or condominium form of ownership.

Pictures of the Comparables used in the chart mentioned above.

Exhibit 2
continued

WILKES STREET TOWNHOUSES

Townhouse Comparables Map

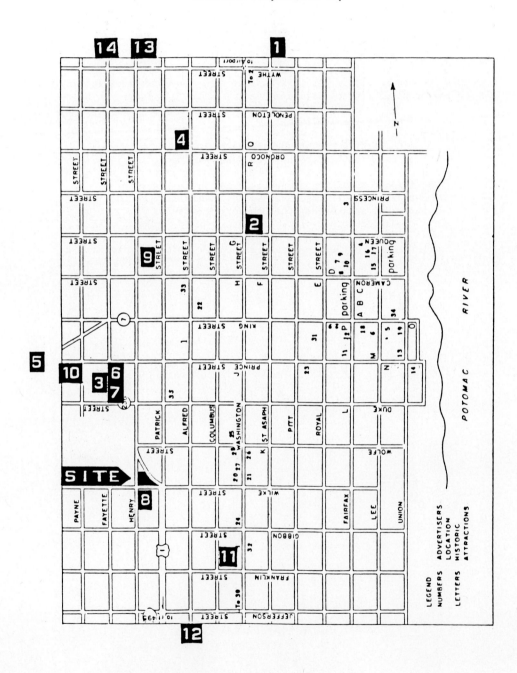

Exhibit 2
continued

Project Name	No. of Units(1)	Average Price(2)	Average Finished S.F.	Average S.F. Price(2)	No. Sold/ Months It Took
WILKES STREET	25	$ 94,500	1277 SF	$ 74.18	N/A
(Site)		COMPARABLES			
(1) WATERGATE OF ALEXANDRIA	150(C)	$102,500- 138,500	1370 SF	$ 99.75	68/16 mo.
(2) BROCKETTS CROSSING	42(C)	$112,000- 175,000	820 SF	$136.59	42/9.5 mo. Sold Out
(3) PORT CITY MEWS	11(C)	$110,000- 122,500	1500 SF	$ 77.34	10/6 mo.
(4) COOPERS ALLEY	11(C)	$110,000- 129,000	1175 SF	$102.13	3/8 mo.
(5) COMMERCE STREET	5	$ 96,000	1135 SF	$ 84.58	4/4 mo.
(6) SOUTH FAYETTE STREET	4	$108,000	1400 SF	$ 77.14	4/2 mo. Sold Out
(7) SOUTH FAYETTE STREET II	4	$ 89,500	1008 SF	$ 88.79	4/3 mo. Sold Out
(8) OLDE TOWNE WEST (3)	39	$ 67,500	1200 SF	$ 56.25	39/3 mo. Sold Out
(9) 220-222 NORTH PATRICK	2	$ 89,000	1350 SF	$ 65.93	2/1 mo. Sold Out
(10) CENTENNIAL ROW	12	$100,000	1100 SF	$ 90.90	10/6 mo. Sold Out
(11) WASHINGTON SQUARE	39(C)	$ 95,000- 120,000	1100 SF	$ 97.72	37/6 mo. Reserved
(12) GUILFORD GREEN	32	$103,000- 131,500	1350 SF	$ 86.67	16/8 mo.
(13) OLD NORTH PORT	38	$ 88,500	1400 SF	$ 63.22	38/9 mo. Sold Out
(14) PORTNER PLACE	22	$104,500	1300 SF	$ 80.38	Just Opened

NOTES: (1) C denoted Condominium.
     (2) Where projects have sold out the most recent resale price has been shown, where prices have risen on existing projects the most recent known contract price has been shown.
     (3) This project was on urban renewal ground and therefore the builders had profit and sales limitations. Not built to suit the market at all, but so low priced it sold out anyway.

Exhibit 2
continued

(1) WATERGATE OF ALEXANDRIA

(2) BROCKETTS CROSSING

(3) PORT CITY MEWS

(4) COOPERS ALLEY

(5) COMMERCE STREET

(6) S. FAYETTE STREET

(7) S. FAYETTE STREET II

(8) OLDE TOWNE WEST

Case 4

Savannah West

On Friday, August 12, 1977, Alison Porter, a three-year veteran of Chemical Bank's "Real Estate Bank" with medals and scars to prove it, faced the unpleasant prospect of another working weekend. She had just returned from a trip to Savannah, Georgia, where she met with Willy Welsh, an Atlanta developer. Welsh was anxious to get approval for a $3 million construction loan so that he could begin work on Savannah West, a 216-unit "California-style" garden apartment complex in Savannah.

Welsh felt it essential to get started for several reasons. Rumors were afloat that other developers were preparing plans for multi-family projects in Savannah. Welsh wanted to be the first one in the ground and possibly scare off competition. Pressure to start also came from his subcontractors. He had promised them a September 1 starting date. Welsh knew that if the project did not start on time, he could not hold the subcontractors to their initial bids. In addition, if there were a delay, the subcontractors might find other work, and he would have to begin anew the delicate, frustrating job of hiring and scheduling subcontractors to conform to a ten-month construction timetable. Welsh was also anxious to get started because the take-out commitment from the Empire State Savings Bank had a time limitation. The $3 million commitment from Empire Savings specified completion of the construction by September 1, 1978. By starting September 1, 1977, Welsh would have ten months to complete the construction, plus a two-month buffer to absorb possible delays.

During her trip to Savannah, Porter promised Welsh a quick answer. Porter had scheduled a meeting of the loan committee for Monday, August 15. At that meeting the committee would either turn down the loan or give it tentative approval. The members of the loan committee would rely heavily on Porter's memorandum explaining the key issues.

WILLY WELSH

Willy Welsh began working in construction during the summers while he was in high school and college. After graduating from the Georgia Institute of Technology, he joined a construction company in Atlanta. In 1968 at the age of thirty-two, he went into partnership with Harry Barnes, an experienced contractor who built apartments and light commercial properties. Welsh became president of the company a year later.

In 1970 Welsh created Engineered Concepts, a general contracting firm. He immediately won a bid for the construction of a $5 million, 280-unit apartment development. His firm also took on the supervision of a 288-unit apartment complex as part of a joint venture agreement. Since 1972, Engineered Concepts has completed construction on over $25 million of property. Welsh has also set up a subsidiary which manages income-producing properties (see Exhibit 1).

Welsh came in contact with the Chemical Bank in 1976. At that time, Chemical Bank was involved in the troubled Greenbriar Apartments, a 400-unit garden apartment development in Atlanta. A local savings and loan had issued a take-out, contingent upon 80% occupancy by July 1, 1976. The Thomas Herbert Company, Inc. of Atlanta, Georgia, the developer, ran into serious cost overruns and untimely delays. At the same time, a competing project in the neighborhood came on stream ahead of schedule and drew away potential tenants. When July arrived, the project was less than one-half completed and only 15% occupied, thus canceling the savings bank's commitment.

Without the permanent financing to bail them out, Chemical Bank, the largest of the group of banks involved in the construction financing, realized Herbert would not be able to repay his loan. Chemical also discovered that several of the key subcontractors were displeased with the developer. In an effort to save the project, Chemical decided to step in and arrange for someone else to finish the work. A deal was struck with Herbert, relieving him of personal and corporate liability, and Chemical obtained a deed in lieu of foreclosure. Chemical assigned David Hancock to take charge of the work-out. An old college classmate in the real estate department of one of Chemical's correspondent banks in Atlanta steered Hancock to Willy Welsh.

Welsh's people, in close consultation with Chemical, reviewed the Greenbriar project and agreed to complete construction on a fee basis for $3.5 million. Welsh recommended several design changes that he felt would improve the marketability of the apartments. Hancock agreed, and Welsh proceeded with construction.

Dramatic changes ensued. The project was completed within five months and within the stipulated budget. Welsh's property management subsidiary put together an outstanding marketing program and achieved a 40% occupancy in four months and 90% occupancy in nine months. A suitable purchaser was then found, and Chemical Bank received full repayment on its loan.

CHEMICAL BANK

Chemical Bank is the fifth largest bank in New York, and the sixth largest in the United States in terms of both capitalization and deposits. In July 1977, it had over $23 billion in deposits and over $30 billion in assets. These figures represent an 11% growth in deposits and a 15% growth in assets during the prior twelve months.

Several departments at the Chemical Bank are organized as "separate banks." There is, for example, a "Metropolitan Bank," a "Corporate Bank" and a "Trust and Investment Bank." In September 1976, Chemical Bank set up a "Real Estate Bank." The prior two years had been rough ones for the bank's real estate department. The recession of 1974-75 led to a large volume of real estate problem loans, especially loans made to Real Estate Investment Trusts. The "Real Estate Bank" represented management's recognition of the need for more specialized and sophisticated personnel to deal with existing and new loans in real estate.

By the end of the following year, the "Real Estate Bank" employed 200 people, including 110 loan officers, each of whom was responsible for a specific geographic area in the United States or Canada. In 1977, the "Real Estate Bank" managed a $1.45 billion asset portfolio. Most of this portfolio was inherited. One of the major achievements of 1977 was upgrading this portfolio by reducing loans to Real Estate Investment Trusts from $490 million to $332 million.

In addition to making loans, the "Real Estate Bank" provides a full line of banking services to people in the real estate industry such as lock box facilities, short-term investment management and lines of credit. In creating this separate entity, Chemical Bank hoped to increase its flexibility and improve its service to customers. The goal of the "Real Estate Bank" is to attract new customers on a nationwide basis and to develop and maintain broad customer relationships.

When David Hancock, who had handled the Greenbriar work-out, learned that Willy Welsh was preparing to start a new project in Savannah, Georgia, and had already secured a take-out mortgage from the Empire State Savings Bank, he decided that he had found a stable, competent new customer for the bank. He contacted Alison Porter, detailed the successful Greenbriar work-out, and praised Welsh's efficiency and thoroughness. Porter immediately contacted Welsh and set up a meeting.

SAVANNAH

The city of Savannah is located on the Savannah River, twenty miles upstream from the Atlantic Ocean. It is rich in historical tradition, having been established in 1733 as a Port City in the Georgia colony. Founded by General James Oglethorpe, Savannah was America's first "planned" city and retains today the squares and original street plan.

Savannah is the second largest city in Georgia with a population of 218,000. Eighty percent of these people live in Chatham County. Since 1970 the population of Chatham County has grown at approximately 1% per year. The increase has been mostly in the 20-34 age group. Approximately 60% of the increase has been families with incomes between $12,000 and $20,000. Following the national trend, household size in this area has been declining from 3.5 in 1970 to an estimated 3.2 in 1978. Single family housing starts in Chatham County are expected to average about 500 per year during the next several years.

The major sources of employment are the port and related distribution facilities, manufacturing, tourism, and the military. All four areas of employment are growing. The port handles 10 million tons per year, adds about $73 million to the Savannah economy and is currently undergoing a $27 million expansion. The 193 industries that manufacture products in and around Savannah include American Cyanamid, Continental Forest Industries and Savannah Foods. This sector of the economy received a boost from the recent improvements in the Federal and state highway network, especially the construction of I-16 giving truckers direct freeway access to I-95 and the rest of the Federal highway system. Tourism has grown, especially among foreigners who are taking advantage of the devaluation of the dollar. The Hunter/Stewart army base has always been a major but erratic factor in the Savannah economy. A dramatic build-up is presently underway. The prospects for this army base are enhanced by the fact that the Senator from Georgia is Chairman of the Armed Services Committee. The median per capita income in Savannah is projected to rise in the years ahead. Unemployment in the civilian work force is estimated at 7.6%, which is close to the 7.4% state average.

SAVANNAH WEST

As vacancy rates began to rise in the Atlanta area, Willy Welsh looked for new opportunities. On a visit to his family in Savannah, Welsh talked with rental agents and learned that the market for apartments was getting tight. There had been little or no multi-family construction in Chatham County in over three years, since the failure of a 200-unit garden apartment project. As a result, vacancy rates in existing apartment complexes were dropping

Median Family Income (Including Military Population) Savannah SMSA

Constant Dollars

	1975 (actual)		1980 (projected)		1985 (projected)	
	# Families	Income	# Families	Income	# Families	Income
Bryan	2,206	$7,432	2,342	$8,852	2,342	$10,272
Chatham	59,960	$8,720	65,042	$9,802	67,844	$10,844
Effingham	4,432	$8,944	5,086	$10,624	5,640	$12,254

rapidly, from 7% in 1972 to 5% in 1974, and then down to less than 4% in 1976. As far as Welsh was concerned, the market "felt good."

Welsh was determined to move fast. In a short time, he zeroed in on an 11.8-acre property in Chatham County just south of Hunter Army Air Base. This location was excellent, he believed, for a 216-unit garden apartment development. It is only 6.5 miles from the Savannah business district. Shopping is available along Abercorn Extension and at the enclosed 750,000 square foot Oglethorpe Mall. Although the property is close to Hunter Army Airfield, noise does not seem to be a problem (see Exhibit 2).

Welsh surveyed the multi family developments in the area and found that vacancies were down to 1%. He felt that he could build a complex that would "completely out-class them" and still rent at a comparable or slightly higher rate (see Exhibit 3). In aiming at what he defined as the "semi-luxury" market, Welsh claimed: "I know what they want. Not the old, stuffy, fake-genteel style so prevalent in Savannah. Our 'California-look' will sweep them off their feet" (see Exhibit 4).

Based on his survey of neighboring properties, Welsh estimated that he could achieve gross revenue of approximately $600,000 and net income before financing of close to $400,000 (see Exhibit 5). He then estimated his costs as shown in the

table. Based on this analysis he negotiated for and purchased the 11.8-acre tract for $172,000.

THE TAKE-OUT

Welsh took his plans and projections to New York to look for permanent financing. He contacted the Empire State Savings Bank, which then hired an Atlanta appraiser to do an appraisal of the property and the project. The appraiser concluded that a 216-unit garden-apartment complex constituted the highest and best use of the property. He further stated that when completed, the complex would have a market value of $4,000,000: $200,000 for the land, and $3,800,000 for the improvements (see Exhibit 6).

Empire Savings then offered to provide $3 million of permanent financing at 9-1/2% interest for a twelve-year term with a balloon at the end (10.23% constant). Empire offered this financing in the form of a floor-to-ceiling first mortgage. Empire would advance $2,550,000 (the floor) after July 1, 1978 and prior to September 1, 1978. To receive this floor payment, Welsh was required to meet all the terms of the loan covenant including satisfactory completion of all of the construction. Before releasing the $450,000 balance of the mortgage, Empire insisted that occupancy at Savannah West be such that the collectable rentals from the rental units in

Development Cost Estimate, Savannah West

Land (12 acres+-) zoned for 216 units, with on-site water, sewer, and drainage	$172,000
Construction and site development	2,578,000
Architectural, engineering and inspection	20,000
Construction interest ($3,000,000 x .5 x 9%)	135,000
Legal and accounting	20,000
Construction loan and permanent loan fees	45,000
Banker's fee	30,000
	$3,000,000

the buildings shall be at least $552,000 per annum on a nonfurnished basis, exclusive of concessions, and the space is rented on a basis so that if the buildings were 100% rented the annual rentals would be at least $601,200.

This ceiling loan would not be made later than January 30, 1979. Welsh secured this $3 million take-out commitment by depositing $30,000 in a non-interest bearing account. That deposit will be forfeited if the loan is not consummated.

THE DECISION

Like most construction lenders, Chemical Bank did not like to tie up its money in long-term loans and therefore expected most developers to secure take-out financing before applying for a construction loan. Now that Welsh had this permanent financing arranged, he only needed approval from Alison Porter and he could begin construction. In fact, Welsh was so confident of his new relationship with Chemical Bank and so anxious about local competition, that he was prepared to begin construction while waiting for all of the paperwork to be completed. If need be, to get things underway, Welsh was willing to provide some of the initial financing himself. The Savannah subcontractors would be told of the Chemical commitment and asked to postpone their billings for eight weeks.

Porter had reservations about this strategy. She had heard that Savannah subcontractors were inexperienced, undercapitalized and sometimes surly. Would they make a reliable source for the initial financing? In case of problems, would Welsh's proposed strategy lead to mechanics' liens[1] "getting in ahead" of Chemical's claim?

On the positive side, Welsh was exactly the kind of customer Chemical's "Real Estate Bank" was looking for. Chemical was committed to expanding its direct lending in the South Atlantic region. Although the bank had tended to confine most of its activity in that region to participations in loans generated by local correspondent banks, the continuing strong development in the South Atlantic region and the low level of construction activity in the Northeast had led Chemical to take a more aggressive approach. Welsh might be exactly the right person on whom Chemical should take a chance. He had the potential to become a major regional developer. Here was Chemical's chance to become his bank.

Porter's memorandum, however, would have to concentrate on the specifics of this loan. Did the project make sense financially and otherwise? How helpful was the Empire take-out in minimizing Chemical's risks? What importance should she put on the appraisal showing that the completed property would be worth $4 million?

The loan committee would also want to know about Welsh. What was he putting into the project? What kind of profit was Welsh expecting to make on this project and when would he make it? How valuable was his personal guarantee?

The committee would also expect Porter to recommend terms. What would be an appropriate interest rate relative to prime? What kind of covenants would protect the bank? What covenants would be acceptable to Welsh?

The loan committee liked its officers to begin with a recommendation, rather than just presenting undigested facts. Porter checked her notes and began to write.

---

[1]If a person supplying certain types of labor or material for a building, such as a plumber or electrician, has not been paid within a legislatively designated time period, that person can place a mechanic's lien on the property. Clear title to the property cannot be obtained until this claim is settled. In practice, construction lenders often require a certification of clear title with each draw.

EXHIBITS

1. Willy Welsh: personal balance sheet.

2. Map of Savannah area.

3. Comparable apartments.

4. Description of improvements.

5. Income projections.

6. Appraisal of Savannah West Garden Apartments (excerpt).

7. Summary of key clauses in Chemical Bank's standard commitment letter for a construction loan.

QUESTIONS FOR DISCUSSIONS

1. As Alison Porter, would you recommend that Chemical Bank make this loan? What are the key financial assumptions?

2. Assuming you make the loan, what terms and conditions would you impose?

3. Assuming you reject the loan, do you believe the project will be built?

Exhibit 1

<u>William Welsh - Personal Balance Sheet</u>
<u>($000 - July 30, 1977)</u>

Cash	370	A/P	1
A/R	162	Loans Against	
Insurance Policy		Life Insurance	3
(cash surrender value)	8	Mortgages Against	
Stock and Securities*	1,275	Real Estate	5,973
Real Estate Owned**	7,761	Net Worth	3,599
	9,576		9,576

<u>Income Statement</u>
<u>($000)</u>

Salary	$110
Bonuses and other payments	
from Engineered Concepts	300
Other	6
	$416

<u>Personal Data</u>

Married, 2 children, age 40
Residence: 12 Fairview Road, Atlanta, Georgia

---

* Description of Security	Cost	Estimated Market Value
Georgia Power Bonds	$10,000	10,000
Engineered Concepts		1,213,000
Oilwell - Halsey Project	38,000	1,000
Welsh Property Management Co.		51,000
		1,275,000

** Real Estate Owned	Estimated Market Value
60A Sumpter Road	
Clayborn County, Georgia - zoned apartments	112,500
Approximately 36 acres on Old Arkansaw Road	108,900
288 unit apartment complex	
Clark County, Georgia	2,042,500
395 unit apartment complex - under	
construction - Dekalb County, Georgia	5,496,783
	7,760,683

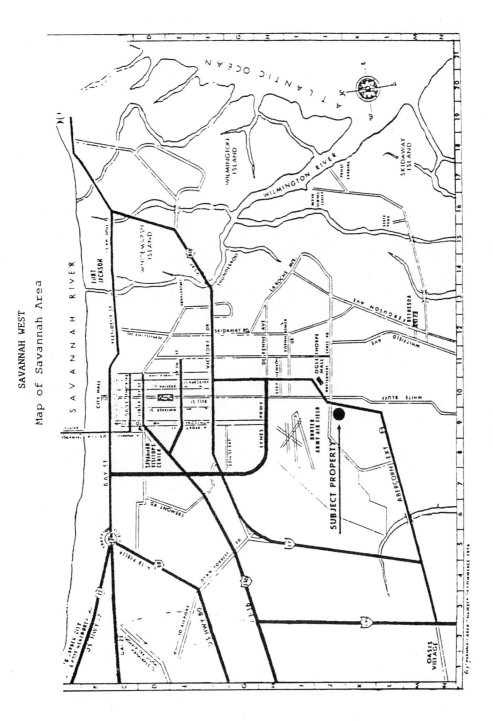

SAVANNAH WEST
Map of Savannah Area

Scale: 1" = approximately 4 miles.

Exhibit 3

Comparable Apartments

The following chart is a summary of the Rent Comparables. The rental
schedules have been analyzed as follows:

Comparable No.	Size	1 BR Rent/Sq. Ft.	2 BR Rent/Sq. Ft.	3 BR Rent/Sq. Ft.
1	172 units	$.28	$.25	$.24
2	278 units	.26	.22	.17
3	160 units	.25	.23	.22
4	58 units	N.A.	.23	.22
5	238 units	.21	.18	N.A.
6	232 units	.29	.20	.20
7	216 units	.27	.24	N.A.
8	168 units	.26	.24	N.A.
9	102 units	.25	.24	N.A.

The rent comparables are judged to be similar to the subject with regard to
pertinent features such as location, quality and type of construction, and
amenities. More detailed information about #6 and #7 follows.

Comparable #6

Project: Spanish Villa
          10599 Abercorn Street extension
          232 units

Type & Size	Rent Monthly/Annually	Monthly Rent/Sq. Ft.
64 - 1 BR, 1 Bath, 664 sq. ft. Gdn.	$195/$2.340	$.29
138 - 2 BR, 1-1/2 Bath, 1,200 sq. ft. TH	$245/$2,940	$.20
30 - 3 BR, 2-1/2 Bath, 1,336 sq. ft. TH	$265/$3,180	$.20

Remarks: Project estimated to have been completed in 1972. Buildings are two
story with all stucco exterior. Occupancy is reported at 100%. Tenant
responsible for all utilities, including water. Standard fully equipped
kitchens, including frost-free refrigerator. Drapes included. Amenities
include clubhouse, two pools, laundry room and playground. April 1 rental
increase put in effect.

Exhibit 3
continued

Comparable #7

Project: Club Riviera
          1230 Mercy Boulevard
          216 units

Type and Size	Rent Monthly/Annually	Monthly Rent/Sq. Ft.
116 – 1 BR, 1 Bath 720 sq. ft. (Aug.), Gdn.	$195/$2,340	$.27
100 – 2 BR, 2 Bath, 1,005 sq. ft. (Aug.), Gdn.	$245/$2,940	$.24

Remarks: Project completed in 1970. Buildings are two story with brick at first level and wood shingle mansard roof at upper level. Occupancy reported at 100%. Tenant responsible for all utilities. Standard fully equipped kitchens. Drapes included. Amenities include clubhouse, two pools, laundry, and volleyball court. Rent increase effective in January 1977.

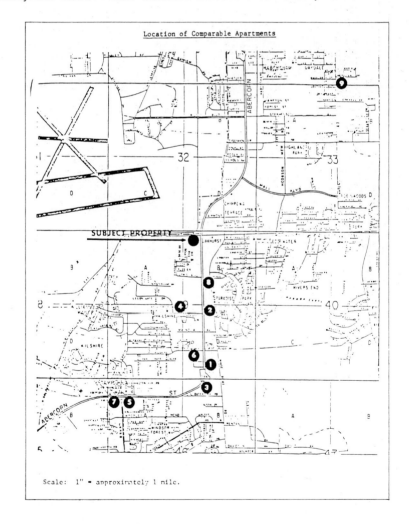

Location of Comparable Apartments

Scale: 1" = approximately 1 mile.

Exhibit 4

<u>Description of Improvements</u>

The subject is to be improved with a fifteen building, 216 garden unit apartment project, plus clubhouse and auxiliary improvements. Gross building area is approximately 202,244 square feet. A summary of the improvements is as follows:

Total Apartment Area	192,372 square feet
Clubhouse	800 square feet
Paving	130,000 square feet+
Hallways	9,072 square feet
Screen Porch Area	10,368 square feet

Unit Apartment Area

24 - 1 BR units	630 square feet
24 - 1 BR units	707 square feet
72 - 2 BR units	882 square feet
72 - 2 BR units	959 square feet
12 - 3 BR units	1,109 square feet
12 - 3 BR units	1,202 square feet

Foundation:	Poured concrete foundation on slab.
Exterior Walls:	5/8" exterior plywood over frame structure.
Floors:	Concrete slab at ground level, 1.5" L.W. concrete on 5/8" plywood deck over 12" floor joists (24" O.C.) at upper level.
Floor Covering:	Synthetic carpeting on all floors including bath except kitchens which have vinyl tile.
Roof:	Truss system with asphalt shingles on 0.5" plywood decking.
Windows:	Aluminum framed, vertical sliding.
Insulation:	Ceiling insulated with 6" blow-in and walls with 3" batts.
Interior Walls and Ceiling:	5/8" painted gypsum board walls; stippled finish ceilings.
Baths and Plumbing:	Lavatory units with vanity, mirror and small medicine cabinets. Fiberglass wainscot at tubs. Assume copper water lines and cast iron soil and waste line. Individual electric fuel hot water heaters (Rheem); 30 gallon capacity for 1 BR units; 40 gallon capacity for 2 BR and 3 BR units.

Exhibit 4
continued

Kitchens:	Single bowl sink, free standing electric range, double door refridgerator, dishwasher, range hood and exhaust fan. Plywood wall and base cabinets.
Electrical:	Assume minimum 125 amp circuit breaker panel per unit.
Heating and Air Conditioning:	Heating & air-conditioning system utilizes an upright closet type air handling unit, with an outside mounted condenser. Distribution is through overhead insulated ducts, with a central return air vent. Total electric 1.5 to 2 tons per unit (Rheem).
Patios/Balconies:	All units have screened in patios or balconies.
Swimming Pool:	Assume 800 square feet, minimum, concrete deck, fence enclosure, approved filter system.
Landscaping:	Finished landscaping and grounds are typical. Several large mature trees have been saved.
Walks:	4" concrete slab.
Clubhouse:	Clubhouse includes large recreation room, rest rooms, office and utility area.
Remarks:	In the two bedroom floor plan, which is available at 882 square feet and 959 square feet, 36 of the 72 smaller units have 2 bathrooms in lieu of 1 bath with laundry room. Also, 36 of the 72 larger units have 2 bathrooms in lieu of 1 bath with laundry room.
Age/Life:	Economic life judged to be 40 years.

Exhibit 4
continued

LG 1 BEDROOM

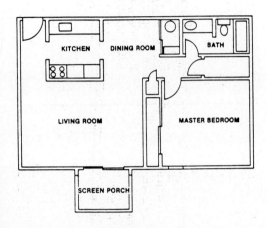

LG 2 BEDROOM, 2 BATH

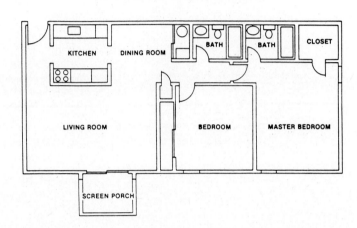

SM 1 BEDROOM

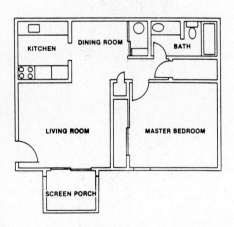

SM 2 BEDROOM

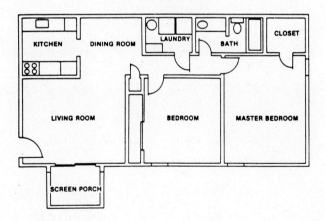

Exhibit 5

Income Projections

The following rental schedule has been utilized:

1 BR, 1 BA	630 sq. ft.	x	$.30/sq. ft./mo.	=	$189/mo., Say $190
1 BR, 1 BA	707 sq. ft.	x	$.30/sq. ft./mo.	=	$212/mo., Say $210
2 BR, 1 BA	882 sq. ft.	x	$.25/sq. ft./mo.	=	$221/mo., Say $220
2 BR, 2 BA	882 sq. ft.	x	$.26/sq. ft./mo.	=	$229/mo., Say $230
2 BR, 1 BA	959 sq. ft.	x	$.25/sq. ft./mo.	=	$240/mo., Say $240
2 BR, 2 BA	959 sq. ft.	x	$.26/sq. ft./mo.	=	$249/mo., Say $250
3 BR, 2 BA	1,109 sq. ft.	x	$.24/sq. ft./mo.	=	$266/mo., Say $265
3 BR, 2 BA	1,202 sq. ft.	x	$.24/sq. ft./mo.	=	$288/mo., Say $290

The monthly per square foot rent of the various subject units is in the upper range of the comparables.

Gross annual income is projected as follows:

24 - 1 BR Units	@	$190/mo.	x	12 mos.	= $ 54,720
24 - 1 BR Units	@	$210/mo.	x	12 mos.	= 60,480
36 - 2 BR Units	@	$220/mo.	x	12 mos.	= 95,040
36 - 2 BR Units	@	$230/mo.	x	12 mos.	= 99,360
36 - 2 BR Units	@	$240/mo.	x	12 mos.	= 103,680
36 - 2 BR Units	@	$250/mo.	x	12 mos.	= 108,000
12 - 3 BR Units	@	$265/mo.	x	12 mos.	= 38,160
12 - 3 BR Units	@	$290/mo.	x	12 mos.	= 41,760

Potential Gross Income $601,200

Exhibit 6

Correlation and Final Value Estimate

The indication of value from the three approaches are as follows:

Cost Approach	$4,095,000
Income Approach	$3,980,000
Market Approach	$3,760,000

(See explanation of the approaches below.)

In estimating the Market Value of the subject project, we have given consideration to all three indications of value. In our judgment, the Income Approach is the most reliable indication of value. The Cost Approach and Market Approach set the upper and lower range of value and are felt to be less reliable. Therefore, it is our opinion that the Market Value of the 216-unit apartment development, known as Savannah West Garden Apartments as of April 22, 1977, was:

FOUR MILLION DOLLARS
($4,000,000)

Divided as follows:

Land	$ 200,000
Improvements	$3,800,000
Total	$4,000,000

Cost Approach: This estimate is based on, "an analysis of cost data obtained from developer/contractors who are knowledgeable of the cost of building apartments. The cost of constructing semi-luxury multi-family apartments" in this area, for example, "range from $13.00 to $16.00 per square foot depending on quality and type of construction and size of units, excluding paving, landscaping, and indirect cost." A complete breakdown of the costs leading to the $4,095,000 estimate is included at the end of this exhibit.

Income Approach: "In order to estimate the value of the subject property by the Income Approach, it is necessary to determine Market Rent typical to the subject neighborhood (Exhibit 3). . . . The comparison is made on the basis of gross rent per square foot per month." Based on this survey of comparable apartments, the appraiser concluded that the rents shown in Exhibit 5 "represent market rent" and that the $397,889 net income before financing was reasonable. The appraiser then looked at the net income of four comparable properties that were recently sold and concluded that a 10% capitalization of net income best reflects the current market. He then made the following calculations:

Net Income:	$397,889 / .10 = $3,978,880
Indicated Value, Income Approach, Rounded:	$3,980,000

Exhibit 6
continued

Income Analysis

Projected Gross Rent Income	$601,200
Less Vacancy/Collection (5%)	30,060
Total	$571,140
Auxiliary Income* ($10/unit/mo.)	26,400
Effective Gross Income	$597,540

Expenses

Management Fee	$ 29,900	
Salaries/Taxes	18,500	
Taxes	41,915	
Insurance	8,950	
Sanitation	10,750	
Pest Control	2,100	
Utility Common	8,600	
Maintenance, Redecorating	25,600	
General Expenses	26,000	
Total	$172,315	
Reserves**	$27,336	
Total Expenses and Reserves	199,651	
Net Income		$397,889

---

* Auxiliary Income figured as follows:

	Per Month
Furniture rental	$ 600
Laundry Income	600
Cleaning fees	700
Miscellaneous	300
Total	$2,200
	x12
Auxiliary Income	$26,400

** Reserves

Roof:	2,500 squares (10' x 10') @ $25/20 years	=	$ 3,125
Mechanical	$200/unit/15 years	=	2,880
Appliances	$400/unit/12 years	=	7,200
Floor Covering:	14,950 sq. yds. @ $5.25/sq. yd., 8 yrs.	=	9,811
Paving:	14,400 sq. yds. @ $4.50/sq. yd., 15 yrs.	=	4,320
Total			$27,336

Exhibit 6
continued

Market Approach: "An investigation has been made of sales of properties which possess characteristics similar to the subject. The comparison process is based on a gross rent multiple basis. . . . Adjustments are made for time of sale, location, size, utility, condition of improvement and other factors which, in our opinion, influence value."

Sale Number	Gross Rent Multiple
1	5.51
2	6.50
3	5.63
4	5.72

The Appraiser estimated that Savannah West could be sold for a rent multiple of 6.25 leading to the following calculation:

Projected Gross Income (Exhibit 5):	$ 601,200
Estimated Gross Rent Multiple:	x6.25
Value by Market Approach:	$3,757,500
Rounded to:	$3,760,000

The foregoing description is a simplified summary of the appraisal. The appraisal itself runs to 45 pages plus exhibits.

Reproduction Cost New

Total Apartment Area (192,372 Sq. Ft. @ $15.00)	=	$2,885,580
Hallway Area (9,072 Sq. Ft. @ $5.00)	=	45,360
Clubhouse (800 Sq. Ft. @ $18.00)	=	14,400
Pool (1 @ $12,000)	=	12,000
Tennis Courts (2 @ $10,000)	=	20,000
Paving and Parking (14,450 Sq. Yds. @ $4.50)	=	65,025
Landscaping, finished site work, etc.(est. @ 5% of $3,042,365)	=	152,118
Total Direct Construction Cost		$3,194,483
Indirect Costs:		
Construction Loan Interest (10% of $3,194,483 x .60)	=	$ 191,669
Miscellaneous, including Entreprenurial Profit, Loan Fees and off-site overhead:	=	507,923
Reproduction Cost New		$3,894,075
Less Depreciation, None Observed		-0-
Depreciated Reproduction Cost New		$3,894,075
Plus Land Value		200,000
Value Indicated by Cost Approach		$4,094,075
Rounded to:		$4,095,000

Exhibit 7

Summary of Key Clauses in Chemical Bank's Standard
Commitment Letter for a Construction Loan

General Terms and Conditions

1. Amount of the loan $_____.
2. Construction of the improvements shall commence within 30 days of the loan closing.
3. The loan shall mature in_____months and interest shall be payable monthly on the outstanding balance at a rate of_____% or_____% plus the prime rate.
4. Loan will be secured by a first (second) mortgage or deed of trust.
5. Signed commitment letter together with a commitment fee must be returned to lender within_____days.
6. The loan closing shall be held within 60 days of the date of issuance of this letter.
7. All leases shall be assigned to Lender.

Fees

1. A commitment fee of $_____shall be deemed earned by Lender upon Borrower's acceptance of the commitment letter. If loan does not close Lender may retain all of such good faith deposit as liquidated damages.
2. Borrower agrees to pay all fees, commissions, costs, charges, taxes and other expenses incurred in connection with this commitment letter and the making of the loan. These fees include: a. Lender's New York counsel and local counsel, b. appraisal fees, c. survey fees, d. title examination fees, e. mortgage title insurance, f. hazard insurance, g. bond premiums, h. mortgage and transfer taxes, i. recording fees and charges.

Some of the Usual Conditions for the Commitment

1. Joint and several guarantee of payment of the note by the principals and their wives.
2. Joint and several guarantee of completion of the improvements.
3. A permanent loan commitment for the long-term mortgage financing.
4. An appraisal indicating a value in the real property equal to not less than $_____.
5. 100% payment and performance bond.
6. Final plans and improvements approved in writing by independent inspecting architects and engineers designated by the Lender.
7. Current certified financial statements of Borrower and all guarantors.
8. Evidence of compliance with all zoning, environmental and other laws, ordinances, rules and regulations.
9. A detailed breakdown of the cost of the improvements and an itemization of non-construction and land costs. In no event shall the amount of the loan exceed these estimated costs.
10. Evidence from utility companies and municipalities servicing the Premises that water, sewer, electric, telephone and gas service will be available upon completion.

Exhibit 7
continued

11. Full insurance on the property in the form of an "all-risk," 100% nonreporting policy.
12. All instruments and documents affecting the premises, securing the loan or relating to the development and construction shall be subject to the approval of the Lender's New York counsel and the Lender's Local Counsel.

During Construction

1. Borrower shall furnish a revised survey showing location of foundation, plus an affidavit from the surveyor that set-backs conform with zoning restrictions.
2. All contracts shall be assigned to the Lender. Borrower shall furnish all such information about the architect, construction manager, general contractor and subcontractors as the Lender requests. All these people shall be subject to approval by the Lender. All shall continue performance in Lender's behalf under their respective contracts without additional cost in the event of a default by the Borrower.
3. Advances shall not be made more frequently than monthly shall be based upon inspections and certifications by the Supervising Engineers. The total amount retained from Borrower by Lender shall, in no event, be less than 10%.

Grounds for Termination

1. Lender may terminate commitment if Borrower misrepresented any feature.
2. Lender may terminate commitment if an adverse change occurs to the premises.
3. Lender may terminate commitment if any part of the premises is taken for condemnation or if any person connected with the loan is involved in bankruptcy or insolvency.
4. Borrower shall keep permanent loan commitment in full force.
5. Loan may become payable immediately upon sale or transfer of the property.

Chemical Bank does not require all borrowers to conform to all of these terms and conditions. On the other hand, it may insert additional terms and conditions in a specific loan commitment to cover unique or unusual situations.

PART II
FINANCING THE PROJECT

In Part I of this casebook, we became acquainted with the real estate industry and its participants. We were introduced to income property and property held or developed for sale. We examined closely the role of the entrepreneur and the basics of financial analysis. Cases featured a variety of land uses and included both new and rehabilitation construction. We concluded with a case involving a lender.

In this Part II, we will build on this base, extending our financial analysis tools to include discounted-cash-flow analysis and accounting. Our primary focus will be the various forms of financing used in real estate. Cases will include both urban and suburban land development settings. Part II begins with an introduction to the sources of financing for real estate investments.

Where do the funds for real estate come from? How does the developer or buyer of property obtain them? In this note we will introduce the major providers of debt and equity capital in the changing world of real estate development.

CAPITAL FOR REAL ESTATE INVESTMENTS

Each time someone develops, improves, purchases, or refinances a piece of real property, he or she must raise or contribute capital. The dollars involved are enormous. As estimated in *The Changing World of the Real Estate Developer*, the value of U.S. residential property is on the order of $5 trillion. The value of all U.S. property, including commercial property, is certainly in excess of $7 trillion. If only 5% of this property value were developed, improved, sold or refinanced in a given year, this would require $350 billion in new financing transactions per year.

Real estate investments are financed through a combination of debt and equity capital. The use of debt, or borrowed money, is very important in real estate, and a substantial majority of the new capital flowing into real estate is normally in this form. By year-end 1987, U.S. properties were supporting about $2.75 trillion in mortgage debt. The balance of the property value, of course, represents the owner's equity capital.

Each individual transaction may be financed with up to 100% debt, or in some instances, 100% equity capital. Real estate developers often seek to borrow 100% (or more) of the cost of the project. (This is called "financing out.") Major foreign and institutional investors will often pay 100% of the purchase price of a property in the form of equity. However, most transactions involve both debt and equity capital, with debt usually in the majority.

Debt Capital

When completed properties are bought and sold, the most common form of debt financing is the mortgage loan, usually a long-term or permanent loan. When properties are being developed or improved, however, the different phases of development involve different sets of risks. Three broad categories of mortgage loans have evolved to fit them. These are the **acquisition/bridge loan,** the **construction loan,** and the **permanent loan**.

The typical development project may progress through a series of loans beginning with an acquisition/bridge loan. Reflecting the uncertainty involved in the beginning of any project, the loan may be relatively expensive. This is followed by a construction loan, which may or may not be provided by the same lender. Monitoring a construction loan involves specialized capabilities on the part of the lender, and the terms of the loan generally reflect the risks involved and the management needed to oversee the loan. The construction loan is "taken out" by the permanent loan. Here the project is already built, most of the uncertainties are out of the way, and a longer term and lower rate are usually available. There still may be risks, however, particularly if the development is not fully leased.

The capital market for mortgage lending has changed greatly in recent years. Different types of lenders have emerged as major providers of debt capital. The table on page 117 presents the outstanding loan balances at year end 1987 by institutional holder category. We will distinguish the very large national market in residential mortgage lending from the much smaller and more fragmented market for commercial lending. From this data can readily be seen the relative importance of residential lending (including farm-based lending) and the obvious importance of the commercial banks and thrift institutions as lenders.

In the table on page 118, we can examine recent changes in the relative share of the mortgage-lending market. From data on year-end mortgage balances of the major investor groups, we may compare the period prior to 1979 with the more recent period 1979-1987.

The year 1979 represented the beginning of both a period of volatility in interest rates and a period of change in banking regulation. Thus the year 1979 marks the beginning of today's debt market environment. Despite high interest rates, this period produced a dramatic increase in debt financing. From a net increase of $151 billion in 1979, by the second quarter of 1987, the net yearly increase for real estate financing overall was on the order of $263 billion.

In the following paragraphs, we will review briefly the major providers of debt capital and note a number of major changes which may be observed in the tables.

Thrifts. Thrifts are Federal- or state-chartered savings banks, mostly small. Their traditional role is to take in savings from small depositors and make mortgage loans, predominantly on residential property. Whenever interest rates have increased, these institutions have tended to lose deposits to higher yield investments (a process called disintermediation). Banking regulations now allow thrifts to bid for deposits in money-market accounts. This means they can obtain deposit money to lend, but only at high rates. The net effect of these changes appears to be a significant decline in market share -- from about half of all new mortgage loans to about 30% at present. Because thrifts are small and often lack specialized expertise, they are not particularly active in commercial or construction lending.

Commercial Banks. Commercial Banks have remained steady participants in the mortgage market. Combined with the thrifts, these institutions now hold about half of the new mortgage loans, down from 70%. Both the commercial banks and the thrift institutions now are able to sell or syndicate their mortgage loans in the secondary market. As a result, they very likely still originate and service a high percentage of the volume, but now commonly will sell off a portion of their mortgage portfolios to other investors. Prior to 1979, this was not widely permitted. Compared with other groups, commercial banks are very active in construction lending.

Government. Government has increased its holdings of mortgages. These are financed through the sale of mortgage-backed securities with some degree of

Mortgage Credit Outstanding

1987 (Billions)

Source	residential	non-residential	total	% of total
Thrifts	$673.4	$149.8	$823.2	30.0%
Banks	336.1	243.4	579.5	21.1%
Government	799.6	8.7	808.3	29.5%
Insurance Companies	43.9	154.8	198.7	7.2%
Other	276.1	59.2%	335.3	12.2%
Total	$2,129.1	$615.9	$2,745	100.0%

"Other" includes pension funds, REIT's, mortgage companies and private individuals
Source: Federal Reserve Bank

government backing. This mechanism has been greatly increased in recent years and has resulted in a new and highly liquid national mortgage market. Several agencies are involved -- FNMA (Fannie Mae), GNMA (Ginnie Mae), and FHLMC (Freddie Mac), each of which provides differing products and services. Some states and local agencies have originated their own loan programs based on tax-exempt bond issues. By and large, the agencies themselves do not originate loans, but establish criteria for loans they will purchase. These "underwriting" criteria may include the creditworthiness of the borrower, valuation of the property, and the size, term and interest rate of the loan. Government agencies rarely get involved in commercial or construction lending.

Pension Funds and Insurance Companies. Pension funds and insurance companies together represent the second group to have increased holdings of mortgages. Within the "Other" category, pension funds have increased their share of the dollar volume of mortgages. A portion of this represents purchased loan portfolios and mortgage-backed securities, although both pension funds, through advisory firms, and insurance companies are also originators of mortgages. Fueled by the 1979 Employment Retirement Income Security Act (ERISA), pension funds have grown dramatically in size during this period. Their participation as lenders is small, but growing, and they are also investing in volume directly as equity owners of properties. This group is active in commercial real estate and construction lending.

From this recent experience, it is possible to project some future trends. In the residential sector, the banking and thrift industries will continue to be the prime originators of new loans. Their underwriting trends will increasingly emphasize standardization of debt products to facilitate use of the various secondary markets. At the same time, the number of "standard" mortgage products is increasing. Borrowers will choose among conventional fixed rate and variable rate mortgages, loans with deferred payment features, such as shared appreciation mortgages, and various government sponsored and/or supported loans.

In the commercial, industrial, and land development sectors, the picture will be very different. Construction lending will continue to be the province of commercial bankers with the organizational capability to control construction and credit risks. Construction lenders will continue to re-

Net Increase in Mortgage Credit Outstanding

(Billions)

Source	1970-1978 average	% of total	1979-1987 average	% of total
Thrifts	$42.9	49.3%	$39.3	$26.9
Banks	18.3	21.0%	39.3	26.9%
Government	11.1	12.8%	50.4	33.2%
Insurance Companies	4.0	4.6%	10.3	6.7%
Other	9.3	10.7%	12.6	8.3%
Total	$87.0	100.0%	$125.1	100.0%

"Other" includes pension funds, REIT's, mortgage companies and private individuals
Source: Federal Reserve Bank

quire either a permanent "takeout" loan or substantial credit backing for the project or both. Rates will continue to be variable, almost without exception, and maturities will be short. Many lenders will avoid this market entirely.

Permanent loans for income property will be obtained from a very wide range of sources. As indicated in the tables, the commercial market is divided among the four classes of private lending institutions, with no one group having dominance. A new group of lenders -- organizations which will package loans for participation by smaller banks, thrifts and pension funds -- is also becoming significant.

The objectives of these institutions vary widely, as do the objectives of the borrowers. Loans will become increasingly diverse in their details, as the imaginations of borrowers and lenders produce new ways to meet these objectives. Loans will have combinations of features designed to assure adequate total income to the lender in either inflationary or non-inflationary periods. Maturities will remain short, interest rates variable, and lenders will continue to seek various types of participations in future appreciation.

Equity Capital

The debt markets provide over $250 billion in new financing each year, but another $50-plus billion of equity capital is also required for new real estate investments. As noted above, large pools of capital, such as pension funds, have been attracted to real estate for its inflation-hedging characteristics. Large pools of foreign capital also participate in hopes of preserving asset values. Despite the great attention these investor groups receive, they actually contribute only about $5-10 billion per year.

The bulk of the equity funds comes from developers themselves and from individual investors. The developers typi-

cally invest their own cash as working capital for projects. Usually they expect to invest their profits as well -- at least for a time. Many developers are also major property owners and will routinely reinvest cash flow from their portfolios. In fact, some of the major commercial real estate portfolios built in the 1960's and 1970's produce more cash flow than can be prudently reinvested in development ventures.

Individual investors participate in much the same way as developers, involving themselves as principals in individual properties or as partners with developers. Real estate syndication, the practice of organizing investment partnerships to purchase and develop properties, has enjoyed rapid growth since 1982. The Real Estate Securities and Syndication Institute (RESSI) reported that the top ten brokers in 1987 sold $3.4 billion worth of syndications through offerings registered with the U.S. Securities and Exchange Commission (SEC). Perhaps three times this amount was sold privately.

Investments in the public and private categories are quite different. Public offerings involve extensive formal documentation and review by the SEC. They are usually structured for many small investors, each contributing as little as $2,000. These funds have been used primarily to acquire existing properties, avoiding the possible pitfalls of construction and leaseup risk. Returns emphasize tax-sheltered cash flow and capital appreciation. Overall returns are lower than in the private placement investments. A group of major syndication firms called the "Big Six" accounts for a major share of this market. These firms offer one partnership after another through established marketing organizations, often led by major Wall Street brokerage houses.

Private placements are exempt from securities registration procedures under the provisions of the various federal and state securities laws. Private placements may nevertheless be quite formal and extensive in their documentation and in their marketing programs. These placements often involve the services of a syndicator, a firm or individual who organizes the partnership, structures and documents the investment, and coordinates the marketing program. Many small syndicators have entered the market since 1981, often working with licensed "broker-dealers" who sell the partnership units on a commission basis. Many developers organize investment partnerships themselves, thus avoiding the syndicator's often substantial fees.

Most private syndications appeal to wealthy investors. Many are structured exclusively for participation by "accredited" investors, as specified in a 1981 law. Other syndications require minimum income or net-worth limits which must be met by prospective investors. At the same time, many investments are informally negotiated between developers or promoters and individuals and existing investor groups. These informal private investments may require little documentation. A large portion of the private equity funds are used for new development ventures, although many also are used for acquisition of existing properties and "resyndication" of older properties.

The rapid growth in syndication investments may be traced in part to the tax incentives prevalent in the 1981-1986 period that increased depreciation allowances for income producing real estate and created tax credits for rehabilitation projects. Many investors moved into real estate after becoming disillusioned with oil and gas investment about this same time. It now seems that a demographic bulge of investors in their prime earning years is getting rich enough to appreciate the multiple benefits of real estate.

It should be noted, however, that real estate partnerships have been popular investment vehicles at various times in the past. Syndication has declined somewhat since these tax incentives were eliminated in 1986. However, syndication is likely to remain a substantial source of funds for future real estate investment.

CONCLUSION

For the developer, particularly the small developer, the equity syndication market is making an important contribution. In the absence of this vehicle, only the best-capitalized developers would be able to obtain financing, and small developers would have to take in major partners. For the present, the availability of individual investors through equity syndication permits developers a choice.

Large developers and institutions will continue to have major advantages in the development market. Most important of these is the ability to build ahead of the market. As each new building is completed and leased, the capital may be rolled into the next building. As noted above, a large real estate firm's internally generated funds may be sufficient to support a stream of new investments.

Large or small, today's real estate developer has to search long and hard for both debt and equity capital. In an efficient capital market, only the best proposals with the strongest sponsorship will be financed. In this era of scarce capital, lenders and investors will take a lot of convincing.

Case 5

Park Place

In April 1982, J. W. Kaempfer, Jr. had his mind on responding to leasing proposals for space in his new office building, scheduled for completion in March 1983. He was greatly relieved that the owner of the land under the building had finally executed an agreement to subordinate to the permanent lender. The takeout financing was thus assured, and he could postpone further worries about bankruptcy.

Mr. Kaempfer was now working out of the new offices of The Kaempfer Company in the heart of Washington's Georgetown. "We've evolved a lot in the last thirty-six months," he reported, "from being a small builder-developer to having well over $100 million in the pipeline today."

The Great Northwest Land Company had become The Kaempfer Company in the spring of 1981. While there were now fourteen full-time employees in the office, it was clear that Mr. Kaempfer was still very much involved in all aspects of the business. Within one two-hour span, he was observed to handle a wide variety of matters, ranging from inquiries into the whereabouts of the truck keys and final approvals for the company Christmas party, to negotiations involving financing for a major new downtown commercial project. Unlike the cartoon image created by Richard Lyon, landscape architecture student, after reading the Joey Kaempfer case, Mr. Kaempfer actually works at a constant high level of energy. He is usually juggling several tasks at once. And when concentrating on numbers, he will tap his fingers rhythmically, in concert with his calculator punching.

ORGANIZATION

Many changes had occurred and new faces appeared since late 1978 when the first case was written. As the pace and volume of work continued to rise, Mr. Kaempfer knew that he had to build a stronger organization. In addition to introducing weekly staff meetings, which he described as "one of our major leaps forward," cash needs of the organization began to be projected a full twelve months ahead.

As a measure of the growth of the organization, total overhead grew more than eight-fold between 1978 and 1981, from $99,000 to $800,000. Much of this increase was due to the salaries of new staff members. Since late 1978 the number of office employees had increased from four to thirteen. John Nicolosi had continued as Joey's right-hand man and Vice President. As Joey found less time to spend at the construction sites, John's role as the link between the office and on-site activities became more critical.

Foremost among the moves made by Mr. Kaempfer to develop the organization was the addition of an old business school classmate, John Gardner, in September of 1981. Described by Joey as the "number two man" in the class, Mr. Gardner came on at a substantial salary commensurate with his ten years of solid real estate experience. His last four years had been spent managing the shopping center portfolio (which included twenty-five properties) of a large Real Estate Investment Trust based in the Washington area.

Mr. Gardner's background in marketing, leasing, and property management would effectively complement Joey's strong intuitive abilities. Joey also hoped that he would provide a very useful sounding board. Due to his more conservative orientation, Mr. Gardner would also become a moderating influence on Joey. Both John and Joey agreed that their arguments and discussions had been helpful. In describing his decision to change jobs, John offered: "Giving up certainty for an uncertainty is clearly difficult. But I know the real estate business well enough, and Joey well enough to make a judgment about his talents and abilities. He's a very talented and creative person who can do things that very few people in the business can."

Within the new structure, as Mr. Kaempfer describes it: "Gardner is supposed to make the organization happen, while I make the deals happen. Of course, the lines get blurred, and we do some of both." As for the future direction of organizational development, Joey quoted Mao: "A journey of a thousand miles begins with a single step." Mr. Gardner pointed out that organizational development in the real estate field is different from other businesses. There is a fear of building up overhead expenses. "We don't want to have to do deals just to cover overhead," he explained. "That's what gets a lot of developers in trouble. We'll develop projects, then hire staff..."

In the meantime, much hard work is required. Joey elaborates: "Fourteen hour days are not uncommon -- I have one or two each week. More often, I have eleven or twelve hour days. I don't know people who work as hard as I do, but I love it. I'm not suffering -- and I suppose when the time comes that I don't like it any more, I'll stop."

RESULTS OF EARLIER PROJECTS

The Wilkes Street Townhouse (Old Town Station) project was sold. In Joey's November 1978 meeting with his partners there was some debate on the matter. But Joey was not as optimistic as his partners on the future of the housing market, and decided to sell the project. The project yielded nearly $80,000 in profit which stayed within the company to cover overhead expenses. At that time, the sum was nearly enough to cover an entire year's overhead. It turned out to have been the right decision. "The project really was too fancy for the area," Joey explained. And its performance in the market supported this assessment (see Exhibit 1).

In August 1979, the sale of the last of the Guilford Green townhouses was being closed. The broker involved asked Joey if he would be interested in selling the Union Street Townhouse (Waterford Place) project -- a potential buyer had expressed interest. Somewhat surprised, Joey agreed to think about it. He calculated the total existing investment by his company and his investor partners including debt and simply added $1 million to that figure. The buyer accepted the $2.7 million price tag, and the deal was closed in October.

Joey considered what happened next "a real shame." The buyer, a well established general contractor, failed to foresee the coming rise of interest rates and the volatility of the housing market. Instead of moving quickly to build and sell units, they acted slowly, believing they might fetch higher sales prices later. "They would have made a bundle of money on Union Street if they had built it quickly. We thought they would make $1.5 million. I gave them nineteen serious contract offers, but they thought they could make more money later so they allowed the offers to lapse. I would have at least sold enough to cover construction costs." In the twenty-six months following the sale, only seventeen units were built, two were sold, and one occupied. Not surprisingly, the project was foreclosed.

Another project sold by Joey was the 5.2 acre Lucas property. The property had been bought by Joey for a price of $7,000 per potential unit, and it was sold for $23,000 per unit.

Two projects had advanced. The 9.8 acre country club parcel in Fairfax County had been approved as a seventy-four unit luxury townhouse project, with construction scheduled to begin in Spring, 1982. Construction did commence on the thirteen acre McLean farm, which became a fifty unit luxury townhouse project named Evans Mill Pond. As of early 1982, five units, including two models, had been built, but none had yet been sold.

THE NEW ENVIRONMENT

Over the past few years, several factors had had a major impact on the real estate industry. Central had been the continued rise of interest rates. The prime lending rate -- to which developers' borrowing rates were increasingly tied -- had risen to in excess of 20%, and still stood at 16.5% in the spring of 1982. Home-buyer mortgage rates had also increased substantially, causing a virtual freeze in the new home construction business. In addition, the Washington housing market had softened dramatically.

When asked what was currently troubling him most, Joey was quick to respond: "The housing market is terrible. You can't sell any houses, and even if you can, you're paying a third of your profit to the bank, and more in brokerage fees." He complained that at best he could hope for a 10% profit out of the Evans Mill Pond project, while he had originally projected 20%+. He added that there were very big risks involved: "To make one million dollars at Evans Mill Pond, we're taking two to three million dollars in risks. That's exactly backwards. My history in the housing market says that you risk one million to make three million..." Would the market rebound? "It's scary. I think it will come back, but I don't know whether the kind of housing that I am comfortable with [high quality/luxury] will come back."

In addition to the increased costs of borrowing money, the structure of financing deals had also changed. Lenders were participating more actively, either through taking an equity position in the financed project or a portion of the future profits. Developers had come to accept these sacrifices in order to secure base interest rates low enough to make their developments feasible.

The tax environment had also changed dramatically. For new commercial developments, the 1981 tax act provided for 15-year cost recovery. This provided a major increase in the tax benefits for owners of new income-producing properties. This was resulting in a major increase in syndicated equity investments for institutional investors and in turn contributing to an upswing in office development across the country.

While certainly affected by the financial climate, Joey claimed to have little trouble in adjusting to it: "Development is still a matter of assessing what you think you can do, and then making it happen. We have not reacted to prime. We just keep doing deals, and somehow we make them happen." As for the increased participation of lenders: "I suspect that it is easier for me to arrange financing on a big deal now that there is lender participation. The lenders have gotten very greedy, and along with their greed, they've dropped some of their caution. No, I have had no problem accepting lender participation."

The changing business climate and local market outlook caused a shift in the strategy of the Kaempfer Company. A reorientation to stress commercial projects was charted. This change prompted one of Joey's usual financial backers to drop out of all new deals. Described by Joey as being too conservative, he wanted no part of any commercial development ventures. Another partner also dropped out of the picture. As a result, on his most recent deals, Joey has worked primarily with two of his original partners, although all remained friends.

The newest Kaempfer Company pipeline projects are commercial, and are significantly larger than any completed projects to date. They also reflect a broadened geographic scope, with one project slated for Baltimore, and others (though still very tentative) possible in other cities. Joey is clearly pleased with his progress and the growth of his company. And he is optimistic about the future. With tongue very much in cheek, he offered: "In twenty years, people are going to say, 'If only Gerry Hines had kept his nose to the grindstone, he could have been another Kaempfer!'"

PARK PLACE

Though he had not been actively seeking a commercial project, by the summer of 1979 Joey was starting to look around. Wilkes Street had been sold, and as Joey put it: "We'd made some money, we could breathe easy, and we thought it was time to nose about." In July, he heard about a piece of land for sale in Rosslyn, a densely developed office center just across the Potomac River from Washington. This property seemed to be an excellent starting point for Joey in the booming Washington office market. The 22,000 square-foot site was being used as a parking lot, and was zoned to allow for development to a floor area ratio of 3.5.

After some investigation, Joey found out that the land was held subject to a long-term ground lease. In November he went to Florida with hopes of negotiating purchase of the fee ownership. The Union Street project had just been sold, and with his and two partners' shares of the $1 million capital gain available, Joey now had a significant sum to work with. The 99-year lease still had 91 years to run, and stipulated payments to the landowner of $43,000 a year until 1986, when an adjustment tied 100% to the Consumer Price Index would increase payments to around $90,000. Joey was unable to negotiate the purchase of the fee, but his lawyers assured him that the owners would have to subordinate to a bona fide permanent mortgage. Based on this, Joey purchased the leasehold position for a $375,000 purchase price from the local group that controlled it. He paid $25,000 down in December, and closed the deal in March, 1980.

In the meantime, Joey had begun a serious process of self-education in commercial property development. "I talked to everyone I knew -- I talked to leasing agents about what the best thing to build would be, and went to look at other buildings and tried to teach myself the business."

It became clear to Joey that he needed to build a bigger building than the existing zoning would allow. Existing buildings surrounding the site had used density transfers (transferred development rights permitted under local zoning laws) to get up to fifteen stories. In hopes of getting increased density, Joey went to the Arlington County Planning Department. He met with the Director, and offered: "Look, this is what I can build by right -- it's a lousy building for me, and it's a lousy building for you. Tell me what it is you need me to do to get some density transfer, and I'll do it."

The planners indicated that a donation of land suitable for a public park would allow him to use the associated development rights. Through a broker, a 10,000 square foot parcel a few blocks from the site was acquired for $500,000. Expecting to gain only the 35,000 square feet of development potential associated with the park site, Joey instead was able to negotiate a 63,000 square foot transfer from the County. Other deals were made to gain additional density rights: A $50,000 donation was made to provide operating support to another local park; ramps for the handicapped were added to the plans for the areas fronting the streets; and extra landscaping was committed for the site. After six months of adjusting, Joey had secured the rights to develop 165,000 net leasable square feet. The County issued final approvals for the Park Place plans in March of 1980.

The architects chosen for Park Place were described by Joey as being "not too innovative...but what they design, you can build." They came up with a 13-story building which would sit on three underground levels of parking. The ground floor would include 9,200 square feet of retail space, and the remaining twelve stories would include office space (see Exhibit 2).

PROJECT FINANCING

Then came the task of securing financing. "We were ready to go for financing in the summer of 1980. We did get offers for $14 million, and up to $16 million, but the numbers just didn't work." (See Exhibit 3) Joey wanted a permanent loan more in the $18 million range and would wait until such financing was available. Luckily, he could afford to wait, since the actual carrying costs of the project were very low at that point. "We were not carrying very much. It was actually costing us only around one and one-half percent a year to carry it. The land lease was so low that the parking income almost fully covered it. So we had the $375,000 leasehold cost in the deal, plus some architectural fees and other overhead. But when you're carrying a $20 million deal at $10,000 a month, you don't feel incredibly pressed."

It was a full year before a permanent loan could be secured. In June 1981, a commitment was made by a pension fund to provide an $18.4 million permanent mortgage, with a 35-year term, and interest rate of 13.5%, plus 30% of any cash flow in excess of the base projections (see Exhibit 4). Joey was very pleased with the terms: "Based on what is available, it is an extremely favorable loan. It means that annually, the first $275,000 to $300,000 in cash flow is ours. Then, above that, we get 70%, while they get 30%." When asked if the lender had perhaps been too generous, Joey responded: "No, they got an extremely strong location...and they're going to get their required internal rate of return."

Several issues had arisen during the loan negotiations. At the outset, the lender expressed deep concern over Joey's lack of a track record in commercial devel-

opment, no less in any development of this scale. "The lender said: 'Look, you're a nice guy -- we're really charmed -- but look, you've never built an office building. And we don't know that you can lease it up, or that you know what the hell you're doing. So why don't you take some of your fat from the deal and bring in an outside partner who has some large-scale development experience.'...So, I was in a bit of a panic -- what was that partner going to want? Fifty percent of the deal?"

Joey had another idea. During this time, he had been taking bids from general contractors for the construction contract, and had narrowed the field to five. He saw an opportunity in working with one of the contractors who had a development track record, but who had recently come upon hard times. Joey recounted his offer: "Instead of making you bid for the contract, we can negotiate it and guarantee you the deal. In addition, we'll give you limited partner status with five percent of the deal -- in return for your signing on as co-developer." The offer was accepted, and a construction contract was signed in May 1981. The lender was also satisfied, and extended the loan commitment the following month.

Joey had also negotiated a construction loan with a commercial bank, which would offer the loan when permanent financing contracts were signed. The terms of the construction loan were also very favorable, with the interest rate set at 0.5% above prime, and a 0.25% fee going to the bank.

All was not clear sailing however. The permanent loan commitment was made contingent on the land-owner agreeing to subordinate lease payments to the mortgage debt service. As it turned out, the land-owner, who had been unhappy with the terms of the lease and was hoping to renegotiate it, refused to sign the necessary subordination papers (even though a provision of the lease required him to do so). The effects of this wrinkle multiplied rapidly. As long as the landowner refused to subordinate, a permanent loan agreement could not be signed, and in turn, the construction loan would be held back.

The inability to conclude the permanent financing had already caused a six-month delay in the start of construction. Joey was confident that he would eventually win subordination from the land-owner, even if it meant going to court. Discussions of an outright sale of the fee interest in the property were opened, but the asking price of $1.25 million was far above the $600,000 Joey was willing to pay. After all, he felt with the land encumbered by a lease that only cost $43,000 per year he would be wasting money to pay any more. While pondering legal action in the midst of continued slow negotiations with the landowner, Joey secured an open line of credit from the same commercial bank that had offered the construction loan at an interest rate set at 1.5% above the prime rate.

Borrowing on the open line of credit, Joey started construction at Park Place in August 1981. He was concerned with having the project completed by the second quarter of 1983, as stipulated in the permanent loan agreement. And as it was, Joey feared that the six-month delay might prove costly, since the market was showing signs of softening, and three new buildings were under construction or announced for the Rosslyn area. The market had been strong: rents in Rosslyn were at $19 per square foot, up from the $15 level eighteen months earlier, when Joey was first considering the project. But Joey was concerned about the competition which was soon to come on the market.

In April 1982, the landowner finally agreed to subordinate. The financing arrangements would therefore become firm. Construction had proceeded thus far as planned, and Joey began to feel certain that Park Place would indeed be completed on schedule in mid-1983. His priority would now shift to leasing the commercial space that was being created.

LEASING

In May 1981, Joey had entered into an agreement with a local real estate brokerage firm, granting it exclusive leasing agent status on the Park Place project. The firm agreed to have 30% leased by November, and 50% within one year. Now, one year later, none of Park Place had yet been leased. Joey was not pleased with the agent's performance, and intended to replace them soon.

Sitting at his desk, Joey reviewed the Park Place situation. He was growing a little nervous knowing that the building would be ready for occupancy, and none of it was yet leased. For a moment he wondered if the recently begun construction of the 400,000 square foot "Silver Slipper" office complex across the street from his Park Place would interfere with its prospects. He was not truly concerned though, since the Silver Slipper would not be available for occupancy before late 1984. Three other buildings were of more immediate concern. One, a nice 30-story office tower had recently opened fully leased at rents ranging from $18 to $21, with subleases of up to $24. This was encouraging.

However, other projects faced trouble. While considerably further out from downtown Washington, one building would be completed within 90 days, and no tenants were lined up. The proposed rents were $19-20, and Joey predicted that "some lender is going to be holding an empty building for quite some time." Another building was under construction only three blocks from Park Place -- further away from the Metro subway stop. It was expecting to draw $23 per square-foot for its 130,000 square feet of net rentable area. Though it looked to be a nice building, it was not slated for completion until after Park Place would open. Joey reaffirmed his confidence in his project: "It's a good looking building, with great views, and a beautiful location one block from the new Metro. It's a major gateway to Washington, and has lots of promise." He felt that it would be ideal for a single tenant, but was not sure how long he could wait to see if one turned up.

In the meantime, three options had surfaced for leasing parts of Park Place, but none had materialized into a prelease agreement. Early on, a prospective tenant had expressed interest in leasing the penthouse floor. Joey felt that it would be foolish to commit his most valuable space to a single-floor lease that early. He offered the tenant a lease of the top three floors, with the tenant becoming responsible for sub-leasing that space which was not needed. In addition, Joey asserted that the lease would have to include a provision allowing him an option to expel the tenant nine months prior to occupancy for a fee. This would cover the possibility of accommodating a large single tenant prospect which might come along later. The tenant found these conditions unacceptable and was not heard from again.

Another interested tenant was the U.S. Postal Service, which wanted to lease the ground floor. Joey considered the option only briefly. He knew that the ground floor retail space would not be easy to rent, but he felt strongly that a post office would not be appropriate: "A post office is not classy enough to have on the ground floor of this kind of an office building. So we turned that one down."

A third option involved a potential single tenant. Joey was approached by a company which needed 250,000 square feet. They wanted to know if Joey would be interested in building an 80-foot walkway across to an adjacent building which would have 100,000 square feet becoming

available at about the same time that Park Place would be ready for occupancy. The company would then lease space in both buildings to meet its needs. After discussions were held with the owners of the adjacent building, and after architects and County officials were consulted, the proposal was deemed possible, though at a cost of over $150,000. Joey formulated an offer for the tenant. Although he was enthusiastic at the prospect of having a single large tenant, he was concerned about the clear risks of the plan: "It would have been a big commitment on our part. We weren't going to be able to do all that for our own health! We determined that we could rent them the building, but that it would require a six month deposit, and they would have to pay for the bridge up front. These conditions were made because the bridge might be an improvement that we'd never use if they left the building." The deal fell through at this point, with the tenant unwilling to meet Joey's conditions.

Joey now turned his attention to the latest proposals to be received. A national association wanted to lease 60,000 square feet, taking the first four office floors, for $20 per square foot. Perhaps of more significance, they wanted to have the building bear their name. In addition, they wanted to buy an equity position in the project. A second association wanted two floors at the same rental rate and also wanted an equity participation.

These offers raised many major issues for Joey to consider in formulating formal proposals. He would have to reassess the optimal position for the company in the project, and determine what any changes in that position would imply about the future direction of the organization.

EXHIBITS

1. Notice of public sale.

2. Excerpts from leasing brochure.

3. Excerpts from loan proposal.

4. Permanent financing commitment.

QUESTIONS FOR DISCUSSION

1. How is the entrepreneur doing at the time of this case?

2. What actions should he be taking during the next six months?

3. What concerns appear to have motivated the lender?

Exhibit 1

Exhibit 2

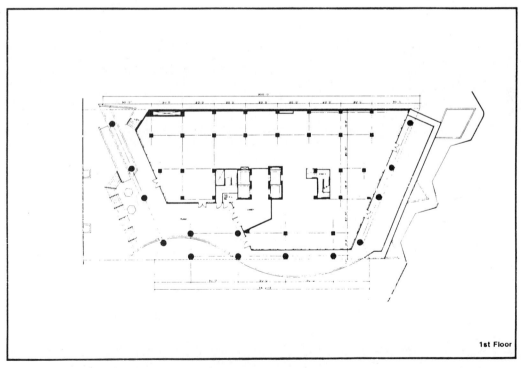

1st Floor

Park Place

Exhibit 2
continued

Park Place

. . . the last, best, most exclusive address in Rosslyn.

The Kaempfer Company presents a sleek, new thirteen story office building and park on the last available commercial space in downtown Rosslyn. Park Place, available for occupancy in late 1982, offers the latest in building design along with an ideal location for firms with business activities in Washington or Northern Virginia.

LOCATION

1655 North Fort Myer Drive
(Between North Fort Myer and North Lynn at Arlington Boulevard/Rt. 50).

Minutes from downtown Washington, the Pentagon, Crystal City and the office complexes of Northern Virginia.

One and one-half blocks from the Rosslyn Metro Station.

Within walking distance of major hotels, fine restaurants and specialty shops.

Overlooks a specially created park featuring earth sculptures.

Offers a panoramic view of Washington facing the Iwo Jima Memorial and the Potomac.

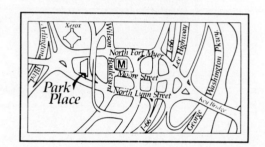

BUILDING SIZE

Approximately 164,700 total rentable square feet on twelve floors and penthouse.

Typical floors of approximately 14,000 rentable square feet.

Over 12,000 square feet for potential retail use.

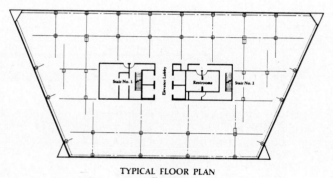

TYPICAL FLOOR PLAN
(Floors 4–12)

BUILDING FEATURES

Energy conserving Variable Air Volume HVAC system with zoned and individual floor-by-floor controls.

Unique trapezoidal design maximizes view.

Balcony areas on each floor.

Four high-speed elevators, and attractive brick lobbies on each floor.

Full sprinkler coverage and a sophisticated fire prevention system.

Three levels of underground parking.

OCCUPANCY

Late 1982.

Exhibit 3

```
                          PARK PLACE
             Rosslyn, Arlington County, Virginia

                  Pro Forma Income and Expense
                      (1984 Stabilized)


INCOME
                        Rentable      Rent per SF
                         _Area_     (Plus Electricity)        Total_

    Office               144,800         $20.50          $2,968,400
    Office Penthouse      10,000          23.00             230,000
    Retail/Restaurant/Bank 9,200          22.00             202,400
    Storage                1,500           8.00              12,000
    Parking            150 spaces   $65.00/space/month       117,000

    TOTAL GROSS RENT                                     $3,529,800
    Vacancy @ 3%                                            105,894

    GROSS OPERATING INCOME                               $3,423,906


OPERATING EXPENSES

    Management (3% of Gross Operating Income)     $102,717
    Operations
       Security                                     16,500
       Janitorial @ $65/SF(office only)             92,880
       Elevator Maintenance                         12,000
       Operating Personnel; chief engineer @
         $22,000; 2 maintenance @ $30,000;
         2 parking attendants @ $24,000;
         all plus benefits @ 20%                    91,200
       Sewer and Water @ $.08/SF(office only)       12,384
       Electrical for Building                      24,000
       Repairs and Replacement @ $.25/SF(office only) 38,700
       Insurance @ $.09/SF(office only)             13,932
       Real Estate Taxes @ $1.31/SF(office only)   202,788
       Gross Receipts Tax @ $.0025 x gross rental
         income                                      8,560
       Utilities Paid by Tenants                         0
       Miscellaneous @ $.15/SF(office only)         23,220

                                                   $638,881


NET INCOME AVAILABLE FOR DEBT SERVICE                    $2,785,025
```

Exhibit 3
continued

PARK PLACE
Rosslyn, Arlington County, Virginia

Development Budget

	Project Total	Cost Per Gross SF[1] (251,124)	Cost per Net SF (154,800)
LAND COST			
Acquisition[2]	$ 1,300,000	5.17	8.40
Real Estate Taxes	142,500	.57	.92
Subtotal	$ 1,442,500	5.74	9.32
BASE BUILDING			
Soil Testing/Borings	$ 12,000	.05	.08
Base Bldg. Shell & Garage	9,750,000	38.83	63.06
Architects			
Mech/Elect Engineers	290,000	1.15	1.87
Structural Engineers			
Permits and Fees	120,000	.48	.76
Developers Fee	500,000	2.00	3.23
Material Testing	18,000	.07	.12
Civil Engineering/Survey	30,000	.12	.19
Landscaping & Drainage & Park	150,000	.60	.96
Park Construction	75,000	.30	.48
Contingency	300,000	1.19	1.94
Subtotal	$11,245,000	44.78	72.64
TENANT DEVELOPMENT			
Tenant Construction	$ 1,654,000	6.59	10.68
Space Planning & Working Drawings	86,000	.34	.55
Work Above Standard	101,000	.40	.65
Misc. Expense	10,000	.04	.06
Contingency	54,000	.22	.35
Subtotal	$ 1,905,000	7.59	12.31

[1] Includes Parking
[2] Land Acquisition Components:
    Subordinated leasehold 22,000 s.f.
    Land in Fee 10,000 s.f. (provides FAR and bonus density credit)

Exhibit 3
continued

Development Budget, Cont'd.

	Project Total	Cost Per Gross SF[1] (251,124)	Cost Per Net SF (154,800)
FINANCING			
Lenders Fee-Const. Loan	$ 180,000	.72	1.16
Commission-End Loan	50,000	.20	.32
Lender's Inspection Fee	20,000	.08	.13
Lender's Legal	40,000	.16	.26
Appraisal	23,000	.09	.15
Subtotal	$ 313,000	1.25	2.02
LEASING MARKETING			
Lease Commissions/Fee	$ 561,000	2.23	3.62
Lease Concessions	228,000	.91	1.47
Advertising/P.R.	20,000	.08	.13
Legal (Lease)	15,000	.06	.10
Contingency	34,000	.14	.22
Subtotal	$ 858,000	3.42	5.54
GENERAL AND ADMINISTRATIVE			
Project Legal	$ 60,000	.24	.39
Project Accounting	20,000	.08	.13
Project Insurance	44,000	.18	.28
Title Insurance/Fees	25,000	.10	.16
Misc. Expense	10,000	.04	.06
Subtotal	$ 159,000	.63	1.03
OPERATIONS DURING CONSTRUCTION			
Income			
Expenses			
Lease Assumptions NET	$ 650,000	2.59	4.19
Income Abatement			
Contingency			
Ground Lease	65,000	.26	.42
Interest Expense	2,052,500	8.17	13.26
TOTAL PROJECT COST	$18,690,000	74.43	120.74

[1] Includes Parking

Exhibit 3
continued

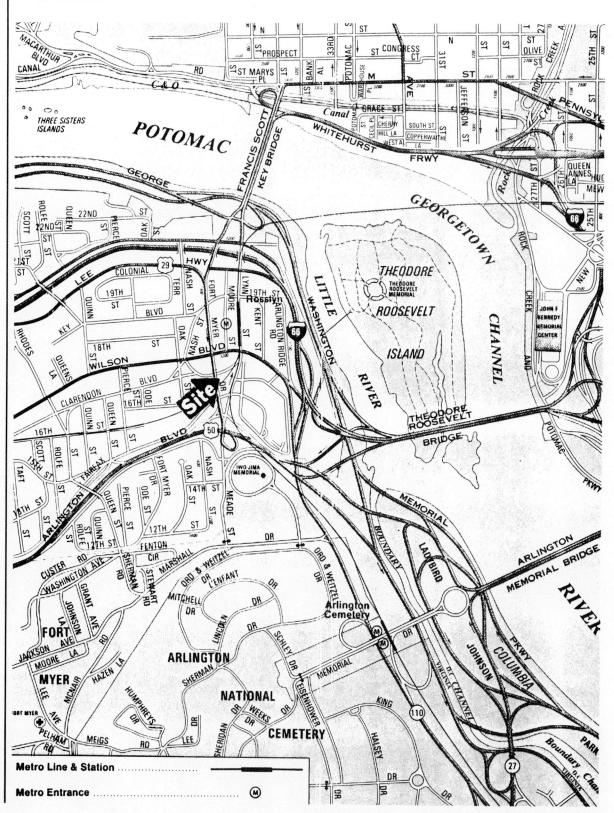

Metro Line & Station ....

Metro Entrance .... Ⓜ

Exhibit 4

Permanent Financing Commitment
(Introductory Paragraphs Deleted)

<u>Loan Amount</u>: $18,400,000

<u>Term</u>:   Thirty-five (35) years, with payments to be made in
equal monthly installments of $208,993 including principal
and interest in order to retire the loan by maturity.

<u>Call Option</u>:   The note and mortgage will provide that the
entire remaining indebtedness, plus accrued interest, shall,
at Lender's option, become due and payable at par, without
penalty, at the end of the 15th loan year, provided Borrower
is given at least nine months prior written notice of Lender's intention to exercise this option.

<u>Interest Rate</u>:   13-1/2% (thirteen and one-half percentum) per
annum.

<u>Additional Interest</u>:   Commencing on the 1st anniversary of
the loan, Lender shall annually receive 30% of the annual
gross income from operations of the subject property in excess of $3,435,000 per year, exclusive of any pass throughs
for electricity, operating expenses, real estate taxes and
ground rent, as additional interest.   Said additional interest shall be in addition to the 13-1/2% per annum interest
charged and shall be paid within 90 days of the end of each
calendar year as determined by audited CPA operating statements.   In the first and last loan years during which said
additional interest is applicable, there shall be a proration
of said additional interest based on the number of calendar
months in the loan year falling within the calendar year for
which the operating statement is applicable.

At the time of payoff of the loan either through voluntary
prepayment by Borrower or exercise of the call option by
Lender, but not at the expiration of 35 years or the time the
loan fully amortizes, Lender shall receive as additional
interest 30% of the net proceeds from either a sale of the
subject property to a bona fide third party or a refinancing
of the subject loan.   Net proceeds from a refinancing shall
be the net new loan amount less the outstanding principal
balance of the subject loan.   Net proceeds from a sale shall
be the net sale price less the outstanding principal balance
of the subject loan.   It is understood by both Borrower and
Lender that for the purposes of computing the net proceeds
from a sale or refinancing, the dollar amount to be used as
the net new loan amount or net sales price for the purposes
of this paragraph shall be a minimum of $24,500,000, notwith-
standing the actual net proceeds from such sale or refinancing.   In the event of a payoff through means other than a

Exhibit 4
continued

Park Place Associates
July 14, 1981
Page 3

sale or refinancing (e.g., a cash payment), Lender shall be
entitled to receive as additional interest 30% of the difference between $24,500,000 and the outstanding principal bal-
ance of the subject loan.

Tax Deposits: Monthly payments are to include a sum equal to
estimated monthly charges for future real property taxes and
assessments. This amount will be adjusted at closing so that
beginning with the first payment under the loan, subsequent
monthly deposits of one-twelfth of the annual taxes and
assessments will account for the entire taxes and assessments
when due. All such tax escrow deposits may be commingled
with Lender's other funds and shall bear no interest.

At the time of the loan closing, Lender will waive the
requirements for monthly tax deposits by separate letter subject to:

   (a)   prompt payment of mortgage installments
         when due and Borrower not being in de-
         fault in performance of any of its other
         obligations under the loan documents; and

   (b)   receipt by Lender of tax receipts or
         other proof of timely payment (such as a
         copy of the tax bill and cancelled
         check) within 60 days of each tax due
         date.

Prepayment: Except for regular amortization, no additional
payments may be made to principal for the first fifteen (15)
loan years. In the event that Lender does not exercise its
option to call the loan, at any time after the fifteenth
(15th) loan year, additional payments may be made to be
credited to principal on any interest payment date and with
sixty (60) days' prior written notice. In the event of such
prepayment, either in full or in part, a premium of 5% of the
amount so prepaid shall be charged during the sixteenth
(16th) loan year. Such premium shall decrease 1% per annum
thereafter to a minimum of one percent (1%). Prepayments
will be credited to installments of principal in the inverse
order of their maturity. To the extent permitted by law,

Exhibit 4
continued

Park Place Associates
July 14, 1981
Page 4

Such prepayment premium shall be payable regardless of
whether the loan is prepaid voluntarily or involuntarily,
except that no premium shall be required on prepayments
occasioned by condemnation awards or proceeds from fire
and/or casualty.

Security: A first and valid lien upon the fee simple interest in real estate commonly known as the Zinnamon Property
containing approximately 22,018 square feet located in
Arlington, Virginia, at the convergence of North Lynn Street
and North Fort Myer Drive immediately south of 17th Street,
having frontage on all three (3) such streets, to be improved
with a 12 story plus penthouse office building containing
approximately 252,800 square feet gross area and approximately 164,000 square feet rentable area, and 3 below-grade
garage levels for approximately 150 cars.

Because the interest of Borrower is that of a lessee, Lender
will require that all parties having an interest in the fee
simple title also sign the mortgage papers without personal
liability. The final legal description of the mortgaged
premises must be approved by Lender.

Title and Documents: Title and all documents, agreements, or
other instruments used in conjunction with or related to this
transaction, including, without limitation, the partnership
agreement of Borrower and the ground lease, shall be approved
by Lender. Lender is to be furnished with a title insurance
policy containing no exceptions, other than those approved by
Lender, issued by a company or companies acceptable to it
with provisions for such reinsurance as Lender may require.

Lender's Right to Refinance: In the event Borrower wishes to
refinance the subject property prior to the date the loan has
been paid in full, Borrower shall first notify Lender in
writing, which notice shall specify the amount of the refinancing requested. Lender shall then, within 60 days after
receipt of such notice, either issue its commitment for such
refinancing or notify Borrower that it does not wish to provide such refinancing. In the event Lender notifies Borrower
it does not wish to provide such refinancing (the failure of
Lender to issue its commitment within said 60 day period

Exhibit 4
continued

Park Place Associates
July 14, 1981
Page 5

shall be deemed such notice), Borrower shall be free to refinance the subject property at any time within 120 days
after the expiration of such 60 day period through an
alternative source upon such terms as Borrower deems acceptable, subject to all other terms and conditions of this commitment. In the event Lender issues its commitment for
refinancing, if Borrower does not accept said commitment,
then Borrower shall be free to refinance the subject property
through an alternative source within 120 days after the date
Lender's commitment for refinancing was issued, provided the
terms of the refinancing through such alternative source are
more advantageous to Borrower than the terms of the commitment issued by Lender. In the event refinancing through an
alternative source is not consummated within the aforesaid
120 day time periods, then prior to consummating any refinancing Borrower shall again afford Lender the right to
provide such refinacing in accordance with the terms of this
paragrpah. The fact that Lender may provide refinancing
shall not affect Lender's right to receive additional interest on the refinancing of the subject property as hereinabove
provided.

Lender's Right to Purchase: In the event Borrower wishes to
sell the subject property prior to the date the loan is paid
in full, Borrower shall first notify Lender in writing of
Borrower's desire to sell, such notice to be accompanied by
an offer to sell the subject property to Lender containing
the relevant terms of sale. Lender shall then, within 60
days after receipt of such notice and offer, either accept
said offer or notify Borrower that it does not wish to purchase the subject property in accordance with the terms of
said offer (failure of Lender to so notify Borrower shall be
deemed a rejection of the offer). If Lender does not accept
said offer, then Borrower shall be free, for a period of 120
days thereafter, to enter into a contract to sell the subject
property at a price and on terms not less advantageous to
Borrower than those stated in the offer made to Lender. If
such a contract is not executed within said 120 day period,
then Borrower shall again offer the subject property to
Lender in accordance with the terms of this paragraph before
contracting to sell the property to a third party. The fact
that Lender may purchase the subject property shall not

Exhibit 4
continued

Park Place Associates
July 14, 1981
Page 6

affect Lender's right to receive additional interest on a
sale of the subject property as hereinabove provided.

Management: Management of the property shall be in all
respects acceptable to Lender throughout the loan term.

Mortgage Demand Clause: Title to the mortgaged premises
securing the loan contemplated herein shall not be changed by
sale, assignment or otherwise, without the prior written consent of Lender. Change of title by devise or descent or by
transfer of limited partnership interest to members of the
immediate families of the General Partners shall not be considered a violation of this clause. Transfer of any general
partnership interest in the borrowing entity or transfer of
more than thirty percent (30%) in the aggregate of the limited partnership interest in the borrowing entity shall be
considered a sale of the premises for all purposes of this
commitment. Should the mortgaged premises be sold without
the prior written approval of Lender, Lender shall have the
right to require the balance of the loan to be immediately
paid in full. If permitted by local law, provision to this
effect shall be included in the documents securing this loan.

Security Agreement: As additional security, Lender will
receive a first lien on all fixtures, equipment, furniture
and furnishings, and any additions or replacements thereto,
which are owned or leased by Borrower, and are (to be) located on the premises described above and are to be used in
the operation of the premises.

Annual Statements: Annual operating statements of this property, prepared and certified by a CPA satisfactory to Lender,
are to be forwarded to Lender within ninety (90) days after
the end of each calendar year. This requirement shall be
included as a covenant in the security instruments.

Survey: A certified survey of the entire property by a
Registered Surveyor, or his equivalent in states not having
Registered Surveyors, showing an acceptable state of facts
and the location of the improvements, easements, and any en-
croachments, is to be furnished by Borrower at least two
weeks prior to closing.

Exhibit 4
continued

Park Place Associates
July 14, 1981
Page 7

Insurance Requirements: The loan documents shall provide for
fire and extended coverage, rent loss insurance and for other
insurance coverage, including war risk insurance, if available, as Lender may require from time to time, in amounts and
with companies acceptable to Lender. The policies shall contain a standard mortgagee clause and shall be deposited with
Lender throughout the life of the loan together with re-
ceipted insurance bills evidencing payment thereof within 60
days of each due date.

Personal Liability: Borrower and its partners shall not be
personally liable for payment of the debt.

Plans and Specification: Prior to the start of construction, (i) Lender must approve final working plans and specifications which shall be in substantial agreement with preliminary plans, specifications, and descriptions accompanying
the application for the loan, and (ii) at Lender's option,
an independent architect selected by Lender shall review and
approve such plans and specifications on behalf of Lender.
All architect's fees, costs and other expenses related to
such review and approval will be paid by Borrower.

Completion: Prior to disbursement of the loan proceeds, all
building and site improvements are to be completed to Lender's satisfaction in accordance with final plans and specifications as approved by Lender (and Lender's architect, if
applicable), and satisfactory proof that the completed improvements comply with all ordinances, building codes and
zoning requirements shall be furnished to Lender.

During construction, Lender is to be provided with satisfactory periodic inspection reports prepared by an architect or
engineer satisfactory to Lender showing the improvements are
being built in accordance with the approved final plans and
specifications. These reports will be paid for by Borrower.

Lender understands that upon disbursement of the loan amount
as provided for below, all office tenant areas nay not be
fully completed for occupancy by tenants. Lender specifically agrees to disburse the loan amount with 125% of Lender's estimate of cost to complete the unfinished tenant areas

Exhibit 4
continued

Park Place Associates
July 18, 1981
Page 8

to be deposited in an interest-bearing escrow account with an
escrow agent and on terms acceptable to Lender. Lender further specifically agrees to give Borrower twelve months from
the date of the loan closing to qualify for release of this
completion holdback by completing all unfinished tenant areas.
Borrower may request disbursements from the escrow account
upon completion of tenant areas not more frequently than one
time per month and in amounts not less than $50,000.00. At
Lender's option, funds will be disbursed only upon Lender's
receipt of certification from an independent architect
selected by Lender that said architect has inspected the work
and the work has been properly completed. All architect's
fees, costs and other expenses related to such inspection and
certification will be paid by Borrower. In the event Borrower does not qualify to have the entire escrowed amount
released, the remaining escrowed funds shall be treated as
prepayment of principal (without penalty) and the monthly
installment mentioned in Term above will be adjusted to
amortize fully the amount of the loan after such prepayment
over the remaining loan term.

Disbursement Contingent Upon Leasing: Prior to the closing
of the loan, Lender will require all general partners of the
borrowing entity to enter into and jointly and severally
guaranty a master lease of the entire improvements for a term
of not less than 10 years at an annual gross rental of
$3,540,000 with utilities paid by the tenant. Said lease
shall be approved by Lender, be in full force and effect and
be specifically assigned to Lender. Said lease obligations
will be reduced as space is leases (pursuant to leases with
not less than a three year term) to third party tenants acceptable to Lender on a basis that would equate to a gross
annual rent roll of $3,540,000 with utilities paid by the
tenant.

Such master lease and any substitute leases shall at Lender's
option either be superior to the mortgage or shall be subordinate to the mortgage, in which latter event the Lender
shall grant the tenants non-disturbance rights so long as the
tenants are not in default and the tenants shall agree to
attorn to Lender or its successors.

Exhibit 4
continued

Park Place Associates
July 14, 1981
Page 9

At the time of closing, Lender shall be furnished with an
estoppel certificate signed by all tenants confirming that
the leases are in full force and effect, that the tenant is
in possession and paying rent on a current basis, that there
has been no prepayment of rent, and that Borrower is not in
default in its obligation under the lease.

Financing Sign: Lender   Inc. shall be
permitted to place a suitable sign on the subject property
during the term of construction indicating their participation in the permanent financing.

Secondary Financing: No secondary financing shall be placed
on the subject property without Lender having the right to
approve the second mortgagee and the terms of said second
mortgage, such approval not to be unreasonably withheld.
Failure to secure such prior review and consent shall, at
Lender's option, cause all secured indebtedness, including
any prepayment fee that may be due, as provided in this commitment, to be immediately due and payable. This requirement
will be incorporated in the mortgage instrument.

Tri-Party Agreement: This loan will be pre-closed by means
of a buy-sell agreement to be entered into between Borrower,
the interim lender, and Lender, which agreement shall be
satisfactory in form and substance to Lender.

Commitment Fee: As part of the consideration for the issuance of this commitment and for Lender's obligation to loan
the money in question, a commitment fee of $368,000 (2% of
the loan amount) will be paid by Borrower to Lender (which
may be commingled with Lender's other funds) at the time this
letter is accepted, with the understanding that such fee
shall be returned to Borrower (without interest thereon)
only (i) if Lender fails to approve the ground lease for the
subject property, provided such ground lease has been submitted by Borrower to Lender and Lender's Counsel for review
within thirty (30) days after the date of Borrower's acceptance of this commitment (Lender agrees to use its best
efforts to review said lease within 30 days after receipt)
or (ii) after the loan has been properly closed and delivered in accordance with the terms and condtions of the com-

Exhibit 4
continued

Park Place Associates
July 14, 1981
Page 10

mitment, including payment of all fees and expenses, provided
such closing and delivery take place before March 31, 1983,
subject to ninety (90) days extension for force majeure, the
date on which Lender's commitment hereunder terminates, time
being of the essence hereof. In the event Borrower fails to
close for any reason not the fault of Lender on or before
March 31, 1983, subject to ninety (90) days extension for
force majeure, Lender shall keep the aforementioned commitment fee as and for its complete and liquidated damages. The
closing and delivery of this loan shall take place not
earlier than January 2, 1983.

One-half of the commitment fee shall be in the form of cash.
The remaining half may be in the form of an unconditional,
Irrevocable Letter of Credit by a bank and in a form satisfactory to Lender and expiring not earlier than April 30,
1983, or ninety (90) days thereafter in the event of force
majeure as above provided. The Letter of Credit must be payable on presentation with absolutely no accompanying documentation, with payment only by wire transfer to a bank
account designated by Lender.

<u>Legal</u>: All legal matters, including the required mortgage
documents, other loan documents (leases, if applicable) and
an acceptable ALTA title insurance policy from an acceptable
title insurer are subject to the approval of Lender. Lender
shall also be represented by Counsel of its choice from the
state in which the property is located. Counsel will be
responsible for drafting all loan documentation for Lender's
approval and providing all other attorney's services necessary in Lender's opinion to facilitate the closing of this
transaction. At the closing, Counsel must be in a position
to deliver an attorney's opinion acceptable to Lender regarding the validity of the loan, specifically including
Lender's ability to make the loan under applicalbe laws and
regulations, and covering such other matters, including, but
not limited to, the organization in good standing of the borrowing entity and the authority of the General Partner to act
on its behalf. Whether or not the transactions contemplated
hereby are consummated, Borrower agrees to pay all costs
involved in the closing of this loan, including, but not
limited to, the fees, expenses and disbursements of Lender's

Exhibit 4
continued

Park Place Associates
July 14, 1981
Page 11

Counsel, recording fees, title insurance premiums, title
examination fees, appraisal fees and survey costs.

<u>Binding Commitment</u>: Borrower agrees that upon acceptance of
this commitment, it shall become binding and that the loan
will be closed in accordance with its terms and conditions.
Where terms and conditions of this commitment differ from the
loan as applied for, this commitment shall prevail.

This commitment shall not be assignable or otherwise transferable by Borrower. This commitment shall not become effective unless it is accepted in writing by Borrower on or
before Aug, 14, 1981. Such acceptance is to be made by signing and returning to the Lender the attached copy of this
commitment along with the commitment fee mentioned above.

Discounted Cash Flow Analysis

This note examines contemporary methods of real estate financial analysis. Many real estate lending and equity investment decisions rest in part on projections of investment performance over time. Using these projected financial results, we will apply measures of valuation and return which explicitly consider the time value of money. These measures of return involve the discounting of future dollars to reflect their present worth.

Many real estate professionals still make their investment decisions on the basis of relatively simple return measures, such as those presented in Note 1, Static Financial Analysis. However, the widespread availability of microcomputers and "spreadsheet" software has in recent years made computer modeling of complex investments both practical and rewarding. Previously, financial modeling involved the use of a specialized consulting service or laborious hand calculations. With the new tools, frequent revisions and tests (called "sensitivity analyses") are now quite easy to do.

For developers, the tools of discounted cash flow analysis present an important opportunity to present their proposals in a good light. For investors, the opportunity is to be fully informed about a range of possible outcomes. For lenders, these tools facilitate the more efficient consideration of any issues being negotiated. This note contains three sections:

Section I introduces the **time value of money** and the calculation of present values.

Section II reviews the art of preparing **financial projections** of investment performance over time.

Section III presents **valuation and return measures** based on financial projections.

I. THE TIME VALUE OF MONEY

In real estate, developers and investors must commit large sums of money at the beginning of a project in exchange for uncertain and variable returns over time. In this section, we will introduce the concept of time value of money and develop the mathematical tools to determine the present worth of these future returns.

The Concept

Most people recognize, at least implicitly, that there is a time value associated with money. They do this every day in commerce when they answer the following: "Would you rather have a sum of money, say $100, today? or tomorrow? or a year from now?"

Most people prefer having the money earlier, rather than waiting for it, because if they have it, they can invest it, earning a return in the meantime. At a minimum, they can deposit the money in a savings account, earn interest, and then withdraw both the original sum ("principal") and the interest for use at a later time. If the $100 were deposited at 5% annual interest, a total of $105 would be available after one year.

Some people might prefer to wait for their money. For example, they might prefer having "forced savings" for some possible or specific future use. This is not necessarily an irrational view, but one which imposes a cost on the person taking it. This cost, the foregone interest, is what is meant by the **time value of money**. In the balance of this section, we will develop the mathematical tools to measure that value.

Future Value

Up until now, we have examined real estate income and costs in a static state. We have not been concerned with the timing of cash flows. As illustrated above, cash received earlier is worth more than the same amount received later. The same is true of cash flowing in the reverse direction. That is, money paid out early costs more to the payer than the same dollar amount paid out later. If you pay early, you lose the interest that could be earned in the meantime. Measuring the amount of interest that is earned or could be earned over a period of time is how we will measure the time value of money.

We will use the same notation used before for calculating mortgage constant payments, a related time-value calculation:

---

i = interest rate per time period
n = number of time periods
pv = principal amount ("present value")

What will be the future value (fv) of a sum of money deposited today? The amount deposited (pv) will increase over time as interest is earned. Using the simple example of an annual interest rate (i) for one year (n), future value may be calculated as follows:

$$fv = pv\,(1 + i)$$

In this formula, i is represented by a decimal interest rate. Thus in our earlier example of $100 invested at 5%:

$$fv = \$100\,(1 + .05) = \$105$$

For the next year, the value will again increase. This time, however, the base figure earning interest will include the original principal plus the interest earned during the first year. This is known as "compound" interest. Thus:

$$fv_2 = fv_1 (1 + i)$$

Substituting in this equation the original expression for fv_1, this may be restated:

$$fv_2 = pv (1 + i) (1 + i)$$

In the general case, this may be expressed:

$$fv_n = pv (1 + i)^n$$

Thus the future value at any time in the future (after n time periods) will be the present value increased by a compound interest factor, equal to one plus the interest rate per period, raised to the nth power. With this formula, we can calculate future value from information about the principal amount, interest rate and length of time over which interest will be earned.

So far, this is quite straightforward. If we have the cash and invest it, its future worth may be precisely calculated, assuming we actually receive the interest rate used in the calculation. This is not, of course, guaranteed. We may assume a high return and not receive it, or we may assume a low return which is eventually exceeded. Note that a small difference in the rate of interest will compound over time, making potentially a major difference in the future value. Thus, the choice of interest rate is critical to the accuracy of the calculation.

Present Value

More commonly in real estate financial analysis, we have a different sort of problem. We expect to receive amounts of dollars in the future, and we want to compare them with dollars being spent today. Therefore we need to determine the value today of these future dollars.

In the previous equation, we calculated a future value, based on a stated present value, given a stated interest rate and time period. It stands to reason that the reverse may also be done; that is, we should be able to calculate a **present value**, based on a stated future value, given a stated interest rate and time period. Mathematically, this is done by simply transposing the previous equation:

$$pv = fv_n / (1+i)^n$$

Thus, in this restated equation we may calculate what original principal amount (pv) is necessary to generate a specific future amount (fv) after a specific time period (n), given the interest rate (i). Using our previous example, assume we know that the future value will be $105, the interest rate (for this purpose, this is also often called a "discount" rate) is 5%, and the time is one year:

$$pv = \$105 / (1+.05)^1 = \$100$$

The above equation is often converted into a table of present values. To do this, simply let $fv_n = 1$ in our restated equation and calculate the present value of $1 received at various times in the future at various interest rates:

$$pv = 1 / (1+i)^n$$

Exhibit 1 provides present value factors calculated from this formula for a range of interest (or discount) rates and up to 25 years. The present value factor may be multiplied times any future cash flow, thus converting the future cash value to its present value equivalent.

We now are in a position (mathematically at least) to compare amounts of dollars received at different points in time. We can simply calculate the present value of each future amount and make the comparison directly.

Just as in the calculation of future values, the accuracy of the calculation depends entirely on the eventual accuracy of the interest or discount rate selected. The actual outcome generally is of little concern to the analyst. The important issue is to select the interest or discount rate appropriate for the decision at hand. As in the case of the capitalization rate, discussed in a previous note, the choice of discount rate is one which requires careful consideration. We will return to this topic in Section III of this note.

Related Calculations

The same basic equation which relates present and future values may at times be useful in other ways. For example, we may want to calculate the length of time it will take for our given principal amount to increase to a given sum. Or we may want to calculate what rate of interest will be required to achieve a specific sum at a fixed point in time. These calculations might be useful if, for example, a specific contractual payment has to be made at a particular time in the future, and we are establishing an interest-bearing reserve to fund it.

These calculations are not quite as straightforward to make. From examination of the formula, the reader will observe that the calculation can *only* be made through a series of approximations. To solve for the interest rate, knowing the present and future values and the length of time, we must first make a trial calculation, assuming a particular interest rate. If the calculated future value is too high, we must adjust the rate downward; if the result is too low, the adjustment would be upward, and so on. Note that the result will eventually approach the precise answer closely enough to be useful, but the result usually will *not* be mathematically exact.

This is called an "iterative" calculation, and, although it can be done by hand, it is best done with a financial calculator or computer. Note that as your calculator is performing this calculation, it takes several seconds as it runs through a series of iterative approximations.

The mathematics of the present value formula are similar to those of the mortgage payment tables discussed previously. In the case of the mortgage, the principal amount of the mortgage is the present worth of a series of future payments (the "constant" payments or k). Thus, the basic formula would simply add the present value of each of the payments, as follows:

$$pv = k \left(\frac{1}{(1+i)} + \frac{1}{(1+i)^2} + \dots \frac{1}{(1+i)^n} \right)$$

Given the principal balance of the loan (pv), the interest rate (i), and the term of the loan (n), one may calculate the required constant payment (k). As each payment is made, the principal balance outstanding is reduced by the following amount:

$$pv_n = pv_{n-1} (1 + i) - k$$

Thus, by running through a series of laborious calculations, one may determine the amounts of interest and principal in each payment, and the remaining balance of the loan after each. Until the advent of computers, such calculations were normally made using books of tables. Every bank's loan officers had them, but not every borrower. Today, the hand-held calculator will give this information quickly and easily to anyone.

II.   FINANCIAL PROJECTIONS

Making projections of financial performance over time is an art form. Preparing or interpreting a financial projection requires considerable creativity, not simply the mechanical calculation of the numbers themselves. In this section, we will review the mechanics of computing financial projections and identify areas where assumptions and presentation decisions are important.

Preliminary Matters

The basic information needed to begin a financial projection is that studied in Note 1, Static Financial Analysis. In the case of income property, we will need a setup, that is, a stabilized annual cash-basis income statement. In the case of a development project, we will need a capital budget.

As noted previously, we will benefit greatly from using a microcomputer with spreadsheet software. Alternatively, we will need sheets of wide accounting-type paper, pencils and erasers. A hand-held financial calculator may also be very useful. Green eye-shades are optional.

A good first step is to think carefully about the purpose of the financial projection. Who is to use it and why? Important to developers are two general types of financial projections:

1. The **investment analysis** is intended to illustrate the consequences of a particular proposed investment. This type of projection is often used as a selling tool for the developer, seeking to attract lenders or equity investors. Investment analysis projections will be the focus of discussion in this note. Exhibit 2 is an example of an investment analysis prepared to support the refinancing of an office building located in Boston.

2. The **cash flow model** is intended to demonstrate the consequences of a particular set of interacting financial events over time. This type of projection is often a management tool used for planning or to test or confirm feasibility. Lenders, for example, usually want a developer to prepare a projection of cash balances over time to confirm the margin of safety in a particular project. Cash flow models vary widely and must be tailored to a specific situation. Generalization will not be attempted in this note. Exhibit 3 is an example of a cash flow model reflecting the final months for completing an office rehabilitation development, also located in Boston.

The next preparatory step is to develop a format for the projection. The format of the financial projection may vary widely, depending on its purpose. What is the beginning point for the projection? What time horizon is appropriate?

Choosing the time scale is an important step. Projections may be computed on an annual, quarterly, monthly, or even weekly basis, depending on their purpose. Most investment analyses are based on annual returns, although years may be calendar or fiscal, and the first and last years may include a longer or shorter time period. In the case of property being sold, such as condominium units or homes, shorter periods, monthly or quarterly, are usually more appropriate. The cash flow model type of projection usually involves irregular cash flows and will also require shorter time intervals. The time scale selected will generally be laid out on the horizontal axis of the spreadsheet.

The final preliminary step is to develop a chart of accounts for the vertical axis of the spreadsheet. These may include a wide range of items and categories, including operating cash flow, taxable income and income tax consequences, equity and debt financing proceeds, capital budget expenditures, and revenue from sale of the property, either now or in the future. These may be organized as a simple sequence of calculations or as a single-page summary with detailed supporting schedules for those items which involve extended calculations. Selection and sequencing of these items in the presentation is of vital importance.

Projections for Investment Analysis

An investment in income-producing real estate provides up to three components of return:

1. **Cash Flow** to be distributed by the property ownership, independent of income tax consequences;

2. **Tax Effect**, the net increase or decrease in taxes payable resulting from the taxpayer's ownership interest; and

3. **Residual Value**, the net cash remaining, after payment of taxes, (or the net deficit to be made up) upon sale of the property.

Each of these components of return can be affected by uncertain events over time. Real estate investments are fraught with

risk, whether in the form of construction risk, marketing risk, or interest rate risk. Real estate investments also involve typically long time horizons, and an investor or lender may not be able to resell the investment. This illiquidity exacerbates the already large degree of uncertainty as to the actual future financial performance of a particular property.

These risks and uncertainties cannot readily be dealt with in a financial projection. In preparing an investment analysis, we must make precise estimates of these uncertain future events. Some computer modeling techniques, such as the "Monte Carlo Simulation," attempt to take uncertainty explicitly into account, but these are complex and therefore not widely used for decision-making. Instead, most practitioners will use a straightforward financial projection like that in Exhibit 2.

To deal with the uncertainties, most practitioners find it useful to establish a consistent attitude toward them. Depending on the purpose of the projection, our attitude may be to strive to be as "accurate" as possible in projecting future events, to be as "optimistic" as possible (within reason), or, on occasion, to be "conservative." We should attempt to be conscious of the basic attitude suitable for the purpose at hand.

Choices of assumptions and presentation will influence greatly the projections. Some of these factors are discussed in the following paragraphs.

Projecting Cash Flow. Investment analysis generally begins with operating income. The same chart of accounts used in the setup provides a starting point. One problem with this is that the setup is generally drawn up for a typical or stabilized year, and not for any specific year. The analyst may choose to keep matters simple by using the same income as shown in the setup for the first full year of operations, but this is unlikely to prove to be a particularly accurate assumption. A more detailed study of the rentup and development period will often be useful to determine a more realistic first-year cash flow.

In most projections, the early years are the most important. Establishing the baseline expectation for operating income is a very important step. Once the baseline is developed, the next step is to project the observable **trends**, such as inflation, and the predictable changes or **discontinuities** which may be apparent in the market. As discussed in Note 1, Static Financial Analysis, considerable research effort may be required to predict accurately market acceptance of a new development over even a short time horizon.

For income-producing property, inflation is very important to the projection. The effect of inflation depends on the **lease structure** for the property. Short-term leases provide the opportunity frequently to adjust rents. If the market rental rate has increased, whether as a result of inflation or for other reasons, the owner will benefit. Short leases are prevalent in the hotel and lodging, rental apartment, and small-user office building segments.

Increasingly in recent years, long-term leases can also provide inflation protection for owners. This is done through a variety of "escalator" clauses in the lease, including stepped rents and percentage rents. Stepped rents are contractual rent increases, either fixed or tied to an index, such as the Consumer Price Index. Percentage rents, common in retail leases, are rents tied to the dollar volume of sales. This clause has the effect of raising the rent when inflation or physical sales volume increases. Long-term leases also typically have clauses which pass through to tenants most or all increases in operating expenses and real estate taxes. These clauses are called "expense stops" or "bases".

Some long-term commercial and industrial leases may not have escalators. In such cases, the property owner must expect to receive only the fixed rental income for the term of the lease. Although this is often overlooked, rent decreases may also be experienced. In such cases, short term leases are *not* an advantage to the property owner. Short-term leases also mean frequent turnover, with attendant costs to refurbish the space and high overall vacancy experience.

The specific lease structure may or may not be reflected in the financial projections. The cash flow projection in Exhibit 3 calculates income and other items on a lease-by-lease basis. Prepared by a major mortgage broker for a recently rehabilitated office building, this projection is based on detailed supporting exhibits. (These may or may not be included for a particular presentation.) The supporting exhibits calculate income and expense escalation individually for each actual lease and each assumed new lease. At the same time, this projection is quite optimistic, having been prepared for the purpose of supporting an application for a loan increase. In this projection, an 8% average annual increase in market rent levels is assumed. Note that the lender was to receive a fixed base debt service payment plus 50% of annual cash flow from this property.

Most analysts will want a much simpler format, particularly for an initial review. To do this, there are many options. We could, for example, simply calculate the Free and Clear income for this property for its first year of full occupancy. Presumably the 1985 figure would be $1,536,000. From this base, the simplest approach would be to project steady net increases over time. Unless the leases are very short, however, this is unlikely to be accurate. Alternatively, we could assume a standard lease structure, say a five-year term, hold the net income fixed for that period, and then calculate a jump in the rents for the following year. Another simplification would be to ignore the details of lease turnover. The virtue of simplification is that the projection is easier to prepare; in the process, however, it may become more difficult to interpret.

Of all the assumptions to be made in the cash-flow projection, the most important is the choice of the **inflation assumption**. Until 1979, it was considered inappropriate to base investment returns on inflationary increases in net income. More recently, as inflation has become more conspicuously a part of our economic lives, most projections include an inflation assumption in the range of 4% - 6%. It seems to matter little that economists at various points in time would project different figures from this. What matters is that those investing in real estate have become accustomed to this approach.

Exercise: Test what effect the choice of inflation assumption and the simple projection options discussed above will have on the final year income in Exhibit 2. Using an assumed lease structure as a base, try two runs at 4%, 6% and 8% annual inflation. How much different is the projected 1993 Free and Clear income in each case?

Projecting Tax Effects. Many investment projections are prepared on a pre-tax basis, that is, they do not explicitly consider tax effects. For individual investors considering ownership directly or through partnerships, however, tax effects are often an important source of return. This brief discussion will be useful in cases where tax effects are to be considered as a component of return.

Making estimates of future tax consequences is deceptively simple. We typically calculate taxable income based on the cash flow projection and deductions allowable under present law. We then assume an effective tax rate for the taxpayer -- typically 30% - 35% including state taxes -- and assume that any net losses or tax

credits can be applied against other income. In effect, we are assuming that: 1) the present tax laws will continue in effect; and 2) investors will continue to be taxed at the same effective rate as at present.

These assumptions are evidently troublesome. The tax laws change and change frequently. Although the new laws usually try to exempt (or "Grandfather") projects begun under the old laws, this is not assured. The latest tax-law changes, enacted in 1986, illustrate that the effective value of a tax benefit can be substantially altered, even when its availability is preserved. This possibility is especially important to projects involving a particular tax incentive, such as rapid depreciation or investment tax credits. It is possible that other future tax changes will be made retroactive, but the huge number of people involved in real estate investment makes this politically unlikely.

The second assumption, that of effective rates of taxation, is also troublesome. One problem is with an investor's ability to sustain earnings at the level required to benefit fully from tax savings. As people age, their income may decline, and their objectives may also change. Especially for the many investors whose income is presently high, but who are not truly wealthy, the assumption that their effective tax rate will continue for more than a few years must be seriously questioned. Furthermore, tax rates are today at historically low levels. The good news for real estate investment is that future tax rate changes are likely to be upward, and this may not be very long in coming.

Somewhat mitigating these concerns, the tax effects for a particular investment will generally decline over time. The following contribute to this decline:

1. **Depreciation expense**, the major source of non-cash tax deductions, is either calculated by the straight-line method (an equal amount each

year) or by an accelerated method. These deductions will thus remain steady or decline over time;

2. **Amortization expense** for certain development period costs, another source of deductions, is generally taken over periods shorter than the depreciation schedule, and thus in the aggregate will also decline over time;

3. In the usual case of constant payment mortgage financing, **interest expense** tends gradually to decline over time as the mortgage is gradually paid off; and

4. While these expense items tend to remain level or decline, income tends to increase, often sharply, relative to the magnitude of the tax deductions.

As a result of these factors, tax losses tend to be reduced steadily as the investment ages, and at some point taxable income becomes positive. The reader should note that any investment structured to avoid ever producing a taxable profit is of questionable legality today and should be avoided. Generally, the projected annual cash flow and tax effects will as a final step be combined as a projection of After Tax Cash Flow (ATCF).

Projecting Residual Values. The final component of return from a real estate investment is that of residual values. Residual values are those generated by the future refinancing and eventual sale of the property. The most common presentation is to assume a sale of the property at the end of the projection period. In this approach, the assumed sales price is the most important choice to be made. Two methods of arriving at the sales price are frequently seen:

1. A selected measure of original project cost may be escalated over the holding period at the assumed

inflation rate, to result in an assumed replacement value at the time of sale; or

2. Income projected at the time of sale may be capitalized at a rate assumed to be representative of the market at that time, most commonly a rate at the low end of the range for the property type at present.

At the time of sale, taxes will normally be payable. Taxes on sale of assets held for long-term investment are defined as "capital gains" taxes, and have historically been subject to a lower rate of tax. (Although this distinction was eliminated in 1986, it will likely reappear in the future.) In some cases, ordinary income and expenses may also be generated at the time of sale. These might include additional interest or ground rent payable to participating lenders. The calculation of taxes payable at the time of an assumed sale may involve considerable effort.

Residual values may also be realized by refinancing the property or by "swapping" it for another property. In such cases, little or no taxes may be payable. The optimistic analyst may therefore choose to present a residual value *without* offset for tax payments. This may also be appropriate in analyzing returns for tax-exempt investors, such as pension funds.

Frequently the situation will be encountered where a refinancing will be required *prior to* a future sale. Many income properties today are being financed with relatively short-term loans, so-called "bullet" loans. These often mature in five years or less. In preparing a projection, it is therefore necessary to assume that a refinancing will be available at a particular point in time. There is, of course, a huge risk factor in this -- what will happen if the financing is not available? Aside from the availability question, there is real uncertainty about what interest rates will be at the time of refinancing.

The optimistic analyst is often tempted to assume that because the income from the property has been projected to increase, the mortgage amount may also be increased. Thus, at the time of refinancing, the owners would receive a distribution of capital. Since it is merely borrowed money, not income, this cash distribution will not be taxable. Thus, a big risk is converted by the assumptions chosen into a big reward.

At the same time, it does seem reasonable that in the case of a healthy property with a demonstrably increasing income stream, a lender will be available somewhere in the market at a competitive interest rate. Thus, the problem in forecasting these matters seems to be to select assumptions which are internally consistent with each other. It would be unreasonable, for example, to inflate income at 7% per year for 5 years and then to assume that after 5 years a new long-term mortgage will be available at 6% interest. Most analysts tend to be cautious in this area and generally will make the assumption that present conditions in the debt market will continue. Thus, while market rents are usually assumed to increase, interest rates and lenders' required coverage ratios are assumed to remain at present levels or higher.

These areas involve more art than science.

III. VALUATION AND RETURN MEASURES

Based on the financial projections, we are now in a position to draw conclusions about property and investment value and about return on investment. The measures considered here are based on the present value concept presented in Section I. Discussed here are Net Present Value (NPV), Internal Rate of Return (IRR), Profitability Ratio and Rate-Adjusted IRR.

Net Present Value

The Net Present Value (NPV) of an investment is defined as the sum of the present values of the cash inflows (or returns), less the cash outflow (or investment). This may be expressed:

$$NPV = \sum_{n=1}^{n} \frac{CFn}{(1+i)^n} - \text{Investment}$$

By this formula, each of the future returns is individually discounted for the length of time until it is to be received. This is similar to the case of the stream of future mortgage payments discussed in Section I, except the returns are likely to be uneven over time. The reader should note that the returns may be calculated on a before or after-tax basis.

As noted previously, the most important factor in calculating present value is the choice of discount rate (i). We can see in the above formula that, in order to calculate NPV, one must first specify the discount rate. Thus, the term "Net Present Value" alone has no meaning; it must be further specified as NPV at a particular discount rate. It is useful in Net Present Value calculations to think of the discount rate as a "hurdle" rate, that is, the rate which represents the investor's minimum acceptable return on new investments of the type contemplated.

Example: Mr. Aldrich was asked to put up $100,000 for a limited partnership share in a residential development, which is planned to be converted into condominiums after five years. If all goes as planned, his projected combined totals of cash distributions and tax savings will be:

Year	1	$ 4,500
	2	5,500
	3	6,000
	4	6,500
	5	5,500
	6	165,000

If Mr. Aldrich expects to receive at least a 20% return on investments of this type, he will expect a positive Net Present Value at 20%. Should he invest in this particular deal?

Internal Rate of Return

The Internal Rate of Return (IRR) of an investment is defined as the discount rate at which the sum of the present values of the cash inflows exactly *equals* the cash outflow or investment. This may be expressed:

$$\sum_{n=1}^{n} \frac{CFn}{(1+i)^n} = \text{Investment}$$

By this formula, each of the future returns is individually discounted, just as in calculating Net Present Value, and the sum of these present values is made equal to the investment by adjusting the discount rate. As in the case of mortgage calculations, solving for the appropriate discount rate or Internal Rate of Return requires an iterative calculation, a series of successive approximations. To do this by hand, one will normally select two discount rates, perform the calculations, and then interpolate or extrapolate to approximate the IRR. The financial calculator does essentially the same thing, but will run through many iterations until it reaches a predetermined margin of error. The reader should note that in cases of irregular cash flows more than one mathematically "correct" IRR may exist.

Internal Rate of Return is a very popular return measure. It presents in a single number the apparent overall "yield" of the investment, and thus invites comparison with other investment yields which may be available. One would then presumably select investments with the highest Internal Rates of Return. The biggest problem with using IRR as a decision criterion is the so-called "reinvestment assumption." The IRR carries with it the assumption that as returns are received, they can be reinvested in other investments with yields at the same or higher IRR. Particularly in the case of investments with high IRR's, this will often not be true. Investors will often prefer an investment with a lower IRR if the returns are sustained over a longer period of time.

Example: Mr. Aldrich decided not to go ahead with the housing investment, but did mention the opportunity to his lawyer, Mr. Botch, over lunch. Mr. Botch said he might be interested: "It may not meet your 20% hurdle rate, but how much does it yield? Most of my stocks and bonds are yielding less than 10% after tax. Perhaps I should invest."

Profitability Ratio

The Profitability Ratio for an investment is defined as the ratio of the Net Present Value at a selected hurdle rate to the amount of the investment. This may be expressed:

Profitability Ratio =

$$\sum_{n=1}^{n} \frac{CFn}{(1+i)^n} \div \text{Investment}$$

By this formula, each of the future returns is individually discounted for the appropriate time period, and the present values added to calculate the Net Present Value. The resulting NPV is then compared with the amount of the investment. Presumably, the higher the ratio, the better the investment.

The Profitability Ratio is often used to avoid the problems of the Internal Rate of Return. The ratio presents a method of comparing a number of investments which appear acceptable on an NPV basis, but which may be dissimilar in size or pattern of returns. The rankings suggested by the Profitability Ratio often differ from those suggested by IRR. Use of the Profitability Ratio avoids the IRR reinvestment assumption, but the problems of selecting the appropriate hurdle rate for the NPV calculations still remain.

> Example: Mr. Botch had decided to go ahead with the housing investment, which seemed readily to exceed his hurdle rate for new investments of 10% after tax. However, a day later he was offered an opportunity to invest $100,000 in a short-term situation, which would produce about a $30,000 after-tax profit in about a year's time. After considering the risks, Mr. Botch thought that if the housing investment provided effective profitability of 25% on the invested capital, he would stay with it. If not, he would make the switch.

Rate Adjustments

Experienced financial analysts will develop their own techniques for manipulating and interpreting discounted cash flow investment analyses. Several frequently encountered examples are discussed briefly in this final section.

Deferred Investments. In many cases, investments are structured to be paid in over a period of time. In the financial projections, the promoter often presents these investment installments as if they are directly offset against cash flow and tax benefits received in the same year. In the extreme, the investment is portrayed as "free," that is, the investment is entirely offset by returns, usually in the form of tax savings. In most cases, however, the investment installments are guaranteed by the investor, while the returns are by no means guaranteed.

Most analysts in this situation will distinguish between the investment installments and the returns. This is done by discounting the investment and the returns at different rates. For example, one may discount the deferred investment installments at a rate which represents the investor's potential return on temporary investments of cash (such as the current money-market yield), and may discount the returns at a higher rate reflective of the risks and character of the contemplated investment. One may also compute the Internal Rate of Return using the discounted investment figure as the effective initial investment.

IRR Breakdown. Another basic technique is to separately examine each different component of the return. Having calculated the overall Internal Rate of Return, we may then separately discount the cash-flow stream, the stream of tax benefits, and the residual value. The present value of these three components of return, after each is discounted at the IRR, should add up to exactly the amount of the investment (or its present value equivalent).

Thus the present value of each component of return may be expressed as a percentage of the total return ("IRR Breakdown"). From this, we may assess the relative importance of each of the three components of return in contributing to the overall return. This technique exposes which assumptions are critical to any particular investment, and allows judgmental comparisons to be made among investments with dissimilar sources of return.

Rate-Adjusted Returns. A final, similar technique is to select and adjust discount rates and compute net present values separately for various elements of the return. For example, a guaranteed base return on investment might be discounted at a low rate to reflect the high degree of certainty the cash will actually be received; tax deductions, being fixed by law, might also be discounted at a low rate; additional cash flow above the guaranteed base, being more uncertain, might be discounted at a higher rate; and residual values, being highly unpredictable, might be discounted at an even higher rate. In the extreme, each item of return may be discounted at a different rate.

The sum of these various present value calculations represents a composite rate-adjusted net present value. A variation on this is to adjust each stream of returns on an annual basis and calculate from the adjusted returns a rate-adjusted IRR. The rate-adjusted returns depend on techniques which are highly individualized to the needs of each analyst. They must be interpreted with care.

Conclusion

Many other modeling techniques and variations on the concepts presented in this note will be encountered in future years. As microcomputers add power and software is developed to support ever more complex investment analyses, the student of financial analysis should be alert to new developments. As is the case of preparing the investment projections (Section II of this note), interpreting them effectively involves more art than science.

Exhibit 1

TABLE OF PRESENT VALUES
(Value of $1 Received in Year "n" at Discount Rate "i")

Discount Rate i =

Year n =	1%	2%	3%	4%	5%	6%	7%	8%	9%	10%	11%	12%	13%	14%	15%	16%	17%	18%	19%	20%
1	0.990	0.980	0.971	0.962	0.952	0.943	0.935	0.926	0.917	0.909	0.901	0.893	0.885	0.877	0.870	0.862	0.855	0.847	0.840	0.833
2	0.980	0.961	0.943	0.925	0.907	0.890	0.873	0.857	0.842	0.826	0.812	0.797	0.783	0.769	0.756	0.743	0.731	0.718	0.706	0.694
3	0.971	0.942	0.915	0.889	0.864	0.840	0.816	0.794	0.772	0.751	0.731	0.712	0.693	0.675	0.658	0.641	0.624	0.609	0.593	0.579
4	0.961	0.924	0.888	0.855	0.823	0.792	0.763	0.735	0.708	0.683	0.659	0.636	0.613	0.592	0.572	0.552	0.534	0.516	0.499	0.482
5	0.951	0.906	0.863	0.822	0.784	0.747	0.713	0.681	0.650	0.621	0.593	0.567	0.543	0.519	0.497	0.476	0.456	0.437	0.419	0.402
6	0.942	0.888	0.837	0.790	0.746	0.705	0.666	0.630	0.596	0.564	0.535	0.507	0.480	0.456	0.432	0.410	0.390	0.370	0.352	0.335
7	0.933	0.871	0.813	0.760	0.711	0.665	0.623	0.583	0.547	0.513	0.482	0.452	0.425	0.400	0.376	0.354	0.333	0.314	0.296	0.279
8	0.923	0.853	0.789	0.731	0.677	0.627	0.582	0.540	0.502	0.467	0.434	0.404	0.376	0.351	0.327	0.305	0.285	0.266	0.249	0.233
9	0.914	0.837	0.766	0.703	0.645	0.592	0.544	0.500	0.460	0.424	0.391	0.361	0.333	0.308	0.284	0.263	0.243	0.225	0.209	0.194
10	0.905	0.820	0.744	0.676	0.614	0.558	0.508	0.463	0.422	0.386	0.352	0.322	0.295	0.270	0.247	0.227	0.208	0.191	0.176	0.162
11	0.896	0.804	0.722	0.650	0.585	0.527	0.475	0.429	0.388	0.350	0.317	0.287	0.261	0.237	0.215	0.195	0.178	0.162	0.148	0.135
12	0.887	0.788	0.701	0.625	0.557	0.497	0.444	0.397	0.356	0.319	0.286	0.257	0.231	0.208	0.187	0.168	0.152	0.137	0.124	0.112
13	0.879	0.773	0.681	0.601	0.530	0.469	0.415	0.368	0.326	0.290	0.258	0.229	0.204	0.182	0.163	0.145	0.130	0.116	0.104	0.093
14	0.870	0.758	0.661	0.577	0.505	0.442	0.388	0.340	0.299	0.263	0.232	0.205	0.181	0.160	0.141	0.125	0.111	0.099	0.088	0.078
15	0.861	0.743	0.642	0.555	0.481	0.417	0.362	0.315	0.275	0.239	0.209	0.183	0.160	0.140	0.123	0.108	0.095	0.084	0.074	0.065
16	0.853	0.728	0.623	0.534	0.458	0.394	0.339	0.292	0.252	0.218	0.188	0.163	0.141	0.123	0.107	0.093	0.081	0.071	0.062	0.054
17	0.844	0.714	0.605	0.513	0.436	0.371	0.317	0.270	0.231	0.198	0.170	0.146	0.125	0.108	0.093	0.080	0.069	0.060	0.052	0.045
18	0.836	0.700	0.587	0.494	0.416	0.350	0.296	0.250	0.212	0.180	0.153	0.130	0.111	0.095	0.081	0.069	0.059	0.051	0.044	0.038
19	0.828	0.686	0.570	0.475	0.396	0.331	0.277	0.232	0.194	0.164	0.138	0.116	0.098	0.083	0.070	0.060	0.051	0.043	0.037	0.031
20	0.820	0.673	0.554	0.456	0.377	0.312	0.258	0.215	0.178	0.149	0.124	0.104	0.087	0.073	0.061	0.051	0.043	0.037	0.031	0.026
21	0.811	0.660	0.538	0.439	0.359	0.294	0.242	0.199	0.164	0.135	0.112	0.093	0.077	0.064	0.053	0.044	0.037	0.031	0.026	0.022
22	0.803	0.647	0.522	0.422	0.342	0.278	0.226	0.184	0.150	0.123	0.101	0.083	0.068	0.056	0.046	0.038	0.032	0.026	0.022	0.018
23	0.795	0.634	0.507	0.406	0.326	0.262	0.211	0.170	0.138	0.112	0.091	0.074	0.060	0.049	0.040	0.033	0.027	0.022	0.018	0.015
24	0.788	0.622	0.492	0.390	0.310	0.247	0.197	0.158	0.126	0.102	0.082	0.066	0.053	0.043	0.035	0.028	0.023	0.019	0.015	0.013
25	0.780	0.610	0.478	0.375	0.295	0.233	0.184	0.146	0.116	0.092	0.074	0.059	0.047	0.038	0.030	0.024	0.020	0.016	0.013	0.010

Exhibit 2

June 11, 1984

Bedford Building Associates
Cash Flow Projections
(000's)

	1984	1985	1986	1987	1988	1989	1990	1991	1992	1993
Rental Income (1)										
Office	$1,199	$1,603	$1,606	$1,617	$1,737	$1,990	$2,123	$2,136	$2,148	$2,296
Retail	182	273	290	307	358	423	459	474	491	521
Escalation Income (2)	19	43	69	94	97	105	129	167	206	225
Gross Rental Income	1,400	1,919	1,965	2,018	2,192	2,518	2,711	2,777	2,845	3,042
Less: Vacancy @ 2%	26	46	54	63	44	50	54	55	57	61
Plus: Reimbursed Expenses (3)					65	62	72	79	89	95
Effective Rental Income	1,426	1,965	2,019	2,081	2,213	2,530	2,729	2,801	2,877	3,076
Operating Expenses (4)	320	345	375	405	435	470	510	550	595	640
Real Estate Taxes (5)	60	84	105	126	136	147	159	171	185	200
Total Operating Expenses	380	429	480	531	571	617	669	721	780	840
Net Free and Clear (6)	$1,046	$1,536	$1,539	$1,550	$1,642	$1,913	$2,060	$2,080	$2,097	$2,236

NOTES:

(1) Reflects terms of executed leases for 79,877 square feet of building; assumes remaining 2,881 square feet of office space leased by October 1, 1984 at $25.00 per square foot; remaining 3,204 square feet of retail space leased by October 1, 1984 at an average of $21.00 per square foot. The total rentable square feet of the building is now estimated to be 85,962 due to a higher loss factor than originally anticipated. Of leases expiring in 1988 and 1989, all with renewal options are assumed to renew; all others are assumed to turn over to new tenants.

(2) Reflects terms of executed office leases for 69,882 square feet and similar assumptions for 2,881 square feet of unleased office space. These leases contain escalation provisions based on the increase in the pro rata portion of operating expenses and real estate taxes, which are assumed to escalate at 8% per year (see Note 5).

(3) Reflects terms of executed retail leases for 9,995 square feet and similar assumptions for 3,204 square feet of unleased retail space. These leases provide for the payment on a net basis by retail tenants of their pro rata portion of operating expenses and real estate taxes.

(4) Assumes operating expenses in 1984 of $3.80 per square foot, escalating at 8% annually.

(5) Reflects actual tax bill for entire property for 1984, which is $.70 per square foot; assumes $1.00 per square foot in 1985, $1.25 per square foot in 1986, $1.50 per square foot in 1987, escalating 8% per year thereafter.

(6) Net free and clear is before deduction for ground rent.

Exhibit 3

PROJECT: Boston, MA
DATE: 30 July 1985
.11 = Interest Rate on 1st Mtg (thru 12/31/86)
.13745 = Constant on 1st Mtg (after 1/1/87)
6600000 = First Mortgage Note
.095 = Interest Rate on 2nd Mtg
3500000 = Second Mortgage Note

	0 8/86	1 9/86	2 10/86	3 11/86	4 12/86	5 1/87	6 2/87	7 3/87	8 4/87	9 5/87	10 6/87	11 7/87	12 8/87	13 9/87	14 10/87	15 11/87	16 12/87	17 1/88	18 2/88	19 3/88	20 4/88
Costs In Date (8/86)	10770000																				
Constr Basic Bldg	50000	106000	100000	75000	25000																
Tenant Alterations																					
T & E	17500	10000	50000	50000																	
Yankee	30000	100000	95000																		
D O R	30000	155000	135000	80000																	
Marketing Commissions																					
T & E		37500	37500																		
Yankee		56500	56500																		
D O R																					
BayBanks																					
Other																					
A&E, Proj Admin, Misc	113000	33000	34000	15000																	
Financing Costs																					
GMAC	35000												17500				17500				
NEFR	35000																				
Broker	25000																				
Legal																					
Interest																					
1st Mtg	55000	60179	60500	60500	60500	75598	75598	75598	75598	75598	75598	75598	75598	75598	75598	75598	75598	75598	75598	75598	75598
2nd Mtg	0	9896	18683	21997	25338	25538	25741	25944	26106	26259	26431	26593	26755	26917	26917	26917	26917	26917	26917	26917
Operating Costs	10000	19704	72866	23074	24351	36500	36500	36500	36500	36500	36500	36500	36500	36500	36500	36500	36500	36500	36500	36500	36500
Rental Income																					
T & E	-44680	0	0	0	0	0	-48857	-32571	-32571	-32571	-32571	-32571	-32571	-32571	-32571	-32571	-32571	-32571	-32571	-32571	-32571
Yankee		0	0	-44660	-44680	-44685	0	-44680	-44680	-44680	-44680	-44680	-44680	0							0
D O R		0	-12171	-42234	-48685	-48685	-48685	-48685	-48685	-48685	-48685	-48685	-48685	-48685	-48685	-49685	-44680	-44680	-51785	-51785	-51785
T&E/Storage	-333	0	0	0	0	-383	-437	-383	-383	-292	-292	-292	-292	-292	-292	-292	-292	-292	-292	-292	-292
Yank/Storage		0	0	-393	-383		0	-383	-383	-383	-383	-383	-383	0					-383	-383	0
BayBanks																					
Easement		450000		250000	250000					75000											
Devlo Fees																					
TOTAL COSTS / Month	10724937	711883	573085	399351	43638	39677	11228	11432	86554	86554	56819	11918	29580	12227	57457	12404	12404	9304	26804	9304	54367
CUM TOTAL COSTS	10724937	11436820	12495582	13068668	13453219	13501906	13541564	13552792	13564223	13650817	13707636	13719554	13749133	13761375	13818842	13831246	13843650	13852954	13879757	1388906?	3943427
SOURCES																					
1st Mtg	6565000	35000																			
2nd Mtg/old	475000	-475000																			
2nd Mtg/new		1250000																			
Equity	3615956																				
Security Deposit	89359								82385												
CASH BALANCE	20378	118495	15225	47672	29322	15203	29716	38752	55011	18661	27211	18399	26325	-31142	-43546	-5595	-65253	-92057	-101360	-155727	
2ND MTG OUTSTANDINGS	0	1250000	2359896	2778578	3200575	3225913	3251452	3277192	3318128	3338596	3359064	3379532	3400000	3400000	3400000	340000	3400000	3400000	3400000	3400000	3400000
1ST MTG OUTSTANDINGS	6565000	6600000	6600000	6600000	6600000	6600000	6600000	6600000	6600000	6600000	6600000	6600000	6600000	6600000	6600000	660000	6600000	6600000	6600000	6600000	6600000

Case 6

Harry Hooper

Harry Hooper, a real estate broker with the Borne Corporation, was based in southern Connecticut. His firm was a full-service real estate firm, providing commercial brokerage, construction and property management services for clients, as well as developing for its own account. Borne was active in Stamford, northern New Jersey and in several smaller office markets. Mr. Hooper specialized in the sale of office and industrial buildings in suburban locations. He often represented buyers searching for properties in Connecticut and elsewhere.

THE BUYERS

In June 1988, Harry Hooper was conducting searches on behalf of three buyers. One of these, Connecticut General Life Insurance Company, had an established relationship with Borne. Connecticut General was the equity investor and joint venture partner in a number of the company's development properties. Connecticut General was willing to develop or purchase properties for their portfolio on a leveraged or an unleveraged basis. They expected to receive before-tax cash returns on investment significantly above long-term commercial lending rates, after considering the effects of appreciation of their properties. Beginning in 1988, Connecticut General would be treated like any other corporation and taxed at the 34% Federal corporate tax rate.

The second buyer, B.T. Hutton 1988 Income Properties, Limited, was a public real estate limited partnership. The 1988 partnership, now being subscribed, was seeking to acquire office and industrial properties with a target of 50% leverage. Investors in this partnership were typically pension funds and individual retirement accounts and, accordingly, were exempt from Federal income taxes. The stated investment objectives were to provide stable and increasing cash flow and

capital appreciation as a hedge against inflation.

The third buyer was a personal friend of Mr. Hooper's, Mr. Sato Sushimi. Mr. Sushimi and his partner had offices in New York and Tokyo. Their initial objective was to place $25 million for a group of Pacific Rim business associates. Security of principal and inflation protection were the primary investment criteria stated by Mr. Sushimi. The fund was based in the Netherlands Antilles, which resulted by treaty in an effective U.S. tax rate of just 3%. Under U.S. law, however, offshore investors were required to pay normal taxes upon sale of their U.S. real estate holdings.

Each of the three buyers was interested in building a substantial portfolio of income property over time and would prefer to have several properties in a single market such as southern Connecticut. The buyers would have no interest in managing the properties themselves, preferring to contract with Borne for this service. Each buyer also would impose high standards of quality for acquisitions.

THE PROPERTIES

Harry Hooper had for the past three weeks scoured the market for offerings. He found a few properties that he believed were available, but most of the owners merely indicated they would listen to offers. Based on his experience in the market, Mr. Hooper quickly eliminated a number of properties with major problems of energy inefficiency, poor location, parking inadequacy, or poor construction quality, and also some owners he thought were simply curious about the value of their property.

Out of four properties he selected for follow-up discussions, two seemed somewhat promising. One of these was a three-story, multi-tenant suburban office building, and the other a two-story, single-tenant, high-technology facility.

The office building, Friendswood Park One, was a three-story, steel-frame and brick veneer structure built in 1974. It comprised 72,000 gross square feet of building area. Under the standards of measurement used in the Northeastern United States, quoted rentable areas included the tenant's net usable square footage plus an allocation of designated common areas. As a result, the top two floors were quoted at 26,000 rentable square feet (RSF) each and the ground floor at 20,000 RSF. The excess of rentable area above net usable area was referred to as a "load factor."

The structure was of normal appearance for its age and appeared to be in excellent condition. Parking and landscaping seemed fully adequate, and the location enjoyed a good reputation among leasing brokers.

The top floor was leased to a suburban banking firm which had committed for the space before construction. The bank had a 10-year flat-rate lease at $200,000 per year and two 5-year renewal options with rents adjusted to 90% of fair market rent at the time of renewal. The bank was presently paying $18 per square foot. The lease was a "gross" lease, that is, the rent included all building operating expenses and real estate taxes, as distinct from a "net" lease in which the tenant paid expenses. The lease would expire in September 1994.

The other two floors were fully occupied by twelve small tenants with three and five-year leases. The present owner was upgrading the rents for the smaller tenants as the leases were renewed or the space turned over. In the newer leases, the owner had provided expense "stops," escalation clauses which obligated each tenant to pay its prorata share of increases in operating expenses and property taxes over the levels of the initial lease year.

As a result of the escalation clauses and the recent improving market conditions, the owner had increased his aggregate rent and expense collections to $1,237,000 in calendar 1987. Mr. Hooper was shown a current rent roll indicating gross income, including expense reimbursements, of $1,350,000 for 1988 for the property at 100% occupancy. Although Mr. Hooper had not taken the time to review each lease, the owner had suggested that new leases and renewal options would shortly increase the gross rent roll to over $1,500,000.

Mr. Hooper thought these figures seemed plausible, since he had recently negotiated a lease in a new building nearby. The rent was $24 per RSF for a five-year term, although four months of free rent had been given as a concession to that particular tenant. He believed that operating expense bases in leases written in 1988 would probably average $3.50 per foot (excluding property taxes). Property taxes in Friendswood, he expected, would be about $2.00 per square foot in 1988.

The owner was asking $16 million for the property, but was willing to give some financing to the buyer. The existing first mortgage of $4.2 million had originated in December 1977. This loan carried an 8.5% interest rate and 30-year amortization schedule and could be assumed by the buyer. The owner asked a minimum of $3 million cash down. The balance would be secured by a purchase money mortgage at 10.5%, with interest only for ten years. This mortgage would be subordinated to the existing first mortgage. The owner's stated reason for selling was his desire to retire to a secluded tropical island, while relinquishing the responsibilities of managing real estate.

Mr. Hooper believed the price might be reduced a bit through negotiation, but anticipated the need to add his brokerage commission of 3% of the sales price. He therefore decided to do his initial analysis based on an all-cash gross purchase price of $16 million, which he thought would be acceptable to the seller. He anticipated $1 million of the purchase would be attributable to land.

Mr. Hooper had inquired about the possibility of obtaining new first mortgage financing for the office property. The best fixed rate he found was for intermediate-term financing (5-7 years, typically) at a rate of 10% interest with an amortization schedule of 25 to 30 years. For long-term financing, he had been quoted either a floating interest rate of 1-2% above the prime rate (prime was presently at 9.5%), or a fixed rate with equity participation.

A typical participating loan would feature a fairly high loan-to-value ratio and a fairly low coverage ratio requirement, perhaps as low as 1.10 times the base-debt service. The loan would require a relatively low interest rate, perhaps 8.5-9%, and a 30 to 35 year amortization schedule, plus a variable participation in increases in cash flow above pro forma levels. At sale, the lender would receive the remaining principal balance plus ten times the previous year's escalation payment. Lenders making such loans were often pension funds and were looking for effective yields in the range of 12-14%.

The second property was the corporate headquarters for Accudyne, Inc., a manufacturer of fiber optic chips, used in numerous esoteric research and development functions. The owner of the building was a venture capitalist who had accepted title as part of the security for a loan he had made to the company in its early years. The company had turned out to be stable and profitable, but not a growth company. The owner now wished to redeploy his assets into higher potential ventures.

Mr. Hooper's review of the listing materials provided by the owner indicated the two-story, 120,000 square foot high-tech facility was of steel-frame and curtain-wall construction in excellent condition. He believed it to be well located with adequate parking, loading and access.

Thirty percent of the space was finished for office use. The building was built in 1972 for the company. Accudyne transferred the building to its present owner in mid-1975 and leased it back on a fully-net basis for a 20-year term. For the first ten years, the rent would be $180,000 per year. For the next five years, rent would be $240,000 per year. For the final five years, rent would be the lesser of $300,000 or fair market rental. Mr. Hooper knew this rent level to be well below the present market level of approximately $8 per SF net. All expenses and maintenance were the responsibility of the tenant. Accudyne had the option to repurchase their facility at fair market value on June 30, 1995.

The offering price was firm at $6 million, which included Mr. Hooper's 4% commission on the sale. Some $600,000 of this was attributable to the land, according to the latest property tax assessment. The seller had himself investigated the possibility of obtaining new financing for the property and had found it not available. The existing mortgage was assumable, however, with an interest rate of 8.5% and 30 year amortization of an original amount of $1.8 million. The remaining balance at the end of 1987, after 150 monthly payments, was $1,510,120.

FINANCIAL ANALYSIS

The high-tech property seemed quite a bit simpler, so Harry Hooper decided to begin with it. His first step in financial analysis was always to do a typical or stabilized year pro forma operating statement ("setup"). By subtracting from the scheduled gross rent appropriate allowances for vacancy, operating expenses, replacement reserves and real estate taxes, he would compute the "Free & Clear Income" or "Net Income from Operations" for the property. This figure represented the basic income stream from the property, and Mr. Hooper believed it to be a stable and reliable indicator of value, independent of how a particular property was financed.

In this case there would be no requirement for vacancy allowances, operating expenses, maintenance or real estate taxes, these being all the responsibility of the tenant under the net lease. Accudyne was obliged to deliver the property in first class physical condition at the expiration of the lease if they did not elect to purchase. An arbitration provision would be invoked if the parties could not agree on fair market value at the time of sale. Mr. Hooper therefore decided not to charge a replacement reserve on this property, although he knew many lenders would take a more conservative view. The only other expense often charged to operations would be a management fee for collecting and depositing rents, filing forms and reports and the like. Mr. Hooper chose to ignore this as an internal expense normal to any institutional owner of real property.

Thus the Free & Clear in the first full year would be $240,000. Mr. Hooper then looked at what he believed to be the most basic and important measure of annual return on an income-producing real estate investment -- the Return on Total Assets (ROTA):

Return on Total Assets (ROTA)

$$= \frac{\text{Free \& Clear}}{\text{Total Invested Assets}}$$

$$= \frac{\$240,000}{\$6,000,000} \quad = 4\%$$

This return seemed very low to him. If he were appraising a typical high-tech property, he would very likely choose a capitalization rate in the 8-10% range at present. This would imply a value of the property in the range of 10-12.5 times the Free & Clear income. In this case, there seemed to be other factors to consider,

however, and Mr. Hooper believed there was virtually no chance of a default on the lease. In fact, were the tenant to vacate the property in the near term, the space could be readily retenanted at higher rent levels.

He next considered the impact of financial leverage, assuming the buyer might want to continue the existing low-interest rate mortgage:

Free & Clear:	$240,000
Debt Service (Constant Payment):	($166,085)
Cash Flow After Financing (CFAF):	$73,915

In the case of a constant payment mortgage such as this, debt service had to be computed from mortgage tables or with a financial calculator. The original debt is retired by a series of equal payments, usually monthly installments due at the end of each month. These payments are sufficient to pay the stated rate of interest on the outstanding balance in each period plus an increasing amount of principal in each payment so the final payment reduces the loan balance to zero. Calculating the amount of the constant payment requires the analyst to know typically the interest rate, term of the loan, frequency of payments, and the original balance. By setting the original loan amount equal to 100, the constant payments may be expressed as a percentage. In this case, any loan with an interest rate of 8.5% per year, 30-year amortization period, and equal monthly payments due at the end of each month, will have a constant payment of 0.76891% per month. The annual debt service, (referred to in the industry as the "constant") will therefore be 9.22696%. Hence, the original $1.8 million loan requires a debt service of .0922696 x $1,800,000 = $166,085 per year.

If he forgot his calculator, Mr. Hooper knew he could approximate the constant by adding something to the interest rate. The amount to be added was usually between 0.5% and 1% - greater if the term were short, less if it were long - and also increased as the interest rate decreased. He would have guessed a 9.0%-9.5%-constant in this case from his experience which would, he noted, have been close enough for some useful analysis. Having now computed the cash flow after financing, and using the loan balance at the end of 1987, Mr. Hooper went on to the second fundamental investment return measure -- the "Cash-on-Cash" return or the Return on Equity (ROE)

ROE or Cash-on-Cash Return

$$= \frac{\text{CFAF}}{\text{Equity Invested}}$$

$$= \frac{\$73,915}{\$4,489,880} \qquad = 1.65\%$$

As he expected, the return on equity was lower than the return on total assets. This phenomenon resulted from the condition of "negative leverage," that is, the effective cash cost of the debt (11.00%) was greater than the return on total assets (4.00%), thereby reducing the relative net cash return on the net cash equity investment. The reverse condition of "positive leverage" had the more salutary effect of amplifying the percentage return on equity.

Mr. Hooper observed that U.S. Treasury bonds offered fully guaranteed yields substantially higher than this return and were readily salable by investors when cash needs arose. For many investor classes, this would be a major advantage over owning real estate, with its high transaction costs and lack of liquidity. The bond interest would be fully taxable, of course, so Mr. Hooper proceeded to compute the tax effect for a buyer assumed to be in the 35% tax bracket:

CFAF	$73,915
Mortgage Amortization	39,230
Depreciation	(171,429)
Taxable Income	(58,284)
Tax Savings @ 35%	20,399
CFAF	73,915
After Tax Cash Flow (ATCF)	$94,314

Mr. Hooper computed the principal amount of the debt service above with a financial calculator for the 151st through the 162nd payments on the mortgage. He also knew that the amortization had averaged about $2,000 per month during the period prior to purchase and that he could therefore have approximated this figure if he had needed to do so.

To compute the depreciation, he allocated the appropriate share of the purchase cost to the building and then used the 31.5 year straight line method as required by the Tax Reform Act of 1986 for all non-residential rental property.

After allowing for the savings on income taxes otherwise payable by the owner at an assumed 35% tax rate, Mr. Hooper computed a third basic return measure, the After Tax Return on Equity:

After Tax ROE

$$= \frac{\text{ATCF}}{\text{Equity Invested}}$$

$$= \frac{\$94,314}{\$4,489,880} \qquad = 2.10\%$$

This return measure appeared to compare unfavorably with the yields available from tax-exempt municipal bonds at the time. It seemed obvious that tax benefits would not be a major concern in the analysis.

Harry Hooper was beginning to get discouraged about this particular property, but he knew that the sales price of $6 million was only $50 per square foot of building, well below its replacement cost and below the level of recent comparable sales. From his experience, he expected that when he considered the effects of time and inflation, the return picture would improve dramatically. He could then use the more sophisticated return measures he had learned in an evening program at a well-known eastern design school. He was anxious to put the investment in a favorable light for his clients to consider.

CASH FLOW PROJECTION

Although he now wanted to do a cash flow projection (which he normally tried to avoid), Mr. Hooper did not want to spend a tremendous amount of time. He liked to make a few simplifying assumptions and select a format carefully to save time. For example, he had found that projections of 8-12 years were usually adequate, with little change noted by extending them further. He would often select a few interesting years, such as a year when leases were renewed, or average a number of intervening years, for example, to save time at little loss in accuracy.

In this case, it was clear that the projection should cover the period through 1995 when he expected the sale to occur (see Exhibit 1). To keep it simple, he decided to assume the purchase occurred in mid-1988. For an initial analysis, Mr. Hooper assumed an all-cash purchase. Then, since some of his buyers were willing to purchase on a leveraged basis, he made a second analysis with the buyer assuming

the existing mortgage and thus making an original investment of $4,489,880 in cash. Mr. Hooper also chose to assume a 5% per-year increase in the CPI.

Because of the lease terms, the income remained at below-market levels, but he had yet to consider the likely sale of the property in 1995. This sale would be at "fair market value" and might produce a sizable gain for the owner. What would the sale price be?

Harry Hooper guessed that the market rent for this property would be about $8 per SF net in 1988. If the CPI were a good measure of the escalation of industrial rent levels as well as consumer goods, the market rent in 1995 would, he calculated, reach $11.26 per square foot, increasing at 5% per year. The market rent would therefore be $1,350,816 for the 120,000 square feet. Accudyne would be paying just $300,000 for the space.

Mr. Hooper pondered the choice of a capitalization rate at the time of sale. The building would be then over twenty years old, a negative factor; interest rates would be high, to keep pace with inflation, also a negative factor; inflation would, however, drive up the cost of new, potentially competitive construction, a positive factor, and the inflation protection offered by commercial real estate would argue for a relatively low capitalization rate.

He chose to ignore the possible benefit of the existing low-interest mortgage, although this could possibly be assumed by yet another buyer. The remaining mortgage balance had to be laboriously calculated in the absence of mortgage tables or a financial calculator, but Mr. Hooper knew the annual amortization amount always grew in proportion to the interest rate. If he had guessed the first year to be $15,000 and increased this by 1.085x each year, he could have come quite close. Taking these factors into account, Mr. Hooper appraised the property at sale and calculated the net cash proceeds.

Now, finally, was something pretty interesting. Using a conservative 10% capitalization rate, Mr. Hooper computed that the buyer's original equity of $4,489,880 would be more than doubled in just seven years. This was encouraging, and so he eagerly began to compute the Internal Rate of Return (IRR) and Net Present Value (NPV) return measures he had been taught.

PRESENT VALUE RETURN MEASURES

Mr. Hooper was particularly concerned about comparing the two properties. Therefore he intended to look at them both first on an unleveraged basis and then on the basis of any financing that might be available. Mr. Hooper therefore began by summarizing the combined investment, sale and annual operating cash flows from the investment on an unleveraged basis (see Exhibit 2, Column 2). He then entered these figures into the appropriate registers in his financial calculator, which began to solve for the Internal Rate of Return. Many analysts used this measure of return to compare dissimilar investment flows.

Unfortunately, at this critical juncture Mr. Hooper's calculator batteries expired. Since he was eager to get on with the work, he decided to discount the cash flows manually. To approximate the Internal Rate of Return, he would have to discount the cash flows at two different discount rates and interpolate or extrapolate from there. In an optimistic frame of mind, he decided to try 15% as a discount rate. This also seemed reasonable as a "hurdle" rate; that is, an investor might assume he could earn 15% on alternative investments and use this as a threshold figure for considering a new investment.

Mr. Hooper next had to compute present value factors for each year using the formula:

$$pv = 1 \, / \, (1+i)^n$$

This formula can be used to calculate that decimal which, when increased at a given interest rate i (in this case 15%), for a given number of years n, would by the end of the period have increased to exactly 1.00. This logically would allow one to assess the present worth of a dollar received at a future time.

At this point, Mr. Hooper was able to borrow a simple calculator, which speeded things up, and he proceeded to calculate the discount factors (see Exhibit 2, Column 3) and the discounted cash flows (see Exhibit 2, Column 4). Being careful to include investment flows as negative, he computed the Net Present Value at 15% of the investment as a whole. This NPV at 15% being positive, he knew the effective yield was higher and decided to use 20% for the second discount rate (see Exhibit 2, Columns 5 and 6). Since the NPV at 20% was negative, he interpolated to compute the internal rate of return at 15.28%.

By now the batteries on the financial calculator had revived somewhat, so Mr. Hooper was able to compute a more precise IRR at 15.23%. He noted that the interpolation, which assumed a linear function, was a useful approximation for any practical purpose.

It was clear that the projected appreciation had sharply increased the returns. Mr. Hooper noted that some of this appreciation had already occurred, but was offset by the unfavorable lease terms. He would have to make some further calculations to examine this issue, if it seemed to be significant.

Mr. Hooper had one additional exercise which he found useful, the "profitability" ratio, which would avoid the reinvestment assumption implicit in the IRR. He compared the Net Present Value at a target hurdle rate, in this case 15%, with the amount of equity investment:

Profitability Ratio

$$= \frac{\text{NPV @ 15\%}}{\text{Invested Assets}}$$

$$= \frac{\$77,000}{\$6,000,000} \qquad = 1.28\%$$

Mr. Hooper now began to make the same calculations for the leveraged acquisition of the Accudyne property. He wanted to consider the effect of the buyer assuming the existing first mortgage.

He would then turn his attention to the Friendswood Park property. The seller was thoughtful enough to provide a ten-year income projection (see Exhibit 3). For the Friendswood property, as with the Accudyne, he would begin with an unleveraged purchase. Then he would consider the financing package most comparable with that available for Accudyne. He certainly also wanted to consider the impact of the advantageous financing potentially to be provided by the seller. He was unsure if he should also consider a new participating loan or a variable rate loan for comparison.

He drew up a list of comparative captions for his analyses (see Exhibit 4), summarizing the return measures he thought would be useful in deciding if he could recommend one of these properties to one or another of his clients.

EXHIBITS

1. Projected cash flows, Accudyne, Inc. property.

2. Present value calculations, Accudyne, Inc. property.

3. Friendswood Park One ten-year income projection.

4. Comparative analysis and summary.

QUESTIONS FOR DISCUSSION

1. Based on your analysis of Friendswood Park One, what recommendations should Mr. Hooper make?

2. What additional research would you recommend?

3. What major points would you seek to negotiate on behalf of your buyer?

Exhibit 1

Projected Cash Flows ($000)
Accudyne, Inc. Property

Year:	1989	1990	1991	1992	1993	1994	1995
Free & Clear:	$240	$240	$300	$300	$300	$300	$300
Debt Service:	($166)	($166)	($166)	($166)	($166)	($166)	($166)
CFAF:	$74	$74	$134	$134	$134	$134	$134

Investment:		Residual:	
Unleveraged Purchase:	$6.000	Free & Clear, 1995 Market Rent:	$1,352
Less: Assumed Mortgage:	($1,510)	Value @ 10% Capitalization Rate:	$13,510
		Less: Sale Expenses @ 3%:	($405)
Equity Cash:	$4.490	Net Property Value:	$13,105
		Less: Mortgage Balance:	($1,116)
		Value of Property:	$11,989

Exhibit 2

Present Value Calculations
Accudyne, Inc. Property
Unleveraged Purchase

(1) Year	(2) Combined Cash Flow	(3) Discount Factor @15%	(4) Present Value of Cash Flow	(5) Discount Factor @20%	(6) Present Value of Cash Flow
Investment	($6.000)	1.00	($6.000)	1.00	($6,000)
1989	$240	0.87	$209	0.83	$200
1990	$240	0.76	$181	0.69	$167
1991	$300	0.66	$197	0.58	$174
1992	$300	0.57	$172	0.48	$145
1993	$300	0.50	$149	0.40	$121
1994	$300	0.43	$130	0.33	$100
1995	$13,405	0.38	$5.039	0.28	$3,741
	$9.085		$77		($1,352)

Exhibit 3

Friendswood Park One
Friendswood Associates

Ten Year Income Projection

	1989	1990	1991	1992	1993	1994	1995	1996	1997	1998
Rental Income										
3rd Floor	$597	$597	$597	$597	$597	$847	$847	$847	$847	$847
2nd Floor	650	650	650	752	752	752	871	871	871	1,008
1st Floor	500	500	500	579	579	579	670	670	670	776
Escalation Income	13	30	65	118	191	285	400	539	701	888
Gross Rental Income	1,760	1,777	1,812	2,047	2,120	2,463	2,789	2,927	3,089	3,519
Vacancy @ 3%	(53)	(53)	(54)	(61)	(64)	(74)	(84)	(88)	(93)	(106)
Effective Rental Income	1,707	1,724	1,758	1,985	2,056	2,389	2,705	2,839	2,996	3,413
Operating Expenses	(252)	(265)	(278)	(292)	(306)	(322)	(338)	(355)	(372)	(391)
Real Estate Taxes	(125)	(131)	(138)	(145)	(152)	(160)	(168)	(176)	(185)	(194)
Net Operating Income	$1,330	$1,328	$1,342	$1,549	$1,598	$1,908	$2,200	$2,308	$2,439	$2,828

Exhibit 4

	Accudyne	Friendswood
Unleveraged Purchase Price:	$6000	
Return on Total Assets:	4.00%	
Inflation Assumption:	5.00%	
NPV @ 15%:	$77	
Profitability Ratio:	1.29%	
IRR:	15.23%	
Assumed Mortgage:	$1,510	
Total Debt % of Price:	25.17%	
Cash Required:	$4,490	
Cash-on-Cash Return:	1.65%	
NPV @ 15%:		
Profitability Ratio:		
IRR:		
Secondary Financing:	N /A	
Total Debt % of Price:	N /A	
Cash Required:	N /A	
Cash-on-Cash Return:	N /A	
NPV @ 15%:	N /A	
Profitability Ratio:	N /A	
IRR:	N /A	
Alternative Financing:	N /A	
Total Debt % of Price:	N /A	
Cash Required:	N /A	
Cash-on-Cash Return:	N /A	
NPV @ 15%:	N /A	
Profitability Ratio:	N /A	
IRR:	N /A	

Note 3

Financial Accounting in Real Estate

Most financial decisions made by and about real estate developers depend in part on the analysis and interpretation of financial accounting information. Until now, we have focussed on information provided in the form of financial forecasts or projections -- the *pro formas* for a proposed project. Pro formas are, of course, at least somewhat speculative, and we have learned to be critical in our evaluations of them.

In this next in our series of notes on financial topics, we will turn our attention to a second type of financial information, the *financial statements* for a particular individual or business. These statements are used to present the *actual* record of an individual's or organization's past performance. In real estate development, review of financial statements is often the basis for determining the financial capacity of the firm or individual to play their intended role. Whether they are to be a lender, investor, guarantor, tenant, contractor or buyer, success or failure of the project may depend on this financial capacity and creditworthiness.

In this note we will familiarize the reader with the special accounting issues encountered in the real estate industry and provide some useful methods for analyzing financial statements. This note contains three sections:

Section I is a brief overview of accounting basics, the accounting profession and financial statements.

Section II identifies accounting issues in real estate.

Section III is concerned with analysis of financial statements -- for public companies, private companies and individuals.

In the interest of brevity, many areas considered important to accounting professionals are merely summarized in this note. The interested reader is invited to consult other sources referenced herein.

I. INTRODUCTION

This section provides a brief introduction to financial accounting, the role of accountants and introduces the basic financial statements and the basic principles of accounting.

What is Accounting?

Accounting has been called the "language of business." In real estate or in any other industry, accounting is fundamentally a system of measurement, usually in money terms, of the activities of an individual or organization.

There is no single, universal accounting system. Instead, accounting systems vary widely and are devised to meet the specific purposes of each individual or organization. The simplest accounting system is one's own personal checkbook. Add to this the required state and Federal tax accounting forms and some rudimentary sort of cash budgeting procedure, and you have a complete personal accounting system. In fact, many businesses have no more complicated a system of accounting.

Whether simple or complex, the basic purpose of any accounting system is to enhance management control. Control is achieved through the capacity of the accounting system to produce reports which highlight important management or financial issues and thereby contribute to decision-making about the future or to evaluation of past performance. Therefore, in addition to the basic accounting records and financial reports, many other components may be useful. For example, time sheets, invoices, inventories, budgets and profit-sharing systems all may be considered part of an organization's accounting system. Each of these mechanisms contributes to effective management control.

A second purpose of the accounting system is to convey information external to the firm. In the case of large, publicly owned companies and private companies with a number of shareholders, this purpose is served by publishing quarterly and annual financial statements. These formal statements are the most visible result of the accounting system. The vast majority of individuals and private business entities, however, provide detailed information only to the Federal and state tax authorities. Otherwise, they prepare formal statements only when needed for a particular purpose.

Accountants

All states today provide for the licensing of Certified Public Accountants, or "CPAs." CPAs are the accounting professionals -- roughly analogous to licensed professionals in medicine, law, or architecture. Like these other professionals, CPAs must qualify for their licenses through a combination of education, experience, and examination.

CPAs may work privately as employees of a business, or may provide "public" services such as independent audits or tax services. Regardless of what role the accountant plays, the financial reports of a business entity are the overall responsibility of management, not of its accountants. Accountants must develop accounting policies at the direction of management.

One important role of the independent accountant or CPA is to conduct a company's annual **audit**. Because of the expense,however, an audit is conducted and audited statements are prepared only when they are required. Usually, this will be the case for major private companies and those with public ownership of stock, which fall under the jurisdiction of the Securities and Exchange Commission. Audited statements may also be required by the terms of a particular financing transaction.

It should be noted that the existence of an auditor's certification on a set of financial statements has roughly comparable significance to the presence of an architect or engineer's stamp on a set of drawings. No meaningful warranty against error or misrepresentation is provided; however, there is reasonable assurance that professional standards have been followed. Just as some few professionally designed structures have failed, there have also been situations where accounting systems have failed. On occasion, independent auditors might not be sufficiently inquisitive in their inspections of a company's accounting methods. The result of this can be sudden financial problems or failure, not predictable from the previous financial statements.

Unaudited statements are very common. For example, personal financial statements cannot be audited. Unaudited statements may or may not be prepared according to the current standards of the accounting profession. Even where the highest professional standards are rigidly applied, however, the manager, accountant, or businessperson preparing a set of statements generally has a great many areas in which he or she must exercise discretion. Proper interpretation of financial statements depends on understanding the workings and implications of these areas of discretion.

Financial Statements

Financial statements are regular reports of business performance for a business entity. These consist normally of a set of three related statements plus footnotes. The statements are the balance sheet, the income statement and the statement of changes in financial position. The notes to financial statements are integral to the statements. Each of these elements provides the reader with a different type of information.[1]

The Balance Sheet. The balance sheet presents a snapshot view of a company's financial position at a particular point in time. The balance sheet shows the financial strength of a company by demonstrating what the company owns and what it owes on a certain date.

The **assets** side of the balance sheet shows the resources or valuable property owned by the company (cash, inventory, land, buildings, and so on), while the **equities** side shows the sources of funds used to acquire these resources. This includes amounts provided by creditors (**liabilities**) and amounts provided by the owners or stockholders (**owner's equity**).

The balance sheet, then, is literally a "sheet of balances," based on the fundamental accounting equation:

Assets = Liabilities + Owner's Equity

The Income Statement. While the balance sheet shows the status of a company at a particular moment in time, the income statement reports on the flow of revenues and expenses *over a period of time*. The income statement (sometimes referred to as the earnings report or the statement of profit and loss) records the changes in owner's equity during an accounting period and thus explains some of the differences between two consecutive balance sheets.

---

[1] More detail on the structure and contents of each of the financial statements is contained in *Corporate Financial Reporting and Analysis*, Richard D. Irwin, Inc., 1986, by Professor David F. Hawkins of the Harvard Business School. See also *Accounting*, Richard D. Irwin, Inc., eighth edition, 1988, by Professors Robert N. Anthony of the Harvard Business School and James S. Reece of the University of Michigan Graduate School of Business Administration.

In accounting terminology, "income" is defined as the difference between revenues and expenses. The annual income statement indicates whether the company has had a net profit or a net loss for the year. This is done by comparing the amounts earned during the year (**revenues**) with all the costs incurred (**expenses**).

Statement of Changes in Financial Position. This statement, also called the "Statement of Sources and Uses of Funds", provides a detailed analysis of changes between two balance sheets. The statement of changes in financial position gives a picture of the funds flows within a firm. It shows the sources of funds obtained during the accounting period, and the uses to which these funds were put. The statement is derived analytically from data originally collected for the balance sheet and the income statement. Fundamentally, it involves a rearrangement of accounting data rather than the recording of new data.

The statement of changes in financial position is used both for analyzing the company's investment and financing policies in the past, and for planning the amount, timing, and nature of new financing. Since the funds flow statement is less subject to judgment than the income statement (where, for instance, the choice of depreciation method will have a significant effect on net income) many financial analysts find the statement of changes in financial position very useful. However, since it does not show how net income was earned, it must be used as a supplement to, rather than a substitute for, the income statement.

Notes to Financial Statements. These notes (the "footnotes") are integral and important elements of the financial statements. The notes to financial statements are used to clarify items in the statements and to disclose accounting policies, significant uncertainties, etc. Notes will contain important additional information about a company's business that cannot readily be incorporated in its accounts.

Financial statements are prepared on the basis of a **chart of accounts**. The chart of accounts provides a consistent format for recording a company's transactions. These accounts fall into five basic categories: assets, liabilities, owners' equity, income, and expense accounts. A large number of accounts are regularly maintained by the company and its corporate subsidiaries, partnerships and joint ventures and are aggregated for presentation in the statements.

Accounting Principles

Financial statements may be prepared on either the **cash basis** or the **accrual basis**. As with one's personal checkbook, cash basis accounting is relatively simple. Income and expenses are recognized when the cash is received and paid out. A basic limitation of cash accounting is that one may alter significantly the financial results of an operating period by simply accelerating or delaying the collection or payment of accounts.

Accrual accounting is a more complex system intended to match the income and expenses to the period in which they are incurred. In many businesses, the cash is not received until well after the work is done or the goods transferred. A basic accrual accounting principle, the **matching principle**, seeks to provide a realistic basis for presenting the financial results of business operations by matching revenues and expenses in a given time period.

Simply stated, this is done by "recognizing" (or "accruing") income at the time it is substantially earned and accruing expenses when they are incurred. These accruals are independent of when cash is received or paid out. Much of the complexity of accrual accounting stems from the evolution of the standards and conventions by which these accruals are made and for rationalizing the accrual figures to the receipt and disbursement of cash.

It is important to note that companies may use *both* cash and accrual accounting methods. One may be used for tax accounting purposes, while the other is used for financial reporting. It is normal, usual and entirely ethical for companies to keep two sets of books for these two distinct purposes. In the two sets of books, many different accounting entries will be treated differently for tax accounting purposes than they are for financial reporting purposes.

Standards for the U.S. accounting profession are developed through a system of promulgation and review involving the American Institute of Certified Public Accountants (AICPA) Financial Accounting Standards Board (FASB). Since 1959, the FASB and its predecessors have issued periodic opinions which attempt to improve the clarity or fairness with which statements are prepared. The body of conventions and standards are collectively referred to as "GAAP" standards (Generally Accepted Accounting Principles). Because of the lengthy process of review and comment, changes in accounting standards have tended to lag behind the reporting problems they are designed to correct.[2]

II.   ACCOUNTING IN REAL ESTATE FIRMS

Real estate is a complex and diverse industry, involving large capital transactions and varied organizational forms. These characteristics of real estate have a major impact on accounting practice in the in-

---

[2]Within this chapter, only a brief presentation is possible. Further readings are required for those seeking richer detail. A "programmed learning" introduction to accounting, such as *Essentials of Accounting*, by Robert N. Anthony and Matthew L. Israel, may be useful.

dustry. In this section, we will examine the areas of accounting practice which are particularly important to real estate companies, and therefore to our interpretation of their financial statements.

Areas of Accounting Sensitivity

Most real estate enterprises may be classified simply -- as **sellers** or **holders** of property. Examples of these two basic company types include:

Sellers: Land Sales Companies
              Land Developers
              Merchant Builders

Holders: Investment Builders
              Investors

Accounting concerns are very sharply differentiated between the two groups. Three areas of accounting practice important to real estate enterprises are introduced in the context of the two groups:

Seller Enterprises. The first area of accounting sensitivity relates primarily to the seller type of business. Real estate sales typically are large in scale and involve financially complex transactions. Sales often are completed over long periods of time, and determining exactly when a sale occurs is often difficult. Among the seller group, therefore, *timing of profit recognition* is usually the key accounting issue.

Historically, this area has caused considerable mischief in real estate, even when companies were following all the accounting rules in effect at the time. For example, in the land-sales business, scandals resulted in the 1950s and 1960s when companies were permitted to recognize sales based on only minimal downpayments from buyers. Profit on the sales could properly be recognized at a time when construction of roads and utilities had perhaps not even started. The companies therefore could report high accounting earnings and enjoy a rapid increase in stock value. Maintaining their illusory earnings growth led to the use of unethical sales techniques and the sale of unbuildable land, among other sins.

Holder Enterprises. The holder type of firm is greatly affected by two other areas of accounting sensitivity -- **depreciation accounting** and **valuation accounting**.

Depreciation is the accounting recognition of the "wasting" of an asset, theoretically in recognition of its limited useful life. Land cannot be depreciated; however, buildings and other structures are considered in accounting to be depreciable. Depreciation expense is defined as a non-cash allowance for the diminution in value of the asset during an accounting period. The holding for income or business use of real property assets therefore results in substantial depreciation expenses on a continuing basis. For companies doing this, taxable net income is reduced substantially compared with the same net cash income from a manufacturing or service business. This makes depreciation accounting of paramount importance to holders enterprises. Because they do not generally hold property for long periods, the seller type of real estate firm is generally less affected by depreciation accounting.

One important result of depreciation is to reduce the **book value** (cost minus accumulated depreciation) of the holder's property. At the same time, the **market value** of the property is often increasing, at least in recent inflationary periods. This leads to a third major accounting concern, the valuation of property. The fundamental accounting question is whether to present in financial statements the *cost* of property or instead to estimate its *market value*.

For a holder of real estate, such as an investment builder, this is a particularly critical question. If development projects are successful, the value of the completed properties should be considerably higher than their direct development costs.

In summary, there are three special problem areas of accounting in real estate firms -- profit recognition, depreciation, and valuation of property. Immediately below, accounting standards for these three areas are cited. Included is a more detailed discussion of accounting choices to be made by management of a company.

Profit Recognition

Where for tax purposes a company's management will normally wish to reduce the reported net income, for financial reporting purposes the opposite will usually be true. Management often wishes to increase the reported net, thereby appearing more profitable. This is done by electing accounting policies which accelerate revenue recognition and which delay the accrual of expenses. Revenue in real estate enterprises generally originates from the following sources:

1. Sales of land and developed property;

2. Fees for contractual services;

3. Rental and operating income from investment property; and

4. Interest and other income.

Accounting recognition of profit in the first two categories varies widely and has long been the subject of scrutiny by the accounting profession.

Accounting for Revenues. Prior to 1973, profit on an installment sale of property could be recognized "up front," that is, when only a nominal deposit had been actually received and construction had perhaps not been begun. This resulted in lots of "profits" later becoming "losses." Today[3], such companies must either choose to recognize only a small portion of the profit on the basis of deposit, installment and cost recovery methods or must defer recognition of the sale until stringent requirements are met. These requirements govern the buyer's initial and continuing investment in the property and the seller's continuing involvement with the property sold. A wide variety of companies, including those who sell condominiums while under construction, are affected by these rules. Sales which are entered into by the company, but not recognizable at present, must be disclosed in the footnotes.

A second area of significant variability among real estate companies is in revenue from contractual services. Generally, accountants for such companies must choose to recognize profit from a contract on an installment basis, such as cash or percentage completion, or on the completed contract method. The latter method will recognize profit only after the work is complete, and is therefore typically used for tax accounting purposes.

> Example: At year's end a construction firm has completed 50% of the physical work on a particular contract and has received payment for 25% of the estimated total. The estimated profit on the contract is $100,000. Depending only on a choice of accounting policy, the firm could show profit from this contract for the year as follows:
>
> Completed contract method: $0
> Installment or cash method: $25,000
> Percentage completion method: $50,000

Footnotes are an integral part of a set of financial statements. Accounting Principles Board Opinion No. 22, "Disclosure of Accounting Policies," requires disclosure in the footnotes of the methods used to compute revenue from sales of property and contracts. Other disclosures may be important to real estate companies, especially the breakdown of revenue by line of business. Revenue from normal operations must also be distinguished from revenues from non-recurring sources.

Expense Accounting. The "matching principle" of accounting requires that accountants relate costs to the source and timing of recognition of revenue. In real estate, this is made difficult by the long production cycle from the start of construction to completion of a sale or execution of lease. It is normally a long time from the time when costs are incurred to the time when related revenue is realized. The method of accounting which seeks to match expenses to future revenues is called **capitalizing**. A capitalized expense is carried as an asset on a company's balance sheet until the property is sold. It is then accounted for as a cost of property sold.

Since 1979, companies have been required to capitalize interest as part of the cost of acquiring assets that need a period of time to be brought to the condition necessary for their intended use. Capitalization of interest is not permitted for assets in use or ready for use, or for assets not undergoing the activities necessary to be made ready for use.

Since 1982, companies have also had to capitalize indirect project costs if they clearly relate to a project under development. Costs such as general and administrative costs that do not clearly relate to a project under development should be expensed as incurred. Capitalized costs are assigned to the components of a project with which they are specifically identified. Land costs and other common costs should be allocated to the components on the basis of the relative fair market value of each component benefited.

---

[3]See Financial Accounting Standards No. 66, *"Accounting for Sales of Real Estate,"* 1982.

Depreciation Accounting

As noted above, tax considerations are particularly important in real estate because of depreciation. Financial statements will normally show the cost of the real estate as an asset on the balance sheet. The balance sheet also shows as an offset to this cost the amount of accumulated depreciation of the asset. This is the sum of the depreciation charges to date. All newly acquired or developed real estate placed in service after December 31, 1986, is depreciable for tax purposes over a 27.5-year statutory period for residential-rental property or a 31.5-year period for all other real property. For financial reporting purposes, longer useful lives of 30 to 50 years will usually be applied. These are intended to approximate the actual useful life of a particular structure. Frequent changes in Federal tax law have occurred and are likely to continue to occur. These will have major effects on depreciation accounting, as well as other areas.

Depreciation contributes to a complexity in interpreting accounting reports -- that of **deferred taxes**. Most companies will tend to choose accounting policies which will reduce the computed net income when reporting for tax purposes and increase it when reporting to potential investors, lenders, or the general public. When book income differs from tax income, deferred tax is created. For financial reporting purposes, the typical owner of income property will choose a straight-line method of depreciation and a relatively long useful life. Such an owner will therefore typically carry a deferred-tax account on his balance sheet. This is a liability account since it represents future taxes to be paid on income already recorded in the financial statements, but not for tax purposes.

Other examples of policy choices which commonly result in deferred taxes include: installment-sales revenue recognition (see above); and capitalization of development costs such as interest and real estate taxes.

AICPA's Accounting Principles Board Opinion No. 11, "Accounting for Income Taxes," requires disclosure of the cause of the deferred tax item. This will normally be found in a footnote to the statements.

Valuation Accounting

Accounting for valuation impacts on financial statements of real estate companies very substantially. Real estate held for conversion or sale must be valued differently by accountants from property held for investment. Values of real estate held for sale may presently be carried on the books at historical cost, or, if less than cost, at present market value or net realizable value. The accounting profession is considering requiring that real estate inventory should not be carried at an amount in excess of net realizable value. This value would be based on the estimated selling price plus other revenue from the project, reduced by the costs to complete, carry to the expected time of sale, and dispose of the property.

Real estate held for investment must presently be carried on the books at historical cost. Public real estate companies are permitted to present supplementary current value financial statements in addition to the cost-based statements. Valuations are usually based on appraisals conducted by qualified outside consultants and will indicate the market value of the properties in a portfolio. The difference between the net worth computed in this manner and that computed in the conventional GAAP accounts is called **revaluation equity** or "unrealized appreciation." If current value information is used in the form of financial statements, it must be part of a comprehensive system and not be presented piecemeal. Current value information should include tax effects.

Joint venture investments must also be valued for reporting purposes. For a controlling joint venturer, the investment is normally consolidated, as are the accounts of a subsidiary corporation. For non-controlling venturers, the basic choice is between use of the "equity" method in which the investment is carried at its value including undistributed profits, and the "cost" method in which no adjustments are made until cash is actually received.

III. ANALYSIS OF FINANCIAL STATEMENTS

This section contains a brief introduction to analysis of financial statements. Knowing the choices available to accountants and company management, the analyst must seek to ascertain the financial health of the company. Discussed below for each of the three basic types of financial statements are some of the most common analytic techniques and some of the most important questions to be asked. These may be useful for both real estate and non-real estate companies, and the concepts are equally applicable to the statements of individuals and partnerships.

Balance Sheet

The balance sheet contains assets, liabilities, and stockholders' equity accounts. Analysis of the balance sheet assets normally focuses on the composition of assets and liabilities over time. One basic area of concern for the analyst is always liquidity. For industrial firms, working capital (current assets less current liabilities) is an important indication of liquidity. How much capital can be readily deployed if needed?

A favorite tool of the analyst is ratio analysis. Changes over time in a ratio, such as the "current ratio" (current assets divided by current liabilities), are often thought to be important indicators of change in a company's fortunes. Real estate companies do not typically distinguish

current from non-current assets and liabilities; however, the analyst may derive his or her own useful working capital indicator from footnote disclosures.

Another area of analytic interest is the "mix" of assets. What types of property does a real estate firm hold? What other assets does it own? How much are the properties worth? How are they valued on the books?

Analysis of liabilities also involves a mix analysis. The analyst will be concerned with the amount of short-term, as opposed to long-term, debt on the balance sheet. A real estate company will usually present an analysis of its debt in a footnote. Individuals do not normally disclose fully such information in their personal statements. Historically, how much of the cost of its property has the company borrowed? Are the interest costs fixed or variable?

A third area of balance sheet analysis relates to the sources and priorities of a company's capital. The analyst will often examine the debt-to-equity ratio. Normally, lenders will have priority over preferred and common stockholders. A high debt ratio often indicates increased risk to the stockholders and greater volatility of earnings of a company. How much capital has been paid into the company? How much capital has been raised by retained earnings? What is the debt-to-equity ratio?

A final area of analysis is valuation of a company. The net assets or book value of a corporation (assets less liabilities) may be related to the number of shares of stock outstanding, giving an indication of value. The actual market value of the shares will often differ from this book value per share. What does the stock price indicate is the value of the company? How much are the properties worth? For the individual, of course, this latter may be the most critical of all the questions.

Income Statement

The income statement contains the revenues and expenses of a company matched by accrual accounting to the accounting period. Analysis of the income statement often will focus on trends over time and on ratio analysis.

The most basic investigation is into profitability. The analyst will typically examine the profit margin -- net income divided by sales. Within any particular industry, profit margins may be compared among companies. In the case of real estate companies which hold properties for income, the cash-flow margin as a percentage of revenue is often considered important. Profit margin analysis is very important in analyzing real estate companies which sell properties or services. What is the profit margin shown in the company's income statement? What is the cash flow margin?

A second area of ratio analysis relates income to debt payments. The "coverage" ratio may be defined as the net operating income before financial payments divided by the required interest payments. For a company holding property, this is normally computed using the net cash operating income before any depreciation expenses. The related debt payments may also include retirement of a portion of principal. What coverage ratios are indicated in the income statement?

A third step in analyzing the income statement is to consider the sources of a company's revenue. Disclosure of lines of business is required and may be found in the footnotes. There is only one proven method of analysis of footnotes -- they must be read. In what lines of business does the company compete? Is this consistent with your impression from analyzing its balance sheet? How important is each of the lines of business?

A final analysis of importance to real estate companies is to consider the differences between book and tax accounting. A quick indication of the importance of this is to examine the deferred tax account. Analysis of the sources of deferred taxes will be found in the applicable footnote. Which accounting policy choices have had the greatest impact on deferred taxes shown in the balance sheet and the income statement? For individuals and partnerships, future tax liabilities are also important.

Statement of Changes in Financial Position

The third financial statement -- the statement of changes in financial position -- is itself an analysis. Based on both balance sheet and income statement data, this statement indicates the sources of cash to the company and the uses to which the cash was put. Presentation can vary widely, and the interpretation and analysis of the statement will depend on how the company chooses to present itself.

A basic concern will be to indicate cash flow from operations. Typically the statement will begin with net income and will then add non-cash charges. The statement will also usually segregate financing transactions and extraordinary items from the operating cash flow. Into what major categories does the company segregate its funds flow statement? Are there items listed which could be classified differently? To what effect?

A straightforward approach to analyzing this statement is often to focus first on the larger items. These will provide a useful perspective for review of smaller sources or applications of funds. What are the three largest sources and the three largest uses of funds indicated in the funds flow statement? What expectation would you have for the next year?

SUMMARY

In section I of this note we looked at the basics of accounting. In section II we provided an introduction to the accounting concerns particular to the real estate industry. In this section III, we have presented a series of techniques and questions useful to the analyst in interpreting financial statements, particularly those of companies involved in real estate.

Each analyst will, with experience, develop his or her own favorite analytic techniques. The purpose here is to introduce a few basic techniques that will lead quickly to greater understanding of the capabilities and limitations, history and prospects of a company as indicated by its financial statements.

The reader should now be familiar with the location of the various types of information -- whether it is to be found in the balance sheet, income statement, funds flow statement, or in the footnotes. The reader should also be acquainted with the major areas of accounting discretion in real estate -- profit recognition, depreciation of property and valuation. Armed with this knowledge, the reader should be acquainted with a series of basic analytic steps:

1. Examine the cash and liquid assets position of the company in relation to short-term liabilities, sales or other measures of liquidity.

2. Examine the asset mix of the company -- what real estate is held for investment, for sale, and under development, and what other assets are owned. Are the assets worth significantly more or less than their book value?

3. Consider the composition of the company's debt -- short- and long-term maturities -- in relation to the company's cash flow and its ability to refinance maturing debt. Are interest rates fixed or variable?

4. Examine the amount of debt in relation to the cost and the value of the assets and in relation to other sources of capital through analysis of the debt-to-equity ratio.

5. Compare the book value per share with the market value of a company's stock or other ownership equity. What are the earnings per share? the cash flow per share?

6. Examine the profit margin and, if appropriate, the cash-flow margin on sales.

7. Consider the cash flow from operations in relation to interest costs through the coverage ratio.

8. Read the Notes to Financial Statements, considering especially the presentations on accounting policy, composition of debt, lines of business analysis, and deferred taxes.

9. Examine the analysis of cash flow from operations provided in the statement of changes in financial position. Relate this to other major sources and uses of funds.

Finally, the reader should form definite conclusions. The purpose of analysis of financial statements is normally related to a decision -- should I invest? or should my firm do business with this firm or individual? Having completed the basic forms of analysis introduced in this section, a decision will normally be reached. If not, the analyst will surely be in a position to ask good questions and gather any other information which might be needed.

Case 7

Zayre Headquarters Tract

In late May 1979, Dick Reynolds of the Boston office of Gerald D. Hines Interests was preparing a proposal for the development of a 20.8 acre tract of land in Framingham, Massachusetts. He and Jack Griefen, his senior partner, intended to present the proposal at a scheduled June 1st meeting with Stanley Feldberg, Chairman of the Executive Committee of Zayre Corporation. This would be the second formal meeting and the latest of many conversations among the interested parties: Zayre, the owners of the land; Hines, the potential developer, and Brad Griffith, a broker with the Boston firm Leggat, McCall and Werner.

Mr. Reynolds had first been shown the property in December 1978 by the brokerage firm. Zayre purchased the land in 1970, intending to build its corporate headquarters. The company later decided against that, and market conditions made it difficult to sell the property ever since. Zayre had received many inquiries over the years about possible office or industrial development, but no serious offers. Office construction, operating and development costs had risen sharply, and the Boston area continued to feel the effects of commercial overbuilding in the early 1970's. Zayre's desire to see some return on their investment and, during the last year, an increasingly tight office market in the Boston suburbs made it now seem likely that a deal could at last be put together. Dick Reynolds and Jack Griefen had discussed the project frequently and were in general agreement that an office development was the right direction to take. Mr. Reynolds' task was to be specific about a proposal -- land price, building type, rent levels, phasing, etc. -- which would provide the right mix of risk and incentive, acceptable to both Hines and Zayre, and be supportable by the market. Since little of the conversations to date had been reduced to writing, he was particularly concerned that his proposal be favorably received.

GERALD D. HINES INTERESTS

Gerry Hines was born in Gary, Indiana, in 1925. He studied engineering at Purdue University, and moved to Houston to work as a refrigeration engineer. In 1954, using funds he raised privately, he built and leased a small office building. He continued in real estate development on a part-time basis until 1957, when he quit his job with the engineering firm and formed Gerald D. Hines Interests. From the beginning he insisted on producing a quality product, always choosing long-run quality over short-term profit.

By the mid-1960s the Houston economy was growing dramatically, and Gerald Hines was there. He had established himself as a solid, high-quality local developer in his first ten years in the business. With One Shell Plaza, Houston's tallest office building, he began a successful move into the high-rise office market. By 1975 he had become perhaps the premier office developer in the country. A series of prestigious office towers and corporate headquarters served to establish his national reputation. His Hines Industrial unit meanwhile continued to develop the less glamorous industrial and low-rise commercial properties. The Hines reputation for producing the highest quality work attracted numerous corporate clients who wanted a combination of high quality and cost control. This led the Hines organization into Development Management, where the company provides management services for a fee without investing its own capital in the development. A dramatic example of this approach was the recently announced Trade Center in China, where Hines will be development manager for an international development team.

Late in 1977 Jack Griefen became a partner in the Hines organization and opened an office of Gerald D. Hines Interests in Boston. It was felt that to be a truly national development firm, Hines needed representation on the East Coast. Boston was chosen as the base because Jack Griefen was well established there. Although the office was small, it was intended to do a wide range of commercial and industrial projects and draw on the central organization for technical support and financial backing.

Jack Griefen, head of the Boston office, was previously Senior Vice-President of Cabot, Cabot and Forbes. There he had built his experience over a successful twenty-year career, specializing in industrial build-to-suit projects for national clients. Like many other firms who owned land for future development, Cabot, Cabot and Forbes was badly hurt in the 1974-1976 real estate recession, and the firm was extensively reorganized. Mr. Griefen departed in 1977 to join the Hines organization. His prior experience had been in commercial brokerage, as Assistant Commerce Commissioner for the Commonwealth of Massachusetts, and as an executive in the lumber industry. He presently serves as a Trustee of the Urban Land Institute, a national organization of developers in which Gerald Hines was himself very active, and a national director of the Society of Industrial Realtors.

In the fall of 1978, Dick Reynolds and John Kastler joined the Boston Hines organization. After receiving his MBA in finance, Dick Reynolds worked for New England Life, where he was second Vice-President for real estate finance. He has been active with the Greater Boston Real Estate Board and headed the local Building Owners and Managers Association. As a junior partner, he served as project manager for Hines/Boston and was involved in the origination, negotiation, and development of office and industrial properties.

John Kastler was manager of construction, supervising building projects under development. He was a graduate civil engineer, a member of the American Society of Civil Engineers and the American Society of Plant Engineers, and had over 20 years of construction management experience.

For its initial venture, Hines/Boston developed 100,000 square feet of manufacturing and 200,000 square feet of research and development space for Prime Computer in suburban Boston. This project was now nearly complete, and the office had several promising development opportunities it was pursuing. Among these were a 50,000 square foot speculative industrial facility, several other 15- to 20-acre sites suitable for industrial or office projects, a 15-story, 300,000 square foot office tower, and build-to-suit possibilities for major clients. With the improving real estate economy in the Northeast, Mr. Griefen was optimistic about prospects for the expansion of Hines/Boston activities over the next 5 to 10 years.

When asked by the casewriter about the risks and rewards of the development profession, Mr. Griefen pointed out the tremendous growth of the Hines organization over the past twenty-five years. He commented: "There are opportunities in the development business that are beyond the opportunities in most aspects of industry -- if it works. If it doesn't, you go in the tank. Real estate is a high-risk business, but the compensations are very attractive."

Mr. Griefen had been exposed to both risk and reward in his real estate career. The Hines office was not yet fully established in the Boston market, and he and his colleagues knew that each project they undertook was critical to their track record. The Hines/Boston organization expected to be especially cautious when it came to acquiring land or building on speculation.

ZAYRE

Zayre Corporation was one of the nation's largest mass merchandisers with annual sales of $1.4 billion and total assets of $476 million. The company's principal business was operating a chain of neighborhood-oriented discount general-merchandise stores. The origins of the firm dated back to 1919 and a wholesale hosiery business started by Max Feldberg and his brother Morris. They began operating a chain of retail outlets in 1929. Thereafter, the business expanded, acquiring other retail operations, and evolved into a chain of ladies' specialty stores. By the early 1950's, Max's son, Stanley, and Morris' son, Sumner, had completed military service and school and became involved in the family business. They convinced their fathers that the discount chain was going to be an important and growing part of the retail market, and in 1956 they opened one of the first mass-merchandising stores in the nation.

The Zayre chain began with that first store in Hyannis, Massachusetts, and experienced rapid growth. The company made its initial stock offering to the public in 1962. Since then, the operation has expanded to the current 251 department stores in 25 states, and in recent years, a number of other chain operations. Zayre financed this growth primarily through leases, real estate and equipment borrowings, and corporate bond issues. Company sales have steadily increased from $1.05 billion in 1975 to $1.40 billion in 1979 (see Exhibit 1).

Despite the public stock ownership, the Feldberg family continued to exercise substantial control, owning 32% of the capital stock. Family members always held key management positions. However, in 1978 Stanley Feldberg was succeeded as President and Chief Executive Officer by Maurice Segall, a non-family member and former Executive Vice-President of American Express Company. Stanley Feldberg became Chairman of the Executive Committee. Sumner Feldberg was Chairman of the Board, while Max, one of the co-founders, was Honorary Chairman.

Each Zayre store contained approximately 100 merchandise departments. Stores ranged in size from 45,000 square feet to 130,000 square feet, and the gross area of all Zayre discount department stores was 18.7 million square feet. Most of the stores were in suburban strip shopping centers.

Zayre also owned and operated specialty store chains. The "Hit or Miss" chain was the largest with over 200 stores, selling off-price brand name women's apparel. The company projected the addition of fifty more "Hit or Miss" units for 1979. In 1977, Zayre started "T.J. Maxx," a chain of family-apparel "supermarkets." There were now eighteen of these stores with ten more planned for 1979. Other specialty operations were "Beaconway," a chain of thirty-two fabric stores, and "On Stage" and "Nugents," women's apparel chains which together totaled thirty-two stores.

The Zayre organization was originally located in Boston, but moved out in 1960 to Natick, a western suburb. There they built a warehouse and corporate headquarters. By the early 1970's Zayre had offices in three locations in the Natick-Framingham area and were looking for suitable land nearby to consolidate their offices in one facility. They identified a potential site in Framingham, across from one of their existing offices. This parcel totaled 20.8 acres, but involved multiple owners.

Brad Griffith, a commercial real estate broker, had participated in the initial acquisition and described his role: "When I got involved, part of the property had already been offered to Zayre. In fact, they had an option on it, but that one piece was not enough. I then went out and assembled the rest of the site from eight owners. The land was originally zoned for residential use, but the owners had been approached so many times about selling and/or rezoning, that they all got together and made an agreement that they would all only sell together, and had their properties rezoned about a year before I approached them."

Zayre bought the entire property in 1971 for $1.1 million, or about $1.25 per square foot of land area. The company considered this a high price, but one justified by their intended use for a corporate headquarters. Zayre proceeded to plan a home office of 275,000 square feet to be constructed in two phases. The company went ahead with the design and permits until 1974, when the recession led the company to reconsider and eventually drop the plans for centralizing. The entire 20.8 acres had been on the market since that time. The company was asking a price of $2.2 million. This price represented Zayre's book value, including carrying and related costs. For the next three years there was no substantial interest in the property and in fact no significant market for any commercial land in suburban Boston. Brad Griffith recalled, "We didn't sell a piece of land during that period, and we sell a substantial amount of land."

THE MARKET

When Hines/Boston first began to consider developing the Zayre tract in December 1978, a low-rise office or research and development facility had looked most appropriate. In the past six months, however, there seemed to be a dramatic change in the office market. There was very little vacancy in first-class suburban office space and a shortage of building sites in preferred locations. Developers were naturally responding to this, however. A survey conducted by students at a well known eastern design school identified proposed projects with a potential of about 3 million square feet in the suburban market. Most of these sites, however, were considered unlikely to be developed quickly because of access or environmental problems. The April 1979 Building Own-

ers and Managers Association (BOMA) report (see Exhibit 2) for the suburban market showed only a 0.2% vacancy in the 1.5 million square feet of first-class space, zero vacancy in the lower cost R&D range, and 1.58% in the total suburban market of 4.2 million square feet.

In considering the potential of the Zayre parcel, Dick Reynolds knew that Boston's office market had major downtown and suburban segments, typical of major cities, but it also had a number of other significant sub-markets. These sub-markets were important in Boston because of its fragmented town government political structure, with widely varying local tax levels and attitudes toward development. The rough coastal terrain and the colonial origins of the road network also affected local site development costs and accessibility.

The premier location for suburban office development was the so-called "gold coast" section of Route 128, Boston's original circumferential highway. This sub-market included the area along Route 128 from its intersection with Route 2 southward to where it crosses Route 9. The "gold coast" had good access to downtown and to the most affluent residential areas of suburban Boston. Most developments were high-image office parks or research and development facilities. Many of Boston's prominent high-technology firms began in this location. This market contained essentially no vacant space and few, if any, available building sites. There were some development proposals in the 100,000 square foot range, but none that seemed certain to go ahead.

The Route 128 North sub-market lies north of the Route 128/Route 2 intersection. Most of the office development centered around Burlington and Lexington. The New England Executive Park at the intersection of Route 3 and Route 128 and the Burlington Woods Office Park under construction a few miles away both contained land for future expansion.

The South Shore sub-market consists of the area south of Boston and eastward from the intersection of Route 128 and Route 1. With limited accessibility either to Boston or to upper income suburbs, this area had relatively little speculative office development.

A final sub-market, the area west of Route 128 to Interstate 495, included the Zayre Headquarters Tract. Historically, there was little office development beyond Route 128. However, the lack of easily developable land in the Route 128 "gold coast" seemed to be increasing the demand for office space farther out. This area was close to high-income residential neighborhoods, and the Massachusetts Turnpike provided good access to downtown Boston and Route 128. There were currently proposals for large office developments in Natick, but none appeared certain.

Dick Reynolds had paid close attention to these market factors. As a result of the recent tightening of the office market and the lack of substantial short-term competition, he now believed it likely that the Zayre Tract would be marketable in the near future for either first class office space or for one-story, lower profile office/industrial space.

CONSTRAINTS ON DEVELOPMENT

In December 1978, a studio course on suburban land development conducted a short design/development feasibility study[1] for the Zayre Tract. Hines and Zayre executives participated in this exercise in which each student made his or her own assessment of the market potential and the physical constraints of the land, and then proposed a development program and master plan. The major areas of concern for

construction on this parcel, as identified by the student work, included zoning and community attitude, traffic impact on the adjacent Speen Street, and certain specific site conditions, especially a transmission line easement. Their assessment of these constraints is described here and illustrated in Exhibit 3.

Based on interviews with the town planning staff, the students concluded that office use of any type for the site would be acceptable to the town from the perspective of land use, and would not involve a special permit or site plan review procedure. The zoning code of the Town of Framingham was in the process of being revised, and the students recommended that planning for the site anticipate meeting the proposed standards, a draft of which was obtained. The major change relevant to the proposed development was a reduction of the required parking ratio from 1 stall per 150 square feet to 1 stall per 250 square feet of office area. Hines' own requirement for marketability was for 3.5 to 4.0 parking spaces per 1000 rentable square feet of office space.

The town appeared particularly concerned with the impact of future development on town services. The town had been able to maintain excess capacity in sewered areas, and had therefore been able to approve all applications for new connections, despite an area-wide moratorium within the Metropolitan Sewer District. However, as growth continued, large developments in the future might be faced with limited sanitary sewer availability. The town's policy on storm water favored natural drainage and non-structural control measures. The twelve-inch storm sewer along Speen Street was not considered adequate to accept run-off from the site if it were extensively surfaced. Therefore it was concluded that any development plan would have to accommodate storm water on the site.

The traffic impact of a major development of Speen Street was also identified

---

[1] Material in this section based on an analysis by Yunghi Epstein.

as a major concern of the town. As an important access road to the Massachusetts Turnpike and a major local connector, Speen Street was heavily used and congested during peak hours. An existing office complex near the Zayre parcel already created peak traffic loads on the street. A development which did not aggravate the peak traffic problem and did not burden Speen Street with multiple access drives was preferred. Resolution of the traffic impact issue was felt to be essential for the town to accept a development plan.

The site was characterized as gently sloping with intermittent vegetation posing no major difficulties for construction. The existing vegetation, in particular the Pine grove along Speen Street, was considered a potential asset if preserved and incorporated into the site plan. Although the topography of the site did not present a building constraint, the steep profile of part of Speen Street did limit the possibilities of entrance locations to the flatter slopes at the east and west ends of the site.

The most significant site constraints were the transmission line and drainage easements along the eastern edge of the property. Together these constituted 6.5 acres, about one-third of the site. Use of the transmission line easement for parking was possible only if the supports were raised to create the required 35 foot clearance. A cost of $12,000 for each support had been suggested to the students by the utility company. Another potential problem was posed by the restriction on vegetation within this easement. The town usually required extensive parking lot landscaping. Use of the easement for parking also created problems in siting the buildings. With a large area of parking in the easement, it was difficult to provide a balanced relationship of parking area to building entrances without wasting space. From the students' design studies, it appeared that a multi-story structure with a single entry was better able to exploit this

configuration, than would multiple entry, single-story structures.

The visual impact of the transmission lines was another important issue. The poles and wires did not seem to reinforce a strong, positive image for a first-class office park. Careful selection and screening of the entrance would be necessary to create an appropriate impression. Even so, the view from the Massachusetts Turnpike was directly through the easement area. Access from the turnpike was also more circuitous than would be desired.

Having completed their assessments of the market and site constraints, the students made a variety of design proposals. These proposals had been developed within a short period of time and illustrated Dick Reynolds' view of the basic alternatives for the site, ranging from lower cost, one-story office/industrial development to a higher cost, multi-story office park. Site plans which illustrate two of these development strategies are included in Exhibit 4.

HINES' VIEW OF THE DEAL

From Hines' perspective, the basis for making a deal on this property would be to make a distinction between land development and building development, with different sets of risk and rewards associated with each. Hines believed that with a building product there is less risk because it can be used right away. Land, however, requires a minimum of one year to develop for its eventual use, and the risk cannot be managed as well. As Dick Reynolds explained, "Land development is more of a venture capital risk and can mean huge profits, but there are also huge risks. If it (land) hits the market at the wrong time and place, it can't be moved. There is a lot of land with roads and utilities that's still sitting vacant. Developed land is an extremely illiquid asset, and the costs of carrying it chew into the value."

In this view, Zayre already owns the land and so, in effect, has already taken the risk of land development. Their costs have been increased by the long carrying period. As Jack Griefen put it, "Now their problem is how to recover their investment in this land, which cannot be sold as small parcels because of the site constraints, like drainage, road access, easements, and so on, which have to be handled all at once."

Brad Griffith outlined what he saw as three alternative approaches available to Zayre: 1) straight sale at $2.2 million; 2) locate a corporate user for a major office facility; or 3) become a partner, assuming some of the risk of development, as well as enjoying some of the benefits of success. Brad did not think a developer could pay the full price in a straight sale because he would need a margin to cover carrying costs. A major corporate user didn't appear likely to turn up in the near future, and so therefore he believed the third option was the most reasonable one. He felt that the challenge to the developer in this situation was to structure a deal that gets the present owner the highest price for the land and still allows a development to be economically feasible.

The approaches that Hines/Boston had been exploring were to buy or lease the land from Zayre. In either case, Hines would take down the land over a period of a few years and pay incrementally more for each phase. The total return could equate with Zayre's book value, although they would not receive the full price at one time. The amount that Zayre would ultimately get would be a function of the appreciation of the land that was created by the development. Jack explained: " The risk is that we might only get one building put up, and then say business is going to hell, and we're not going to put up the others. Therefore, we're only going to buy one-third or one-fourth of the land. But the three-fourths of the land that would be left would be worth more per unit than originally because we will have demon-

strated that a development is feasible. The land would have increased in value by the very fact that we're putting an office building on 25% of the site. On the other hand, there is the risk that if we build a building and it stands vacant for five years, it doesn't do the land any good. That's the risk Zayre has to take. We'll be risking about $14 million of building, and they're risking $3 million of land."

The student presentations in January and again in April had made Dick Reynolds more optimistic about the site's potential. On May 14th, Zayre and Hines sat down for the first time to discuss in general terms how the companies might work together. Mr. Reynolds had sent Stanley Feldberg a memorandum of that meeting (see Exhibit 5). This outlined an approach to a staged land purchase, but no specific response had been received.

In preparing for the upcoming meeting, Mr. Reynolds reviewed a preliminary analysis he had done in early May. He compared average development costs in the Boston area for the two building types being considered:

	1-Story	Class A 3-Story
Land	$7/SF	$10/SF
Building	35/SF	42/SF
Soft costs	8/SF	12/SF
Total	$50/SF	$64/SF

Mr. Reynolds thought that the one-story development could be rented for $6.25 per square foot, with tenants paying operating expenses and real estate taxes, while first class space could probably rent for $12.00 per square foot, gross. He estimated operating expenses in the class A structure at $2.50 and real estate taxes as $1.40 per square foot. Using these figures, both development types could produce similar capitalization rates, but the three-story office could support a higher land cost. He believed that mortgage financing would be available at 10.25% or 10.5% interest for a 30-year term for about 80% of the total cost for either approach.

He estimated that only 13.0 acres of the 20.8 acre site were usable. The transmission line and drainage easements eliminated about 6.5 acres, and an internal roadway to service a multi-building development would probably require another 1.5 acres. Assuming a three-to-four-story development, the 13.0 usable acres could support 225,000 square feet of building based on a land-to-building area ratio of 2.5:1. A 225,000 square foot office development with a land component of $10.00 per square foot could then create a prepared land value of $2.25 million. Mr. Reynolds estimated that the interest carry on the base land plus other land development costs would be about $300,000. Assuming a margin of 20% of final value, land development profit would equal $450,000. Subtracting the total land development costs of $750,000 from the prepared land value gave a raw land value of about $1.5 million. Thus raw land value would be about $6.60 per square foot of building or about $115,000 per net buildable acre. This cost seemed to be acceptable for an ambitious program of exclusively first-class office development.

In his preliminary analysis in early May, Dick Reynolds had outlined a land development venture in which Zayre would contribute the land at its base value of $1.5 million. Upon sale of the developed land to third parties or building development by Hines, Zayre would receive interest on the base value of the land plus perhaps a half interest in any additional land value created. As above, Mr. Reynolds assumed that land development profit would be 20% above the carrying costs. Zayre would receive the interest carry plus half of the profit. Hines would receive its share of the

increased value as compensation for accomplishing the land development program. In effect, Hines' share of the land development program would be 10% of the total prepared-land value. If Hines did proceed with a building development program, this 10% would be applied as a discount on the land cost. However, Zayre was not interested in a purchase price based on the raw land value because it did not adequately maximize the recapture of their investment, so this option was eliminated.

Mr. Reynolds saw two other feasible approaches to the deal. In both, Zayre would continue to assume the risk of land development and therefore would receive any additional land value created by the development. The first approach was for Zayre to sell the land to Hines in stages, based on a prepared-land value of $10.00 per square foot of building. This alternative was discussed at the May 14 meeting and is described in Exhibit 5. The other approach would be for Zayre and Hines to form a joint venture for the total development. This would most likely be on the basis of a ground lease. Zayre's investment would equal the prepared-land value. The ground rent could be based on a preferred yield, which Mr. Reynolds thought might be about 9%, or some share of the cash flow proportionate to Zayre's investment. Mr. Reynolds knew he should be ready with the specifics of a ground lease and cash flow distribution in case Zayre became interested in that approach.

JUNE 1ST

The development seemed to have momentum. It would be crucial for Hines/Boston to have detailed proposals to discuss with Zayre at the June 1st meeting. Mr. Reynolds knew from experience that there are critical decision points in any development process which make or break a deal. He added, "When you look at a site and are trying to decide what to do, success lies in the fine eye of someone who can make a judgment. There are no real comparables, because every piece of real estate is different. The developer must ask himself how his site is different and how he can take advantage of that difference."

EXHIBITS

1. Zayre corporation annual report (excerpts).

2. BOMA office occupancy survey.

3. Site analysis.

4. Site plans.

5. Letter from Dick Reynolds to Stanley Feldberg.

QUESTIONS FOR DISCUSSION

1. What are the key ingredients of a successful deal to develop this property?

2. What proposal should the developers make?

3. What are Stanley Feldberg's objectives for a land transaction? Refer to Note 3, Financial Accounting in Real Estate, and to Exhibit 1 as needed.

4. What bargaining stance should the Zayre executives take? What results do you expect?

Exhibit 1

Zayre Corp.
Five-Year Summary

Fiscal Year Ended Last Saturday in January
(Dollars in thousands except per share amounts)

	1979	1978*	1977*	1976* (53 weeks)	1975*
Summary of Operations:					
Net sales	$1,394,109	$1,261,301	$1,160,572	$1,084,011	$1,045,541
Cost of sales, including buying and occupancy costs	1,076,658	987,259	907,913	855,895	832,103
Selling, general and administrative expenses	270,545	234,487	212,825	196,655	190,417
Interest costs:					
Debt (net of $229 capitalized in 1975)	11,913	9,653	10,001	11,142	16,078
Capital leases	8,069	8,060	8,290	8,184	8,152
Total expenses	1,367,185	1,239,459	1,139,029	1,071,876	1,046,750
Income (loss) from continuing operations before income taxes	26,924	21,842	21,543	12,135	(1,209)
Provision for (recovery of) income taxes	12,907	10,844	11,315	6,234	(830)
Income (loss) from continuing operations	14,017	10,998	10,228	5,901	(379)
Discontinued operations:					
Income (loss) from discontinued owned credit plan, net of applicable income taxes	–	–	–	(36)	168
Loss on disposal of owned credit plan, net of applicable income taxes	–	–	–	(1,880)	–
	–	–	–	(1,916)	168
Net income (loss)	$ 14,017	$ 10,998	$ 10,228	$ 3,985	$ (211)
Average number of common and common equivalent shares outstanding	5,111,790	4,989,588	4,955,553	4,881,859	4,870,425
Net income (loss) per common share:					
Primary					
Income (loss) from continuing operations	2.71	2.18	2.04	1.17	(.10)
Income (loss) on discontinued owned credit plan	–	–	–	(.39)	.03
Net income (loss)	$2.71	$2.18	$2.04	$ .78	$(.07)
Fully diluted					
Income (loss) from continuing operations	2.57	2.08	1.95	1.17	(.10)
Income (loss) on discontinued owned credit plan	–	–	–	(.39)	.03
Net income (loss)	$2.57	$2.08	$1.95	$ .78	$(.07)
Stores in Operation:					
Zayre Discount Department Stores	251	252	255	254	258
Hit or Miss	210	173	118	87	62
T.J. Maxx	19	10	–	–	–
On Stage/Nugent	33	31	36	34	36
Beaconway	32	34	42	44	46
Shoppers' City Supermarkets	8	9	10	10	10
Other Financial Data:					
Current assets	$ 302,402	$ 288,530	$ 258,227	$ 231,617	$ 233,459
Current liabilities	$ 145,062	$ 139,788	$ 117,994	$ 102,035	$ 108,701
Working capital	$ 157,340	$ 148,742	$ 140,233	$ 129,582	$ 124,758
Current ratio	2.08	2.06	2.19	2.27	2.15
Shareholders' equity	$ 142,543	$ 128,014	$ 117,030	$ 106,842	$ 102,840
Number of common shares outstanding at year-end	5,028,420	4,961,694	4,927,744	4,914,667	4,864,767
Equity per common share	$27.60	$25.05	$22.99	$20.98	$20.37

Exhibit 1
continued

Zayre Corp. Consolidated Balance Sheets		January 27, 1979	January 28, 1978*
		(In Thousands)	
ASSETS			
Current assets:			
	Cash	$ 22,977	$ 23,541
	Marketable securities	13,676	11,996
	Accounts receivable	5,526	4,735
	Merchandise inventories	253,999	242,324
	Prepaid expenses	6,224	5,934
	Total current assets	302,402	288,530
Property, at cost:			
	Land and buildings	40,440	40,077
	Leasehold costs and improvements	25,973	23,368
	Furniture, fixtures and equipment	96,874	90,922
		163,287	154,367
	Less accumulated depreciation	72,218	71,061
		91,069	83,306
Leased property under capital leases, principally real estate		124,268	121,325
	Less accumulated amortization	50,254	45,552
		74,014	75,773
Other assets		3,878	4,265
Goodwill		4,880	4,880
TOTAL ASSETS		**$476,243**	**$456,754**
LIABILITIES			
Current liabilities:			
	Current installments of long-term debt	$ 9,249	$ 9,994
	Accounts payable	73,299	76,124
	Accrued expenses and other current liabilities	46,403	38,767
	Federal and state income taxes	10,574	9,756
	Obligations under capital leases due within one year	5,537	5,147
	Total current liabilities	145,062	139,788
Long-term debt, exclusive of current installments:			
	General corporate debt	36,915	39,785
	Equipment promissory notes	36,323	31,796
	Real estate mortgages	26,913	27,241
Obligations under capital leases, less portion due within one year		87,649	88,930
Deferred income taxes		838	1,200
SHAREHOLDERS' EQUITY			
Series B cumulative convertible preferred stock, par value $1, authorized 60,000 shares, issued and outstanding 57,659 shares		58	58
Common stock, par value $1, authorized 8,000,000 shares, issued and outstanding 5,028,420 and 4,961,694 shares		5,028	4,962
Additional paid-in capital		16,995	16,399
Retained earnings		120,462	106,595
	Total shareholders' equity	142,543	128,014
TOTAL LIABILITIES AND SHAREHOLDERS' EQUITY		**$476,243**	**$456,754**

Exhibit 2

APRIL 1979

GREATER BOSTON REAL ESTATE BOARD

BUILDING OWNERS AND MANAGERS ASSOCIATION
OF GREATER BOSTON

SURBURBAN OFFICE OCCUPANCY SURVEY

Classification	# of Bldgs.	Total S.F Rentable Area	Total S.F Vacant Area	% of Vacancy	Total S.F Vacant & for Sublease	% Vacant and for Sublease	Total Government Occupancy	Government Occupancy as % Total Area
$12 and up	12	1,454,515	2,889	0.20	600	0.04	6,000	0.41
$10 to $11.99	25	1,671,231	38,790	2.32	--	--	82,170	4.92
$ 8 to $ 9.99	21	854,475	15,825	1.85	--	--	69,059	8.08
$ 7 to $ 7.99	2	7,400	--	--	--	--	--	--
$ 6 to $ 6.99	1	80,000	9.354	11.70	--	--	--	--
$ 5 to $ 5.99	4	80,129	--	--	--	--	--	--
$ 3 to $ 4.99	3	79,627	--	--	--	--	--	--
TOTAL	68	4,227,377	66,858	1.58	600	0.01	157,229	3.72

Exhibit 2
continued

APRIL 1979

GREATER BOSTON REAL ESTATE BOARD

BUILDING OWNERS AND MANAGERS ASSOCIATION
OF GREATER BOSTON

OFFICE OCCUPANCY SURVEY

Classification	# of Bldgs.	Total S.F Rentable Area	Total S.F Vacant Area	% of Vacancy	Total S.F Vacant & for Sublease	% Vacant and for Sublease	Total Government Occupancy	Government Occupancy as % Total Area
DOWNTOWN:								
$12 and up	13	6,261,065	264,804	4.23	—	—	41,468	0.66
$10 to $11.99	17	3,603,354	211,874	5.88	21,770	0.62	216,307	6.13
$8 to $9.99	22	1,822,526	121,313	6.66	11,100	0.70	99,885	6.26
$7 to $7.99	7	495,644	106,907	21.57	—	—	70,914	14.31
$6 to $6.99	5	376,788	28,000	7.43	—	—	200,000	53.08
$5 to $5.99	6	555,563	59,000	10.62	14,000	2.52	125,209	22.54
$3 to $4.99	2	559,243	12,087	2.16	1,800	0.32	281,000	50.25
TOTAL	72	13,674,183	803,985	5.88	99,140	0.73	1,034,783	7.57
BACK BAY:								
$12 and up	4	1,403,799	2,036	0.15	1,147	0.08	15,726	1.12
$10 to $11.99	5	3,262,829	166,323	5.10	—	—	1,000	0.03
$8 to $9.99	9	1,267,838	92,805	7.32	23,194	1.83	53,756	4.24
$7 to $7.99	4	553,664	263,494	47.59	—	—	31,000	5.60
$6 to $6.99	9	334,368	41,077	12.28	382	0.11	55,143	16.49
$5 to $5.99	2	169,395	141,042	83.26	—	—	3,353	1.98
$3 to $4.99	3	48,339	5,287	10.94	—	—	—	—
TOTAL	36	7,040,232	712,064	10.11	24,723	0.35	159,978	2.27
GRAND TOTAL	108	20,714,415	1,516,049	7.32	123,863	0.60	1,194,761	5.77

Exhibit 2
continued

APRIL 1979

GREATER BOSTON REAL ESTATE BOARD

BUILDING OWNERS AND MANAGERS ASSOCIATION
OF GREATER BOSTON

OFFICE OCCUPANCY SURVEY

Classification	Owner Occupied	Per Cent Owner Occupied	Total Store S.F. Area	Total Store Area Vacant	% Total Store Area Vacant
DOWNTOWN:					
$12 and up	1,030,022	16.45	272,935	16,914	6.20
$10 to $11.99	511,802	14.52	50,842	10,531	0.30
$ 8 to $ 9.99	174,733	9.59	161,574	9,264	5.73
$ 7 to $ 7.99	121,660	24.55	55,519	6,830	12.30
$ 6 to $ 6.99	5,200	1.38	57,311	5,339	9.32
$ 5 to $ 5.99	57,600	10.37	27,265	--	--
$ 3 to $ 4.99	10,800	1.93	10,500	--	--
TOTAL	1,911,817	14.00	635,946	48,878	7.69
BACK BAY:					
$12 and up	324,195	23.09	7,296	--	--
$10 to $11.99	1,613,782	49.46	10,266	--	--
$ 8 to $ 9.99	557,884	44.00	62,610	--	--
$ 7 to $ 7.99	2,400	0.43	29,600	6,180	20.88
$ 6 to $ 6.99	3,400	1.02	97,254	2,900	2.98
$ 5 to $ 5.99	25,000	1.48	5,706	--	--
$ 3 to $ 4.99	130	0.27	18,043	--	--
TOTAL	2,526,791	35.91	230,775	9,080	3.93
GRAND TOTAL	4,438,608	21.43	866,721	57,958	6.69

Exhibit 3

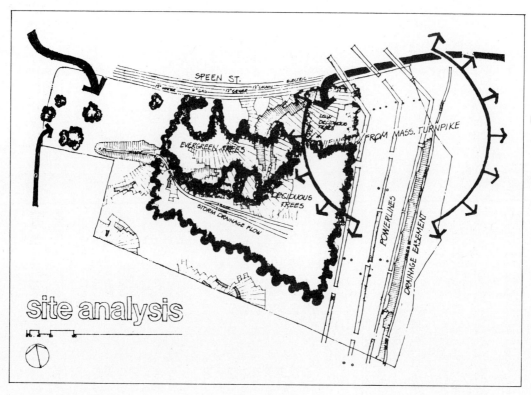

site analysis

drawing by: Michael Brooks

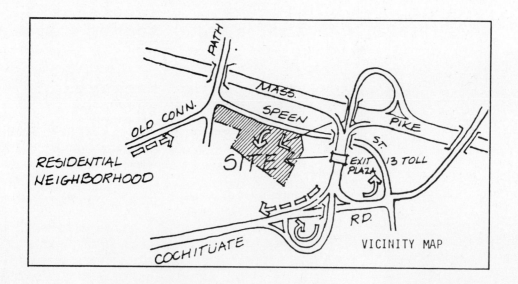

VICINITY MAP

Exhibit 4

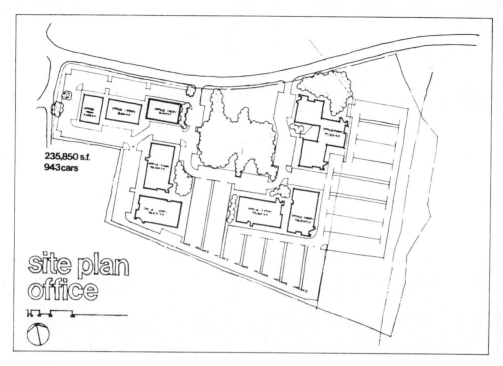

235,850 s.f.
943 cars

site plan
office

drawing by: Michael Brooks

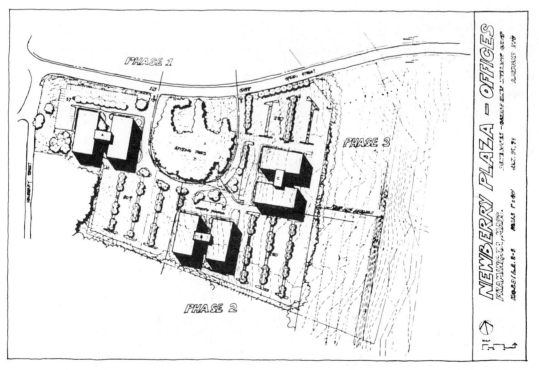

drawing by: Raymond Hsu

Exhibit 5

Gerald D. Hines Interests   Two Faneuil Hall Marketplace   Boston, Mass. 02109   617-723 3055

May 15, 1979

Mr. Stanley H. Feldberg
Chairman of the Executive Committee
Zayre Corporation
270 Cochituate Road
Framingham, MA

RE: The Site
      Speen Street
      Framingham

Dear Mr. Feldberg:

In keeping with our meeting of Monday, May 14, the following outlines the
acquisition and development program we discussed:

1.   A total acquisition price for the entire parcel would be established at
     $2,250,000 based on the master plan for 225,000 sf of office building in
     three phases. While we believe this master plan to be feasible, should
     further investigation result in physical or legal constraints which
     reduce the allowable square footage, the total price will be adjusted.
     Of course, if this adjustment significantly reduces the overall price, we
     recognize that Zayre must retain the right to reconsider this program.

2.   A development schedule would be established for a phased program of
     acquisition based on the initiation of construction of phase 1 in
     September 1979 and the initiation of construction of succeeding phases
     within one year of completion of the preceeding phase so long as that
     preceeding phase is producing income from at least 75% of the space. The
     intended maximum schedule would therefore be:

       phase 1 land takedown September 1979

       phase 2 land takedown June 1981

       phase 3 land takedown March 1983

     While we believe that the actual development program will proceed more
     rapidly than this, initiation of the schedule is subject to receipt of
     the necessary approvals and permits for construction of phase 1. We ask
     that the schedule be extended for any delay in the initiation of phase 1
     construction caused by elements beyond our control, but, in any event,
     Zayre shall retain the right to terminate this agreement if phase 1 has
     not begun by May 1980.

Exhibit 5
continued

Mr. S.H. Feldberg
May 15, 1979
Page two

Should any phase not achieve 75% income production within one year of completion, the succeeding phase would be given an extension of up to one year subject to an escalation in the scheduled land price for that phase; a suggested basis for that escalation is to set the price for the land under the extended phase so that it maintains the same proportion of total building value as did the initial phase. If this extension and land price escalation were required by phase 2, the land price for phase 3 would remain on the original basis so long as development returned to the original time schedule. Otherwise the land price for phase 3 would escalate in the same manner as phase 2.

3. Upon initiation of construction of each phase, we would purchase in cash the pro rata portion of the site based on our established overall price and scheduled total square footage. While we anticipate a three phase program in equal segments, we would appreciate the flexibility to adjust our purchase to reflect slightly smaller or larger buildings as the market may require. Naturally, the remaining parcels must retain the physical and legal attributes necessary for reasonable future development. Our agreement will provide that, should we be unable to proceed with succeeding phases in accordance with the established price and schedule, the development agreement would be terminated and we would lose all rights to the remaining site.

4. While it is intended that our acquisition and development proceed on a phased basis, it is understood that certain site improvements may have to be built with phase 1, which costs are applicable to phases 2 and 3. These costs shall be apportioned among the phases and that amount applicable to later phases shall be built by us during phase 1 and deducted from the phase 1 land price.

It is the intent of the proposal to maximize the land investment return to Zayre and realize this return in cash as quickly as development can progress. Our benefit, of course is the development of long-term investment in the buildings.

We look forward to your favorable response and a mutually beneficial relation-ship.

Yours very truly,

Richard W. Reynolds

RWR/tt

cc: J. Brad Griffith
    William McCall
    John J. Griffin

PART III
STRUCTURING THE OWNERSHIP

In Part I of this casebook, we became acquainted with the real estate industry and its participants. We were introduced to income property and property held or developed for sale. We examined closely the role of the entrepreneur and the basics of financial analysis. Cases featured a variety of land uses -- high and low density housing, as well as office -- and both new and rehabilitation construction.

In Part II, we built on this base, extending our financial analysis tools to include discounted cash flow analysis and accounting. We became familiar with urban and suburban land development and with the major forms of financing which may be used. We concluded with a case involving negotiation of a joint venture between a developer and a land owner.

In Part III, we will begin to apply the tools we have developed to determine the feasibility of the project. Cases in this Part III involve developers of a wide range of products with varied financial and organizational structures. We will study the elements of feasibility analysis -- design and market analysis -- and then study the various forms of organization available to the development project, and the implications of taxation. With these elements in hand, we will be able to negotiate the structure of the real estate venture and the allocation of risks and rewards. We will begin with a brief overview of feasibility analysis and negotiation.

I. FEASIBILITY ANALYSIS

Before the investor, land-owner or lender sits down with the developer to negotiate the terms of a proposed real estate deal, they will each want to study its **feasibility**. Will it work? And if so, what will be the rewards? What are the likelihood and consequences of failure?

Feasibility studies for real estate development involve much more than just financial analysis. Studies may involve the work of several different consulting disciplines, each examining a different aspect of a project.

Other studies are quite informal, involving primarily intuitive judgments and "back-of-the-envelope" numbers. Whether simple or elaborate, the feasibility study will always include at least two elements: physical and economic analyses. In many instances, the feasibility study must also include a third area, that of regulatory feasibility analysis.

These three areas may be further subdivided during a study, but are generally useful as areas where conclusions may be drawn about the basic questions -- Can it be built? (or is it suitable for its intended use?) Do the numbers work? Can it be approved? In the case of a fully developed formal feasibility study, these classifications generally represent the areas of concentration of several disciplines of study.

Even in the simple case in which the experienced practitioner is merely making judgments about a particular proposal, it is useful to structure one's thinking along similar lines. Following is a brief discussion of the three areas -- physical, economic and regulatory feasibility.

Physical Feasibility

Can it be built? Is it suitable for the intended use?

Physical feasibility analysis will normally involve the preparation and evaluation of initial schematic-design studies appropriate to the particular class of property. In the case of a land development, an analysis of the site will be carried out by an experienced civil engineer or landscape architect. Consideration will be given to access, utilities, topographic and soil conditions, and other factors which will influence the subdivision and/or site design.

In the case of a building development, the developer's initial site and marketing assessment will normally establish the desired building area and the various program elements, that is, the number of dwelling units, hotel rooms, rentable areas, parking spaces, amenities, etc. Architectural studies will illustrate the number of floors, massing, exterior materials, and perhaps also the intended structural system. Study of construction costs and structural feasibility may also be appropriate at this stage.

The level of detail in the physical feasibility study will depend on how experienced the principals are with the type of development. An unusual site or building type or a new or innovative product or design will usually require considerable study. A relatively standard real estate product with proven market acceptance may need little or no formal study. A simple judgment by an experienced developer about the capacity and marketability of a site may be all that is needed. However, even when a multifaceted formal study is conducted, the developer's judgment will be the key to its interpretation. Note 4, Location, Design, and Market Analysis provides a more detailed treatment of design analysis.

Economic Feasibility

Do the numbers work? Can the project be financed?

Economic feasibility is normally studied in the context of relatively simple numbers. As discussed in detail in Note 1, Static Financial Analysis, a project capital budget will normally be drawn up at an early stage. For this purpose, the feasibility study may include research into the major cost components, land and acquisition costs, construction costs and indirect development costs, such as professional services, financing and carrying costs.

In the case of income producing property, a setup will generally be prepared. The setup measures the net income produced by the property in the stabilized pro forma year. This will normally involve at least some systematic market research to determine comparable rent levels, operating expenses and real estate taxes, and the time it will take for new space to be absorbed in the market.

In the case of property developed for sale, the focus of a feasibility study will be on assessing the eventual sellout revenues and the pace of sales. Again, it is normal for a systematic study of comparable projects to be carried out at this stage. The revenue estimate will be compared with the capital budget to produce an assessment of profit margin.

In addition to the study of comparable property, the feasibility study may also involve research on both supply and demand for the particular type of property. While examining comparables, the market researcher will usually identify all present and proposed developments which may potentially be competitive with the project. With this measure of future supply, the researcher will then determine recent historical absorption rates and thus judge the time over which the supply will likely be absorbed.

In new and growing markets, where the historical absorption experience may be misleading, market researchers will often base a demand estimate on underlying demographic and economic measures. Such studies will variously focus on population growth, household formation, per-capita income and purchasing power, job creation trends, etc. A demand estimate of this kind should always be tested against the realities of the market. For example, if the economic analysis indicates rapid growth in retail sales, this should manifest itself in crowded parking lots in existing retail centers or in a rapid increase in new retail development proposals. The experienced practitioner will avoid reliance on a totally theoretical study of demand. Note 4, Location, Design, and Market Analysis provides a more detailed treatment of market analysis.

Regulatory Feasibility

Can it win approval from the regulatory authorities?

Sometimes the most important area of feasibility analysis lies in determining what approvals are necessary for the project and whether they may be obtained. Examples of this situation may be found in many American cities with prime downtown office districts. Locations near the center of business activity are generally preferred by office tenants, and thus, if approvals can be obtained, a new office tower there will be favored over one further removed. Similarly, if highway interchange access can be arranged, a low-value piece of warehouse or agricultural land will become a highly profitable retail center.

Regulatory authorities and public agencies are sometimes also directly involved in a project. For example, in assisted housing developments and in disposition of surplus government property, the governmental decision-making process becomes the center of development activities. At other times, the regulatory process is more peripheral in importance.

Feasibility studies in this area usually center on zoning and infrastructure approvals. Zoning laws are enacted by local government for various purposes. Zoning laws may regulate the uses to which land may be put, the density, height and other features of proposed buildings, parking, sewage and other waste-disposal facilities, and the process of obtaining permits. Even if a proposal is fully in compliance with zoning, the permitting process may be extensive. Where a project does not comply in every respect, a zoning "variance" may be needed.

Infrastructure -- the road and utility networks which serve the larger community -- is generally provided by public agencies and authorities. In a locality where growth is occurring, new road, water and sewer projects are expected to be carried out over time. Even in mature urban areas, new and replacement facilities must continuously be put in place. Coordination of these projects with the needs of new developments is an important problem for both the agencies and the developers.

Regulatory feasibility studies are often carried out by lawyers and design consultants. These professionals will often concentrate on a particular land use type and a particular locality in an effort to be effective in representing their clients. Because a great deal of specialization exists in this area, selection of the appropriate consultant will depend greatly on the particular situation. In situations where the regulatory processes are central to the success of a development proposal, experienced developers will attach considerable importance to this area of study.

Having done some formal study or at least some thinking in each of the major areas of feasibility analysis, the developer can now make an overall assessment. Will the project work? If not, can it be altered to make it work? From this study, the developer will formulate a development proposal which he or she believes is feasible. This proposal will then be presented in a positive light to potential lenders, equity investors or property owners who may be in a position to participate.

II.   NEGOTIATING THE VENTURE

With their own feasibility studies or assessments complete, the land-owner, investor or lender is now in a position to negotiate the venture arrangements with the developer. Within the scope of this brief overview, we cannot deal thoroughly with the topic of negotiation *per se*. Approaches to negotiation vary widely, and the subject is broad enough to require book-length treatment. The interested reader is referred to *Getting to Yes*[1], an excellent short treatment of the subject. For an interesting contrast, refer to *Winning through Intimidation*[2] by Robert Ringer. It is perhaps most important in understanding the art of negotiation to remember its objective -- to reach agreement.

Reaching agreement requires a meeting of the minds. This is not always easy. Consider a negotiation between two small boys over who will own a single piece of candy. Two developers sometimes will negotiate in a similar vein, because each wants a fundamentally different result from the other. A developer and a lender, by contrast, may find it much easier to negotiate agreement, since in at least one important respect both want basically the same result.

The boys negotiating over the candy must find and focus on other interests in

---

[1] Roger Fisher and William Ury, *Getting to Yes* (New York, N.Y.: Penguin Books, 1981).

[2] Robert Ringer, *Winning through Intimidation* (New York, N.Y.: Fawcett, 1979).

order to reach agreement. For example, one may not really be hungry at the moment, and would be willing to accept a future consideration in return for relinquishing his claim on the present candy. Instead of viewing the situation as a "zero-sum" game, with one winner and one loser, success in negotiation produces two winners -- both boys are happy, even though only one got the candy.

Components of Agreement

Achieving a realistic focus on interests is often the key to negotiating successfully the real estate venture. In a typical deal, three general categories of interests must be considered and agreed upon: money, risk and control. Once these items have been negotiated, they must be recorded in the form of a written agreement.

Any written agreement, even an abbreviated letter of intent, will contain a number of written descriptions. These will set out the type of agreement and the basic intent of the undertaking. As discussed in Note 5, Organization and Taxation, agreements may reflect a particular ownership structure, such as a partnership or joint venture. Other types of agreement are also important, including the Option to Purchase, the Purchase and Sale Agreement, the Lease, Master Lease or Ground Lease, the Mortgage Loan and even the Management Contract. Each of these agreements may be used as the vehicle for the developer and investor to initiate or carry on the real estate venture.

The parties to the agreement will be identified. The property involved will be described, together with any encumbrances, such as mortgages, easements, etc. A surveyed plan and legal description are often attached. Longer agreements will often contain a whole series of definitions, which will specify the meaning of terms used in the agreement. Finally, signatures and the date of the agreement will be provided. With the basic descrip-

tions complete, the written agreement must serve to record the negotiation of the three categories of interests.

Money. Agreements will always specify the allocation of consideration or interests in money. The most conspicuous item, interest in profits, is only one of a number of money interests which must be specified. In a partnership, interests may be specified in profit and loss, cash flow, and in proceeds of refinancing or sale. Other cash payments may be made between and among parties in various forms, such as loan advances, contributions of capital, purchase price or deposits toward purchase price, interest or rent payments, or commissions or fees. Various contingent payments may be involved. Finally, liabilities may be assumed as a component of consideration.

An agreement will always specify the time for performance. It will state when the deed will be delivered, the construction completed, or the guarantee expires, etc. Timing of payments is important of course, as are accruals or other deferred payment provisions. Agreements may also set forth conditions of performance of the buyer or borrower. A Purchase and Sale Agreement may be subject to the buyer obtaining financing, for example.

Risks. Many provisions of a real estate venture agreement deal with the allocation of risks. The major risks include those of construction, marketing and financing. Security interests, such as mortgages or ground ownership, afford a means of allocating broad categories of risk.

Specific risks may be allocated by stating a condition to performance. For example, by accepting a Purchase and Sale Agreement with a financing contingency, the seller of a property is assuming the risk that the buyer may be unable to obtain financing.

Other means of allocation of specific risks include warranties and representations. The developer may guarantee construction completion or agree to advance funds needed in the event of a slow rentup, for example. Warranties and guarantees may be backed up by security interests in other property or assets, as well as by mortgages or ground ownership. Unforeseen conditions may also be dealt with in the agreement. The seller of an existing building may warrant it to be in sound structural condition, or may represent that no leases or hazardous waste exist, for example.

Control. The final major area of interests is the allocation of control. Agreements will generally state the management responsibilities of the parties. Who does what? This may be done along functional lines -- construction, marketing, accounting, etc. -- or by specifying management control of the entity itself. Liabilities of general and limited partners will be set forth, as well as any other limitations of liability.

An agreement may also allocate control of specific items. This can be done by reserving specific approval or veto rights. It may also be done by specifying voting rights and interests and providing a forum for exercise of those rights, such as formal partners' meetings, a board of directors, or a management committee. Other provisions may reserve particular approvals for financing, leases, or other important items.

The list of items contained in the above paragraphs is, of course, only a beginning.

But it does give an idea of how many areas there are in which interests will be found during negotiation of the real estate venture. Any and all of these interests may be as important to the success of a particular negotiation as the more conspicuous interest in profit.

Closing the Deal

Developers and lenders, investors or property owners must devote considerable effort to exploring each other's interests. Since each will have independently studied the feasibility of the development, their points of view as to various risks and rewards will necessarily be different. These differences provide opportunities for the parties to add value to the venture. A developer who is quite comfortable in his assessment of costs may find it relatively easy to eliminate what may be a major investor concern.

The combination of differing interests and differing viewpoints affords an almost endless list of possibilities for reaching agreement. It should be noted that even if the parties reach agreement early, and ignore many of their interests, these interests will arise subsequently as legal documents are prepared or as events transpire. There are few shortcuts in this process, and patience and thoroughness will be rewarded. While it is always possible for parties in a negotiation to end up in the position of the two boys and their candy, they certainly have a great deal to discuss before reaching this conclusion.

Case 8

Brea Specialty Center

This case was prepared by John McMahan, Lecturer in Business Administration at the Stanford University Graduate School of Business. Reprinted with the permission of Stanford University Graduate School of Business, (c) 1976 by the Board of Trustees of the Leland Stanford Junior University.

The letter from the general partner had come as a complete shock to Bill Reynolds, and he still wasn't certain what course of action to take. Bill was a very successful entrepreneur who had recently become a limited partner in Specialty Center Associates, a group that had been formed to develop specialty shopping centers throughout Southern California. After months of searching, the group had optioned the land for its first project (a specialty center in Brea, California) at a price of $820,000. Additional months of planning had gone into the project, and construction was scheduled to start in January 1976.

Now, in early December 1975, the general partner had sent Bill and the other limited partners a letter indicating that they had been approached by a major insurance company to develop an office building for its Southern California regional headquarters. The partners were being asked to vote on whether to accept the office building proposal or proceed with the specialty center project. Bill began to go over the background of the events that had led up to the current situation.

THE PROPERTY

The site for the proposed project was located in the city of Brea, California (see Exhibit 1). The property consisted of approximately 12.5 acres of gently rolling land at the northeast quadrant of Imperial Highway and the Orange Freeway (see Exhibit 2). It was bordered by the Orange Freeway on the west, Greenbriar Lane on the north, Loftus Flood Control Channel on the east, and a 9.84-acre site for a 125,000 square foot convenience shopping center on the south. To the west across the freeway, Homart, a subsidiary of Sears, was developing a 1,000,000+ square foot enclosed mall as a regional shopping center (see Exhibit 3).

The property was zoned GC-PD (General Commercial, Precise Development) which permitted a broad range of commercial uses, subject to obtaining approval of a precise development plan for the site. All utilities were available to the site, and soil tests indicated that the property was buildable.

ECONOMIC CHARACTERISTICS OF THE BREA AREA

Brea was located in Orange County, the fastest growing major metropolitan area in California. Although there had been a general slowdown in population growth in Southern California, only a slight slowing had occurred in Orange County. Population projections indicated Orange County would continue to be among the fastest growing areas in California (see Exhibit 4).

The cities of Brea, Placentia and Yerba Linda were growing considerably faster than the Orange County average. Because these communities had a substantial amount of undeveloped land area, higher-than-average rates of population growth were expected to continue into the future.

The major types of employment of persons residing within a five-mile radius of the subject site were professional and technical, followed by craftsmen, foremen, and operatives (see Exhibit 5). In 1970, the median family income of these residents was $13,314, higher than the average of Orange or Los Angeles County; 9.6% of the residents made over $25,000 annually. These residents also had a higher average level of education than the average resident of 0range or Los Angeles County.

Per-capita retail sales for Orange County had been increasing each year since 1969, although a portion of this increase was attributable to inflation (see Exhibit 6). Per-capita sales in selected shopper goods categories and restaurant sales were considerably lower in Brea than in other communities or the county as a whole. This was generally attributed to the lack of facilities offering this type of merchandise and to fewer first-class restaurants in the Brea area (see Exhibit 7).

THE PROPOSED SPECIALTY CENTER

Specialty Center Associates was composed of a group of investors who had been searching for some new, innovative area of real estate investment where they could develop investment "packages" that would work well in a variety of locations. After analyzing several possibilities such as mini-warehouses, racquetball courts and others, they selected specialty retail centers.

Characteristics of Specialty Centers

Specialty shopping centers were a relatively new concept in shopping development that had gained rapid acceptance in many parts of California and other states. Most specialty centers contained 100,000 to 200,000 square feet, with retailers involved in women's wear, gifts, household wares, jewelry, and other specialty retail fields. There were often several outlets carrying the same type of merchandise in each center. In addition to the shops, there were usually two or three restaurants. Typically, specialty centers had no "anchor" tenant such as a department store, variety store or supermarket. There also were very few national chain stores, such as were common in regional or community centers. Most of the retailers were local or regional, generally selling relatively high-priced merchandise. For this reason, specialty centers generally appealed to higher-income families.

Another characteristic of specialty centers was that they were developed around some type of architectural "theme." Many of the early specialty centers had been developed in converted buildings which provided the theme (e.g.. Ghirardelli Square in San Francisco). Tourist expenditures usually provided a high proportion of their sales volume.

More recently, several specialty centers had been developed in non-tourist, suburban locations, directed at higher-income residents from the surrounding area. In Southern California, these included Lido Village in Newport Beach, South Coast Village in Costa Mesa, Village Fair in Laguna Beach, Villa Marina Center in Marina Del Rey, and Plaza De Oro in Encino. Most of these centers enjoyed high occupancy at relatively high rents per square foot (see Exhibit 8).

Design Concept for the Proposed Center

The design concept for the Brea Center called for a split-level center around an open mall (see Exhibit 9). The lower mall level consisted of 68,000 square feet of gross leasable area, including 10,000 square feet of mall restaurants. (Gross and net areas were the same in this center.) The upper mall level had 28,000 square feet of gross leasable area for shops plus two 8,000 square foot detached restaurants. The mall area contained 8,000 square feet on the upper level and a 25,000 square foot "court" on the lower level.

Construction was to be textured reinforced concrete masonry with concrete tilt-up retaining walls in portions of the lower level. All storefronts were to be developed by the individual tenants with an allowance by the developer. In addition to the building, 338,000 square feet of land area was to be devoted to 800 parking stalls, walkways, and landscaping. Construction was expected to be completed by December 1976.

Development Costs

A construction cost estimator had reviewed the plans and estimated that the project could be built for the following costs assumed by the landlord:

	$ per square foot
Building Shell	16.00
Tenant Areas	
Mall Shops	7.00
Mall Restaurants	15.00
Mall Finish	12.00
Free-Standing Restaurants	50.00

In addition to these construction costs, the developer was also allowing $7.50 per square foot for tenant finish in both the shop and restaurant areas. These were:

	$ per square foot
Drywall	$.35
Acoustical Ceiling	.65
Toilet Room	1.25
Storefronts	2.00
Ceiling Fixtures	1.75
Paint-Interior Walls	.25
Carpet	1.25
Total	$7.50

There were also several other costs related to the construction program: $130,000 for landscaping; $420,000 for grading and all other site development costs; $249,000 for developer's overhead; and $150,000 for architecture and engineering.

Exhibit 10 outlines the proposed tenant mix for the center. The minimum annual rental income from these tenants was projected as follows:

	$ per square foot
Mall Shops	$8.00
Mall Restaurants	9.00
Free-Standing Restaurants	9.50

All tenants would also pay "overages" based on a percentage of annual gross sales, depending upon the type of operations (see Exhibit 11). Vacancy was expected to average 15% during the first year of operations (1977) and then stabilize at 7% thereafter.

Under the terms of the proposed lease, all tenants were required to maintain the interiors of the stores, including air conditioning equipment, storefronts, and all doors and windows. In addition, maintenance of exterior wall areas and room maintenance over the stores would be allocated to the tenants. The annual stabilized expenses to be paid by the building owners included the following:

Management Fee	$35,000
Promotion (Merchant's Assoc.)	10,000
Property Taxes (Owner's Share)	15,500
Total	$60,500

Both retail sales and expenses were expected to increase an average of 8% annually after the second year of operations (1978).

A loan commitment for $5,600,000 had been secured from a pension fund. The terms of the loan called for an interest rate of 9%, and a 30-year amortization with a balloon payment at the end of 16 years. The charge for the commitment was 1.5%. Construction financing was available at the same interest rate, but it would cost an additional point.

There were also some other interim costs that would be experienced during the construction period. These included $67,000 for property taxes; $32,000 for legal and accounting; $200,000 for leasing commissions; $50,000 for promotion; and $25,000 miscellaneous, including the land option.

THE LIMITED PARTNERSHIP AGREEMENT

The limited partnership agreement for the Brea project was relatively simple and straightforward. The limited partners were to put up 100% of the equity funds required in exchange for 75% interest in the partnership. The remaining 25% was to go to the general partner in exchange for developing the project. The same formula was to be followed for each of the centers to be developed. All profits and losses, as well as cash flow, were to be split proportionately. Upon sale or refinancing, all proceeds were to go to the limited partners until they got their capital back. The next $350,000 was to go to the general partner with any additional proceeds split proportionately.

The property was expected to be sold at the beginning of the ninth year (1985) based on the 1984 project income capitalized at 8.5%. Sales expenses were expected to be 3.0%. Each of the limited partners and the general partner were in the 50% tax bracket and had sufficient other income to utilize any tax shield. Improvements were to be depreciated over 15 years, utilizing the straight line method. A replacement reserve of $20,000 annually would be charged to the project and would be increased by 8% annually beginning in 1978.

THE OFFICE BUILDING PROPOSAL

In early November 1975, the general partner was approached by a major national insurance company with a proposal to lease 100,000 square feet in a new building to be developed on the subject property. The annual rent would be $6.90 per square foot for a period of 15 years. They agreed to provide a loan of $4,000,000 for 30 years at 9%. They would also arrange the construction financing at the same rate for one point.

The general partner immediately called in the architect and cost estimator to determine how large an office facility could be developed on the site. Two weeks later, a preliminary plan was ready which indicated that a ten-story building with 148,000 gross square feet of space could be developed on the site. This would provide the 100,000 square feet of leasable space for the insurance company, plus 41,500 square feet of speculative net rentable space for other tenants. The cost estimator then came up with the development costs below (assuming a one-year construction period):

Site Development	$654,900
Construction	
Building:	
148ksf @ $21.00	$3,108,000
Tenant Finish:	
41.5ksf @ $8.50	352,800
Developer Overhead:@ 3.5%	144,000
Contingency:@ 5%	213,000
	$3,817,800
Interim	
Property Taxes	$20,000
Insurance	5,000
Interest	180,000
Finance Fees	40,000
Architecture	205,000
Legal Fees	15,000
Leasing Commissions	83,600
Promotion	100,000
Miscellaneous	10,000
	$658,600
Total Project Costs	$5,131,300

The general partner made some pre- liminary checks in the area and deter- mined that the speculative space could probably be rented for approximately $8.40 per square foot. He estimated that the speculative space could rent up to 95% in the first year and thereafter maintain that level. All leases would be for five years with a five-year option at market rent. All tenants were expected to exer- cise their options. Tenants would pay for any refurbishing.

Operating expenses for the insurance company's space would be approximately $150,000 annually and $105,000 for the speculative space at 95% occupancy. Ten- ants would pay for any increase in operat- ing expense over the base year. (The an- nual growth in market rates was expected to be 8% beginning in 1978.) Annual con- tributions to replacement reserves would be $15,000. Operating expense and re- placement reserves were expected to in- crease at 8% beginning in 1978. The building and other capitalized items would be depreciated over 15 years utilizing the straight-line method. Since the insurance company was under considerable pressure to get started on its regional headquarters, they put a deadline of December 31, 1975, on acceptance of their proposal.

The information about the insurance company's proposal had been spelled out in a letter from the general partner to all of the limited partners. In the letter, the general partner recommended accepting the insurance company's proposal, with no major changes in the partnership agree- ment. In order to meet the insurance company's December 31 deadline, the general partner asked the limited partners to return their voting slips prior to De- cember 15. Regardless of the alternative selected, all cash from the limited part- ners would be due by December 31, 1975.

Bill was very confused over the entire matter. He had become quite intrigued with the specialty center concept and knew that if they didn't proceed on the Brea site their whole program would be set back months, if not years. On the other hand, the specialty center had con- siderable risks, particularly when com- pared to an office building with a strong anchor tenant for 70% of the space. Bill knew he could drop out of the partnership altogether, should he so desire, but he had set aside $300,000 cash and wanted to get it invested in real estate as soon as possi- ble. (He expected to earn 15% IRR on pas- sive investments.)

EXHIBITS

1. Location map.

2. Site map.

3. Aerial view.

4. Population projections for Orange County.

5. Census data.

6. Orange County -- per capita sales.

7. Brea market area sales potential.

8. Suburban specialty centers.

9. Brea specialty center plans.

10. Tentative summary of tenant mix.

11. Lease summary.

12. Office building survey.

QUESTIONS FOR DISCUSSION

1. How should Bill Reynolds respond?

2. Which project would you recommend? Why?

3. What is the upside potential of each proposal?

4. What are the downside risks?

Exhibit 1

LOCATION OF PROJECT

Exhibit 2

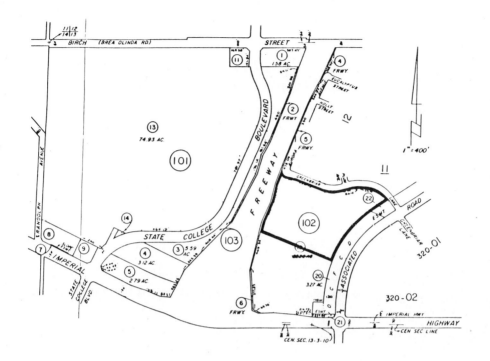

Exhibit 3

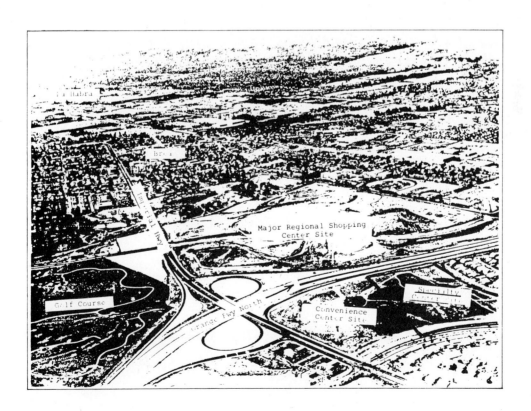

Exhibit 4

Population Projections for Orange County

Population
Growth

	Population			% Increase
	1960	1970	1974*	1970–1974
Brea	8,487	18,447	22,179	20%
Fullerton . . .	56,180	85,826	89,980	5%
Placentia . . .	5,861	21,948	29,832	36%
Yerba Linda . .	N/A	11,856	20,697	75%
La Habra . . .	25,136	41,350	43,606	5%
Anaheim	104,184	166,701	187,382	11%
Orange County .	703,925	1,420,386	1,646,314	16%

Source: U.S. Census and
Orange County Progress Report

* Estimated January 1, 1974

	Population		
Area Covered	1970 Actual	1974 Estimated	1977 Projected
Five-Minute Driving Time	71,600	87,000	102,500
Ten-Minute Driving Time	272,800	305,000	350,000
Five-Mile Radius	174,000	203,000	234,000

Exhibit 5

Census Data

Employment Profile

Field of Employment	5-Mile Radius	No. Orange County	Orange County	L.A. County
Professional, Technical	22.5%	18.1%	19.8%	17.1%
Manager, Administrator	12.0%	9.7%	10.8%	9.2%
Clerical	18.0%	18.3%	17.7%	21.2%
Sales	9.6%	9.3%	9.8%	7.8%
Craftsman, Foreman, Operative	20.6%	25.8%	25.3%	25.7%
Others	17.3%	18.8%	18.6%	19.0%

Source: U.S. Census and
         Los Angeles Times Marketing Research Department

Family Income
1970

	5-Mile Radius	No. Orange County	Orange County	L.A. County
Median Family Income	$13,314	$12,414	$12,245	$10,972
Under $10,000	30.0%	34.1%	35.1%	43.9%
$10,000 to $15,000	30.2%	33.0%	31.2%	27.7%
$15,000 to $25,000	30.2%	26.8%	26.5%	21.3%
$25,000 and over	9.6%	6.1%	7.2%	7.1%

Source: U.S. Census

Education Profile
(persons 25 and over)

	5-Mile Radius	No. Orange County	Orange County	L.A. County
Less than Four Years High School	27.1%	32.2%	29.5%	38.0%
Four Years High School . .	33.6%	36.8%	34.9%	32.7%
One to Three Years College	20.4%	18.0%	19.8%	16.6%
Four Years College or More	19.8%	13.0%	15.8%	12.7%

Source: U.S. Census and
Los Angeles Times Marketing Research Department

Exhibit 6

Orange County – Per Capita Sales

Per Capita Retail Sales

	1969	1971	1973
Anaheim	$2,386	$2,425	$2,682
Buena Park	1,772	2,141	2,410
Fullerton	2,510	2,794	3,500
La Habra	2,197	2,492	2,851
Orange	2,491	2,773	3,859
Orange County . . .	2,029	2,238	2,856
Los Angeles County	1,997	2,122	2,663

1974 Per Capita Annual Retail Sales

Community	Apparel	General Merchandise	Eating and Drinking Places	Total
Brea	$ 7	$ 36	$152	$195
Fullerton	101	419	288	808
Placentia	29	126	142	297
La Habra	135	511	277	923
Anaheim	117	247	377	741
Orange County	113	439	296	848

Exhibit 7

Brea Market Area Sales Potential

The purpose of this analysis is to determine the extent to which the Brea Market Area is able to support the Brea Regional Mall and the Brea specialty shopping center. The basic data were supplied by the State Board of Equalization (sales volumes), Orange County Planning Department (population) and Hobart Development Co. and Village Mall Associates (square footage).

An analysis of these data indicate that there is substantial support in the Brea Market Area for the planned facilities.

I.   Existing Voids in the Brea Market Area

A physical inspection of retail facilities in the market area reveals that there are few retail establishments in the area other than those associated with convenience centers. This is born out in the retail sales of the cities of Brea, Placentia and Yerba Linda. In fact, the retail sales level in Yerba Linda is so low that the State Department of Equalization does not break down sales by merchandise lines for this city. The sales volumes for Brea and Placentia illustrate that a substantial portion of the available retail business is being lost to other areas.

TABLE I

COMPARATIVE PER PERSON RETAIL SALES
1974

Merchandise Lines	Placentia/Brea	Orange Co. Average
Apparel	$19.01	$113
Gen. Mdse.	84.65	438
Household	22.29	101
TOTALS	$125.95	$625

Sources: State Board of Equalization; Orange Co. Planning Department.

Exhibit 7
continued

Thus, in the cities of Brea and Placentia, at least $500 per person in department store type merchandise dollars is being lost to other areas and would theoretically be available for the two centers being planned.

II. Potential Sales/Regional and Specialty Shopping Center

In order to understand the impact of the planned centers in the Brea market area, we have estimated the spending power of the area and compared it with the number of square feet being planned by merchandise lines within the DSTM categories. The sales per person data are based on Orange County's averages as these data are known. The actual per person sales are undoubtedly higher than the Orange County averages because the median family incomes of the Brea market area are higher. Table II which follows shows the total potential sales by merchandise lines for the Brea market area.

TABLE II

MARKET AREA SALES POTENTIAL
(1977)

Mdse Lines	Orange County[1] Total Sales (millions $)	Orange County[2] Sales/Person	Total Market Area[3] Sales Potential (millions $)
Apparel	$ 187	$113	$ 26
Gen. Mdse.	722	438	102
Jewelry & Gifts	49	30	7
Specialty Shops	231	140	33
Household	167	101	24
TOTAL DSTM	$1,356	$822	$192

Sources: [1] State Board of Equalization, State of California.

[2] Orange County Planning Department - Population 1.65 mil.

[3] Larry Brown, Shattuck & Co.
Market area population: 243,000 x sales/person.

Exhibit 7
continued

The regional and specialty centers cannot expect to capture all these sales as there are existing facilities on the perimeter of the market area which will compete for these dollars. The capture rates in Table III below are estimates based on the competitive facilities presently existing in La Habra, Fullerton and Anaheim and the typical square footage devoted to the merchandise lines in the planned centers.

TABLE III

REGIONAL & SPECIALTY SHOPPING CENTERS
MARKET AREA SALES CAPTURE RATE

Mdse Lines	Market area[1] Sales Volume (millions $)	Capture Rate	Potential Sales Reg. & Spec. Centers (millions $)
Apparel	$ 26	60%	$ 16
Gen. Mdse	102	70%	71
Jewelry & Gifts	7	50%	4
Specialty Shops	33	60%	20
Household	24	40%	10
TOTAL DSTM	$192	63%	$121

Sources: [1] From Table II.

[2] Based on "pull power" of the centers and competing facilities.

Exhibit 7
continued

The last step in the anaysis is to divide the sales
potential by the number of square feet planned to determine the
potential sales per square feet of space the merchants may
expect to achieve.

TABLE IV

REGIONAL & SPECIALTY SHOPPING CENTERS
ESTIMATED SQUARE FEET BY MERCHANDISE LINES

Mdse Lines	Regional[1] # Sq. Ft.	Specialty[2] # Sq. Ft.	Total # Sq. Ft.
Apparel	133,000	20,000	153,000
Gen. Mdse	590,000	–	590,000
Jewelry & Gifts	30,000	10,000	40,000
Specialty Shops	87,000	28,000	115,000
Household	25,000	12,000	37,000
TOTAL SQ. FT. (Excluding Restaurants)	865,000	70,000	935,000

Sources: [1] Based on "typical regional centers.

[2] Preliminary Brea Specialty Shopping Center plans.

Square footage estimates for the regional center are based
on typical centers in Los Angeles and Orange County.

Exhibit 7
continued

TABLE V

POTENTIAL SALES VOLUME/SQ. FT.
REGIONAL & SPECIALTY SHOPPING CENTER

Mdse	Sales Potential[1] (millions $)	# Sq. Ft.[2]	Sales Potential Per Sq. Ft.
Apparel	$ 16	153,000	$105
Gen. Mdse	71	590,000	120
Jewelry & Gifts	4	40,000	100
Specialty Shops	20	115,000	174
Household	10	37,000	270
TOTAL DSTM	$121	935,000	$129

Sources: [1] Table III

[2] Table IV

Thus, after using low sales per person figures and relatively low capture rates the sales dollar volumes for the merchants of the regional and specialty centers are potentially high.

III. Restaurant Sales

There are presently seven (7) full service dinner house type restaurants within the market area. Assuming these restaurants are typical they would expect to average about 1.2 million dollars in sales each year or a total of $8,400,000 in business. The Brea market area has potential for $38,000,000 in sales for restaurants serving liquor. (Estimated population 234,000 x $162.00 per person = $38 million). Thus, the proposed restaurants in the specialty shopping center have almost $30,000,000 of restaurant sales potential to draw upon. (List of major restaurants in the market area follows).

Exhibit 7
continued

MAJOR FULL SERVICE RESTAURANTS

BREA MARKET AREA

(1) The California Restaurant
     1400 So. Harbor Blvd.
     La Habra   870-0910

(2) Marie Callender's
     126 Yerba Linda
     Placentia   996-0500

(3) Reubens (Coco's)
     501 N. State College Blvd.
     Fullerton   870-0433

(4) Velvet Turtle
     1450 No. Harbor Blvd.
     Fullerton   871-9340

(5) Rembrandt's
     909 E. Yorba Linda
     Placentia   524-2090

(6) Red Onion
     1446 N. Harbor Blvd.
     Fullerton   870-6150

(7) Dal Rae Restaurant
     2151 No. Harbor Blvd.
     Fullerton   870-1711

Mall restaurants are expected to experience sales of $125 per
square foot beginning in the stabilized year (1977).

Exhibit 8

Suburban Specialty Centers

PROPERTY NAME
AND LOCATION:

Lido Village
3420 #4 Via Oporto
Newport Beach, California

PROPERTY
DESCRIPTION:

This one and partial two-level center features old
European architecture and opened in July 1973. The
center consists of a partial redevelopment of numerous
old shops on a tree lined brick street. The new
section contains a five-level parking structure with
free validation from most shops.

Gross Leasable Area . . . . . 103,000 sq. ft.

TENANT MIX:

Three restaurants, including The Warehouse, men's and
women's shops, boutiques, gifts, specialty food market, etc.

LEASE DATA:

80% to 85% leased at an average rent of $12.00 per
square foot. Upstairs rents are from $0.60 to $1.20
per square foot less than the ground floor rents.

TENANT
EXPENSES:

Tenant pays all expenses except base year taxes.

Exhibit 8
continued

PROPERTY NAME
AND LOCATION:

        South Coast Village
        3800 Plaza Drive
        Costa Mesa, California

PROPERTY
DESCRIPTION:

Open walkways, with a winding cobblestone street, provide access to the single-level mall shops and to the three-level mercantile building.

This center opened in August 1973. Buildings are of highly stylized contemporary design with extensive use of natural wood siding, complemented by wood shingled roofs. Landscaping is moderate.

Gross Leasable Area . . . . . 130,000 square feet

Total Number of Units 60

Parking Ratio . . . . 4.3 spaces/1,000 square feet of G.L.A.

TENANT MIX:

Several restaurants represent 27% of the square foot area , with men's and women's apparel shops, jewelry, shoes, housewares, plant shop and art oriented shops comprising the remainder of the center.

LEASE DATA:

This center is approximately 90% leased. Average minimum rent is $8.50 per square foot.

TENANT EXPENSES:

Tenant is responsible for all expenses including taxes, insurance, utilities and common area maintenance.

Exhibit 8
continued

PROPERTY NAME
AND LOCATION:

      Village Fair
      1100 South Coast Highway
      Laguna Beach, California

PROPERTY
DESCRIPTION:

This two-level with subterranean parking open mall specialty center opened in December 1974. The Old World English theme is executed through use of heavy textured stucco with natural wood detailing and double hung wood window sash.

Gross Leasable Area . . . . . 41,000 square feet

Total Number of Units 65

Average Store Size . . . . . 630 square feet

Site Size . . . . 2 acres

Parking Ratio . . . . 5.61 spaces/1,000 square feet G.L.A.

TENANT MIX:

Three dinner houses and one fast food outlet, heavy representation of galleries and gift shop appealing to the tourist trade, limited number of men's and women's apparel shops, very limited number of shops featuring household specialty items.

LEASE DATA:

95% leased with waiting list for main level shop space.

Average minimum rents are from $10.00 to $12.00 per square foot annually.

TENANT EXPENSES:

Tenants pay tax increases over base year, utilities, and pro rata share of common area maintenance.

Exhibit 8
continued

PROPERTY NAME
AND LOCATION:

       Villa Marina Center
       Northeast Corner Lincoln Boulevard
       and Marina Freeway
       Marina Del Ray, California

PROPERTY
DESCRIPTION:

       This single-level, open mall, specialty/convenience
       center opened in October 1973. The architectural
       design is slightly nautical in nature with concrete
       block construction and wide overhangs above store
       entries, decorated with "pier" piling supports and
       heavy wood beams.

       Gross Leasable Area . . . . . 149,750 square feet

       Total Number of Units 41

       Site Size . . . . 13 acres

       Parking Ratio 4.48 spaces/1,000
                               square feet G.L.A.

TENANT MIX:

       Anchor tenants include a Sav-On drug, Vons grocery
       market and a United Artists theater. Included in the
       remaining tenancies are several restaurants, a limited
       number of apparel shops, plus numerous hobby, crafts
       and leisure time oriented shops; also community service
       facilities with a laundry, cleaners, print shop and
       travel agency.

LEASE DATA:

       Percent Leased 100%

       Rents . . . . $5.40 to $10.00
                               per square foot

       Average Minimum Rent . . . . $6.35 per square foot

TENANT MIX:

       Tenants are responsible for all expenses including
       taxes, insurance, common area maintenance, plus
       interior and exterior maintenance.

Exhibit 8
continued

PROPERTY NAME
AND LOCATION:

> Plaza De Oro
> 17201 Ventura Boulevard
> Encino, California

PROPERTY
DESCRIPTION:

> This one and two-level specialty center opened in mid-
> 1973. Extensive landscaping and Spanish architecture
> with rough timbers and mission tile roofs characterize
> the center with an early California theme. Surface
> parking is provided along periphery of the site with
> offsite parking along Ventura Boulevard.
>
> Gross Leasable Area . . . . . 61,237 square feet
>
> Total Number of Units 30
>
> Site Size . . . . 4.91 acres
>
> Parking Ratio 4.49 spaces/1,000
> square feet G.L.A.

TENANT MIX:

> Tenants consist of fashionable dress shops and
> boutiques; men's clothing, both traditional and high
> fashion; two unique restaurants offering indoor and
> outdoor dining; a tobacconist; several shoe shops; gift
> shops with imports from European countries; a jewelry
> shop offering distinctive costume jewelry and semi-
> precious stones; and other shops featuring plant-life,
> resort wear, optical items, books, art objects and a
> music shop.

LEASE DATA:

> Rents are uniform at $6.00 per square foot per year
> with percentage rents varying between 5% and 6%.
> Substantial overage rents are being generated at the
> present time. Occupancy is approximately 95%.

TENANT EXPENSES:

> Tenants pay pro rata share of tax increase over base
> year, insurance, utilities, merchants association and
> common area expense.

Exhibit 9

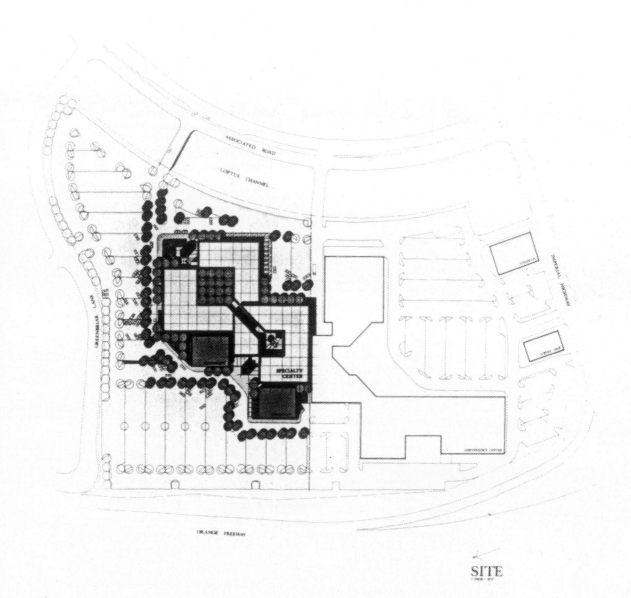

Exhibit 9
continued

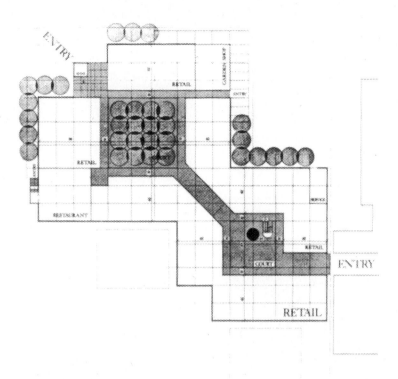

LOWER LEVEL

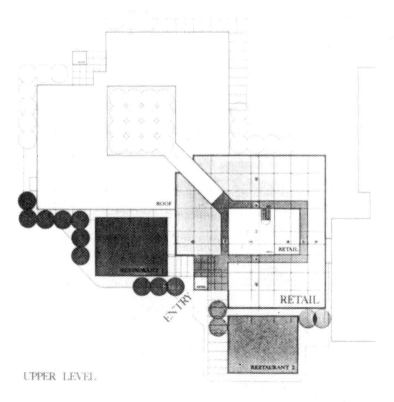

UPPER LEVEL

Exhibit 10

TENTATIVE SUMMARY OF TENANT MIX

Approximate No. of Tenants	Categories	Approximate GLA	%	Avg. % Rent
	Restaurants & Food:			
2	Free Standing	16,000		9.5%
3	Restaurant & Food Service	10,000		9.0%
5-7		26,000	23%	
	Specialty Foods:			
4-6	Cheese Shop; Bakery; Specialty Liquor; Coffee; Tea & Spice; Nut Shop; Candy; Health Foods; Specialty Meats; Fish & Poultry	8,000	7%	8.0%
	Apparel:			
8-12	Women's	12,000		
2-3	Men's	4,000		
2-4	Shoes & Other	4,000		
12-19		20,000	18%	5.5%
	Household:			
4-8	Gourmet Cookware; Culinary Shops; Stoneware; Furniture; Lamps; Antiques; Memorabilia; Decorator; Linen Shop; Imports; Clockshops; Household Accessories	12,000	11%	3.0%
	Jewelry & Gifts:			
6-10	Conventional Jeweler; Matches; Custom Jewelry; Specialty Jewelry; Pottery; Crystal; Gifts; Imports; Candles; Cards; Etc.	10,000	9%	8.0%

Exhibit 10
continued

Approximate No. of Tenants	Categories	Approximate GLA	%	Avg. % Rent
	Arts & Crafts:			
8-12	Galleries; Artistic Glass; Wrought Iron; Minerals; Shells; Sculptor; Print & Litho; Wood & Metal; Macrame; Needlecraft; Leather Craft; Carpet Craft; Yarn Shop; Winemaking; High Fashion Textiles; Winemaking; Sewing Supplies; Etc.	10,000	9%	8%
1	**Plant Boutique:**	3,000	3%	8%
	Services:			
6-8	Slenderizing Salon; 2 or more Beauty Salons; Fingernail Care; Cosmologist; Photographer; Travel; Optometrist; Etc.	8,000	7%	--
	Miscellaneous:			
10-15	Musical Instruments; Smoking; Stationers; Camera; Books; Toys; Luggage; Game Shop; Coin & Stamp Shop; Flowers; Party Goods; Tennis Shop; Back Packing; Bike Shop; Kite Store; Golf Shop; Etc.	15,000	13%	8%
56-86		112,000	100%	

Exhibit 11

Summary of Items in Specialty Center Form
Lease, Related to Analysis

Documents Referred
to in the Exhibit

    1. Form Lease

    2. Merchants Association By-Laws

Term

    Lease to continue for fifteen years and to begin 30 days
after the occupancy date, or on the date on which Lessee
shall open its store for business, whichever is earlier.

Minimum Annual Rent

    Payable in 12 equal monthly installments in advance, com-
mencing on the date the lease term commences.

Percentage Rent

    Percentage rent computed by multiplying the percentage by
gross sales in each calendar month. The amount by which
this total exceeds the minimum monthly rent paid is the
amount, if any, of percentage rent due. There shall be no
lease provision for the recapture of taxes or any other
expenses paid by the tenant from the amount of the percentage rent available.

    While payable on a monthly basis, percentage rent is
adjusted annually on the basis of annual gross sales.

Real Estate Taxes

    Tenant to pay annually its proportionate share of real
estate taxes on the leased premises and underlying land.
Tenant is further responsible for his pro rata share of
common area taxes and assessments which shall be included in
the common area expenses. Tenant shall pay all property
taxes and assessments on furniture, fixtures and other
equipment on the premises.

Utility Services

    Tenant is responsible for all charges for water, gas,
sewers, electricity. light, heat, air conditioning, power,
telephone, trash removal, and other services. Where possible, contract for services will be made in the tenant's
name. However, utilities furnished by the landlord will be
payable on a pro rata basis by the tenant.

Exhibit 11
continued

Common Area Expenses

Tenant shall pay a monthly charge based upon the size of leased premises' floor area as a common area charge. At the end of each calendar year, actual common area costs will be calculated on a pro rata basis and an adjustment made between actual cost and tenant payment. Pro rata share is calculated by dividing tenant floor area by total gross floor area. In the event vacancies occur, landlord shall have to pay common area expenses for vacant store.

Most important among common area expenses are general maintenance and repairs, cleaning, sweeping, gardening, real and personal property taxes and assessments on the improvements and land comprising automobile parking and common areas, insurance, and a 10% allowance of all the foregoing costs to cover landlord's administrative and overhead expenses.

Insurance

Landlord is required to carry fire, extended coverage, vandalism, and malicious mischief coverage on tenants' premises within the shopping center. Tenant shall reimburse landlord for all insurance expense. Furthermore, the tenant individually is required to maintain all coverage on all fixtures and equipment installed by tenant. Tenant is also required to carry and pay for liability and property damage insurance within the limits of not less than $500,000/$200,000/ $50,000, plate glass insurance, equipment insurance, sign insurance, etc.

Merchants Association

Tenants are required to join and maintain membership in the shopping center's merchants' association and to pay assessments to be established by the lessor. In no event shall the assessment exceed $0.20 per sq. ft. of floor area of the premises per year. Landlord is required to maintain membership in the merchants' association and to contribute 25% of all assessments collected from association members. Contributions shall not be less than $4,000 nor more than $10,000 per year.

Repairs and
Maintenance

Tenant must repair and maintain everything included in his premises including the roof and exterior walls, carpeting, terrazzo or any other special floor covering, air conditioning, and heating equipment, conduits, storefronts, windows, sash, doors, etc. Common area repairs and maintenance are included in the common area expenses.

Exhibit 12

Survey of Office Buildings in the Fullerton-Brea Area

Identification	Location	Sq. Ft. Size	Leasing Begins	Rent Sq. Ft. Per Mo.	Occu-Pancy
Hillcrest Office Park (2 story garden office building)	1370 Brea Blvd. Fullerton, CA	34,800	11/74	$.70	40%
Valencia Bank Building (2 Story garden office building)	1235 No. Harbor Blvd. Fullerton, CA	27,000	6/74	$.67	92%
Brashear's Office Center	1400 No. Harbor Blvd. Fullerton, CA				
7 Story Tower		119,000	1968	$.65	96.5%
9 Story Tower		120,000	7/75	$.72	31%
Chapman Financial Center (2 story garden office building)	2651 Chapman Ave.	60,000	9/75	$.65	10%
Hunt Wesson Building (9 story office tower)	2600 E. Nutwood Ave.	206,700	1970	$.60-$.65	100%

Note 4

Location, Design, and Market Analysis

This note provides a brief introduction to location, design, and market analysis for real estate development. Developers must assess locational qualities, design opportunities and market support in the acquisition, development and operation of property. These areas of analysis may be applied to any land use as well as to an existing building or operating property. This note is organized into three sections:

Section I is concerned with the analysis of **location**: the physical, economic and regulatory context of a particular site. The primary objective of location analysis is to determine the most likely uses for a piece of real estate and any limitations imposed by its local and regional settings.

Section II introduces the **design** process, including consultants responsible for design, decisions on land use and density, and design criteria for five generic project types: residential, retail, office, industrial, and lodging.

Section III addresses **market** analysis and introduces the specific market issues pertinent to the five generic project types discussed in section II. Market analysis may also serve to establish design criteria for a proposed site.

Copyright (c) 1988 by the President and Fellows of Harvard College.
This note was written with the assistance of research associate Paul Mehlman.

I. LOCATION ANALYSIS

"Location, location, location" is the real estate professional's answer to the questions posed by a piece of real estate. Often this adage is interpreted narrowly. Location is seen simply as a prominent street address or a desirable neighborhood. The concept of location as it applies to real estate value, however, is broad and multi-faceted. Location encompasses the physical, economic and regulatory context of a property. Synthesis of these contextual factors provides the developer with a framework for establishing initial use scenarios for a site.

Location and Real Estate Value

Why is location such a key determinant of real estate value? The answer to this question lies in the physical nature of real estate as a commodity. Unlike most other goods which are bought and sold, real estate is fixed and immobile. Every site represents a singular geographic entity characterized by a unique set of locational attributes. While participants in real estate markets often evaluate projects against "comparable" properties, no two properties are exactly identical. To the extent locational attributes differentiate two pieces of real estate, their economic usefulness will be differentiated as well.

The uniqueness of a given location is augmented by the limited availability of sites for development. In theory, any site can be acquired if appropriate financial, political and legal arrangements can be negotiated. At a given point in time, however, only a fraction of the total number of sites are actively offered for sale. During a given year, for example, not more than 5 to 6% of all residential properties change hands. The scarcity or abundance of available locations in an area is a key factor in establishing real estate value.

Locational Attributes

The locational attributes offered by a given site determine its suitability to a given type and intensity of development. A developer considering a project must assess locational factors at a variety of levels: site, neighborhood and regional. Criteria applicable to each of these frames of reference are outlined below:

Site. The basic physical attributes of a site -- size, shape, topography and landscape -- often impose fundamental restrictions on its appropriate use. A narrow hillside lot will probably not be viable as a site for an industrial park due to constraints on access and expandability. The same site, however, may work well as a residential subdivision taking advantage of potential desirable views.

Use scenarios for real estate are also impacted by existing man-made conditions on a site. The developer must make an initial assessment of existing buildings and other remnants of prior use. Do these structures need to be removed or can they be incorporated into the overall use scenario?

Developers should consider the extent to which factors such as zoning may constrain development of a site. An experienced developer will be able to make a qualitative evaluation of the relative ease or difficulty of obtaining necessary approvals and variances.

Neighborhood. The characteristics of the area surrounding a site normally will exert a strong influence on its development. An urban context may suggest very different land uses and densities as compared with a suburban or rural setting. A developer's initial ideas for a site should incorporate judgments about the physical, economic and demographic characteristics of the surrounding neighborhood. Is the population and density of use around a site increasing or decreasing? What are the relative income levels in nearby areas?

What is the makeup of the available work force?

In many instances the use of a site may be influenced by its proximity to other developments or amenities: a lake-front, a city's financial district, a major manufacturing facility. For certain developments proximities are necessary. A convenience retail center, for example, requires immediate adjacency to a residential area.

Transportation routes through the neighborhood surrounding a site represent a critical variable in formulating a development scenario. How easy is the site to get to? Is there parking available on site or nearby? Is it convenient to public transportation? These factors control how users gain access to a site and hence reflect significantly on its potential use and capacity.

Regional. Transportation networks -- highways, waterways, airports and rail systems -- provide means for interaction or linkage between a site and its larger regional context. Where such linkage is available, the developer must consider the impact of regional economic and demographic factors upon a proposed development.

The manner in which a site physically interfaces with regional transportation networks exerts a significant influence on the type and scope of development which that site will support. Sites differ greatly as to the relative expense required to bring goods and people by major transportation networks. A site that is directly tied to the regional transportation network is potentially available to a greater number of users and is convenient to the general regional flow of goods and materials. Such a site has a strategic advantage for land use where accessibility is critical.

Certain developments require strategic siting in order to minimize costs associated with transportation and accessibility. A manufacturing facility, for example, ab-

solutely must have access to an appropriately skilled labor force. It is beneficial also, but not essential, if raw materials are available nearby.

Analysis of the site, neighborhood and regional location of a piece of real estate provides the developer with a means for determining development scenarios for that property. At this stage, these scenarios are usually conceptual and very preliminary in nature. Once an initial determination of use is made, design and market analysis can be applied to refine the development scenario into specific goals and objectives.

II. DESIGN ANALYSIS

The design process involves the translation of a development concept for a site into plans and guidelines for buildings or land improvements. The initial phase of this process -- design analysis -- addresses both the technical feasibility of a project as well as the physical and aesthetic appropriateness of the project for its intended market. The results of design analysis usually take the form of specific proposals for density, site utilization and building type.

Planning and Design Consultants

Although some developers are organized to do their own design work, generally the planning and design process is executed by specialized design consultants. These consultants work in collaboration with the developer and other members of the development team. Depending on its scope and complexity, a project may require input from a variety of professionals. The paragraphs below summarize the basic categories of design services.

Architects. Architects deal with the planning and design of buildings. They are responsible for both aesthetic and functional concerns, including plan layout, massing, detailing and compliance with zoning and safety codes. Generally, architects coordinate their work with a variety of sub-consultants: site engineers, structural engineers, mechanical and electrical engineers, systems specialists, etc. Computer-aided design (CAD) and other sophisticated new computer technologies, now play a significant role in contemporary architectural practices.

Architects are licensed in each state through competitive examination. Architects generally have undergraduate degrees plus graduate professional degrees from accredited schools. The most publicly recognizable works of contemporary architecture are the public buildings and high-rise towers designed by "name" architects, such as I.M. Pei and Philip Johnson. Architecture, however, encompasses the full range of scales and building types. Many architectural firms specialize in certain kinds of design services: hospitals, laboratories, single-family homes, etc. A skilled architect can add value to the simplest prefabricated warehouse or apartment block.

Landscape Architects. Design issues involving land development at relatively low densities are the competence of the landscape architect. Landscape architecture encompasses a wide range of scales from regional planning to the design of small gardens and plazas. Landscape architects have formal professional degrees and are licensed by state registration boards.

The most publicly recognized works of the profession are spectacular public spaces, parks and gardens. The seventeenth century formal gardens of France and the metropolitan green spaces designed by Frederick Law Olmstead provide historical examples of landscape architecture at a grand, public scale. More important to developers today is the profession's competence in creating livable land design for housing developments and emerging high-quality business and industrial parks.

Urban Designers/Planners. Urban designers and city planners deal with issues of large scale development and multi-building projects within an urban context. These design professionals usually focus on planning context, access and building forms. Urban designers are usually also professionally trained architects, landscape architects and city planners who have attained post-professional or specialized degrees from accredited design institutions. Many architecture firms offer urban design and planning capabilities as part of their services.

Interior Designers/Space Planners. Interior designers and space planners provide design services for planning the interior arrangements of spaces in larger buildings -- generally urban or suburban office buildings, but also hotels, public buildings and marketing facilities, such as stores and showrooms. Typically, space planners are retained by developers and corporate clients. Space planners generally have architectural or interior design degrees and may be licensed by state registration boards. Many architecture firms also offer space planning services.

Issues in Design Analysis

Design analysis seeks to assess the feasibility of a development concept with respect to design criteria. This assessment encompasses three primary areas of consideration:

1. What is the density of construction that a site can accommodate, and is this density appropriate to a developer's proposed use?

2. What building types -- high-rise, low rise, loft, etc. -- and what construction types -- wood frame, masonry, steel frame, etc.-- best suit the density and functional needs of a project?

3. What is the optimal configuration of building types and density upon a site?

Design analysis starts with a detailed evaluation of a site's physical characteristics and legal restrictions. This process of documenting a site is often referred to as **site analysis**. In location analysis the developer makes assumptions about the ability of a site to accommodate a certain use scenario. Site analysis evaluates and tests these assumptions in detail.

Assessment of the physical attributes of a site forms a key part of site analysis. The size, shape and topography of a piece of real estate determine to large extent the relative ease and appropriateness of adapting it to a particular use and density. Major natural features of a site, such as streams, ponds and rock outcroppings, may provide amenities or detriments to certain development scenarios. Other physical characteristics, such as climate, vegetation, soil conditions and drainage, will also effect a site's amenability to different uses.

Site analysis should provide a comprehensive assessment of a site's man-made as well as natural features. Few sites are devoid of some form of human intervention. Most sites available for development have passed through a variety of land uses. Buildings and other existing man-made structures should be evaluated with respect to their viability or potential for adaptive reuse. Some human interventions may impact extremely negatively upon development, for example, the presence of toxic wastes.

Site analysis must consider in detail the legal and political parameters governing utilization of a site. The introduction to Part III, Feasibility Analysis and Negotiation, has already referred to zoning and infrastructure issues pertinent to site development. Regulatory factors such as zoning may effect a wide range of variables including land use, building height, density, setbacks, sewerage, parking and automobile access. These restrictions are generally enforced by public ordinances which require variances in order to be superseded. Other legal constraints on land use, such as easements, air rights and mineral rights may originate from deed provisions.

Once site conditions have been documented through site analysis, the results are used to assess the feasibility of adapting the site to the proposed use. The development scenario must be converted into a building program which accounts for all of the space needs of the project. Square footages and technical requirements for interior and exterior functions can then be tested against site constraints.

The final step in design analysis is the consideration of building types and site configurations appropriate to the proposed use. This process usually involves the development of schematic designs for the site and buildings. Issues of construction cost, and project scheduling (phasing) should be reflected in these initial proposals, as well as assumptions about marketability, amenities, etc. Often the design process initially includes consideration of several alternatives. These must ultimately be reduced to a single solution that maximizes economic, aesthetic and functional performance.

The Design Cycle

Design progresses through a series of five stages -- schematic design, design development, contract documents, bidding and construction. The **schematic design** stage develops the general scope, configuration and character of the project. These designs are used to obtain public approvals and financing as well as to generate rough cost estimates. Often these preliminary designs undergo numerous changes in order to satisfy all the concerned parties. This cyclical process of review and revision is referred to as the **design development** stage. It is during schematic design and design development that the fundamental questions of design analysis -- density, building type and site configuration -- are addressed and finally resolved.

Once all the necessary approvals and financing are obtained, **contract documents** (working drawings and material specifications) are developed. These documents are used to **bid** or negotiate contracts for construction of the actual building and are the basis for building permit review and approvals. During the **construction** period, design firms may provide services in the field as inspectors or owner's representatives in order to insure that work is executed satisfactorily.

Most developers enter into contractual arrangements for design and construction services. Traditionally the owner-architect agreement assumes a triangular relationship among the owner, the architect and the contractor. The standard form contracts are coordinated in an effort to allocate responsibilities, risks and rewards of the job. Some construction firms, referred to as design-build companies, possess in-house design capabilities.

Projects where time is critical may be fast-tracked. Fast-tracking involves compressing the contract cycle such that the design and construction phases overlap. In a fast-track project certain elements, such as sitework and foundations, will be constructed while other portions -- the building, the exterior envelope and interior finishes -- are still being designed.

Design Criteria

Different uses require different functional and aesthetic design considerations. Here we will briefly consider some of the design issues for specific use scenarios. The sections that follow outline design criteria for five generic project types.

Residential. In urban areas, residential developments generally take the form of high-rise towers, mid-rise apartment blocks and clustered or zero-lot-line townhouses. Suburban residential developments usually consist of single-family lots and homes, townhouses and garden apartments.

Generally, residential developments hinge on a well configured site plan. In a single family suburban subdivision, for example, the site plan must reconcile a variety of conflicting variables: unit density, land development costs, site amenities and unit sales price. A certain minimum level of density is required on the site in order to achieve reasonable economic returns. As density increases, cost per unit is reduced, allowing greater profit margins or reduced sales prices. Increases in density, however, tend to diminish site amenities such as trees and seclusion. Reductions in site amenities translate into reduced marketability. In most residential developments, a certain level of market analysis will be useful to determine an appropriate mix of product type, density and amenities.

Infrastructure is critical to most residential use scenarios. Residences should be adequately serviced by automobile access, yet arranged to minimize exposure to noise and danger from through traffic. Design of common areas -- sidewalks, parking facilities, laundries, recreational facilities and lobbies -- also impacts the quality of the residential experience. In tract housing developments, it is desirable to cluster buildings to minimize street and utility work and thereby reduce development costs.

Typically a residential development will offer a variety of units incorporating different numbers of bedrooms and baths. The mix of units may be derived from data obtained in the market analysis. The aesthetic character and quality of construction for the individual units should also correlate to marketing objectives. Certain regions may be amenable to new design concepts while others may be characterized by strongly traditional housing preferences.

Buildings of four or more stories are generally required at densities above about 30 units per acre. These require elevators and are of class A (fireproof) construction. Lower density buildings (below about 20 units per acre) are usually light frame construction and are walkups.

Units in larger buildings must be configured to maximize efficient use of space. Bathrooms and kitchens may be 'stacked' next to those of other units to reduce plumbing requirements. Where possible, space allocated to hallways, fire stairs and other common circulation elements should be minimized.

Retail. Retail developments are distinguished by their scale and drawing power. Such projects generally fall into specific categories: regional malls; community shopping centers; neighborhood shopping centers; specialty centers; and free-standing stores. This section considers the specific example of a regional shopping center -- the largest category of shopping center, generally in the range of one million square feet or more.

Market expectations and site capacity combine to establish the projected amount of gross leasable area (GLA) for a potential shopping center site. Early stages of design focus on allocating land area to service various uses in the proposed program: buildings, parking, access roads, landscaped areas, buffer areas and land held for further expansion. Once it is determined that the site can accommodate the proposed program, the design emphasis shifts to consideration of how the various uses should be located on the site.

At a functional level, shopping center design strives to facilitate the movement of pedestrians, cars and goods shipments.

Typically, such facilities are configured with single story buildings and all on-grade parking. Where land prices are high, multi-level parking structures and two level store areas may prove to be economical. On rare occasions one encounters a high-rise configuration as at Water Tower Place in Chicago or Trump Tower in Manhattan. In such instances, internal visual orientation and ample and conveniently located vertical circulation become the critical factors in the project's design.

Buildings should be situated on the site such that they are central to parking and visible from major vehicular traffic routes. Analysis of traffic flows resulting from the center should be conducted to determine the most convenient points of access to parking areas and loading facilities. The analysis should also consider whether local roads around the site are sufficiently sized to accommodate traffic generated by the center.

Design of the actual buildings in a regional shopping center focuses on the placement of the anchor tenants. These stores are usually department stores, such as Sears, Wal-Mart or Filenes. Anchor tenants are situated within comfortable walking distance from each other with smaller satellite stores arranged along the connecting axes. As few as two and as many as six anchors may be involved.

Shopping centers cater to both merchandisers and shoppers and should be pleasant and convenient for both groups of users. Tenant areas must have flexibility to accommodate varying space needs (modular design) and should be well supported by loading and service areas. Pedestrian zones, both internal and external, should create a colorful vibrant atmosphere for shopping. These public spaces provide the center with a sense of identity and coherence which can potentially set it apart from other competing regional centers servicing the same area. In many localities the regional shopping center has come to function as a major political and social meeting ground, much as the town commons of a by-gone era.

Office. Office uses are serviced by a diverse range of real estate products: high and mid-rise towers, rehabilitated older buildings, and suburban office parks. For all office building types, successful design is based on efficient layouts and services for tenant needs. Flexibility is important to accommodate changes in tenancy and in use of the space by each tenant.

Generally, multi-tenant office buildings should be able to service both small and large tenants. The distance between interior corridors and exterior window walls must be deep enough to accept offices and reception areas for small users (as little as 1000 square feet), yet not too deep as to create an unreasonable floorplate for larger users. Many developers consider 45' the optimum depth. Interior cores and elevator lobbies should be laid out to be as efficient as possible while providing access to the largest potential number of tenants. Mechanical, electrical and telephone systems should also allow for maximum flexibility in different arrangements.

The quality and convenience of public areas -- lobbies and exterior plazas -- is critical to the market acceptance of a multi-tenant building. Elevators must be sufficient in number, capacity and speed to meet peak use requirements while avoiding oversizing which results in excess operating and construction costs. Pedestrian movement in and around an office building should be unencumbered without compromising building security.

Finish materials in public areas must be commensurate with the standards of the anticipated tenancy. Material selection is also important for controlling operating costs. Durable materials typically increase construction outlays while reducing subsequent maintenance expenses. As competition has increased among speculative office buildings, higher design standards have evolved in formerly

mundane areas such as bathrooms and parking facilities. Some developers now provide special features such as art in the common areas, roof decks, and site amenities such as jogging/exercise facilities, picnic areas, etc. Combined with high quality tenant spaces, these features are intended to sustain high occupancy levels over time.

Industrial. Industrial parks, warehouses and single-user industrial facilities comprise the majority of the industrial sector. This section considers design issues for planned industrial parks, the most sophisticated form of industrial development.

Usually located peripheral to towns and cities, industrial parks service a wide range of uses, principally warehousing, manufacturing, and research and development. Multi-tenant office buildings, corporate headquarters, hotels, medical facilities and shopping areas are also often encountered. Tenant-landlord arrangements vary in different industrial parks. In many parks, the developer erects standard industrial structures and leases them to prospective tenants. In other parks, the developer sells or leases land to tenants and allows them to build their own facilities to suit their specific needs.

In all industrial parks, site layout is a key design factor. The network of streets within a park should access all potential parcels and should be sufficiently sized and engineered for truck traffic. Efficient layout of streets, railroad spurs (if provided), parking areas and utilities will save development costs and minimize loss of land. At the same time, open space and buffer zones must be provided.

Where the developer is providing buildings for an industrial park, care must be taken to develop designs appropriate to the anticipated tenant mix. Manufacturing and warehousing businesses focus their space requirements on operational considerations: ceiling clearances, appropriate square footages, properly sized and configured loading facilities, etc. R&D companies typically seek out a more up-scale, people-oriented, business park. Attractiveness of landscaping, quality of building materials, and seclusion from surrounding businesses are potentially key selling points for R&D tenants.

If tenants are building their own facilities, the developer typically provides standards for type of industrial operation, site coverage, setbacks, loading area configuration, etc. Such guidelines prevent a tenant from undertaking construction or operations which might compromise the use of the industrial park for other tenants. Covenants enforcing design guidelines are usually included in the lease or sale documents.

Lodging. Hotel and motel design centers around minimizing operating costs while providing an ambiance that is convenient and attractive to patrons. Transient commercial developments are primarily differentiated from one another by the scope and quality of their public areas: lobbies, restaurants, etc. The configuration and finish materials of these spaces should be commensurate with anticipated clientele and room rates. A multi-story atrium lobby, for example, would probably be inappropriate for an economy motel.

A second level of differentiation is in the size and configuration of the rooms. Hotels and motels usually provide a mix of rooms types based on market research. Linking doors between adjoining rooms can provide added flexibility. Increasingly, high-end hotels are tailoring rooms to specific users. The recent proliferation of suite hotels for business travelers exemplifies this trend.

Rooms should blend spaciousness with efficiency. Usually bathrooms are stacked back-to-back to reduce plumbing costs. Furnishings which resist dirt and permit vacuuming without moving insure ease of room cleaning. Maintenance is also facilitated by minimizing the distance from rooms to service elevators, linen closets, and trash chutes.

Wherever possible, parking areas should be sized to handle the peak guest load in addition to any visitor parking for dining, conference and banquet facilities. Vehicular drop-off areas should be convenient to the lobby area and should incorporate ample area for short-term parking and loading.

The design criteria presented here are far from exhaustive[2]. As noted, market research often plays a key role in establishing objectives for the design process. Regardless of how much research is involved, however, success is often determined by the intuition of a seasoned developer and his or her design consultants. Beauty is in the eye of the beholder -- but the sense of vision necessary to see beauty *before* it's there is an absolute necessity for the developer.

III. MARKET ANALYSIS

Market analysis provides a framework for predicting the performance of a piece of real estate based upon its locational attributes and market circumstances. The principle objective of market analysis is to measure the supply and demand factors that may effect the developer's ability to sell or lease a project.

A market study usually begins by defining the **market area**: the geographic domain in which the proposed use for a given site directly competes with other properties. The market area may be as restricted as an individual neighborhood, in the case of a small residential development, or as broad the entire nation, in the case of a major company looking for a corporate headquarters.

---

[2]For a more comprehensive overview of design analysis see John W. McMahan's *Property Development*, second edition, (New York, N.Y.: McGraw-Hill, 1989).

Demand for real estate within a given market area is determined by the number of buyers and tenants seeking space. Generally, demand for a given type of project is estimated based upon historical **absorption** in a market area. Economic and demographic trends may also provide a basis for evaluating future demand. Market areas with increasing population and income levels are likely to have expanding space needs.

Supply considerations in a market area focus on the effects of competition from other projects. The **vacancy level** indicates the degree to which the supply of space in a market area is servicing demand. A low vacancy level may mean that supply is deficient and there is potential for a new project. Assessment of market area supply factors should also consider the specific characteristics of the projects that will compete with the proposed development. What amenities do these projects offer? How do their sites compare to the site of the proposed project?

Evaluations of supply and demand are necessarily based upon data that represents the state of the market at present. Real estate markets, however, are dynamic and may change quickly in response to a variety of factors: an upturn in interest rates, competing projects planned or underway, etc. Since a proposed project will come on line at a time in the future, estimates of supply and demand must endeavor to predict market conditions when the project is going to be actively sold or leased.

The final step in market analysis is to draw specific conclusions. The most important conclusion is a predicted **capture rate**, that is, the share of market demand which a development can reasonably expect to capture. Of course, many other conclusions may be drawn from an assessment of competitive properties. These will enable the developer to make specific assessments of the marketability of a proposed development and, if necessary, alter the project's underlying design or marketing concepts.

The details of market analysis vary significantly for different use scenarios. The sections that follow identify the key market analysis variables for the five generic project types discussed in Section II of this note.

Residential

The first step in analyzing the market for a housing development is to determine the market area. This is usually done by considering the proximity of the proposed site to centers of employment. In an already established residential area, emphasis is placed on an assessment of completed developments.

The demand for housing in a market area can be measured as a function of growth in the number of households. Most local planning agencies (redevelopment authorities, city and town planning departments) regularly publish forecasts of population and household growth. Demographic forecasts should be compared with census records of past growth. Census tract information and other data can also be correlated to the market area to ascertain its socio-economic characteristics: employment profile, ethnic character, age and income distribution, etc. These factors help to define the character, price range and density of housing appropriate to the market area.

Household growth provides a baseline measure of demand. In addition to this, however, an allowance should be made for the replacement of deteriorated housing stock. In recently developed residential areas this factor will be small. In older neighborhoods, the need for rehabilitation of residential buildings and removal or demolition of marginal units comprise an important component of future demand. By comparing the final assessment of demand with data on housing supply, a residential market analysis can quantify unmet demand within a market area.

Once overall demand has been verified, residential market analysis focuses on the characteristics of competing developments. These should be surveyed with respect to location, number of units, density, size of units, quality of construction, amenities, parking arrangements, special features (fireplaces, appliances, etc.), price and sale terms. Critical variables for market analysis are the rate of absorption -- units rented or sold per month in the market area -- and the price or rent level per square foot for competing projects.

Comparison of the attributes of a proposed project to those of competing developments will determine the portion of market demand which it can expect to capture. Market capture rates may be influenced by intangible factors such as timing and marketing. Projections for reasonable market capture rates may provide a reason for adjusting the scope of the proposed project to reduce the risk involved in undertaking it.

Retail

As noted in the previous section, there are many different types and scales of retail development. Market factors differ significantly among the various kinds of real estate products that support retailing. An urban department store has very different market analysis criteria from a convenience shopping mall in a residential neighborhood. As before, we focus here on the regional shopping center as a generic example of market analysis for a retail development.

Assessment of retail demand for a regional center begins with definition of the center's trade area -- typically the area within 15-30 minute travel time to the site. Large or specialized retailers may have much larger trade areas, of course, while convenience shopping is done closer

to home or work. The success of a regional center depends on its ability to capture retail expenditures by consumers within the trade area.

Census and sales tax data are available for retail expenditures and can be used to calculate the total retail expenditures by trade area residents. Usually it is helpful if retail purchase figures are broken down according to types of merchandise: apparel, general merchandise, household goods etc. These historical figures should be tested against socio-economic trends -- population growth, changing income levels, changing employment characteristics, etc. -- which might impact upon trade area retail expenditures in the future. The total retail expenditures by trade area residents represents a maximum potential level of retail activity. In reality, of course, a significant percentage of these expenditures occurs outside the trade area.

A regional center captures shopping demand in four basic ways:

1. Stimulating growth in retail expenditures by residents of the trade area;

2. Increasing the size of the trade area by reduction of sales prices or increased scale or specialization;

3. Capturing sales from competing centers; and

4. Capturing more of the retail dollar flow leaving the trade area.

All of these methods necessitate competing with other retail developments in or near the trade area. Market analysis for a regional center should incorporate a survey of other centers accessible to trade area residents. This survey should address center size, major tenants, rents, quality of overall design, quality of stores, number of parking stalls per square foot, etc. It is important also to determine or estimate sales volume for each center.

Figures for actual retail sales within the trade area may be generated by a survey of centers within the trade area. One can also multiply the total square footage of retail space in the trade area by estimates for annual sales dollars per square foot. Comparison of these figures to the total retail expenditure by trade area residents provides a means of evaluating whether the market is saturated or has room for expansion.

The result of this is a quantified estimate of unmet sales potential which may be captured by a proposed center. This forecast necessarily involves many qualitative judgements relative to advantages and disadvantages of the site, strengths and weaknesses of anchor stores, etc. Once the sales projection is determined, the appropriate size of the center can be fixed.

A final step in market analysis for a regional center is the development of marketing strategies regarding store mix and timing of the center's opening. Store mix should derive from consumer preferences in the trade area as ascertained by interviews and surveys of trade area shoppers. Where the trade area for a center is characterized by a mix of socio-economic levels, the center must cater to a broad cross-section in order to achieve success. Store mix scenarios should accommodate any planned phasing of a center's opening. Phasing of construction permits the developer to bring more space on line to match the actual growth of demand. Developers may opt to "buy position" in a trade area by erecting a small number of stores in advance of a center's full-fledged entry into the trade area retail market.

Office

Unlike housing and retail developments, office buildings do not cater to a well defined market or trade area. Banks, law firms and many other businesses may prefer to be located in a city's central business district. Many other companies, however, can carry out their daily activities in any section of a metropolitan area. Accordingly, market analyses for office developments must address issues of supply and demand at a metropolitan-area scale.

Evaluation of demand for office space usually derives from an assessment of historical absorption. Markets for office space tend to be cyclical, passing through periods of robustness, followed by over-building and high vacancy rates. Over an extended period, however, absorption data provides a good indicator of the status of an office market at a given point in time. In addition, the observation of a low vacancy rate typically indicates an office market ready for new development.

Absorption data should be broken out according to types of office space. Market studies may employ a grading system for building quality -- class A, class B, etc -- or may focus on geographic sub-markets. Often absorption experience will vary from one type of office development to another.

Absorption expectations should be adjusted to account for the time frame of a proposed project. Factors that might affect the marketing of future office space -- new office construction, changing office employment levels, etc. -- must be evaluated to project the likely rate of absorption when a new project will come on line.

Once the analysis has estimated the likely demand for new office space, supply factors must be evaluated to determine the viability of a proposed project. Any new office building must compete for tenants with other new developments. It will also compete with vacant space in existing buildings. Future and existing buildings that will vie for market share with the proposed project should be surveyed with respect to location, gross, and net rentable area, vacancy levels, rent levels, lease terms, parking, amenities, etc. This data is commonly published by lease brokerage firms. More difficult is the problem of surveying future buildings -- which ones will actually be built and when?

Predicting the ability of a proposed office building to capture market demand necessitates many subjective judgements. Desirability of the site address and quality/price comparison with competitive buildings must be carefully weighed. Marketing and lease concessions (rent rebates, landlord build-out allowances, etc.) play a significant role in drawing tenants. If there is a major anchor tenant for the building, certain firms may be attracted for reasons of prestige or desired proximity. Anticipated tenant mix may also dictate the size and character of a proposed project.

Industrial

As with office buildings, demand for new industrial developments may be gauged by historical absorption experience. Absorption data for acreage in existing industrial parks within a metropolitan region may be broken down by types of industry -- distribution, manufacturing, and R&D -- or by geographic area. Since different industry groups have differing space needs, the market analysis may serve to guide the developer in structuring an industrial park that best suits the requirements of potential tenants. For speculative or multi-tenant buildings, a survey of absorption pace and remaining vacant space is needed.

As with office projects, historical absorption data for industrial parks or buildings should be projected forward to account for the time frame in which a proposed property will enter the market. Factors that may effect regional demand for industrial land include demographic changes in the regional labor force, changes in transportation networks, revision of local tax laws, etc.

The attractiveness of an industrial development to certain tenants depends to a large extent on how the locational attributes of the project correlate with the tenant's operational needs. Industrial firms display a variety of orientations in their disposition toward site location:

1. Market-oriented -- firms which locate near the market for their final product.

2. Resource-oriented -- firms which locate near resources required for production of their product.

3. Transportation-oriented -- firms that require proximity to highways, railroads, waterways, etc.

4. Labor-oriented -- firms which locate near where economical labor is available.

5. Non-oriented -- firms not motivated by production or distribution costs. This last group may be more influenced by the cost of real estate, local executive housing conditions, etc.

Market analysis for an industrial project should identify an industrial client base suited to the site and region. Regional growth of employment and land use in these target industries should be evaluated to verify the demand assumptions made from absorption data.

Market capture estimates for the target site should be determined through a survey of competing sites. This survey should document overall site size, land available for expansion, cost of land and buildings, accessibility to transportation, proximity to residential neighborhoods, etc. Using the competitive survey, the project site should be evaluated for its relative advantages and disadvantages. The competitiveness of the project in the overall market will determine appropriate sales prices, rent levels and time expected for lease-up.

Lodging

The viability of a hotel or motel development depends upon the continuing ability of the project to attract guest revenues. Room revenue forms the principal income stream for both hotels and motels. Bars, restaurants and other ancillary facilities comprise secondary profit centers.

The market area and clientele base appropriate to a particular location is usually dictated by relatively obvious conditions of proximity, such as adjacency to a convention center or a major tourist attraction. Demand for hotel/motel space within the market area is determined by assessing the room night requirements generated by visitors to that area. Demand figures should be projected into the future by accounting for factors that might change

visitor levels: growth in business volume, a new convention center, etc.

A survey of competitive developments in the market area should document occupancy, number of rooms, rates, amenities and overall quality. Combining data on the total available room nights in the market area with figures for anticipated visitor levels will determine whether there is sufficient excess demand to warrant a new project. Increasing room rentals combined with sustained occupancies in the 75% range generally indicate a strong market ready for a new property.

Published Sources of Market Data

Property Types	Publications
Residential	*National Economic Projections Series* National Planning Association *Expense Analysis of Apartment, Condominium and Planned Unit Developments* Institute of Real Estate Management
Retail	*Directory of Shopping Centers in the U.S* National Research Bureau *Shopping Center Today* Monthly Periodical "Survey of Buying Power" in *Sales and Marketing Management*
Office/Industrial	*National Real Estate Investor* Monthly Periodical *Directory* Society of Industrial Realtors
Lodging	*Trends in the Hotel Industry* Pannell, Kerr, Forster and Company *Worldwide Lodging Industry* Laventhol and Horwath

Market capture estimates for a proposed hotel/motel provide a basis for determining the appropriate number of rooms. This figure should be sufficient to meet peak demand, but not so much as to result in excessive vacancies during slow periods. Generally the newest property in an area will always attract customers for a period. Sustaining this at profitable room rates depends on a reasonable overall capture requirement.

A successful hotel/motel development, of course, depends not only on the soundness of the development concept, but also on good management. A strong management organization may overcome limitations posed by poor location, mediocre design, or miscalculated demand estimates. No piece of land and no architectural masterpiece can overcome poor operating management.

Conclusion

Where location analysis assesses a project in broad generalities, market analysis considers issues of project viability in detail. The results of market analysis inform the design, marketing and subsequent operation of a project. Market analyses should be formulated and interpreted creatively by the developer in order to realize solutions that provide the highest real estate return.

· CHADWICK · LEAD · WORKS ····· BOSTON ·

In November of 1979 Robert Yelton and Harry Standel, principals of the Bay Group, were reviewing the status of their Chadwick Building development in downtown Boston.   This development was a 55,000 square foot historic commercial structure which was being rehabilitated under the historic preservation provisions of the 1976 Tax Reform Act. The Chadwick Building was their first project since they had formed the Bay Group in 1977.

The Chadwick Building originally had been built as two structures -- the Whiting Building, constructed in 1875, and the somewhat larger Chadwick Lead Works, constructed in 1887. The buildings had been combined in 1944 by breaking through their common party wall and had housed low-grade tenancies until very recently. By 1978, the downtown Boston office market was very tight, and potential tenants were becoming much more receptive to leasing space in rehabilitated structures. The Bay Group contracted to purchase the property in 1978 and took title in 1979.

Knowing major changes would be forthcoming, some of the existing tenants had elected to remain. Bay's efforts also resulted in some new leases. The new lease agreements provided that rents would continue at a lower level until the Bay Group completed its planned capital improvements.   Mr. Yelton was presently negotiating with interested parties for the remaining major spaces and thought it reasonably certain that they would accept the lease offers he had made. With most of the space in the Chadwick Lead Works now either occupied or very close to being leased, the principals were moving ahead with construction. Although it was difficult to maintain tenant services during construction, they expected work to be substantially completed by July 1980.

Financing for the project was scheduled to close in just a few days. The financing included a permanent mortgage of $1,050,000, which would fund at completion. In the interim, a construction loan of $850,000 would be advanced monthly as the project progressed. Finally, an equity syndication would provide a total of about $355,000 in net proceeds. With the imminent closing of these financial transactions, Mr. Yelton and Mr. Standel expected to be able to recover their personal cash used in getting the development underway.

In the coming weeks, the principals intended to set the strategy for their next project, a similar property located nearby. They were pleased with the results of the Chadwick Building, feeling that their concept had been proven and the vital "track record" established. At the same time, they were disappointed at how little profit had been achieved, especially in view of the risk they had taken and the high level of personal involvement that had been required to get to the present state of completion. They were pleased that their investors would receive a high return, but for the next project, they wanted to achieve a more significant front-end profit.

HISTORIC REHABILITATION LEGISLATION

The Tax Reform Act of 1976 included a section entitled "Tax Incentives to Encourage the Preservation of Historic Structures." This section fundamentally changed the economics of rehabilitating historic properties. The key provision allowed five-year depreciation of the rehabilitation costs of qualified historic properties. This provision assured substantial tax losses to the ownership and thus provided a significant Federal subsidy for historic rehabilitation. To be eligible, a property had to meet one of the following criteria:

1.   Listed in the National Register of Historic Places;

2. Located in a registered national historic district and certified by the Secretary of the Interior as being of historic significance to the district;

3. Located in a local or state designated historic district, under a statute which has been certified by the Secretary of the Interior, and certified by the Secretary of the Interior as being of historic significance to the district.

The law also required that the rehabilitation work be approved by the Secretary of the Interior as a "certified rehabilitation," consistent with the historic character of the property or the historic district in which it was located. These provisions applied to any property located within a registered historic district, unless it was specifically determined not to be of historic significance by the Secretary of the Interior. Demolition of historic structures was not prohibited; however, the act disallowed any deduction for doing so and prohibited any accelerated depreciation on the replacement structure.

The Tax Reform Act required the Secretary of the Interior to make certifications with respect to the historic character of buildings and structures, the rehabilitation of historic buildings and structures, and the preservation criteria of state and local statutes. Within the Department of the Interior, the Office of Archaeology and Historic Preservation was given the responsibility for developing the standards and procedures for implementation. The Technical Preservation Services Division of that office was responsible for creating regulations and administering the process.

The regulations created a two-part "Historic Preservation Certification Application" to determine eligibility for the tax benefits. Part One, "Evaluation of Significance," required a description of the physical appearance and a statement of the historical significance of the proposed building. Part Two, "Description of Rehabilitation," required information on the proposed rehabilitation or preservation work to be done. This included extensive photos and detailed descriptions of how the proposed work will affect the existing historic features. The two parts of the application could be submitted together or separately.

Properties listed on the National Register of Historic Places automatically qualify as certified historic structures. The process for nominating a property to the register begins with the local agency, which in Boston is the Boston Landmarks Commission. The local agency advises the property owner and provides assistance in preparing the application materials. In areas without a local agency, the state historic preservation office, here the Massachusetts Historical Commission, is responsible for initiating the process. After receiving the application from either a local agency or property owner, the state office evaluates its historic significance. If the state office decides to nominate the property, the application is forwarded to the National Register Office of the Department of the Interior, where the final decision is made. Buildings not on the National Register, but at least 50 years old and located in either a national historic district or in a state or locally designated historic district, could also qualify for the tax benefits.

Part Two of the application concerned the quality of proposed rehabilitation. The regulations established "Standards for Rehabilitation" which defined generally the criteria for designation as a certified rehabilitation (see Exhibit 1). The final certification of a rehabilitation is not granted until the work is completed and documented.

With the regulations in place and administrative procedures defined, the tax incentives for historic rehabilitation were officially available. As a practical matter, however, it required two more tax bills -- the technical corrections of 1977 and the Revenue Act of 1978 -- to make the tax incentives finally usable. These modifications had the effect of sharply reducing the tax impact of selling a property after the five-year depreciation was exhausted.

For older buildings which were *not* found to be eligible for the historic register, a second tier of rehabilitation tax incentives was created. A 10% investment tax credit (ITC) was available for the entire rehabilitation cost and could be combined with a conventional accelerated-component depreciation schedule. The 1978 legislation excluded residential rental properties and required that at least 75% of the existing external walls remain in place as external walls. If the building were a designated historic structure, the rehabilitation had to be certified by the Technical Preservation Services Division.

Note: Although five-year depreciation was replaced by a system of Investment Tax Credits in 1981, the provisions of this section remain substantially accurate as of 1988.

USING THE TAX INCENTIVES

Mr. Yelton was enthusiastic about the intent of the legislation, but felt that the only real advantage to having a building designated "historic" was the five-year depreciation provision. This, he believed, would be a major help in getting financing. In marketing the Chadwick Building, he found that while many users were interested in older buildings, their interest seemed to have little to do with the official historic designation. He said, "The appeal of these older buildings is more in their character. The tenants would be interested in the space whether it was built 20 or 100 years ago." He was concerned also that the certification process could involve significant delays in preparation of the application documents and in waiting for approval by government agencies.

The Chadwick Lead Works was one of the first properties to apply for certified historic structure designation under the historic preservation legislation. It had been identified as being historically significant in the process of placing the Custom House Historic District on the National Register. As a result, the Chadwick application for historic structure status was processed without delay. The Bay Group submitted the entire application on January 12, 1979, to the Massachusetts Historical Commission and received notice from the Office of Archaeology and Historic Preservation on February 9, 1979, that the building qualified as an historic structure.

Approval of the Part-Two application took longer as minor modifications in the plans were requested by the state. On March 21, 1979, the proposed Chadwick rehabilitation was approved by the Massachusetts Historical Commission, and Mr. Yelton was notified of Federal approval about two months later. Since then, however, the number of applications for historic structure certification had steadily increased, and the time required for approval was increasing. The Massachusetts Historical Commission estimated that 60 to 70 properties had been designated historic structures thus far, and as of November 1979 an equal number were in progress. However, the Chadwick Lead Works was the first actually to be developed.

THE CHADWICK BUILDING PROJECT

The Bay Group first became interested in the Chadwick Lead Works in 1977. Prior to that time, the building had housed retail, light manufacturing, and warehousing space. In 1978, with the property under agreement, the partners leased the first office space in the Chadwick Building, and they proceeded to close on the purchase in April 1979. The purchase price was $274,000, and the seller took back a purchase money mortgage of $156,000. This obligation would be retired out of the initial draw on the construction loan.

Mr. Yelton described the Bay Group's approach to development: "We're a young development company without much cash. So we look for ways to do a building without putting much equity into it. In the Chadwick Building, we were willing to put in a lot of time, and we knew we could get others to put in time on a speculative basis." Mr. Yelton wanted the Bay Group to have design, construction, and building management expertise in-house; he and his partner believed these areas were essential to rehabilitation projects on this scale. Mr. Yelton had been trained in architecture and in business administration at well-known eastern graduate schools. Mr. Standel was an experienced construction manager and property manager.

The partners believed construction management was particularly important to their business. To plan for all of the unknowns in rehabilitation work would require substantial investigation and design time. They believed that large general contractors were reluctant to bid on rehabilitation work without large contingencies and would usually request change orders when they encountered anything unexpected. Bay Construction, the in-house general contractor, was able to make modifications to the work as needed and maintain direct control of construction costs. In addition to providing control over each phase of a project, the separate corporate entities, Bay Development, Bay Construction, and Bay Management were sources of additional income. As estimated in the equity offering circular, their combined compensation and fees in the Chadwick project could gross $250,000 before office overhead costs.

The capital improvements planned for the Chadwick Lead Works were extensive. The design, prepared by Bay's in-house architect, featured a three-story entrance court, reconditioned and new elevators, and new mechanical systems. The design and other aspects of the development program were described in detail in the mortgage loan package (see Exhibit 2 and Exhibit 4). Mr. Yelton prepared this package in early 1979 to assist in arranging financing. By November, some basic construction work had been accomplished, but construction of the major improvements would not begin until the closing of the construction financing agreement.

While they were arranging financing, the partners continued their leasing efforts. By November of 1979, leases were signed for 20,076 square feet of the total rentable tenant space of 44,800 square feet. Leases for 15,094 square feet of the remaining space were reasonably certain. (Exhibit 3 presents the current rent roll.) Most leases were for a five-year term, and all included annual operating cost escalators, as well as a provision to increase the base rent when the major improvements, such as the atrium/entrance court and lobby, were completed. Leases longer than five years included an adjustment to the base rent after the first five years based on the consumer price index.

The remaining space in the building included the Bay Group's offices and a block of first-floor space which could not be rented until the atrium/entrance court was completed. The Chadwick Restaurant had recently opened after spending a considerable sum on its own improvements. This space was built out by Bay Construction and was very attractive. The restaurant appeared to be doing well, and its management had expressed interest in taking some of the basement space.

Rents for rehabilitated space had been increasing along with the general increase in downtown Boston, but Mr. Yelton thought it was necessary to keep the rents slightly below the top market rents in the initial rent-up period. The current annual gross rent and operating expenses were

$135,445 and $70,000 respectively. Since the rehabilitation was being done incrementally, no tenants would be displaced during construction. When the improvements were completed, the final rent levels would become effective.

PROJECT ECONOMICS AND FINANCING

Mr. Yelton's view of the project economics had changed since he had prepared the original mortgage package. Originally, he had estimated the total development cost at just under $1.5 million. He now believed that the construction cost would not increase, but the soft costs had increased, especially the financing costs.

The bulk of the project cost would be financed by the permanent mortgage of $1,050,000. Because interest rates had recently increased, Mr. Yelton believed the project now had a competitive advantage in the 10.5% interest rate committed in May 1979. Permanent financing of $1,050,000 had been committed by State Mutual Life Assurance Company of America at a fixed rate of 10.5%, with a 25-year term, but callable after 15 years. The commitment provided for an initial disbursement of $850,000 at completion. The final disbursement of $200,000 would be withheld until gross annual rent reached $343,691, with tenants paying an average of $8.13 per square foot.

Mr. Yelton now felt confident that the construction loan of $850,000 was in hand as well. Construction financing was to be provided by New England Merchants National Bank. The commitment was for $850,000 at a floating interest rate, 2% above the small business prime rate. Despite recent dramatic increases in interest rates, the lenders' commitments had held up, and a three-party financing agreement was scheduled to be signed in just a few days.

Syndication of the equity had also just been completed, netting $308,812.50 after $28,687.50 in commissions. Three earlier investor limited partners had contributed an additional $45,000 some months before. Mr. Yelton and Mr. Standel had contributed $45,100 in partnership capital as well, and had loaned additional funds to the partnership. Any such loans remaining would eventually be repaid from project cash flow. The investors as a group were to receive the bulk of the tax shelter and any remaining cash flow for the first five years of operations. They would receive half of all subsequent proceeds.

Getting all of this put together had been made difficult by the lack of financial strength at the outset. Each partner had contributed substantially all of his savings and personal borrowings to the effort. The partners expected to recover these funds from project financing and cash flow.

The most positive change in the project economics was that leasing had progressed ahead of schedule, and market rent levels had escalated. The cash flow from the building was therefore better than anticipated. In the mortgage package, Mr. Yelton had estimated the gross potential rent at $345,000 and net income from operations at $161,900. He now believed these figures would be significantly higher. He knew, for example, that a 22,000 square foot lease in a rehabilitated building had just been signed for $16 per square foot. This property was only a few blocks from Chadwick, though in a somewhat better location. He also knew that other building owners were becoming more aggressive in measuring space and were allocating common areas to the tenant rentable areas. Implementing this policy would add 10-20% to the Chadwick rentable areas.

THE SYNDICATION

Although historic rehabilitation was a relatively new area for syndication, Mr.

Yelton and Mr. Standel both had extensive experience in low and moderate income housing syndications. They believed syndication was the best way to generate the equity needed for the Chadwick Building development. The five-year depreciation made this attractive for tax-oriented investors, and the appreciation potential of commercial property provided a significant advantage over low and moderate income housing projects. These normally have cash flow restrictions, questionable residual value and often cannot be refinanced for twenty years or more. Unlike commercial development, however, the investment risk in housing syndications was believed to be low.

While the risk is greater in commercial rehabilitation, Mr. Yelton believed it was not significantly different from the risk of other private development. Although rehabilitated buildings were sometimes assumed to involve greater risk because of major structural uncertainties, his experience was that this is almost never the case in commercial buildings. These usually have a straightforward structural system and were often designed to carry warehouse loads. Their simple, open plans were readily convertible to modern office space, while maintaining the character of the older structure.

Usually few modifications had been made to these structures over the years because they were not considered desirable office space. There were often complications in rehabilitated buildings which wouldn't occur in new construction (such as the local utility's steam line easement which runs through the basement of the Chadwick Building), but in his opinion these rarely posed major problems. Structural uncertainties could usually be resolved by a competent structural engineer after exposing the condition to scrutiny. Mr. Yelton believed that the existing structure resulted in a shorter construction time in a rehabilitation project and made its total cost more predictable than that of new construction.

The Limited Partnership Agreement for the Chadwick Building Company was executed on April 19, 1979, and the equity syndication offering was prepared in September for distribution to potential investors. A total of $337,500 of limited partnership interests were offered in 15 units of $22,500 each. Three previous investor limited partners had already contributed $45,000. A minimum purchase of one-half unit, or $11,250 was specified. Robert Yelton and Harry Standel were the general partners. The marketing of the units was informal, and most of the investors were either friends of the partners or their professional consultants.

Under the terms of the agreement, the limited partners were to receive 95% of the profits and losses and cash flow, after an incentive management fee and after repayment of advances from the general partners. This 95% was allocated 20% to the early group of three investors and 75% to the latest group. When the investor limited partners had received total cash equal to their investment, most likely at the expected time of refinancing in five to seven years, their interest reverted to 50% thereafter, allocated similarly. Mr. Yelton said that this represented a normal deal for a syndication. The limited partners received a high rate of return, primarily through income-tax savings in the early years, and a 50-50 split of the "futures."

The projections of financial performance in the offering memorandum (see Exhibit 5) were very conservative in Mr. Yelton's view. Yet they indicated a very high return for the investors. The cash flow from the project would be needed for a time to return the cash advances made by the general partners, but the tax shelter was automatic. Once the certified costs were spent -- estimated at $1,289,000 -- the depreciation, $257,822 per year, would automatically produce tax deductions, which would be allocated 95% to the limited partners. These investors were all in the 50% tax bracket on marginal income. Therefore, even if the cash flows never materialized, the investors would get a return just from their tax savings.

THE FUTURE

The Bay Group's two principals were optimistic about the potential for doing more historic rehabilitation projects. The firm had one project it could point to, and was in the process of making plans for a second -- the Bedford Building. This property was located nearby and was in many ways similar to Chadwick Lead Works. Mr. Yelton said, "In the Chadwick Building we preferred to get it syndicated quickly and get our money out." In the Bedford Building, they would look for a higher total return on their personal and financial investment.

As Mr. Standel put it succinctly, "What should we do differently next time?"

EXHIBITS

1. General standards for historic preservation projects.

2. Loan package.

3. Current rent roll.

4. Architectural plans.

5. Offering memorandum (excerpts).

QUESTIONS FOR DISCUSSION

1. Did the historic certification make a significant contribution to this project? Would it have gone ahead without the tax subsidy?

2. Assuming Chadwick will be completed by July 1, how much cash will have been spent for all purposes during the entire development process? What are the sources of this cash?

3. When will cash flow likely be available to distribute to the limited partners?

4. What will be the pattern of tax losses for the limited partners? Is this a good investment for them?

5. What would happen if there were a cost overrun of $150,000?

Exhibit 1

GENERAL STANDARDS for Historic Preservation Projects

The following general standards apply to all treatments undertaken on historic properties listed in the National Register:

1. Every reasonable effort shall be made to provide a compatible use for a property that requires minimal alteration of the building structure, or site and its environment, or to use a property for its originally intended purpose.

2. The distinguishing original qualities or character of a building, structure, or site and its environment shall not be destroyed. The removal or alteration of any historic material or distinctive architectural features should be avoided when possible.

3. All buildings, structures, and sites shall be recognized as products of their own time. Alterations which have no historical basis and which seek to create an earlier appearance shall be discouraged.

4. Changes which may have taken place in the course of time are evidence of the history and development of a building, structure, or site and its environment. These changes may have acquired significance in their own right, and this significance shall be recognized and respected.

5. Distinctive stylistic features or examples of skilled craftsmanship which characterize a building, structure, or site, shall be treated with sensitivity.

6. Deteriorated architectural features shall be repaired rather than replaced, wherever possible. In the event replacement is necessary, the new material should match the material being replaced in composition, design, color, texture, and other visual qualities. Repair or replacement of missing architectural features should be based on accurate duplications of features, substantiated by historical, physical, or pictorial evidence rather than on conjectural designs or the availability of different architectural elements from other buildings or structures.

7. The surface cleaning of structures shall be undertaken with the gentlest means possible. Sandblasting and other cleaning methods that will damage the historic building materials shall not be undertaken.

8. Every reasonable effort shall be made to protect and preserve archeological resources affected by, or adjacent to, any acquisition, protection, stabilization, preservation, rehabilitation, restoration, or reconstruction project.

Exhibit 2

Exhibit 2
continued

The restored Chadwick Building, combining two of Boston's historic structures, offers business, professional and institutional tenants a distinguished physical environment in which to locate.

The Whiting structure at 172 High Street was built in 1875 in Italianate style after the plans of Architect Geoffrey Young. The refined facade designs draw together the detailed masonry ornamentation and subtly paired windows into an expressive arcade effect.

The Chadwick Lead Works was erected in 1887 for the manufacture, sales and distribution of ammunition. Lead shot was formed from molten metal during its fall from the top of the beautiful tower. William Preston designed the building with Romanesque arched windows, rough stone and terra cotta ornamentation.

As one of the most significant buildings of Boston's financial area Historic District, the Chadwick Building offers a dignity and character that can not be recreated.

LOCATION

At the corner of High and Batterymarch Streets, in downtown Boston's financial district, the Chadwick Building is adjacent to the region's major financial institutions and within easy walking distance of the City's major shopping areas on Washington Street and Quincy Market, the Boston Waterfront, and Government Center.

Exhibit 2
continued

Since the commercial construction boom began in the '60's with the construction of the State Street Bank Building, one block away, this area has undergone rapid transformation until now, with the completion of the Federal Reserve Plaza and plans for a South Station arena/convention/hotel complex, it has become the recognized locus for business development.

The Chadwick Building is extremely conveniently situated for public and private transportation.

Automobiles: Major highways are easily accessible from the Central Artery, which has an exit onto High Street. Within a 5-minute walk, there are over 5,000 public and private parking spaces, the closest being the inexpensive High Street Boston Municipal Garage.

Public Transportation: South Station, with its bus, rapid transit and commuter train service, is a 3-minute walk from the Chadwick Building.

Airport: Logan International Airport is a 10-minute taxi ride from the Chadwick Building and is accessible from the South Station Rapid Transit Station.

DESIGN FEATURES

The Entrance Court

The entrance to the building from High Street will be through a dramatic three-story semi-enclosed garden. From an intermediate level, this elegant entrance court makes accessible the commercial space along its perimeters by two levels of walkways. The focus of this space is the office lobby for the newly constructed office interiors above.

The conversion of the Chadwick to first class commercial space has provided the opportunity to create this three-story semi-enclosed entry garden. The adaptation of the original Romanesque brick arch expression to the entrance court maintains the design integrity of the original and adds a timeless dignity to a dramatic new feature.

Exhibit 2
continued

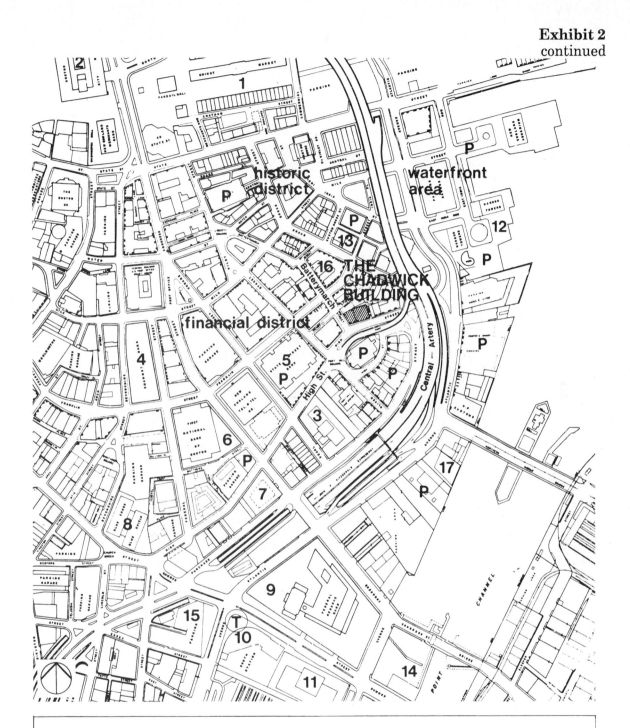

1. FANEUIL HALL MARKETS	10. SOUTH STATION TRANSPORTATION CENTER
2. CITY HALL	
3. TRAVELERS BUILDING	11. STONE & WEBSTER BUILDING
4. SHAWMUT BANK BUILDING	12. HARBOR TOWERS APARTMENTS
5. STATE STREET BANK BUILDING	13. FAIRMONT HOTEL PROPOSED
6. FIRST NATIONAL BANK BUILDING	14. ARENA/CONVENTION SITE
7. KEYSTONE BUILDING	15. CONVENTION HOTEL SITE
8. 100 SUMMER STREET	16. BATTERYMARCH BUILDING
9. FEDERAL RESERVE PLAZA	17. SHERATON BUILDING

Exhibit 2
continued

The Ground Floors

The two ground floors will open onto the entrance and
its garden court, and can be entered from Batterymarch
and High Streets. The second level will have a recessed
arcade/patio along Batterymarch Street. This area could
be utilized by a restaurant for sheltered outside service.
Major retail uses on these floors could all face onto the
Entrance Court, creating an activity focus for the public
spaces.

These floors have 12-14 feet of clearance to the heavy
timber floor construction that lends itself well to being
exposed as a design feature. A loading dock, at the rear
of the building, is accessible from Wendell Street.

The Office Floors

The third through the seventh floors are available for
single or multi-tenant space. The office spaces are open
and light and easily partitioned to accommodate professional, institutional or commercial uses. The suites
will be distinguished by the exceptional features of the
building - high ceilings, hardwood floors, a variety of
arched and many lighted windows, and the options of
exposed brickwork and heavy timber ceilings. Views are
toward the financial district and the waterfront. The
building has windows on all four sides. The third floor
has balconies which overlook the entrance garden, and
the seventh floor has additional skylight lighting.

Service areas contain passenger and freight elevators,
lavatories and storage areas. Space is available for up
to eight tenants per floor, as follows:

	Gross	Multi-tenant
Level 1	9,450 s.f.	8,500 net rentable s.f.
Level 2	7,850 s.f.	6,600 net rentable s.f.
Level 3	7,900 s.f.	6,600 net rentable s.f.
Level 4	8,600 s.f.	7,300 net rentable s.f.
Level 5	8,600 s.f.	7,300 net rentable s.f.
Level 6	5,350 s.f.	4,200 net rentable s.f.
Level 7	5,350 s.f.	4,300 net rentable s.f.

Exhibit 2
continued

January 15, 1979

THE CHADWICK BUILDING
172-184 HIGH STREET
BOSTON, MASSACHUSETTS

INCOME		INITIAL LEASES	YEAR 2 LEASES	
Level 1	*1800 s.f.	$ 8,600	$ 8,600	
	6200 s.f.		43,400	(plus percentage)
Level 2	*4900 s.f.	44,000	44,000	(plus percentage)
	1800 s.f.		15,500	
Level 3	6600 s.f.		52,800	
Level 4	7300 s.f.		58,400	
Level 5	*4500 s.f.	30,000	38,000	
	2800 s.f.		22,400	
Level 6	*2950 s.f.	11,875	16,875	
	1350 s.f.		10,800	
Level 7	*3600 s.f.	21,150	28,800	
	700 s.f.		5,600	
	*17750 s.f. (leased)			
	44000 s.f. (total)	$115,625	$345,175	
Vacancy			17,275	

EXPENSES		
Heat	$21,000	$27,000
Electricity (Public)	6,000	13,000
Water and Sewer	1,000	2,000
Janitor and Main.	3,000	17,500
R.E. Taxes	18,000	75,000
Elevator	2,000	2,500
Insurance	5,000	9,500
Mgmt. Exp.	6,400	17,000
	$62,400	$166,000

NET INCOME	$53,225	$161,900

Exhibit 2
continued

January 31, 1979

THE CHADWICK BUILDING
172-184 HIGH STREET
BOSTON, MASSACHUSETTS

Seven Stories   55,000 square feet gross building area
                                     44,000 square feet net rentable
                                     10,668 square feet land area

Historic Designation, United States Park Service

Mortgage Requested: $1,110,000.00

Uses: Level One and Two - Restaurant and Retail Space
            Levels Three thru Seven - Office Space

Construction Proposed:

        - Central Entrance Court
        - New Office Lobby
        - New Elevator
        - Public Spaces
        - Tenant Improvements

Leased Space: 17,750 s.f. Net Rentable
                     Average of $6.50 per s.f. = $115,625

Available Space: 26,250 s.f. Net Rentable

Developers:

        Bay Development Corporation
        184 High Street
        Boston, Mass. 02110
        Robert H. Yelton, Harry M. Standel, principals

Architects:

        Richard W. White, Architect/Planner
        184 High Street
        Boston, Mass. 02110

Attorneys:

        Lee Kozol
        Friedman & Atherton
        28 State Street
        Boston, Mass. 02108

Exhibit 2
continued

January 15, 1979

THE CHADWICK BUILDING
172-184 HIGH STREET
BOSTON, MASSACHUSETTS

PROJECT COSTS	YEAR I	YEAR II
Acquisition	$276,000	$ 276,000
Construction	130,000	1,074,000
Architectural & Engineering	12,000	78,000
Legal	4,000	18,000
Interest During Construction	6,000	25,000
Taxes During Construction	6,000	10,000
	$436,000	$1,481,000

FUNDING SOURCES		
Equity	$ 30,000	$ 371,000
Purchase Money Mortgage	156,000	
Mortgage	250,000	1,110,000
	$436,000	$1,481,000

Exhibit 2
continued

page four   NEW ENGLAND REAL ESTATE JOURNAL   1978-1979 Commercial Report

Rates over $9 for totally rebuilt space with strong demand in Boston

APRIL 1978
GREATER BOSTON REAL ESTATE BOARD

BUILDING OWNERS AND MANAGERS ASSOCIATION
OF GREATER BOSTON

Office Vacancy Survey

Classification	# of Buildings	Total Sq. Ft. Rentable Area	Total Sq. Ft. Vacant Area	% of Vacancy	Total Sq. Ft. Vacant & for Sublease	% Vacant and for Sublease	Total Government Occupancy	Government Occupancy as % Total Area
DOWNTOWN:								
$12 and up	4	2,887,282	304,216	10.53	8,000	0.28	--	--
$10 to $11.99	14	5,240,776	318,906	6.08	17,330	0.33	209,628	4.00
$8 to $9.99	22	3,179,459	264,270	8.31	55,614	1.75	108,793	3.42
$7 to $9.99	13	1,059,188	92,440	8.73	--	--	87,222	8.23
$6 to $6.99	15	1,071,672	187,656	17.51	4,200	0.39	97,857	9.13
$5 to $5.99	7	787,733	152,552	19.37	30,000	3.81	244,119	30.99
$3 to $4.99	3	899,243	32,303	3.59	--	--	357,000	39.70
TOTAL	78	15,125,353	1,352,343	8.96	115,144	0.76	1,104,619	7.30
BACK BAY:								
$12 and up	2	287,078	--	--	--	--	--	--
$10 to $11.99	3	2,747,854	325,367	11.84	--	--	15,726	0.57
$8 to $9.99	8	1,384,701	70,960	5.12	--	--	--	--
$7 to $9.99	5	467,260	116,057	24.84	--	--	25,000	5.99
$6 to $6.99	5	283,716	64,262	22.65	4000	1.41	--	--
$5 to $5.99	8	312,014	150,214	48.14	--	--	34,675	11.11
$3 to $4.99	3	46,103	5,873	12.74	1400	3.04	--	--
TOTAL	34	5,528,726	732,733	13.25	5400	0.10	78,401	1.42
GRAND TOTAL	112	20654079	2085076	10.09	120544	0.58	1,183,020	5.73

Exhibit 2
continued

```
                              APRIL 1978
                    GREATER BOSTON REAL ESTATE BOARD

                BUILDING OWNERS AND MANAGERS ASSOCIATION
                         OF GREATER BOSTON

                  Vacancy Survey -- Supplemental Data


                                               Total Store      Total       % Total
                                       %         Sq. Ft.      Store Area    Store Area
Classification    Owner Occupied  Owner Occupied   Area        Vacant        Vacant
-------------------------------------------------------------------------------------

DOWNTOWN:

$12 and up           445,054         15.41         65,085        9,124        14.02
$10 to $11.99      2,358,512         45.00        170,737        5,807         3.60
$8 to $9.99          255,066          8.02        226,331       17,750         7.84
$7 to $ 9.99         161,857         15.28         71,700        2,000         2.79
$6 to $6.99           93,679          8.74         88,806        5,962         6.71
$5 to $5.99            1,800          0.23        102,895       25,781        25.06
$3 to $4.99           30,800          3.43         12,500        3,500        28.00

TOTAL              3,346,768         22.13        738,054       69,924         9.47


BACK BAY:

$12 and up           283,812         98.86          --            --            --
$10 to $11.99      2,324,640         84.60          7,898         --            --
$8 to $9.99        1,020,824         73.72         72,216        7,700        10.66
$7 to $ 9.99         119,000         25.47         23,570        8,000        33.94
$6 to $6.99            2,100          0.74         61,682        4,850         7.86
$5 to $5.99           27,000          8.65         38,169          800         2.10
$3 to $4.99              350          0.76         18,570         --            --

TOTAL              3,777,726         68.33        222,105       21,350         9.61

GRAND TOTAL        7,124,494         34.49        960,159       91,274         9.51
-----------
```

Exhibit 2
continued

NEW ENGLAND REAL ESTATE JOURNAL　　1978-1979 Commercial Report

Ramsey reports that office rents are going up and will go higher

By R. DUFF RAMSEY

(Mr. Ramsey, formerly an executive with the Codman Co., is an office leasing specialist and heads his own company in Boston.)

Buy low, sell high. Developers who bought sites in 1975 or 1976 and bought design and construction in 1977 or early 1978 for delivery in late 1978 or 1979 will do very well.

Office rents are going up and will go higher, faster in the next six months (after that who

knows?). The reason for the jump is the basic economics of supply and demand. The specifics and timing will vary according to location, but the general trend applies to both urban and suburban markets.

DOWNTOWN BOSTON

The sage broker I quoted last year in this column who said "Downtown is a year behind 128" has been proven right. The demand has increased dramatically while the production has virtually ground to a halt. Buildings containing 1.25m s/f of space became ready for occupancy in 1977 after peak completion of over 4m s/f in 1975. Completions in 1978 total 550,000 s/f only because of a few months delay of the Federal Reserve Bank in actually occupying its new tower.

No office buildings will be completed in 1979 or 1980 in Boston proper, the first blank years since 1963! The 15 year building boom, during which 18¼m s/f of office space was created, has come to an end. No new private office towers have even been announced.

The only office building projects in the works (planning) are:
1. State Transportation Building in Park Plaza.
2. Federal Office Building of up to one million s/f; possible location on lower Washington street.
3. Urban Investment & Dev. Co. proposal for 600,000 s/f as part of its Copley Square air rights project.

It is unlikely that any of these projects will be ready for occupancy before 1982.

DEMAND

The renewed vigor of the national and regional economies has resulted in one of the best leasing years of the decade. The new developer buildings at 175 Federal st. and 60 State st. have both passed 80% rent-up within a year of their doors' openings, even with rents at a premium over the previous market level. Equally important has been the virtual elimination of the overhang of vacancy left over from buildings completed in 1975 and 1976, including One Federal st. and 100 Summer st., as well as large vacancies in some of the older

modern towers.

The most significant deals of the past year have been announced within the past quarter. One was the move of the Sheraton Corp. headquarters from their own older building to 60 State st. The other was the move of Touche, Ross & Co.'s Boston region office to the Shawmut Bank's One Federal tower; less than five years ago they vacated downtown for Wellesley Office Park.

The tenants for the new buildings came from both existing towers and from old buildings. The resulting vacancy in existing towers has largely been swallowed by pent-up expansion of other tenants in the same buildings. The older buildings have not been as fortunate. But the survivors will do well in 1979, 1980 and 1981.

RENT LEVELS

Rent levels in the financial district towers have held in the $10 to $12 psf range (New York) since 1970 when adjusted for tax and energy escalation only. This has meant no provision for interest and construction cost escalation over the same interval caused by

inflation. This spring, when several new buildings passed 75% lease-up, quoted rents were increased $.50 to $1 psf, although real increases were less because of escalation base revisions.

As little or no resistance has been encountered to the new rates, a general round of increases of an additional (real) $1 psf can be expected this fall or winter. This will result in an effective range of $12 to $15 (NYS) psf for tenants of 5,000 to 20,000 s/f who negotiate in 1979. Penthouses and deluxe smaller suites with special views will rent for $15 to $18 psf (NYS).

The best of the pre-WWII buildings have recently broken the psychological barrier of $10 psf (NFF) for turnkey space. In the next year, the market for first class older buildings will be $10 to $11 psf, while the second class buildings struggling since 1970 on $6 to $7 psf rents will move up to a range of $7.50 to $9 psf for average remodelled space.

Exhibit 2
continued

THE PRINCIPALS

BAY DEVELOPMENT CORPORATION

Robert H. Yelton who resides at 152 West Concord Street,
Boston, Massachusetts is the President of Bay Development
Corporation. Mr. Yelton has been the President of Arch-
plan, Inc. - a subsidiary of State Street Development
Company of Boston since 1973. In that capacity he had extensive experience in developing real estate complexes
financed by state and federal programs, including the responsibility for the land assembly, planning and design,
construction co-ordination, and processing of over $50
million of subsidized multi-family complexes. Mr. Yelton
has also worked as a development consultant to the World
Bank, the Arabian American Oil Company, community groups
and public agencies. He is a graduate of Harvard Business
School, Harvard Design School and the University of Cin-
cinnati.

Harry M. Standel who resides at 115 Bellevue Street in
Newton, Massachusetts, is the Vice-President and Treasurer of Bay Development Corporation. Mr. Standel has
been Vice-President of Continental Wingate Co., Inc. with
total responsibility for the management of over 3500 residential units. In this capacity he has participated in
all aspects of the processing and development of over $70
million of subsidized multi-family housing. Previously,
Mr. Standel was responsible for contracting for CWC Builders, Inc. - a company involved in the construction of federal and state financed residential complexes. In the
above capacity he produced over 2500 apartment units. An
engineer by training, Mr. Standel graduated from Boston
University and did graduate work at Northeastern University.

Exhibit 2
continued

BAY DEVELOPMENT CORPORATION

184 HIGH STREET

BOSTON, MASSACHUSETTS

Bay Development Corporation was formed in early 1977 as an organization dealing with all aspects of real estate development. The principals and staff bring to the corporation years of experience in development, construction and management of some of the most innovative and successful projects in the northeast.

By maintaining effective working relationships with planning, building and zoning officials, state and local environmental boards and historic commissions, financial agencies and community groups, the principals of Bay Development Corporation have made possible the development and management of over 75 million dollars in mortgage value of real estate projects. These include large scale new construction as well as the rehabilitation and conversion of institutional buildings, commercial and hotel structures and residential development.

Bay Development Corporation brings to a project trained professionals in the area of finance and economic analysis, planning, engineering, architecture, construction management, tenant management and marketing.

Exhibit 3

LEASE SCHEDULE (November 1979)

TENANTS	COMMENCE-MENT DATE	FLOOR	AREA (S.F.)	TERM YEARS	INITIAL RENT		FINAL RENT		% OPERATING COST INCRSE. ASSIGNED
					$TOTAL	$/S.F.	$TOTAL	$/S.F.	
BOSTON BLUE PRINT	12/1/78	1	1,800	5	8,559	4.75	12,163	6.75	4%
CHADWICK GARDENS	6/1/79	2	4,900	10[1]	44,000[2]	9.00	44,000[2]	9.00	10
ASSOCIATED PRESS*	4/1/80	3	6,984	10[1]	62,856	9.00	62,856	9.00	16
COMPUTER SERVICES OF AMERICA*	3/1/80	4	8,110	5	56,770	7.00	79,990	9.00	18.6
DOROTHY A. PIKE	9/15/79	5	636	5	3,816	6.00	5,088	8.00	1.5
D. PIKE & CO.	9/15/79	5	2,772	5	16,362	6.00	22,076	8.00	6.6
A.V. DESIGN ASSOC.	8/1/79	5	1,612	5	10,962	6.80	14,508	9.00	3.8
BOSTON ARCHITECTURAL TEAM	3/1/78	6	3,325	5	23,700	7.12	29,925	9.00	7.6
MARKETHOUSE DESIGN	10/1/78	7	429	5	2,574	6.00	3,432	8.00	1
RICHARD WHITE, ARCHITECT	10/1/78	7	429	5	2,574	6.00	3,432	8.00	1
VANASSE/HANGEN DESIGN	5/1/79	7	2,384	5	16,328	6.00	21,456	9.00	6
RESTAURANT BROKERS OF AMER.	11/18/78	7	1,050	5	6,300	6.00	8,400	8.00	2.5

* Pending: Draft Leases Presented

1 Base rent adjustment after first five years proportional to change in Consumer Price Index

2 Plus Percentage Rent: based on Gross Annual Sales, paid monthly, on following schedule:

GROSS SALES	% DUE AS RENT
$0-650,000/yr.	0%
$650-750,000/yr.	5%
$750-850,000/yr.	7%
$850-950,000/yr.	9%
$950,000 +/yr.	11%

Exhibit 4

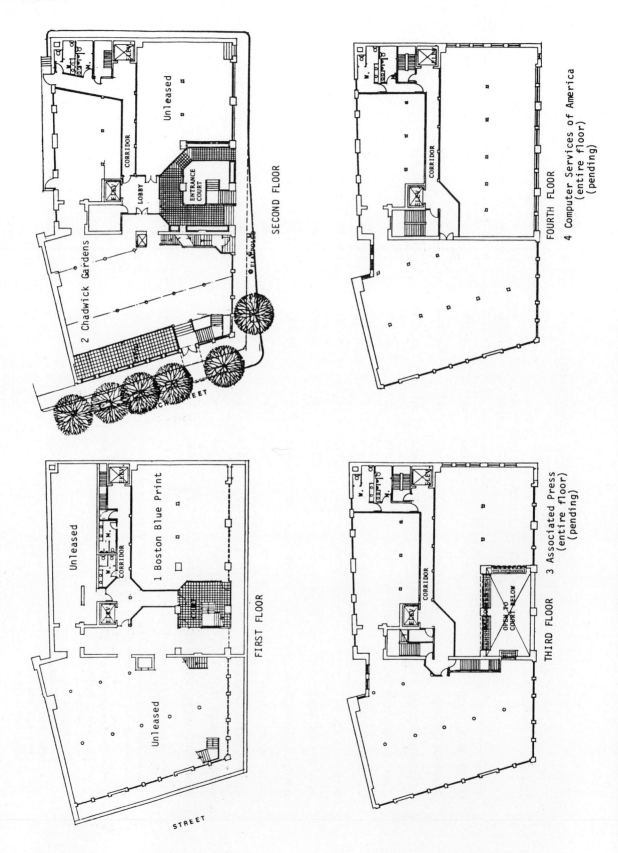

Exhibit 4
continued

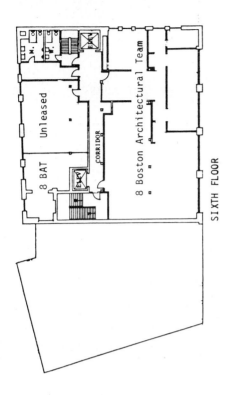

SIXTH FLOOR

8 BAT

Unleased

8 Boston Architectural Team

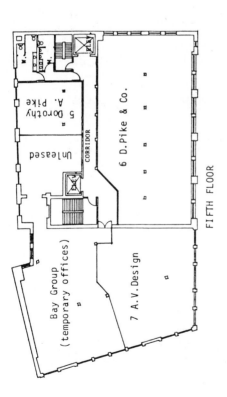

FIFTH FLOOR

Unleased

5 Dorothy A. Pike

6 D. Pike & Co.

Bay Group (temporary offices)

7 A.V. Design

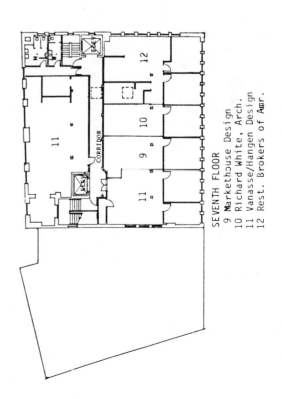

SEVENTH FLOOR
9 Markethouse Design
10 Richard White, Arch.
11 Vanasse/Hangen Design
12 Rest. Brokers of Amr.

Exhibit 5

Excerpts from Offering Memorandum (September 1979)

USE OF PROCEEDS

The anticipated aggregate capital contributions, ($382,500 if all of the Interests offered hereby are sold) will be applied as follows and in the following order of priority. See also "Compensation and Fees to the General Partner and Affiliates" and "The Project" - "Terms of the Purchase":

1. $21,000 to be paid to Bay Development Corp. ("BDC") as reimbursement for the cash required for Mortgage Commitment, provided by "BDC".

2. $7500 to be paid to "BDC" as reimbursement for the appraisal required by "SML" and paid for by "BCD".

3. $10,000 to Bay Development Corporation as reimbursment, on a non-accountable basis, for legal, printing and other direct out-of-pocket expenses incurred in connection with this Offering.

4. $28,687.50 to broker-dealers (which may include "BDC") as commissions for selling Limited Partnership Interests.

5. $10,125 to "BDC" as a syndication fee.

6. $68,400 to Bay Management Group, Inc. ("BMG") for rent-up fees and commissions earned by it or due or paid to real estate brokers.

7. $40,500 to "BMG" for additional management services to the Partnership during the three year period commencing at initial rental of the Project.

8. $11,000 to "BDC" for supervision of the business affairs of the Partnership prior to the closing of the permanent loan.

9. $50,000 to "BDC" as reimbursement for the fees paid to architectural and engineering consultants.

10. $90,287.50 to "BDC" as a development fee.

The financial projections annexed hereto assume that all of the Interests offered hereby are sold and that each Limited Partner is entitled to report his distributive share of the Partnership's losses on the assumed time schedule. If less than all of the Interests are sold, the amount and/or timing of these payments would change and, accordingly, the timing of losses resulting from the payment of these items would also change.

See "Risk Factors", "Federal Tax Matters" and the attached Projections - "Assumptions" for additional information about the tax treatment and anticipated timing of these payments.

Exhibit 5
continued

COMPENSATION AND FEES TO THE GENERAL
PARTNER AND AFFILIATES

The following table sets forth the amount and types of fees, compensation, income, distributions and other payments to be received by the General Partner and its affiliates in connection with this offering and the operations of the Partnership. Such fees, income, distributions and other payments are not the result of arms-length negotiation. See "Use of Proceeds" and "Potential Conflicts of Interest".

Name of Entity RECEIVING COMPENSATION (A)	Form and Amount of Compensation (B)
Bay Management Group, Inc. ("BMG")	Management Fees pursuant to the Management Agreement with the Partnership. In addition, BMG may earn supplemental fees based on the Project's operations, equal to one-half of the excess, if any, of net receipts from operations over the payment of all expenses, including, without limitation, the basic management fee.
	Rent-up fees and commissions (to Real Estate Brokers ------------- $68,400.
	Fee for additional management services-------------------- $40,500.
Bay Development Corportation ("BDC")	Fee for supervising business affairs of the Partnership prior to permanent loan closing---------------- $11,000.
	Developer's Fee------------- $90,287.
	Reimbursement of Expenses--- $10,000.
	Syndication Fee------------- $10,125.
	Commission for selling Limited Partnership Interests------- $28,687.
	Reimbursement of Architectural Expenses-------------------- $50,000.

The General Partner will also have a five percent (5%) interest in the Profits, Losses and Cash Flow, if any from operations of the Partnership and a fifty (50%) interest in the net proceeds of any sale, refinancing, condemnation ot other disposition of the Project, or

Exhibit 5
continued

COMPENSATION AND FEES TO THE GENERAL PARTNERS AND AFFILIATES (cont.)

dissolution or termination of the Partnership, after the return of capital contributions to all Partners (less any previous distributions previously made to them). See "Profits, Losses and Distributions".

NOTES:

(A)   For a description of the relationships between the General Partners, their affiliates and the Partnership, see "Participants" and "Potential Conflicts of Interest".

(B)   For a description of the agreements providing for these payments and fees, see "Summary of Certain Provisions of the Partnership Agreement" which are attached hereto.

(C)   Commission will be paid to BDC for Limited Partnership Interest which it sells. Commission on Interests sold by other broker/ dealers will be paid to such other broker/dealers.

Exhibit 5
continued

THE CHADWICK BUILDING COMPANY
(A Limited Partnership)

FINANCIAL PROJECTIONS

The following summary of financial projections are based upon information obtained from sources deemed reliable by General Partners; and include assumptions as to future events which may or may not prove to be accurate. No representation or warranty is made or to be implied as to the present or future accuracy or completeness of these assumptions or as to the results of these projections as they may compare to future actual operations. Each prospective Limited Partner must rely either upon his own analysis of the project or the advise of his professional advisor.

FINANCIAL SUMMARY

The following is a summary of the result of the financial projections attached hereto. This summary is intended only as a quick reference, and is subject to the statements on this page, the assumptions contained herein and, the disclosures contained in the Confidential Offering Memorandum.

The attached schedules analyzing the proposed Project transactions are based, among other things, upon the following assumptions. The more descriptive and informative confidential memorandum should be read in conjunction with the attached schedules, especially "Risk Factors and Federal Income Tax Matters".

Section 56 of the Code (as amended by the Tax Reform Act of 1976) imposes a 15% "minimum tax" in addition to any Federal income taxes otherwise payable on certain "tax preference items". These preference items include one-half of the amount of which net long-term capital gains exceed net short-term capital losses and the excess of accelerated depreciation over straight-line depreciation of depreciable real property. The limited partners will be required to take into account their respective share of the partnership's tax preference items. The amount subject to the 15% tax is the aggregate of tax preference items reduced by the greater of $10,000 ($5,000 for a married individual filing seperately) or one-half of the regular income tax paid for such a year.

The reader is advised to consult with his tax advisor for advice as to state and local taxes which may be payable in connection with tax preference items.

Section 1348 of the Code (as amended by the Tax Reform Act of 1976) limits the maximum income tax rate on earned income in the case of individuals to 50%. However, the amount of earned income qualifying for such reduction in rate will be reduced by the amount of the total amount of the reader's tax preference items (as defined above) for the taxable year (subject to certain adjustments under applicable regulations).

Exhibit 5
continued

A LIMITED PARTNERSHIP (cont.)

1. PRINCIPLES OF REPORTING

    The projections are prepared on the accrual method of tax
    accounting, assuming the investors will be admitted as of October
    1, 1979. Further, all the investor units will be sold and the
    total mortgage proceeds will be advanced to the partnership. The
    allocation of losses to an investor limited partner will commence
    upon actual admission to the limited partnership.

2. COSTS, REVENUES AND EXPENSES

    Projected costs, revenues, and expenses are based only on the
    estimates of the General Partners and their consultants.

3. SCHEDULE OF EVENTS

Construction commencement	July 1, 1979
Construction completion	July 1, 1980
Final closing	July 1, 1980
Commencement of mortgage amortization	July 1, 1980

4. FINANCING

    Interim mortgagee: NEW ENGLAND MERCHANTS NATIONAL BANK ("NEM")

    Amount: $850,000 ($+200,000) Interest Rate: Small
                                               Business Prime +2%

    Permanent mortgagee: STATE MUTUAL LIFE ASSURANCE COMPANY OF
                           AMERICA ("SML")

    Amount: $1,050,000 Interest Rate: 10-1/2%

5. DEPRECIATION SCHEDULE

YEAR	BUILDING SHELL	FEES & COMMISSIONS	BUILDING IMPROVEMENTS	TOTAL
1979 (Oct. 1- Dec. 31)	2000	$ 111,487	20,000	133,487
1980	8000	53,400	213,000	274,400
1981	8000		257,822	265,822
1982	8000		257,822	265,822
1983	8000		257,822	265,822
1984	8000		237,822	255,822
1985	8000		64,825	72,825
1986(on)	8000			8,000

5. DEPRECIATION SCHEDULE (cont.)

Assumed dates of construction completion and start of depreciation:

    October 1, 1979   31% complete
    July 1, 1980   100% complete

6. OPERATING SCHEDULE

YEAR	GROSS INCOME	OPERATING & COSTS	DEBT SERVICE INT.	PRINCIPAL	CASH FLOW	DEPRE- CIATION	PROFIT (LOSS)
1979	50,000	20,000	17,000		13,000	133,000	(110,000)
1980	300,000	120,000	95,000	5,000	80,000*	275,000	(195,000)
1981	350,000	166,000	109,000	10,000	70,000	265,000	(196,000)
1982	350,000	166,000	107,000	12,000	70,000	265,000	(196,000)
1983	350,000	166,000	106,000	13,000	70,000	266,000	(196,000)
1984	400,000	181,000	105,000	14,000	100,000	72,000	28,000
1985	450,000*	231,000	104,000	15,000	100,000	8,000	92,000
1986	450,000t	231,000	152,000t	13,000t	54,000	8,000	46,000

*- Required for project completion
t- After refinancing and releasing

7. SOURCES OF PARTNERSHIP FUNDS

    CAPITAL CONTRIBUTIONS:
    General and Original Limited Partners   45,100
    Investor Limited Partners   382,500
    Mortgage   1,050,000
    Operating Net 1979-1980   103,000
    Cash Flow Loan from General Partners   144,000

    Total Funds $1,725,000

8. APPLICATIONS OF PARTNERSHIP FUNDS

    Acquisition   274,000
    Construction   951,000
    Taxes   27,000
    Interest   80,000
    Depreciable Costs
    mgmt. fee, arch. and
    developers fees   220,613

Exhibit 5
continued

8.   <u>APPLICATIONS OF PARTNERSHIP FUNDS</u> (cont.)

Expense Costs
  Appraisal and commitment fees
  commissions, syndicate fee   164,887
                                             _____

TOTAL APPLICATIONS $1,725,000

9.   <u>LIMITED PARTNERS RETURN - 10% SHARE - 50% BRACKET</u>

YEAR	PROFIT (LOSS) 10% SHARE	SAVINGS OR (COST) 50% TAX BRACKET	CASH FLOW 10% SHARE	ESTIMATED TOTAL BENEFITS
1979	(11,000)	6,500	–	6,500
1980	(19,500)	8,750	–	8,750
1981	(19,600)	8,800	7,000	15,800
1982	(19,600)	8,800	7,000	15,800
1983	(19,600)	8,800	7,000	15,800
1984	2,800	(1,400)	10,000	8,600
1985	9,200	(4,600)	10,000	5,400

Total Cash Flow after Tax before Refinancing 41,000 $92,000

Total Benefits Before Refinancing   4,000

Preference Refinancing Proceeds   4,000

1985 Refinancing at 5% Share, 7%/yr. Appreciation   19,000

Total Benefits Through 1985   115,000

1986 On/Residual 5% Ownership Equity/Value $39,000

Estimated Cash Flow Per Share $27,000/yr.

Note 5

Organization and Taxation

Federal income tax benefits are an important source of investment value in U.S. real estate. Yet different kinds of organizations may be taxed quite differently. Corporations, partnerships, business trusts, and individuals may own or develop real estate, and the actual value of the tax benefits may depend on which of these organizational forms is chosen. Therefore, developers and owners of real estate must plan their organizations and structure their transactions with tax considerations in mind.

In this note, we will examine the principles of Federal income taxation and the characteristics of the various organizational forms as they apply to real estate ownership and development. The U.S. Internal Revenue Code has been subject to frequent revisions since 1976. As a result, this area of legal and accounting practice has become exceedingly complex and specialized. In this note, we will not present the definitive word on taxes, but will instead stress broadly applicable principles, both of tax law and of organizations. These principles should remain useful to the reader as details of the law continue to change. *The need for competent legal and accounting professionals to review and advise on particular tax matters cannot be overemphasized.* This note contains three sections:

Section I introduces the principles of Federal income taxation, as relevant to real estate ownership and development.

Section II introduces the organizational forms used for real estate.

Section III examines more closely current tax laws and organizational consequences for the real estate developer.

I. PRINCIPLES OF INCOME TAXATION

This note deals with taxation of income at the Federal level and its consequences for real estate investment and development. In this section, we will review the purposes of Federal income taxation and identify the various mechanisms for achieving these purposes.

Income Taxation and Real Estate

The basic purpose of Federal taxation of income is, of course, that of raising money for the government. An enormous amount of money is raised every year by the U.S. Treasury for national defense, social programs, and transfer payments of various kinds. Income taxes and payroll taxes are the primary sources of revenue.

State and local taxes are increasingly important and vary significantly from one locality to another. The U.S. government does not generally have the power to collect sales taxes or taxes based on the value of property owned. These taxes are largely left to state and local governments, which sometimes also have their own income taxes. Most state income taxes are tied more or less directly to the Federal income tax. These are, in effect, a surcharge on the Federal tax. But in other states -- Massachusetts is an example -- the differences are quite dramatic. This note will be limited to the Federal level.

The Internal Revenue Code has been shaped by many other purposes than simply raising money. Perhaps the most important has been to encourage investment of one kind or another, as distinct from personal consumption expenditures. Especially in recent inflationary times, lawmakers have considered this essential to the long-term economic health of the country. As an example of the incentives

used for this purpose, income from the sale of long-term investments ("capital gains") had for many years been taxed at a lower rate than ordinary income.

In addition to encouraging investment generally, the code also encourages numerous specific categories of investment in various, sometimes conflicting, ways. Examples involving real estate include home ownership and rental property generally, as well as specifically investments in subsidized housing, rehabilitation of older and historic structures, and industrial expansions.

Each of these areas of real estate investment has been the subject of one or more major revisions in the tax code over the last decade. Since 1976, six major tax bills have been enacted by the U.S. Congress, each containing numerous items applicable to real estate. In addition, two technical corrections acts were required in intervening years to make workable the previous round of changes. The major bills are listed below:

Tax Reform Act of 1976

Revenue Act of 1978

Economic Recovery Tax Act of 1981 ("ERTA")

Tax Equity and Fiscal Responsibility Act of 1982 ("TEFRA")

Tax Reform Act of 1984

Tax Reform Act of 1986

Throughout this note, these bills will be referenced to provide some historical perspective on current practice. Not content with matters as they stand, the administrative and legislative branches of government now seem to expect to continue to make changes. The latest round of tax changes was very substantial, and it required nearly two years to sort through a series of competing comprehensive proposals. What has been passed is so complex a set of compromises and so uncertain in its actual effect that further evolution seems inevitable. In short, the reader should stay tuned for further developments.

Rates of Taxation

The U.S. individual income tax is a graduated income tax, the theory of which is that everyone is taxed, but those who have more income are taxed more heavily. Many would believe that this principle was handed down by the Founding Fathers, but in fact, income taxes were generally unconstitutional, except during the Civil War, until the passage of the 16th amendment in 1913. Americans' attitudes toward taxes can generally be summed up by the Boston Tea Party of 1774. Once begun, however, income taxes got quickly out of hand. The maximum rate of 7%, passed in 1913, became 94% in World War II, and was still 70% as late as 1981.

Since 1981, the U.S. Internal Revenue Service has received up to 50% of each incremental dollar of annual income received by an individual. This figure is now scheduled to be reduced to an historic low (in the modern era) of 33% for 1988 income. The following table indicates the tax rates which are scheduled to apply for 1986-8 income. Note that by 1988 the highest marginal income tax rate will no longer apply to those with the highest incomes.

Until recently, most real estate analysts used a standard assumption that most real estate investors would have high incomes and would be in the 50% tax bracket for Federal income taxes. Note that for married couples filing joint returns, the "standard" assumption is now only correct to the extent of 1986 annual income above $172,250. Looking forward from 1986, a more reasonable overall average might be 35%, including state and local income taxes, but this will vary widely depending on each taxpayer's specific situation.

The income tax rates do not include the Social Security payroll tax (FICA). This tax adds to the effective tax rate, and because it only applies to a basic level of income, adds to the effect of non-progressivity of tax rates from the middle to the highest income taxpayers. The FICA tax will increase from the 1986 level of 7.15% on the first $41,000 of income to a 1988 level of 7.51% of the first $45,000 of income per person.

The Federal government also taxes income received by corporations. Corporate income for 1986 will be taxed at up to 46%, the rate that has applied since ERTA. This rate will be reduced to 34% in 1988.

These structural changes in tax rates are the central feature of the Tax Reform Act of 1986. The concept of "graduation" of tax rates has been deliberately abandoned, at least for the present. A major incentive has been created to accumulate capital through earning higher income personally. Once the taxpayer is "over the hump," additional dollars of income are taxed at only 28%. The long-term effect of this is uncertain.

Tax Benefits of Real Estate Ownership

What are the tax benefits which provide incentive for investment in real estate? These may be classed into three groups -- tax credits; exclusions from taxable income; and deductions from taxable income. Each of these categories is discussed conceptually here and in more detail in Section III.

Tax Credits. Tax credits are a very direct form of incentive. A tax credit is a simple and direct offset to taxes otherwise payable. As such, for a tax-paying investor, receiving a tax credit is very similar to receiving cash. The Investment Tax

Tax tables

COUPLE FILING JOINTLY

If taxable income is between	Your tax is	Of the amount over
1986 $0 - 3,670	0%	0
3,670 - 5,940	0 + 11%	3,670
5,940 - 8,200	250 + 12%	5,490
8,200 - 12,840	521 + 14%	8,200
12,840 - 17,270	1,170 + 16%	12,840
17,270 - 21,800	1,879 + 18%	17,270
21,800 - 26,550	2,695 + 22%	21,880
26,550 - 32,270	3,740 + 25%	26,550
32,270 - 37,980	5,170 + 28%	32,270
37,980 - 49,420	6,768 + 33%	37,980
49,420 - 64,750	10,544 + 38%	49,420
64,750 - 92,370	16,369 + 42%	64,750
92,370 - 118,050	27,969 + 45%	92,370
118,050 - 175,250	39,525 + 49%	118,050
175,250 and over	67,553 + 50%	172,250
1987 $0 - 3,000	11%	0
3,000 - 28,000	330 + 15%	3,000
28,000 - 45,000	4,080 + 28%	28,000
45,000 - 90,000	8,840 + 35%	45,000
90,000 and over	24,590 + 38.5%	90,000
1988 0 - 29,750	15%	0
29,750 - 71,900	4,463 + 28%	29,750
71,900 - 171,090*	16,265 + 33%	71,900
171,090* and over	48,998** + 28%	171,090

* Add $10,920 for each exemption over 2 personal exemptions.
** Add $3,603 per exemption over 2 personal exemption to the $48,998 figure.

SINGLE TAXPAYER

If taxable income is between	Your tax is	Of the amount over
1986 $0 - 2,480	0%	0
2,480 - 3,670	0 + 11%	2,480
3,670 - 4,750	131 + 12%	3,670
4,750 - 7,010	260 + 14%	4,750
7,010 - 9,170	577 + 15%	7,010
9,170 - 11,650	901 + 16%	9,170
11,650 - 13,920	1,298 + 18%	11,650
13,920 - 16,190	1,706 + 20%	13,920
16,190 - 19,640	2,160 + 23%	16,190
19,640 - 25,360	2,954 + 26%	19,640
25,360 - 31,080	4,441 + 30%	25,360
31,080 - 36,800	6,157 + 34%	31,080
36,800 - 44,780	8,102 + 38%	36,800
44,780 - 59,670	11,134 + 42%	44,780
59,670 - 88,270	17,388 + 48%	59,670
88,270 and over	31,116 + 50%	88,270
1987 0 - 1,800	11%	0
1,800 - 16,800	198 + 15%	1,800
16,800 - 27,000	2,448 + 28%	16,800
27,000 - 54,000	5,304 + 35%	27,000
54,000 and over	14,754 + 38.5%	54,000
1988 0 - 17,850	15%	0
17,850 - 43,150	2,678 + 28%	17,850
43,150 - 100,480*	9,762 + 33%	43,150
100,480* and over	28,681** + 28%	100,480

* Add $10,920 for each exemption over 1 personal exemption.
** Add $3,603 per exemption over 1 personal exemption to the $28,681 figure.

Source: Internal Revenue Service

Credit (ITC) is the most prominent type of tax credit applicable to real estate investment. The amount of the credit is generally tied to the amount of the eligible investment.

Three investment tax credits are significant today: a credit of 10% for investments to rehabilitate nonresidential buildings over 50 years old; a credit of 20% for investments to rehabilitate certified historic structures, regardless of age, and for residential or non-residential uses; and a credit of 9% for development of new or rehabilitated low-income housing (or 4% if financed with other government subsidy programs).

Exclusions from Taxable Income. This form of tax benefit classifies certain types of income as not taxable in the current year for Federal income tax purposes (although the income may be taxable at a later date). Five major types are important to real estate:

1. **The Federal tax exemption for interest on certain bond issues** of state and local government bodies. Bond issues are sometimes used to make low-interest loans for real estate projects, including industrial, commercial and rental housing developments, as well as to provide financing for middle-income homebuyers;

2. **Installment sales**, in which income from the sale of property may be received over time and, with certain limitations, reported as taxable income only in the year cash is actually received;

3. **The tax-free exchange**, in which a sale of real estate may be structured as a swap of like-kind property;

4. **The "roll-over"** treatment accorded gains on sale of a taxpayer's principal personal residence and the senior citizen's one-time exclusion of up to $125,000 of such a gain;

5. **Capital gains** treatment, in which income received from sale of a long-term investment is taxed at a reduced rate. This is done by excluding a portion of such income (60% in recent years) before computing taxable income. The 1986 law eliminated this treatment, but it will likely be revived in the future and so is listed here.

It should be noted that some of the items of income listed above may eventually be taxed. They may variously be includable as ordinary income in later years, or for estate tax purposes, or may be subject to an alternative minimum tax.

Deductions from Taxable Income. This form of tax benefit reduces the amount of income which is otherwise taxable for Federal income tax purposes. Three major types are important to real estate:

1. **The recovery of capital costs** (also known as depreciation expense): The Asset Cost Recovery System (ACRS), established by ERTA, permits recovery of capital costs as annual deductions from income over specified periods. ACRS was modified by the 1984 and 1986 acts, successively lengthening the required recovery periods. For rental property placed in service after 1986, the capital costs are depreciated on a straight line basis over 27.5 years for residential property or 31.5 years for non-residential property. The system of fixing depreciation schedules, in effect since 1981, replaced a more complex system in which numerous depreciation methods were available for various types of buildings and for components of buildings,

which could be depreciated separately.

2. **The recovery of fees and financing costs** (amortization expense): Some project costs other than the depreciable real estate costs may be recovered over various periods shorter than the standard 27.5 or 31.5-year periods for the real estate costs. Organization costs, for example, are amortized over five years. Other costs, such as fees and commissions, may be amortized over the time in which the matching benefits are received. Costs of obtaining a five-year loan, for example, would be amortized over five years;

3. **The recovery of ordinary business expenses**: In addition to the normal and usual expenses of operating a piece of property, some project costs, such as developer's overhead allowances, profits or bonus arrangements, and fees for providing various services, may be expensed in the year incurred.

It is important to note that none of these deductions from taxable income is really unique to real estate. All non-real estate businesses enjoy the same deductions. What is different about the real estate business is the relative importance of non-cash charges. The business of investing in income-producing real estate inherently involves a considerable amount of depreciation and amortization. For new construction investments, which lack the tax credit featured in rehabilitation, non-cash charges indeed provide the only tax incentive.

Also unique about the real estate business today is the capacity for an owner to generate losses in excess of the amount of cash invested and to offset such losses against other income. Real estate investment is in part exempt from the requirement otherwise established in the 1976

act that losses be limited to the amount the owner has "at risk" in the investment. The 1986 act extends the "at risk" requirements to real estate, but it provides an exception that "qualified non-recourse financing" is considered an amount at risk. Most institutional financing is considered "qualified," so this is a big exception, and real estate will therefore continue to be able to generate losses in excess of the amount invested.

Minimizing Taxes

The three types of tax benefits are important incentives to invest in real estate, rather than in other investments or in consumption. Together they comprise a major form of tax subsidy. Are these tax benefits immoral?

From the standpoint of an oil-drilling investment promoter or a socialist, it might appear so. However, the intent of the U.S. Congress is clear. While many other tax-driven investments have been eliminated since 1976, the legal mechanisms which permit tax-subsidized investment in real estate have been carefully preserved. Even the 1986 act does not end the relative advantage of real estate, though it is greatly reduced. Because it is the law of the land, few if any real estate owners or investors feel guilty about using the tax subsidy.

The case against the tax benefits depends generally on the argument that they are relatively inefficient in accomplishing their desired public purpose. This argument is strengthened by the fact that ingenious promoters have created many methods, usually legal, to increase the amount of depreciation and other non-cash losses from real estate transactions, in order to attract investors interested solely in the tax savings. This has resulted in high profits for promoters and for owners of existing properties, but has not necessarily led to any new investment in development projects.

Since 1976, many of the more unproductive techniques used to increase artificially the tax losses from real estate have been eliminated. Prepayment of expenses, retroactive allocations, excessive interest accruals, uneconomic fees, artificial increases in the cost of depreciable property, and transactions involving tax-exempt entities and related parties have all been eliminated or curtailed in recent years. In addition to eliminating each of these previously-legal techniques, penalties have been established for promoters of abusive tax shelters. Generally, transactions which lack economic substance are not legal today.

II. ORGANIZATIONS AND REAL ESTATE

Developers and purchasers of real estate may choose to organize formally as a corporation, partnership or trust or may choose to operate as an individual proprietor. In this section, we will examine briefly the attributes of these various organizational forms, focusing on their use in developing and owning real estate.

Corporate Organization

A corporation is an artificial "person." A corporation is established under state laws, which generally require reserving the use of the corporate name and filing an appropriate corporate charter and bylaws. These documents, which are made a part of the public records of the state, set forth the purposes of the corporation and provide information about its ownership and officers. Various reporting requirements, such as tax returns and an annual statement of condition, must also be met over time.

While an individual may begin a business as a proprietor at any time, a corporation may only be established with the permission of the state. Once established,

a corporation may continue to exist in perpetuity. Unless provided otherwise in its charter, a corporation's life is not limited by the lifespan of its founders or shareholders.

The corporation is the most formal of organizations. Shareholders have no role in management, except through exercise of voting rights which may be specified in the corporate bylaws. A corporation is generally controlled by a board of directors, the operation of which is specified in the bylaws. Officers of a corporation are generally delegated the responsibility for day-to-day management.

In business, the principal reason for use of the corporate organization is that of **limited liability**. A corporation is owned by its shareholders, but the shareholders are not personally liable for the actions of the corporation. Officers and employees may incur personal liability by their individual actions, but the investor who purchases stock will not lose more than the amount invested.

A second major advantage is the easy **transferability of ownership** through transfer of stock. This advantage has led to the widespread ownership by the public of shares in American business corporations, both directly and through investments in mutual funds.

In real estate, these advantages are frequently offset by a major disadvantage of corporate ownership -- the problem of **double taxation**. As noted in Section I, corporations are themselves subject to Federal income taxes. When corporate profits are paid out to shareholders as dividends, the dividends are taxed again as individual income. A related problem is that losses generated within a corporation cannot be used unless other offsetting income is generated by the corporation.

An exception is made for small business corporations ("S" Corporations), where corporate profits and losses are "passed through" to the shareholders. This eliminates the double-tax problem and makes this at times a useful vehicle for real estate ownership and development. However, there are limitations on classes and numbers of shareholders which limit this usefulness.

These problems lead to a general disinclination to hold operating real estate in corporate ownership. Major exceptions include real estate portfolios and related operations which have grown out of other corporate businesses, particularly retail and hotel chains and construction companies. A number of publicly-owned real estate companies were established in the late 1960s, and while some have become privately controlled once again, others have continued to prosper under public ownership.

The corporate organization is nevertheless very important to real estate developers. Large developers will often organize separate corporations to control risks. A corporation may take on a risky task, such as construction, or a task involving possible liability to tenants, employees, regulators or investors. Thus the developer's major assets may be held in non-corporate ownership, while being shielded from certain liabilities.

The corporate organization offers other advantages as well. Corporate fringe benefit programs, such as pension and profit-sharing plans, health and life insurance, stock options, and other devices enable the corporation to provide a maximum proportion of non-taxable compensation to officers and employees. Bonus and incentive arrangements allow flexible compensation arrangements for key individuals. Corporations operating on a fiscal-year basis will often be able to control the timing of receipt of taxable income by individuals. In the case of a liquidation or in a distribution of property to shareholders, income may be recognized by shareholders at a favorable time.

Corporations may be established for purposes other than business. Corporations may qualify under state law and the Internal Revenue Code (Section 501c) for educational, charitable or other public interest purposes. Such corporations pay no tax on income, but they are required to devote their resources to their public interest purposes. Non-profit corporations have been used for public projects, such as urban renewal, and to create "revolving funds" for such purposes as historic preservation and open space acquisition.

Partnerships

A partnership is defined as a voluntary association of two or more persons to carry on as co-owners a business for profit. A partnership is not legally considered a "person" in the sense that a corporation is.

Two basic types of partnership may be created -- the **general partnership** and the **limited partnership**. General partners in a partnership all have a voice in management of the affairs of the partnership and have unlimited personal liability for actions taken by the partnership. A limited partnership will involve a separate class of partners, limited partners, who have no voice in management and have liability limited to their investment in the partnership.

A general partnership may be established without legal formalities. Two or more individuals may simply begin a business, presenting themselves as partners, and agreeing informally as to the conduct of the business. As time passes, it will generally become necessary to formalize the relationship in a written agreement. Limited partnerships may only be established by means of a written agreement and are subject to the Uniform Limited Partnership Act. In the case of limited partnerships, a written certificate of limited partnership must be recorded with the state.

Experienced legal assistance is important in preparing a proper written partnership agreement. Generally speaking, the partnership agreement will set forth a number of specific items, among them:

1. the name, address and purpose of the partnership;

2. the names of the partners;

3. capital contributions by partners and provisions for withdrawals of capital;

4. the interest of each partner in the profits and losses and cash flow of the partnership;

5. salaries and management responsibilities of the partners;

6. accounting records;

7. banking arrangements;

8. consequences of death, disability, or retirement of a partner;

9. the term of the agreement and provisions for termination of the partnership;

10. any special rights or responsibilities of a partner.

In short, the agreement is intended to establish a complete set of rules governing the conduct of the business and the relationship of the partners to each other and to the partnership.

Just as in the case of shareholders in a corporation, limited partners have no role in management, except through exercise of voting or approval rights which may be specified in the written agreement. Partnerships are otherwise controlled by their general partner or partners, who are also responsible for day-to-day management. Although they have nearly total control,

the general partners have a responsibility, called a "fiduciary" relationship, to treat other partners fairly and reasonably.

Unlike a corporation, a partnership may not continue to exist in perpetuity. Unless provided otherwise in a written agreement, a partnership ends upon death or disability of its partners.

The biggest advantage of the partnership form of organization is in the area of taxation. A partnership is not itself taxed, but is treated as a "conduit," passing its profits and losses through to its partners. Generally, profits and losses are allocated in proportion to partnership interest, but where a valid business purpose exists, allocations may be structured to favor one class of partner over another and also to change over time.

A major disadvantage is the requirement to avoid classification of a partnership as "an association taxable as a corporation." To avoid being so considered, partnerships must avoid having a majority of the following four corporate characteristics:

1. centralization of management;

2. continuity of life;

3. free transferability of interests;

4. limited liability.

Since limited liability and centralization of management are normally important business objectives, partnerships normally specify a limited life and do not permit free transferability of partnership interests. Generally, partnership interests may only be transferred with permission of the general partners. This lack of easy transferability has made public ownership of partnerships generally less attractive, although many public partnerships have been established successfully.

Business Trust

A business trust is a third formal type of organization, much like a corporation, but which also shares some characteristics of a partnership. A business trust is created when capital, such as a parcel of real property, is conveyed to one or more "trustees" who agree to hold title to the capital for the benefit of one or more "beneficiaries."

First used in Massachusetts, business trusts are established under various state laws, which generally require filing an appropriate "Declaration of Trust" or "Trust Deed." Reporting requirements are less than for corporations or partnerships. For example, the trustees are generally identified, as well as the purpose of the trust, but there is no requirement to identify the beneficiaries or to spell out their ownership interests. This can provide a degree of anonymity not available in corporate or partnership organization.

Like stockholders of a corporation, beneficiaries hold shares in the trust in proportion to their contribution of capital. These shares are represented by certificates and are freely transferable. Beneficiaries have no role in management. The trustees act as the equivalent of the corporate board of directors with the power to hire employees and to delegate the responsibility for day-to-day management. Trustees have a fiduciary relationship to beneficiaries.

Unlike a corporation, beneficiaries may not select the trustees. Also unlike a corporation, a business trust may not exist in perpetuity. Generally a trust expires 21 years after the death of all beneficiaries. The liability situation is also unlike the corporation. Generally trustees are personally liable. Beneficiaries usually have limited liability, but particularly if they are active in management, they may have personal liability.

As defined above, a business trust is an "association." As such, a business trust is generally taxable as a corporation. Beginning in 1960, however, the Internal Revenue Code has permitted business trusts to elect to be treated as a conduit, similar to a partnership. This has greatly enhanced the role of trusts in real estate ownership.

Real Estate Investment Trusts ("REITs") are a special category of business trust also created by Congress in 1960. REITs were intended to function much like mutual funds for real estate investment. REITs would facilitate the involvement of many small investors in the ownership of large portfolios of professionally managed, income-producing property. A number of restrictions were imposed. These were intended to limit REITs primarily to real estate, rather than securities investment. To qualify as a REIT, a trust must:

1. have at least 100 beneficiaries;

2. operate as a "passive" investor, rather than itself manage or develop property or act as a broker;

3. invest at least 75% of its assets in real estate interests, government securities or cash;

4. derive at least 75% of its gross income from real estate related sources and 90% from real estate plus securities income; and

5. pay out at least 90% of its net income in the year earned.

The net income paid out to the beneficiaries retains its character as ordinary or capital gain income. The beneficiaries individually pay taxes on this income. A REIT is taxed as a corporation for any taxable income not distributed to its beneficiaries.

As with any business trust, the trustees control the business of a REIT. In practice, however, REITs are often managed on a day-to-day basis by a professional "advisor," a company organized for the purpose. Advisors are generally hired on a fee basis, often structured with incentive compensation. Trustees retain the basic responsibility for investment decisions.

The REIT idea lay relatively dormant through much of the 1960s, but became the center of a major real estate boom from 1968 through 1973. Speculative excess, volatile short-term interest rates, and generally poor loan underwriting contributed to a disastrous crash in 1974. The more conservative REITs have continued to be successful, but the investment appeal of REITs generally was eliminated. Renewed interest has been seen since 1985 on the part of major sponsors, and a new boom in REIT investment may well be in the offing.

Other Non-Corporate Organizations

Two other non-corporate organizational forms will be discussed briefly. These are the sole proprietorship and the joint venture.

Sole Proprietorship. A sole proprietorship is a form of business organization in which the identity of the owner and the business are the same. An individual simply begins without formality to operate a business under his or her own name. Many real estate businesses are operated all or in part through a sole proprietorship. For example, the core business entity of Gerald D. Hines Interests, one of the largest and most powerful real estate development organizations, is a sole proprietorship.

An advantage of the proprietorship is its simplicity. Proprietorships do not pay taxes, but report their results as personal income of the proprietor. The biggest disadvantage is, of course, unlimited personal liability incurred by the proprietor for actions of the business. Other difficulties are presented by the limited lifespan of the organization -- it ends at death of the owner -- and the relatively less advantageous arrangements allowable for employee fringe benefits, retirement plans, etc.

Joint Venture. A joint venture is an association of two or more business entities for a special business purpose. Much like a general partnership, the joint venture may only be formed by a specific agreement, usually written, setting out the specific purposes and limitations of the venture. Many of the same provisions contained in a partnership agreement will usually be contained in a joint-venture agreement. Real estate joint ventures are normally limited to a specific project. A joint venture form of organization is sometimes used on an interim basis, to be replaced later with a partnership or trust.

Unlike the partnership structure, however, the term joint venture may also be applied to purely financing transactions and even to terms of a contract for services. In such cases, the parties agree to share risks and rewards associated with a particular project through an investment or contractual structure which incorporates incentive compensation for both venturers. The joint venturers in such a case might not own the property through the joint venture, but nevertheless agree to share its income and its losses.

III. TAX FACTORS IN REAL ESTATE DEVELOPMENT

In this section, we will examine more closely current tax laws and organizational consequences for the real estate developer. We will follow the same structure provided in Section I, examining the three categories of tax benefit for real estate investment: tax credits, exclusions from taxable income, and deductions from taxable income.

Tax Credits

In 1986, the Tax Reform Act created a two-tiered investment tax credit program for investments to rehabilitate older and historic structures. These ITC's are 10% for non-residential buildings 50 or more years old and 20% for certified historic structures, whether residential or not. The only other tax credit remaining on the books today is the 9% credit for investment in low-income housing (reduced to 4% if other subsidies, such as low-interest financing, are used). No credits are provided for new construction other than housing.

Because the rehabilitation tax credits directly offset up to 20% of project costs, these credits have a major impact on the relative economics of investment in rehabilitation versus new construction. To be eligible, the rehabilitation must be "substantial," defined as at least equal to the purchase cost of the building (excluding land). The rehabilitation must meet the requirement of retaining at least 75% of a building's exterior walls and 75% of interior structural framework.

For the historic credit, the guidelines for rehabilitation issued by the Secretary of the Interior must be followed. Plans must be submitted for advisory review before the fact and certified for compliance after completion. To be eligible, a structure must either be listed individually in the National Register of Historic Places or be found to be a contributing building to a listed National Register Historic District. Formal processing of these listings need not be completed to commence a project, but if they are not eventually completed, tax credits already taken would be reduced. If listing has been completed, but certification of construction is not achieved, the entire tax credit would be lost.

Historic or otherwise, rehabilitation tax credits are earned by the owner of the property at the time it is ready, all or in part, for its intended use and is "placed in service" by its owner. This provides an important benefit to developers in raising equity financing for rehabilitation developments. Investors may be brought into the owning entity, usually a partnership, at any time up to the in-service date and be eligible to share in the ITC. This also places a premium on the developer's completing by year end any construction necessary for the intended use. Additional credits may be earned in subsequent years up to a total project duration of twenty-four months, or in the case of a phased project, up to sixty months. Tenants under leases with at least 31.5 years remaining may also be eligible for credits for their investments.

The amount of the credit received by the property owner (or qualifying tenant) is tied to the amount of the eligible investment (called "qualified rehabilitation expenditures" or "QRE's"). Generally, acquisition costs are not eligible, nor are costs related to new construction or enlargement of a building, nor costs classified as operating expenses. Costs such as leasing commissions and financing fees tied to specific transactions are amortizable over the life of the related transaction and not eligible as QRE's. Construction period interest must be capitalized and is considered a QRE.

Taxpayers who take a rehabilitation tax credit must elect the straight line method of cost recovery (depreciation). QRE's are considered real estate for depreciation purposes and are depreciated over the 27.5 or 31.5-year period. The taxpayer's cost basis in the property for computing depreciation or gain on sale is reduced by the amount of the tax credit.

Tax credits need not be fully consumed in the current year. Unused credits may be carried back three years and forward fifteen years. If a property is sold within one year of being placed in service, 100% of any rehabilitation tax credit taken must be recaptured. After each full year, recapture is reduced by 20%; after five years, there is no recapture.

As will be discussed in a later section, the Tax Reform Act of 1986 limits the use by individuals of tax credits from passive investments. Public corporations and active investors, such as developers, are exempt from this treatment.

Exclusions from Taxable Income

Under current tax laws, certain types of income are not considered taxable for Federal income tax purposes. Four types are important to real estate:

Tax-Exempt Interest. Interest payments received by investors who hold state and local bond issues have traditionally been exempt from Federal taxation. Increasingly over the past 25 years, such bonds have been used to finance private activities with various public purposes in mind. A variety of state and local agencies have been empowered to borrow money by issuing tax-exempt bonds and re-lend the funds to private firms or individuals at below-market interest rates. Some agencies may simply sponsor the bond issue of a private entity, making it exempt from Federal taxes.

These bonds have been used widely to provide loans to developers of low- and moderate-income housing. In recent years, industrial development bonds have also become common. Originally intended for construction of new manufacturing plants, "industrial" bonds are at times used for parking and commercial developments as well. Since interest rates are lower than those for taxable debt issues, tax-exempt financing is naturally very attractive to the borrower.

Notwithstanding the public benefits of these programs, there are problems. In-creasingly, the agencies have been able to issue the bonds relying only on project revenues for repayment. They themselves do not take financial responsibility for the bonds and thus have no financial disincentive to increased use. Competitive pressures among localities have also encouraged wider use. Because the market for tax-exempt investment has become heavily used, the interest rates are relatively high, and the "spread" between taxable and tax-exempt rates has declined in relative terms. Thus, the cost of ordinary government borrowing is increased substantially. The increased usage means the Federal subsidy in the form of aggregate foregone revenues is relatively higher. Finally, because the bonds may be risky, investors naturally prefer the most creditworthy projects. Thus funds may be unavailable for the project most in need of help.

For these reasons, we should expect the use of bonds for private purposes to be sharply curtailed in the future. Housing applications will likely survive with perhaps severe restrictions, but even housing developers should be very cautious in planning any project which needs tax-exempt financing to be feasible.

Installment Sale. Under current law, taxes may be partially deferred in cases where income from the sale of property is received over time. When one or more payments are to be received after the taxable year in which the sale occurs, the taxpayer may elect to report income as the cash payments are received. The gain recognized in each tax year is the proportion of the total gain which represents the percentage of the total purchase price paid in that year. If the seller disposes of the installment obligations, or pledges these obligations to secure borrowings, the remaining income must be recognized.

Example: Ms. Harris wanted to sell her older office building to its lead tenant, who had a particular need to own it, for $6 million. She had a mortgage loan on the property with a current balance of $3,485,000, and would thus realize about $2.5 million in cash, after paying about $10,000 in legal fees associated with the sale. Because she was looking forward to retirement, she preferred now to make passive investments. She could expect a 7% yield on government securities.

Ms. Harris bought the property some eighteen years before from its developer, a close friend of her former husband. She had paid $985,000 in cash and notes that had subsequently been retired. She had also absorbed $25,000 in closing costs. She had occasionally been called upon to replace major building systems, particularly the chiller plant and the boiler, and had redone the windows and the landscaping. According to her accountants, these capital improvements totaled $1,115,000. Over the years, building components had been depreciated at the most rapid rates allowable, and depreciation deductions had totaled $1,325,000 to date. The accountants also provided the following estimate of taxable gain on the sale:

Original Purchase Price	$985,000
Closing costs	25,000
Capital improvements	1,115,000
(Depreciation taken)	(1,325,000)
Tax basis	$800,000
Sales price	$6,000,000
(Selling costs)	(10,000)
Net sales price	5,990,000
(Tax basis)	(800,000)
Taxable income from sale	$5,190,000

Ms. Harris knew from this that after paying off her mortgage loan and paying income tax at a 28% rate on the taxable

gain, she would have about $1,052,000 left to invest. Thus she could anticipate retirement income of about $74,000 per year.

Ms. Harris' advisors suggested she consider structuring her transaction as an installment sale in order to reduce the impact of taxes on her retirement income. Unfortunately, after consultation with her mortgage lender, it was determined that at least enough cash would have to be paid at the closing to enable repayment of the loan balance. Thus she would require at least $3,485,000 plus about $30,000 to pay her legal bills.

The advisors suggested a structure with $4.8 million cash at closing and $1.2 million in purchase money financing at 7% interest. Ms. Harris would thus report a taxable gain of 80% of the prior amount or $4,152,000. After payment of taxes she would thus have a total of $1.3 million invested and an income of $93,000.

This was better, but when she discussed it with her buyer, he indicated he would require the purchase money financing to be subordinated to another loan he planned to put on the property. This introduced an element of risk that was certainly not equivalent to that of the government securities Ms. Harris was contemplating. He asked that she consider what interest rate would be appropriate and get back to him.

Tax-Free Exchange. Based on the tradition of "barter," a sale of property, including real estate, may be structured as a swap of like-kind property. This is often done when a substantial increase in market value has occurred, and the seller wants to keep the sales proceeds invested in real estate. Properly structured, capital gains tax on the sale may be reduced, deferred or eliminated. At the time of the transaction, the cost basis of the old property is carried over to the new one; and when that is finally sold, taxes will finally be paid. Thus up to 33% of the sale value can be kept invested in real estate, rather than paid to the government. A recent rule, the *Starker Rule*, extends the period of time in which an exchange can be made.

To qualify, property must be held for trade or business or for investment. Passive investments, such as stocks and bonds do *not* qualify. If a property is resold too soon after a swap, the transaction may be reclassified. Property exchanged must also be of "like-kind." Based on court rulings over the years, almost any kind of interest in real estate, including land, partial interests, etc., will meet the "like-kind" requirement. An exchange may be partially tax-free, most commonly when there is a difference in the value of properties exchanged. Property which is included in a transaction, but does not qualify as like-kind, is called "boot." Such property would include cash, notes, personal property, or the transfer of liabilities. Such items would be considered taxable to the extent of fair market value, and a proportionate share of the total gain on sale would be recognized.

Example: Instead of an installment sale, Ms. Harris suggested her advisors consider a tax-free exchange. She located a parcel of land, net leased to a shopping center owner who was an old friend. This parcel was priced at $6 million. A purchase money mortgage of $3.5 million was arranged. Because the lease payments were not subordinate to other financing, there was no material risk involved. The net income was fixed, providing a yield similar to that of a government security. In a two-stage closing, her buyer first purchased this land and then exchanged the land for her office building, each subject to its own mortgage.

Structured this way, the transaction was a tax-free exchange for Ms. Harris. If she later sold the land, her tax basis would be the same $800,000 carried over from her office property. The buyer

of the office building was unaffected. The seller of the land recognized an appropriate gain on that sale and paid taxes accordingly. Ms. Harris incurred some costs in excess of normal costs of a sale, because in such a transaction, careful scrutiny of each aspect was required on the part of her legal and tax advisors. However, her annual income for retirement was now $225,000 per year, about triple what it would have been if she had simply sold her property.

Involuntary Conversion. Another type of transaction, the involuntary conversion, is similar in its effect to the tax-free exchange. Involuntary conversions generally include fire damage or other destruction, as well as eminent domain "takings" by government bodies. In these instances, a gain may be deferred if the full proceeds are reinvested in like-kind property within three years.

An involuntary sale or transfer by foreclosure of debt or for non-payment of property taxes does not qualify for this treatment. Because of the prevalence of arson, in cases involving fire, restrictions on reinvestment may be imposed. Generally, however, the use of involuntary conversion treatment gives an owner the option to sell the damaged property, rather than undertake a perhaps risky redevelopment.

Sale of Personal Residence. Gains can be deferred when the entire proceeds of the sale of the taxpayer's principal home are reinvested. To qualify, the new residence must be purchased within twenty-four months before or after the sale. If the new home is to be newly constructed, it must be begun within twenty-four months. The taxpayer must actually occupy and use the new residence. Multiple sales and deferrals are permitted every two years, or more frequently in the case of a relocation required by an employer. The amount reinvested must be at least the amount of the sale price of the old residence, less selling and repair costs.

Taxpayers age 55 or older may elect a one-time exclusion of $125,000 of the gain from sale of their principal personal residence. This permits the elderly to move into smaller quarters or rental accommodations, while retaining capital to invest for retirement income.

Deductions from Taxable Income.

Traditionally, real estate offers three basic deductions from taxable income. They are recovery of capital costs (depreciation), recovery of fees and financing costs (amortization), and recovery of ordinary business expenses. These deductions have been very important in real estate due to the importance of non-cash charges in any real estate investment.

However, continuing the trend of recent years, the Tax Reform Act of 1986 significantly restructured the use of deductions from taxable income. The 1986 act limits the use of losses and credits from *passive* activities to offset income (or, in the case of credits, tax on income) from *active* activities, such as wages, salaries, active business income, and "portfolio" income (e.g. interest, dividends and royalties). Losses or credits from one "passive" activity may offset income (or tax) from other "passive" activities, but only up to $25,000 of "active" income. Any "passive" losses or credits not usable in a taxable year can be carried forward (but not back) indefinitely.

These limitations cannot apply to corporations unless they are S corporations or closely held ("C") corporations. Developers are "active" investors, of course, so the major effect of this change is to reduce the attraction of passive real estate investments for high-income individuals.

The 1986 act also extended a requirement to real estate investment that deductions in each year be limited to the amount an owner has "at risk." In non-real estate investments, this means the

amount of equity an owner has invested. However, all "qualified non-recourse financing" is considered an amount at risk. Most institutional debt is considered qualified, so this limitation will not often apply in the case of real estate.

Let us look specifically at each category of deduction:

Recovery of Capital Costs (Depreciation). Recovery of capital costs, also known as depreciation, is guided by the Modified Asset Cost Recovery System (MACRS), established by the Tax Reform Act of 1986. MACRS permits recovery of capital costs as annual deductions from income over specified periods.

Under MACRS, there are six classes of depreciable personal property: those with recovery periods of 3, 5, 7, and 10 years and eligible to be depreciated using an accelerated rate corresponding to the 200% declining balance method, and those with recovery periods of 15 and 20 years and eligible to be depreciated using a rate corresponding to the 150% declining balance method. However, there are only two classes of depreciable real property: residential real property may be depreciated on a straight line basis over 27.5 years, non-residential real property may be depreciated on a straight line basis over 31.5 years.

With respect to additions or improvements to real property, the Act preserves the prohibition against use of the component method of depreciation. Any deduction for an addition or improvement to a property is to be computed in the same manner as the deduction for the underlying property. Hence a new improvement to an existing non-residential building constitutes non-residential real property and is recovered over 31.5 years, using the straight line method.

Land cannot be depreciated. Unlike a building, land is not considered to have a finite useful life. The allocation of value between land and building therefore has important tax effects and must be defensible under IRS scrutiny. One often-used basis for allocation is the assessed value of the property for real estate tax purposes.

Recovery of Fees and Financing Costs (Amortization). As in other industries, fees and financing costs may be recovered. Because of the large amounts of capital investment required for a development venture, these costs are often significant. Generally, each fee or financing cost may be recovered over the period which matches the benefit involved. These are scrutinized by the IRS, and the accounting industry provides guidelines.

Organization costs, for example, are amortized over five years. Fees and commissions are amortized over periods in which matching benefits are received. Loan fees, therefore, must be amortized over the length of the loan. Syndication fees for the sale of interests in a partnership cannot be deducted.

Recovery of Ordinary Business Expenses. The business expenses incurred in operating a piece of property may be deducted in the year they occur. They are not subject to recapture at transfer or sale. These expenses include professional services, marketing, property management, tenant services, utilities, insurance, maintenance and repair costs, and local real estate taxes. Replacement reserve payments cannot be deducted -- the systems they pay for can be depreciated, however, on the same basis as the underlying property, once the investments are made.

In addition to these expenses, certain other project costs, such as the developer's overhead, profit-sharing or bonus arrangements, and fees for providing various services may be deducted in the year they are incurred.

Alternative Minimum Tax

The Alternative Minimum Tax (AMT) rules are designed to ensure that a minimum tax is paid regardless of a taxpayer's shelter status. AMT is payable on AMT income which is defined as regular taxable income with certain adjustments. "Preference items" are then added back to regular taxable income in calculating AMT income. The act of 1986 tightens the AMT rules which existed under the old law and increases the AMT rate for individuals from 20% to 21%.

The method by which AMT is determined is fairly complicated and need not be explained here, but it is important to note that the changes in the AMT rules may force many taxpayers to compute their tax obligation both ways. Taxpayers will be sensitive to items (the "preference items") which increase their liability under this method, including portions of losses under the passive loss rules and the excess of regular depreciation over alternative depreciation (40 years).

Conclusion

The economic effect of taxes on any real estate deal cannot be ignored. Issues of taxation are intertwined with issues of organization, and the successful developer must chart a course that employs forms of taxation and organization to the advantage of his or her project. Despite the recent tax changes, the properly structured real estate deal can provide significant tax advantages over other forms of investment.

Case 10

The Costa Mesa Project

Joe O'Connor took one last look at the pile of papers on his desk, loaded a bunch of them into his briefcase and decided it was time to go home. It was already 6:30, and he had the long Washington's Birthday weekend ahead of him. This February 1981 weekend, however, would not be much of a holiday for him. He would in fact be working most of the time as he tried to come to grips with whether to proceed as a joint-venture partner on a major, multi-phased office project in Orange County, California.

O'Connor was President and Chief Executive Officer of Copley Real Estate Advisors, the real estate equity investment arm of New England Life. Armed with a Harvard MBA, O'Connor had steadily climbed through the ranks of New England Life's real estate hierarchy and had gained a reputation for shrewd and aggressive investment strategies. He thrived on tough decisions, and he had one to make now. Last month O'Connor had received preliminary information about a 50-acre development project near Irvine, California, and last week his correspondent in California, a Los Angeles mortgage company, sent him the details of the project with the recommendation that he act quickly. "It's one of the last big undeveloped parcels in the county," his contact told him, "and one of the best."

Joe remembered how often he had heard that and how the graveyard of real estate was strewn with "last undeveloped parcels." Still, he had reason to believe that this was a pretty good site, and he liked what his correspondent had told him about the developer and proposed joint venture-partner, Shurl Curci (pronounced Kursee). O'Connor was sufficiently interested in the project to tack on to a trip to Texas a visit to Los Angeles to see the site and meet Mr. Curci. He was impressed with what he saw.

O'Connor also knew that the Orange County office market was weakening and

Copley would be making a big commitment with this project. The total project cost was $122 million, and while Copley's initial investment would be small, he knew that Copley might be required to put in more money as the project progressed. Still, even with these caveats, O'Connor was leaning toward the deal. He knew there was no time to lose. Another major financial institution was also looking at the project and had ordered an appraisal which would take a week or two. His Finance Committee was meeting on Wednesday. Over the weekend, O'Connor had to decide whether he should write up this investment and propose it to the Finance Committee. He had arranged to make one more phone call to Curci on Monday to discuss the final structure of the venture.

COPLEY REAL ESTATE ADVISORS

Copley Real Estate Advisors was started in 1981 to make real estate investments and manage New England Life's $1.9 billion real estate portfolio. The firm was staffed by key personnel from the parent company. The idea behind the spin-off was to create an investment group that could take advantage of many of the opportunities becoming available, such as working as an investment advisor to large pension funds and creating limited partnerships to be sold by New England Life agents. Copley Real Estate Advisors would have the best of both worlds: the flexibility and decision-making structure of a small company, and the staff resources and credit of New England Life.

Whereas most institutional investors tended to buy existing, fully leased properties, Copley generally invested earlier in the development cycle, while the land was being prepared for development and before final decisions about the layout and design of the project were completed. By getting in at this early stage of development, Copley generally assumed greater leasing risks and construction risks. Copley felt, however, that these risks could be quantified and made manageable, especially if one worked with high quality developers. On the other hand, by getting closer to the source and getting involved in the manufacturing of real estate investments, Copley gained access to higher quality projects at a lower cost. With fewer competitors willing to invest in developmental real estate, Copley's experience was that the risk/reward tradeoff was extremely favorable.

In a typical Copley joint venture, a developer would bring to the table a site which he controlled and assurances of most of the requisite permits and zoning approvals. The developer would be looking for an investor/partner with the financial staying power to support a project over time and to bear the risks that are often incurred with development projects. Copley, in return, would put up cash and guarantees to cover the cost of developing the project. In the usual investment, Copley would seek a 50-70% ownership interest, a 12 to 13% cash-on-cash return on its investment and an active voice in the development and management of the project. Copley generally structured its investments so that a developer got a share of the tax benefits proportionate to its ownership position, though occasionally Copley traded off some additional tax benefits for more of the cash flow and appreciation. This ability to allocate tax benefits in a joint venture was, however, becoming more difficult to do under the newly proposed IRS guidelines.

Copley would not hesitate to get involved in long-term, multiphase projects, where the payoff might not be achieved for several years, but they would parcel out their investment in increments to minimize the exposure. Copley would specialize in a dozen or so markets which they knew well and then team up with local or regional developers with excellent reputations and strong real estate roots in their area. Copley would hear about good projects and potential partners through their extensive network of correspondents.

SHURL CURCI

Copley tried to minimize some of the risks of developmental joint ventures by getting involved with partners with good reputations and track records. Shurl Curci, the partner on the Costa Mesa site, had been a principal in Barclay Hollander Curci, Inc., a large West Coast condominium developer and homebuilder. The firm was sold to Castle and Cook in 1969, and Curci stayed on for a few years as a senior executive. In 1973, Curci left the company to set up his own partnerships to develop commercial properties in Southern California. Curci had put together an impressive roster of office buildings, shopping centers and hotels, many of which had been joint ventured with institutional partners.

For the Costa Mesa project, Curci had assembled an impressive team including a prominent leasing company, a well-respected local architect, and a top site planning and engineering firm. He had not yet selected a contractor or a property manager, and O'Connor knew that the construction team would be key in keeping such a large scale project within budget.

THE PROPERTY

The Costa Mesa site had been farmed for many years by a Japanese truck farmer. In 1978, Curci successfully negotiated a 50-year ground lease for 50 acres of the farmstead. The terms included an initial ground rent of $800,000 per year and future rental increases every five years pegged at 50% of the CPI. In addition,

Curci had first rights of refusal for the remaining 115 acres of the property. Curci was able to get his 50 acre parcel rezoned from agricultural to commercial use and by 1981 had obtained most of the necessary approvals for the property. As a result, the site was now in a PDC zone which permitted a variety of commercial and professional uses, so long as a conditional use permit was obtained in accordance with the general plan. The City had tentatively approved a 1.3-million-square-foot office complex to be constructed in phases. Curci's one hang-up with the city of Costa Mesa was compliance with their inclusionary zoning law which required that a certain number of housing units be provided as part of any new commercial development. By the time Curci brought his proposal to Copley, however, he had gotten approval in principle to start developing the first phase of his office project without having to build housing and felt that he could probably get approvals to build all the commercial development before he started the housing. He had also solved most of the traffic and circulation issues of the site to the satisfaction of the municipality.

The site itself was located in a prime office and commercial area about 26 miles southeast of downtown Los Angeles and 4 miles northeast of Newport Beach, a popular residential and office area. The site had substantial frontage on the San Diego Freeway and was near the cloverleaf intersection with the Newport Freeway and within minutes of the John Wayne Airport (see Exhibit 1). Near the property were two very successful commercial projects, South Coast Plaza and Two Town Center, both of which had been developed by the Segerstrom family. The 1,645,000-square-foot South Coast Plaza was the second largest regional shopping center in both size and sales in the Los Angeles area. The Town Center project already included a hotel, twin 15-story towers, restaurants, and a major cultural center. The next phase, slated to commence in the fall of 1983, was to include a 21-story, 462,000-square-foot office tower. The Segerstrom family was planning more than 2 million additional square feet of office space in Costa Mesa over the next few years (see Exhibit 3, Table 5).

As was his style, Curci planned a good solid project -- nothing flamboyant or flashy, but nevertheless a project of high quality and class. The basic concept called for a six-building complex, interspersed with plazas and parking facilities. The buildings would be a combination of low rise office structures, typical of southern California, and a few 12-story high rise focal point buildings. A careful landscaping scheme would tie the complex together (see Exhibit 5) Overall, Curci expected to build about 1,400,000 gross or 1,190,000 net rentable square feet of office space at a total estimated project cost of about $122 million (see Exhibit 2). The estimated build-out period was 3 to 5 years.

As a start, Curci proposed to build a 12-story 258,000 net rentable square foot speculative office building and 1,000 spaces of parking as the center piece of the project. The total construction cost for this first phase was to be $32 million.

THE MARKET

The Orange County office market had grown rapidly during the last five years doubling in size from 8.27 million square feet in 1976 to 17.54 million square feet in 1980. Despite this level of construction, leasing had kept pace until 1980, when the market began to soften and vacancy rates climbed. A market study prepared by a consultant to the developer projected, however, that vacancy rates would be back down to 5% by late 1983 when the first building in the Costa Mesa project was scheduled to be completed (see Exhibit 3).

The market study also pointed out that the current vacancy problem in Orange County was not uniformly distributed, but concentrated in the less developed northwest section which recently had a 15.5% vacancy rate. In contrast, the Newport-Airport-Costa Mesa area had only a 5.8% vacancy rate, and Costa Mesa itself had only a 2.8% vacancy rate.

What concerned Joe O'Connor most, though, was the number of new projects currently under construction. The market study projected that leasing activity would keep up with this new construction, but Joe wanted to think long and hard about the absorption rates projected in the market study and the implications of using a more conservative space absorption assumption.

One other gauge of market conditions that O'Connor felt was important was the amount of land being sold in the area and the prices developers were paying. He had received a letter from a local mortgage banker who served as a New England Life correspondent giving him some information on comparable land sales for the area. Both he and the mortgage banker were, however, aware of the difficulty of making such comparisons (see Exhibit 4).

THE SITUATION

Shurl Curci was now at the stage where he wanted to proceed with the first building in Phase I of his project. That meant proceeding on the initial development and construction of a 258,000-square-foot office building at an estimated cost of $32 million. Curci's proofread showed annual rental rates for the completed office space of $19 per square foot (see Exhibit 2).

Curci knew that most insurance companies were not equipped to make construction loans, and therefore he had begun talking with a major West Coast bank about getting a $25 to $30 million construction loan. Many construction lenders insisted that before they would loan any money, the developer had to secure a

commitment for a long-term mortgage. This was so that when the construction was completed, money would be available to repay the bank. In some joint ventures, Copley would either commit to make the mortgage loan itself or, at least, commit to step up as a lender of last resort. In this case, however, Curci thought the construction lender would make an open-ended construction loan and not insist on a prior mortgage commitment. He knew that O'Connor would prefer this situation, and it would give the joint venture flexibility in securing long-term financing at the optimum time.

Curci expected that it would take at least a year and a half to get started on construction with Phase I and he was looking for a money partner with deep pockets who could stick with him during the 3 to 5 year development stage for the total project. At the moment he was looking for an initial infusion of equity to help him carry the land, prepare site plans, complete road work, and cover other development costs, such as legal fees and permits. This would probably come to about $3- to $4-million.

Curci knew that no lender would lend on raw land, but 3 to 5 year funds for commercial development projects were beginning to open up. Rates were in the 14% range for 3 to 4 year funds and long-term lenders were looking for returns from 15-17%. Longer loan terms tended to include kickers and periodic rate adjustments (see Exhibit 6).

THE DEAL

Most of Curci's recent deals had been structured as joint ventures and he was comfortable with this sort of arrangement. Furthermore, in this case, he felt he was bringing substantial value to the table in addition to his own experience as a developer. He had spent three years working with the municipality to get building approvals, and he had what he thought was an extremely good site, on which he held a leasehold position.

O'Connor was aware that the site had potential and that the leasehold interest had value, although Copley did not normally allow imputed land appreciation as a factor in its investments. In this case, he felt that the short-term prospects for the project might be difficult but that the site probably had good long-term potential for growth in value.

Even with these substantial market risks, O'Connor was leaning toward making the commitment. He thought Curci's estimates of a $3- to $4-million need for equity were low, since it was always difficult to estimate development costs, and there might be unforeseen delays in the project. Actual construction of the project was not expected to begin for a year and a half from this initial equity investment. O'Connor thought Copley's initial investment ought to be more like $6 million, should they go ahead with the deal. This would give Copley more leverage in the project and would help cushion possible increases in costs. He also wondered if he should work out in advance an arrangement if, for example, $9 million of equity was eventually needed.

O'Connor knew that, in addition to the economic factors, there would be some tough issues involved in structuring the joint venture document. These included:

1. **Control**. What should be the division of responsibility and decision-making between the money partner and the developer? Who should have authority for the major decisions (e.g. refinancing, leasing) and who should have authority for the day-to-day decisions? How should Copley exercise control over the project, yet not stifle the developer's entrepreneurial spirit? How much control should Copley exert over other professionals and contractors involved in the project? Basically, all major decisions would be made jointly, and hopefully amicably. But as a last resort, O'Connor always insisted on a provision in the joint-venture agreement allowing either partner to buy out the other if they reached an irreconcilable conflict.

2. **Funding**. Should Copley's participation be in the form of a capital contribution or a loan? Should funding be staged and under what conditions? What will be the source of additional funds to defray cost overruns and other contingencies?

3. **Allocation of benefits and risks**. Who gets dollars out of the project and in what order? How are benefits allocated and in what form? How are losses allocated?

4. **Dissolution**. How does one partner get rid of the other if things do not work out? How would Curci be compensated for the value he had created in this project, especially if it were sold before it was built out? What provisions should be included in case the development partner dies? What provisions would there be for resolving disputes short of dissolution of the partnership?

This weekend, O'Connor would have to make two decisions. The first was whether he should proceed with the investment at all. If the answer to that question was yes, how should he structure the venture to protect Copley but give Curci incentives to stick with the project and make it successful?

EXHIBITS

1. Aerial view.

2. Development budget and income projections.

3. Office market survey.

4. Letter from New England Life correspondent.

5. Architectural and site drawings.

6. Financing information.

QUESTIONS FOR DISCUSSION

1. Should Mr. O'Connor proceed with an investment in this office park in Orange County? What are the potential risks and rewards?

2. If he should invest, how should he attempt to structure the joint venture with the developer?

3. How would you evaluate Copley's overall strategy for involvement in real estate? How does it differ from other institutional investors?

Exhibit 1

COSTA MESA
Orange County, California

MORGAN STANLEY

NORTH

1. Costa Mesa
2. San Diego Freeway
3. Newport Freeway
4. American Bank
5. Great Western Savings
6. Downey Savings
7. South Coast Plaza Hotel
8. Imperial Bank
9. Bristol Street
10. South Coast Plaza Shopping Center

Exhibit 2

February 15, 1981

Development Budget

The following development budget is based on both current construction costs and current market rentals. It assumes the buildout of this land over a period of 3-5 years with all of the development consisting of mid-rise office space totaling approximately 1,190,000 s.f. of net rentable area.

   I. Land: (under long term ground lease)   N/A

  II. Building Development Costs:

     Shell Costs: 1,400,000 s.f. @ $46.60 $64,400,000

     Parking:

      Structured: 509,000 s.f. @ $17.00/s.f.   8,650,000

      Surface: 700,000 s.f. @ $ 2.00/s.f.   1,400,000

     Interior Tenant Improvement Finish:
         1,190,000 s.f. @ $10.00/s.f.   11,900,000

     Site Work   4,100,000

     Total Estimated Building Costs $90,450,000

 III. Indirect Costs:

     Architectural & Engineering   2,500,000

     Ground Lease Payments   4,000,000

     Interest and Indirect Costs   20,000,000

     Lease Commissions   5,000,000

     Total Indirect Costs   31,500,000

     Total Estimated Project Costs $121,950,000

Exhibit 2
continued

Income Projections

(on a stabilized basis, $ in thousands)

	First Bldg. in Phase I	Total Project
Gross Rent @ $19/s.f.		
(Phase I: 258,000 s.f. Total: 1,190,000 s.f.)	$4,902	$22,610
Parking Spaces at $25 net per month (Phase I: 1,000 spaces, Total: 3,900 spaces)	300	1,170
Gross Revenue	5,202	23,780
Vacancy (5%)	245	1,131
Net Revenue	4,957	22,649
Operating Expenses ($4.50)*	1,161	5,355
Net Operating Income	3,796	17,294
Ground Rent	200	800
Cash Flow	$3,596	$16,494
Unleveraged Return on Investment (Phase I: $32 million, Total: $122 million)	11.23%	13.52%

* Operating expenses in excess of $4.50 will be passed through to the tenants.

Exhibit 3

> Excerpts from
> THE OFFICE MARKETS OF ORANGE COUNTY
>
>
> Prepared for
>
> CURCI DEVELOPMENT PROJECT
>
> February, 1981
>
> ---
>
> COOK, MERCER AND DESIMONE
> Economics Consultants
> 300 California Federal Building
> 707 Silver Lake Road
> Laguna Hills, California 90274

Exhibit 3
continued

Table 1

Comparative Office Space Vacancy Rates in the Cities of Orange County

	% Vacancy		
	January 1981	August 1980	January 1980
Northwest County			
Anaheim	21.0%	13.1%	12.6%
Fullerton	9.2	8.3	3.9
Garden Grove	22.6	23.7	22.0
Huntington Beach	10.2	3.0	0.9
Fountain Valley	5.2	12.8	--
Brea	17.1	17.4	--
Other	18.8	32.5	--
Total	15.5%	12.4%	8.0%
Central County			
Santa Ana	7.4%	8.4%	7.2%
Orange	3.3	4.3	7.6
Tustin	8.5	10.1	3.3
Total	6.5%	7.6%	6.7%
Newport – Airport – Costa Mesa			
Newport Beach	7.7%	4.6%	3.0%
Airport	5.5	3.8	6.0
Costa Mesa	2.8	2.6	7.1
Other	17.1	44.8	--
Total	5.8%	4.3%	5.4%
South County			
Laguna Beach – Hills – Niguel	23.2%	17.9%	10.2%
El Toro	20.1	9.1	12.9
Mission Viejo	7.6	10.7	7.9
Other	5.2	6.2	6.3
Total	16.1%	12.4%	9.0%
Total Orange County	8.3%	7.0%	6.3%

Exhibit 3
continued

Table 2

Distribution of the Office Space Inventory in Orange County – January, 1981

	January 1981 Total	January 1981 Vacant	% Vacant
Northwest County			
Anaheim	986,600	207,700	21.0
Fullerton	679,300	62,500	9.2
Garden Grove	169,400	38,300	22.6
Huntington Beach	230,700	23,600	10.2
Fountain Valley	191,600	10,000	5.2
Brea	299,600	51,400	17.1
Other	75,200	14,100	18.8
Total	2,632,400	407,600	15.5
Central City			
Santa Ana	3,310,600	244,800	7.4
Orange	1,500,700	49,700	3.3
Tustin	926,100	78,300	8.5
Total	5,737,400	372,800	6.5
Newport – Airport – Costa Mesa			
Newport Beach	1,945,600	150,300	7.7
Airport	4,901,900	268,100	5.5
Costa Mesa	900,400	25,300	2.8
Other	78,700	13,500	17.1
Total	7,826,700	457,200	5.8
South County			
Laguna Beach – Hills – Niguel	575,600	133,500	23.2
El Toro	246,700	51,300	20.1
Mission Viejo	332,100	25,300	7.6
Other	224,000	11,600	5.2
Total	1,377,400	221,700	16.1
Total Orange County	17,573,900	1,459,200	8.3

Exhibit 3
continued

Table 3

Comparative Rental Rates in Modern Orange County Office Buildings
(Rates quoted in dollars per square foot, per month)

	January 1980	January 1981	% Gain
Northwest County			
Low Rise	$ .85	$1.02	+20.0
High Rise	--	--	--
Central County			
Santa Ana			
Low Rise	1.00	1.13	+15.0
High Rise	1.20	1.38	+15.0
Orange – Tustin			
Low Rise	1.08	1.08	+0.0
High Rise	1.25	--	--
Newport – Airport – Costa Mesa			
Newport – Airport			
Low Rise	1.25	1.26	+0.1
High Rise	1.42	1.70	+19.7
Costa Mesa			
Low Rise	1.33	1.25	−6.1
High Rise	1.23	1.50	+22.0
South Coast			
Low Rise	.91	1.01	+11.0
High Rise	--	1.33	--

Exhibit 3
continued

Table 4

Office Space Absorption Rate
Orange County, 1973–1980 Actual, with Projections for 1981–83

(S.F. Leased Per Year)

	North County	Central County	Newport Airport Costa Mesa	South County	Total Orange County
1973	44,500	206,300	296,100	113,500	860,400
1974	129,000	179,400	298,300	57,500	764,200
1975	70,400	133,100	340,600	30,600	574,700
1976	177,000	251,100	589,000	71,800	1,097,900
1977	198,100	624,000	629,300	71,300	1,522,700
1978	42,700	692,600	945,800	180,800	1,861,900
1979	176,300	621,500	1,946,100	193,300	2,937,200
1980	775,700	737,000	312,200	168,100	1,993,000
Projected[1]:					
1981	373,600	798,300	1,311,800	204,300	2,688,000
1982	411,900	880,000	1,445,900	225,200	2,963,000
1983	450,100	961,700	1,580,100	246,100	3,238,000

[1] Based on a 1973–1980 regression analysis of the total County. The projected values for the County then were pro-rated to the sub-markets based on sub-market share of total County absorption.

Exhibit 3
continued

Table 5

Projection of Current Development Trends
Orange County and the Newport – Airport – Costa Mesa Sub-Market

Orange County Total	1980	1981	1982	1983	1984
Inventory (S.F.)					
Beginning of Year	14,925,300	17,573,900	21,181,500	25,489,500	
New Construction[1]	2,648,600	3,607,600	4,944,600	3,897,200	
End of Year	17,573,900	21,181,500	26,126,100	29,386,700	
Vacant Space (S.F.)					
Beginning of Year	941,500	1,597,100	2,516,700	4,498,300	
New Construction[1]	2,648,600	3,607,600	4,944,600	3,897,200	
Absorption	-1,993,000	-2,688,000	-2,963,000	-3,238,000	
End of Year	1,597,100	2,516,700	4,498,300	4,157,500	
Vacancy Rate					
Beginning of Year	6.3	9.1	11.9	17.2	
Newport – Airport – Costa Mesa					
Inventory (S.F.)					
Beginning of Year	7,458,300	7,826,800	9,991,900	11,262,100	
New Construction[1]	368,500	2,165,000	1,270,200	1,072,200	
End of Year	7,826,800	9,991,900	11,262,100	12,334,300	
Vacant Space (S.F.)					
Beginning of Year	400,900	457,200	1,310,500	1,134,800	
New Construction[1]	368,500	2,165,000	1,270,200	1,072,200	
Absorption	-312,300	-1,311,800	-1,445,900	-1,580,100	
End of Year	457,200	1,310,500	1,134,800	626,900	
Vacancy Rate					
Beginning of Year	5.4	5.8	13.1	10.1	5.1

[1] 1980 values based on published differences in inventory. Subsequent years based on 85% delivery of volume during the year construction begins.

Exhibit 3
continued

SUMMARY OF CONCLUSIONS

The essential conclusions of the study are summarized briefly as follows:

1. The proposed Southcoast Metro Center should commence construction on a schedule that will insure ability to lease and deliver space by late 1983 or early 1984. Market conditions by that time should be favorable for a fairly rapid absorption of space, and the projected vacancy rate by that time should be in the neighboorhood of 5% since the heavy volume of current construction should have been absorbed.

2. In the near term, however (i.e., 1981 through early 1983), the Newport-Airport-Costa Mesa sub-market will be overbuilt, since the volume of current construction of 2.5 million sq. ft. represents about a 2-year supply of space at projected absorption rates. Thus, the vacancy rate will rise rather sharply this year and next, but should begin falling late in 1982, and should continue to decline to about 5% by early 1984.

3. The Newport-Airport-Costa Mesa sub-market is second only in size and importance to the Downtown Los Angeles office market.

   Further, it is the most dynamic and rapidly developing office center in Southern California. Over the last five years, for example, the average annual absorption rate in Newport-Airport-Costa Mesa has been 20 percent greater than the long-term average for downtown Los Angeles, and about equal to the combined long-term absorption rate in Beverly Hills, Century City, Westwood, Brentwood, Santa Monica, and Culver City. Moreover, the absorption rate in Newport-Airport-Costa Mesa and throughout Orange County, has been steadily rising over time.

4. Throughout the sub-market, project scale and quality are on the rise, and the long term outlook for the ownership of investment real estate here appears very bright. The area enjoys premium rents compared with other sub-markets of Orange County, and low cost competition from less well developed neighboring markets has not inhibited growth and rent escalation in the past.

   In both high and low rise buildings in Costa Mesa, Newport Beach, and Irvine, the rental rate typically os 10 to 20 percent higher than elsewhere in Orange County. Today, most of the space in high and mid-rise buildings is going for $1.65 to $1.85 per square foot, per month and in 1982-83, leasing agents anticipate a rent structure of from $1.85 to $2.25 per square foot.

5. For the remainder of Orange County, the outlook is less bright, and a seriously overbuilt condition may emerge – particularly in the Northwest and South sub-markets. In these two sub-markets, vacancies already are high (+ 15%), and scheduled and planned construction is substantially in excess of probable absorption. Thus, there is a real possibility that in these less well developed sub-markets of Orange COunty a level of market distress will become evident fairly soon, and given the limited absorptive capacities, it could persist for some time to come.

Exhibit 4

(Letter from New England Life Correspondent)

TEX MORTGAGE BANKERS
1200 Avenue of the Stars
Los Angeles, California 90067

February 1, 1981

Mr. Joseph W. O'Connor
President
Copley Real Estate Advisors, Inc.
535 Boylston Street
Boston, Massachusetts 02116

Dear Joe;

Pursuant to your request, I have asked Gerard to use his MAI contacts to
provide you with an overview of land values of properties comparable to
your proposed South Coast Metro Project in Costa Mesa.

As you will see, Gerard found very few land sales the size of the 50-
acre Costa Mesa site in Orange County in the last two years. None of
the comparables were precisely identical to the subject property, and
all need adjustments. I would also point out to you that your fifty
acre site is divided into five legal parcels which could be developed or
sold seperately.

With this is mind, I am forwarding the following list of comparables to
you. I hope this information will be useful to you in making your
decision.

Please feel free to contact me if I can be of further assistance.

                                        Very truly yours,

                                        Tex Jones

Exhibit 4
continued

Land Sale of Comparable Properties

Location	Size (acres)	Date of Sale	Total Price ($000)	Price Per Sq. Ft.	Comment
1. San Diego Freeway and Lake Forest Dr.	4.7	12/1980	$3,888	$19.03	Good highway exposure and access, inferior location.
2. Jamboree Blvd. and Kelvin Ave, Irvine	8.6	1/1981	7,335	19.50	Inferior in location. Also Irvine imposes a $2.50 to $5.00 per sq. ft. development fee.
3. Kelvin Ave, Irvine	2.9	1/1981	2,500	20.36	Inferior in location and faces the Irvine development fee. Currently on the market at $25 per sq. ft.
4. San Diego Freeway and Von Karmen Ave., Irvine	34.0	for sale	27,444	18.53	The price is listed $47 million but we feel it can be bought for $40 million. We also subtracted from the price an existing structure which we valued at $12 million. Inferior location plus the Irvine development fee.
5. Anton Blvd., East of Briston Street, Costa Mesa	14.7	6/1979	11,500	18.00	Value at which the property was contributed in a joint venture between Prudential and the Segerstrom Family.
6. San Diego Freeway and Harbor Blvd.	100.0	for sale	100,000	23.00	This property is slightly inferior in location.

Exhibit 5

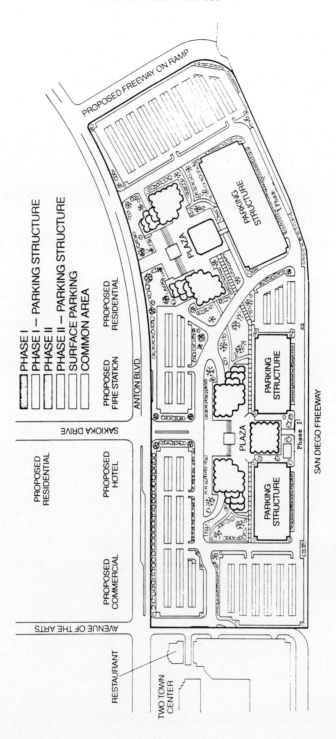

Exhibit 5
continued

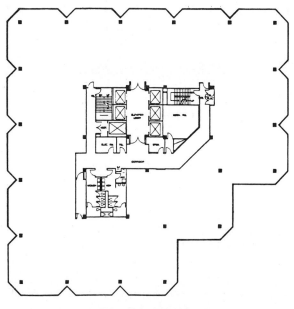

TYPICAL FLOOR PLAN

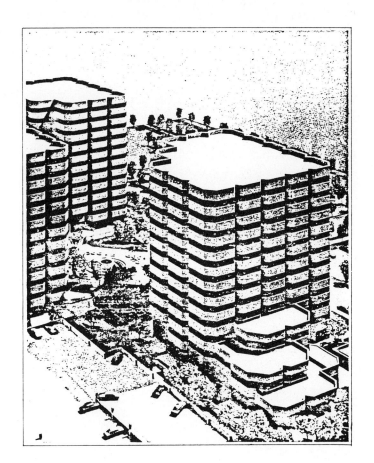

Exhibit 6

Financing Information

Benchmark Real Estate, Inc.   2/12/81

BENCHMARK REAL ESTATE RATES, APARTMENT MORTGAGES

	February 10, 1981	January 13, 1981	December 10, 1980
Interest Rate	Proposed – not available Immediate – 15.25 (FHLMC)	Not Available	Not Available
Fee	1.5 – 2		
Terms (yrs)	Immediate – 30 yrs.		

BENCHMARK REAL ESTATE RATES, COMMERCIAL REAL ESTATE PROJECTS
(Medium–size shopping centers, office buildings, industrial buildings)

	February 10, 1981	January 13, 1981	December 10, 1980
Interest Rate	Mtge. rate + participation or equity adding up to 14.5 – 15.	Mtge. rate + participation or equity adding up to 15 – 17.	Mtge. rate + participation or equity adding up to 15 – 17.
Fee	1 point	1 point	1 point
Terms (yrs)	25–30 yr. amort.	25–30 yr. amort.	25–30 yr. amort.

BENCHMARK REAL ESTATE RATES, CREDIT PROJECTS (all types)

	February 10, 1981	January 13, 1981	December 10, 1980
Interest Rate	Mtge. rate + participation or equity adding up to 14.5 – 15.	Mtge. rate + participation or equity adding up to 15 – 16.5.	Mtge. rate + participation or equity adding up to 15 – 16.5.
Fee	0	0	0
Term (yrs)	30–35 yr. amort.	30–35 yr. amort.	30–35 yr. amort.

* There is an improving tone in the market. At least some lenders are interested in locking in current high yields. Lenders' target for total rate of
return (including kickers) has leveled off to 15% or under. They are willing
to go as low as 12% for the initial rate of return.

Exhibit 6
continued

* Funds are becoming available for straight mortgages with no kickers. Current rate is 14.5 – 14.75 with 5-year and 10-year call provisions. One lender has allocated $100 million through 1983, $20 million this year. He will trade piece of rate for piece of participation if package adds up to 14.75% within two years.

* Funds for deals under $10 million are becoming available. Life companies with smaller pension-fund accounts are open for these.

* Immediates for apartments on straight 30-year loans, no kickers, no calls, are available through FHLMC. Not suitable for proposed construction – rates are only guaranteed for two months.

* On a joint venture hotel deal in Southwest, there is no debt service. Lender provides 75% of cash for 50% ownership, expects 12% cash return in first year.

PART IV
DEVELOPMENT STRATEGY

In the first half of Real Estate Finance and Development, we established a base of fundamental skills. We became acquainted with the real estate industry and its participants, with the many different land use types, and with the roles of the entrepreneur, the developer and the lender. We developed basic and advanced skills in financial analysis, including discounted cash-flow analysis. We became acquainted with the many different forms of organization used in real estate ownership and development.

In the third chapter, we extended our understanding of ownership structuring to include joint ventures and equity syndication investments. We gained experience in applying the tools of feasibility analysis and market research. In the process, we were exposed to the most sophisticated contemporary investment structures which a developer may encounter.

In this final chapter, we will return essentially to basics. This time, however, we will be armed with considerable knowledge. We will now use whatever sophisticated financing and analytic tools which may be appropriate, but we will concentrate on putting these pieces together -- synthesizing strategy for the development. We will once again stress the role of the developer as the agent of change, the manager of the entire development process, from concept to operations. Cases will illustrate this role in a variety of organizational and project settings, including the public sector viewpoint. Simple and complex development programs and various strategic approaches are included, so the reader may derive broadly useful principles and a wide frame of reference. This part begins with a brief introduction to the development process.

INTRODUCTION TO THE DEVELOPMENT PROCESS

The development process consists of the steps by which a property may be altered over time to increase its value or usefulness. Students of this process must learn the practitioner's ability to relate the people and property involved with an appropriate financial structure over time.

As illustrated in the table, "Conceptual Framework for Real Estate Decisions," in the introduction to Part I, The Changing World of the Real Estate Developer, the development process requires a great many decisions, large and small, which must be made over time. These many decisions are interrelated, of course, and perhaps the most important contribution the developer makes is to provide a sense of strategic purpose. The skilled developer must have a sense of vision about property, the ability to ignore the present and see instead the potential future. This sense of purpose provides the unifying element on which the many decisions may be based.

For most developers, strategy formulation is carried out at the project level. Most developers and investors are project-oriented, and a strategic approach to each project will usually be articulated at an early stage. Elements of the development strategy may be numerous. Indeed, the following eight elements of the development process may all be reflected in strategic planning for a project. They include investment decisions -- the developer is an investor, if only of time and energy -- but they also include many decisions unique to development. These decisions are discussed in a rough chronological order as they might become most important in a particular project. Among the most important elements are the basic thinking about products and markets, early consideration of the composition of the development team, and the financial strategy for carrying out the development.

Acquisition

What does the developer do first? It is interesting to note that the investor will often begin by buying a piece of property. Developers rarely do this, but instead will seek to control property through an option agreement with the present owner or to purchase the property using other people's money.

Analysis

Perhaps the more important question is *which* parcel of land or building to pursue. Developers consider many factors in selecting and refining their development strategies. Regional and locational preferences, target products and markets, size of project, and organizational capabilities and limitations are among the usual considerations. While a certain amount of opportunistic response to available properties is only to be expected, the best development projects do not happen by chance. Rather, they are the result of hard work and searching in furtherance of a clearly articulated development strategy. In addition to market research, scheduling, budgeting and design are all important for analysis.

Organization

Providing the organizational and human resources for the development venture is an essential area for decision-making. Many developers think of the composition of their development team as the most important step. As the team is defined, responsibilities are fixed for design, construction, financing and marketing. Given the nature of the project and the in-house capabilities of the developer, certain consulting disciplines and outside contractors will be needed. Internal staffing, including provision for project management, is also important.

Perhaps most important at an early stage is the need to obtain public approvals and permits. Requirements of the approvals process may influence greatly the selection of design and legal consultants. Decision-making in this area is closely related to both development strategy formulation and to design. To the extent the project must be altered in order to win approvals, the entire process may have to be reconsidered.

Design

Design decisions include both the selection of design professionals and guidance of their work. Selection of which disciplines are needed depends on the nature of the task. The large-scale building development may include a full complement -- architect, landscape architect, civil, mechanical, structural and electrical engineer, space planner, interior designer and graphic designer may all be engaged at various points in the process. In other cases, various disciplines may not be needed, and complete architectural and engineering services may not be required.

Once selected, guidance of the design process is very important. Design proceeds through conceptual, schematic, and preliminary stages. After a preferred design has been arrived at, it is developed further, and construction documents are produced. The developer must play an important role in providing effective critiques at the earliest stages of design. This prevents problems arising from the tendency of some design professionals to be either too adventurous or too conservative in early proposals or to become prematurely committed to their initial ideas. Both types of designers need frequent and vigorous feedback.

Financing

Decision-making in this area has been fully considered elsewhere in this volume. Preparation of the initial capital budget and the setup or revenue estimate are es-

sential steps. Beyond this, the typical steps are to identify the amount and source of any debt financing which may be contemplated. With this established, equity funds in various amounts and forms may be arranged. Most developers will prefer to arrange all financing from outside sources first and provide their own equity funds later, if at all, and then only as needed.

Construction

Decision-making in this area centers on the choice of contractor and determining the appropriate contractual relationship. Developers may have their own construction forces and do the work themselves; they may subcontract all or part of the work, serving as construction managers; or they may choose to hire a general contractor. Selection of a general contractor may depend on a combination of factors, including price, availability, experience with similar work, key personnel, and prior working relationships with the developer.

Choosing the form of contract is an important step. The financial protection of a fixed price or guaranteed maximum price for the construction may be very desirable. This protection is only meaningful, however, if the contract documents -- drawings and specifications -- are sufficiently precise so the scope and quality of the construction can be assured. Sometimes the schedule is an important factor, and the work must proceed before all design decisions have been made. In this situation, a fixed price does little to ensure timely completion. Contract terms may be established to deal with a variety of objectives, including schedule, but also such areas as samples, mock-ups, testing, and developer approvals of subcontracts, finish materials, colors, etc.

Marketing

Key decisions in marketing lie in the choice of brokerage firms or individuals, their compensation structure, and the promotional tactics to be used. Depending on the size and type of project, developers may undertake this function themselves or may choose to award an exclusive agency to an outside contractor. Choice of an exclusive agent may be based on competitive proposals, in which compensation, staffing, and competitive offerings are a factor. The intangible factor of "image" of the project and the marketing firm, as represented in personal style and in graphic and promotional materials may also enter into the decision.

Compensation in the marketing industry is traditionally based on commissions. While most brokerage firms publish their "standard" commission schedules, these are negotiable, especially in the case of a major project. Even if marketing is being performed in-house, the developer will want to provide a significant incentive for those responsible for success in the marketing effort. Finally, no matter how well-incented a broker may be, he or she must either provide or be provided with a properly developed set of promotional and marketing materials. These will include advertising, signs, brochures, technical data, sample finish materials, and sample lease or purchase forms necessary to complete the transaction.

Property Management

The final area for decision-making is the choice of property manager. While often overlooked during the early stages of the development cycle, the quality of management service provided to tenants may be the single most important factor in their location decision. Many developers, including virtually all of the major ones,

consider this area so important that they always undertake it themselves. They will do so even in a new market area where the revenue from a single project may not fully cover the associated costs. Those lacking the resources will usually hire a firm with a number of similar properties under management.

Among the areas of concern are decisions about the level of services to be provided to tenants, including optional services. In buildings with rapid turnover, the refitting and refinishing of residential and commercial space must be carried out without disruption to other tenants. Quality and consistency of security services are often important. Energy control and maintenance are essential areas of responsibility for the property manager. Some developers are becoming involved in providing local area network communications capability for new buildings and even linking buildings via satellite. Technical sophistication has become a must for personnel involved in property management.

Conclusion

With all of the above considerations in mind, all that is then needed is execution. The best laid plans will lead to nothing without the commitment to implement them. Finally, when all is said and done, what is needed are the people who will commit themselves and their organizations to the project and see it through. Developers must commit themselves early, take the risks as they come, and see their projects through to completion and beyond. The risks may be incalculable, but with the special sense of vision to see what may be, the developer will reap a great reward.

Tom O'Donnell was perplexed. It was a Sunday night in early January 1978, and he had spent the weekend reading carefully two competing real estate development proposals. The proposals were from private firms to acquire and develop a state-owned parcel of land in Harvard Square, Cambridge, Massachusetts. Each proposal document was about two-inches thick and was expensively produced. Each was accompanied by beautiful architectural renderings and testimonials to its financial feasibility. Each was backed by influential members of the local community. As the senior state official on the Review Board set up to deal with the matter, Tom's opinion would carry considerable weight, but he was unsure how to approach the decision.

The decision by the Project Review Board was an important one. On the state level, this development was seen as an important step toward improving the economic vitality of the state. Locally, the development would provide badly needed tax revenues. And yet, comparisons between the proposals were difficult because no firm guidelines for the submissions had been determined. Both submissions were for large mixed-use developments, but the land uses were different; the formats used in the proposal documents also differed widely, as did the contents, particularly in the area of market and financial information.

The Project Review Board soon would have to decide between the two proposals. The decision, involving ownership of a $40 million dollar development, was rapidly becoming a political *cause celebre* (see Exhibit 1). As Tom O'Donnell sat down to review th proposals once again, he hoped to find an objective way to compare them.

HISTORY OF PARCEL 1B

In 1976 and 1977, unassisted private real estate development activity in New England seemed as rare as a 30-inch snowfall. Except for the well-known Quincy Marketplace retail project, no major developments, private or quasi-private, had been completed during that time. In an effort to counter the regional economic decline, Governor Michael Dukakis and the Commonwealth of Massachusetts were making efforts to move forward on all potential private development projects in which the Commonwealth was an active participant.

One such development was the 4.2-acre parcel of land located in the southwest sector of Harvard Square in the City of Cambridge and owned by the State. This land was known as Parcel 1B. It was being offered for sale to a qualified developer for construction as a mixed-use project. Of the several vacant or underutilized sites which were potentially available for development within the area, Parcel 1B appeared to have significant advantages in terms of location, market attraction, community interest in its success, state and Federal support, realistic scope and freedom from encumbrances. In addition, this was the largest unbuilt parcel in the area and had significant future park frontage. It was therefore seen as the key parcel to the development of the entire sector.

Yet no area was believed to be more uncertain for the private developer to work than Cambridge. Developers in Cambridge had been stopped by legal, governmental and neighborhood actions in the past, even while in the process of construction.

HARVARD SQUARE AND THE PARCEL 1B ENVIRONMENT

As Harvard Square had grown from a colonial neighborhood center to a city and metropolitan center, its character had been altered. By 1978, indeed, the Square was unique. It was a diverse shopping district in a congested, pedestrian-oriented, historic urban setting. Yet it was in the midst of a university campus and surrounded by relatively low-density residential areas, which were themselves diverse. Harvard Square was many different things at once -- a specialty shopping district, a center for entertainment and dining, an entry point for cultural and educational activity, and the focus of an intense street life. In the 1970s many viewed it as a successful urban environment for its residents, for students and for shoppers.

In the early 1960s the Southwest sector of Harvard Square consisted of 17 acres of underdeveloped land. Lying between the center of the Square and the Charles River, the Southwest sector was bounded on its western edge by a residential area known as Neighborhood Ten. The southern boundary was Memorial Drive, adjacent to the Charles River. Along the eastern edge was Boylston Street and the Harvard University Houses. Toward the north was the Harvard Square commercial core. The Southwest sector was covered by vacant brick warehouses and the repair sheds and yards for the "Red Line" subway cars of the Massachusetts Bay Transit Authority. This land represented the largest block of land potentially available for development in the Harvard Square area in more than a century. As such, it was seen by most public officials as a major opportunity, especially so if the MBTA facilities could be relocated.

THE KENNEDY PROPOSAL

In 1964 the John F. Kennedy Memorial Corporation announced its plan to secure 12.2 acres for the proposed John F. Kennedy Library, Museum and Archives (see Exhibit 2, Parcels 1A, 1B and 2A). In this plan, the Parcel 1B portion of the land was to be considered for income producing development. The site was intended to be developed with income producing activities, which would produce badly needed tax revenues. In 1965 a decision was reached to relocate the MBTA yards. During the period from this decision to

1970, little activity occurred toward clearing the site for the Kennedy proposal.

Finally, in 1971 the MBTA relocation program became firm, and the Kennedy Corporation authorized I. M. Pei to begin architectural design studies for the Kennedy complex. When the early schematic proposals were unveiled for the design of the library, an active community and neighborhood debate ensued about the appropriateness of the project as a whole. Controversy centered on the monumental pyramidal design and on the intensity of use that would result from the museum.

Neighborhood Ten, which consisted of mostly upper income residents, had a history of involvement in Harvard Square planning and development. The impact of potential museum and library visitors upon this neighborhood was felt to be severe due to the close proximity of the residential area to the site. The neighborhood began actively to oppose the Kennedy complex. As a response to criticism of the monumental design proposal first submitted, I. M. Pei redesigned the project into three basic parts. These were a building for the School of Government and Institute of Politics, and a separate building for the archives and the related facilities site. This revised plan identified a major area as a memorial park. After this submission of late 1973, serious governmental reviews began.

In March 1974 the preparation of an environmental impact statement for the John F. Kennedy complex began. Ten months later it was released to the community. This document concluded that no negative impacts would occur with the development of the Kennedy complex in the southwest sector. The announced results sparked a renewed intensity in the community debate, and opposing citizens initiated court action to obtain background material under the "Freedom-of-Information" statute in preparation to challenge the results of the E.I.S. in court. However, before any court decision was made, the Kennedy Corporation withdrew the museum proposal from the site.

After this withdrawal, there then ensued a period of ten months in which the possibility of a Kennedy Archives in Cambridge and a museum located elsewhere was exhaustively explored. In November 1975, the final decision was announced to locate the entire Kennedy complex elsewhere.

HARVARD SQUARE DEVELOPMENT TASK FORCE

In the wake of the Kennedy Corporation's decision, the question of the future of the southwest sector of Harvard Square was returned to basics. The City, in the meantime, had formed a task force to recommend public policy for development. This task force consisted of members from Neighborhood Ten, the Harvard Square business community and Harvard University. The land itself had been transferred to the U.S. General Services Administration (GSA) in anticipation of the Kennedy project going forward.

The task force and its consultants drafted the Harvard Square Comprehensive Policy Plan. This document outlined planning objectives for the southwest sector, including land uses, density of development, height restrictions, suggested locations and a use mix for development. The Policy Plan objectives were stated as follows:

1. produce tax generating uses for the City of Cambridge;

2. respect the existing character of the Harvard Square area and adjacent neighborhoods;

3. encourage pedestrian scale activities;

4. complement the existing and projected land uses and building development; and

5. achieve the highest level of design excellence coupled with a sound financial implementation plan.

In 1976, the Commonwealth of Massachusetts acquired title to the MBTA yard site from the GSA by authorization of Housing Act No. 5177. Under this legislation three parcels were delineated: a 2.9-acre parcel for Harvard University's Kennedy School of Government and Institute of Politics, a 5.06-acre parcel for use as a memorial park to the late president, and a 4.21-acre parcel (Parcel 1B) for a tax producing mixed-use development of office, retail, hotel and housing activities.

The legislation also authorized formation of the MBTA Yards Project Review Board to review development proposals for the mixed-use site Parcel 1B. The five-member Project Review Board was to be responsible for its conducting an orderly private developer selection process and making its recommendation to the State's Secretary of Administration and Finance for the disposition of the land. As a first step, the Project Review Board retained consultants and drafted an official request for development proposals.

PHASE I RFP: DESIGN/DEVELOPMENT COMPETITION

This initial RFP, issued in February 1977, covered the first phase of a planned two-part design-developer competition. It invited submissions from teams of architects and developers in an effort to attract high-quality design submissions coupled with financial feasibility. The RFP referred to the Harvard Square Policy Plan as identifying the major considerations for planning, design and development in the southwest sector.

A number of major constraints brought to the developer's attention by this RFP are paraphrased below.

1. **Site Utilization by MBTA**: Parcel 1B, formerly the "Related Facilities Site" in the Kennedy Proposal, is presently occupied by the MBTA Bennett Street garage which shall be demolished in total to grade elevation. The MBTA will have the right to occupy Parcel 1B until January 1979.

2. **Adjacent Land Parcels**: The following is a description of the existing conditions and expected changes:

   Parcel 1A will be developed by the Metropolitan District Commission as the future John F. Kennedy Memorial Park. A 45' pedestrian right-of-way, extending north from the body of the park, will be developed and maintained as pedestrian access from Brattle Square to the park. Parcel 2A, owned by Harvard University, will be developed in two phases. Phase one, presently under construction, is the first portion of the JFK School of Government. In addition, a temporary rapid-transit station will occupy the western edge of the site adjacent to the pedestrian right-of-way. After the Red Line extension is complete, the temporary station will be removed. The Harvard Motor House parcel is occupied by a 72-room hotel owned by Franklin Realty Trust.

   The Eliot Street Block includes a series of small parcels under different ownerships with no immediate plans for development.

   The Cronin's Restaurant Parcel houses a three-story frame building with a restaurant at the ground

level. No plans are known for redevelopment.

The Craigie Apartment Parcel contains sixty apartments in a four-story brick building. It is owned by Harvard University and is leased on the open market. No plans exist to change this use.

The Trinity Realty Trust Parcel is divided into two development sites. Parcel "A" is the site formerly proposed for a Holiday Inn and is owned along with Parcel "B". Both sites are now used as parking lots. Trinity is now planning both parcels for seventy-six units of housing, 18,000 square feet of retail space, 50,000 square feet of office space, and a parking garage of 740 spaces.

The Bay Bank/Harvard Trust Parcel is presently used as surface parking for 126 cars. There are no known committed plans for its development.

3. **Zoning**: Parcel 1B is currently zoned C-3. This classification allows residential and institutional uses. The City plans to alter the existing classification for Parcel 1B to permit development of mixed uses.

4. **Land Use**: Land uses which may be appropriate for development of Parcel 1B are housing, hotel, retail, offices, community service facilities and parking. The exact quantities, location and configuration are not specified in this RFP but are left to the discretion of the proposer. The overall allowable F.A.R. is 3.0 as stated in the Policy Plan.

5. **Parking**: As part of each proposal for Parcel 1B, a parking facility shall be included to accommodate the number of spaces required by

existing zoning ordinance for each proposed use plus a minimum of 350 spaces of public parking which would replace those on grade spaces which exist on site.

6. **Vehicular Access**: At the present time approval for access to the site from Memorial Drive is not committed by the Metropolitan District Commission. If it is determined that such access will be necessary, the Review Board and the City will seek the approvals. No service access will be permitted from Memorial Drive.

7. **Pedestrian Circulation and Open Space**: The general objective for development of a safe, lively and clear pedestrian environment are described in the Policy Plan. Of particular concern will be the treatment of the pedestrian way leading from the JFK Park to Harvard Square, the treatment of the park frontage, and the relationship of the Parcel 1B pedestrian plan to that of Harvard Square as a whole.

8. **Building Height**: The Policy Plan identifies a maximum height range of 60' to 80' as a general range of height and should not be considered fixed or as a constraint on imaginative design. A proposal will be evaluated on its total design quality considering bulk, scale, and density as well as height.

9. **Soil Conditions**: The poor condition of the underlying soil and the high water table may serve to limit building to about one floor below grade.

10. **Public Sector Improvements**: It is the intent of the City to bear the cost of construction and maintenance of the public sector improvements required. However, the City will not pay for any land which may be necessary. These improvements would include public roadways, sidewalks, paving and landscaping within the public right-of-ways, utility improvements and traffic-control systems.

THE SUBMISSIONS

Six development teams submitted Phase I proposals, each with design solutions, development programs and financing plans. After conducting hearings and obtaining testimony from interested community participants, the Project Review Board voted to invite second-round proposals from three developer-architect teams.

Tom O'Donnell felt that the procedure used had led to an initial selection based primarily on design and program issues. He frankly doubted that any of the first round submissions was fully feasible as submitted. One of the losing proposals may well have been financially feasible, since it proposed building only a relatively large retail facility with necessary parking and incorporating several adjacent parcels into the project. However, this proposal was felt to conflict with the objectives of the Policy Plan.

In any event, the three submissions chosen to continue in the competition were judged to be the best solutions and were to be refined in the Phase II competition. The Phase II RFP was issued in early October 1977 with submissions required by mid-December.

The Phase II RFP was much like that for Phase I. Additional details were provided to make firm the required land sales price and property-tax assumptions, which had been left vague in Phase I. In general the second RFP reflected something of a compromise between members of the Project Review Board who wanted the selection to be based primarily on design and program considerations and those who wanted to ensure the project would be built promptly and yield the highest property taxes to the City of Cambridge. As a result, no specific format or detailed criteria were stated in the RFP in either the design or financial areas.

Additional information on constraints was provided in the second stage RFP as follows:

1. **Sale of Land**: The land sale price for Parcel 1B is fixed at $4,162,500. Upon designation, the developer will be expected to pay a non-refundable deposit of $100,000 and will be allowed up to 18 months following designation to obtain all permits and complete design before transfer of the land will be required.

2. **Zoning**: A new Planned Unit Development zoning classification was adopted for Parcel 1B to permit mixed-use development. Formal approval of this zoning change was in part responsible for delay of the start of the second-stage competition from August to October.

3. **Dedication**: At the discretion of the designated developer, 22,000 square feet of the parcel may be donated to the City of Cambridge for road widenings and other improvements along Bennett Street and University Road.

4. **Access**: Proposers should design their schemes to work without a Memorial Drive access, but with the potential to utilize the access if approval is received.

5. **Property Taxes**: The Board has provided a standard set of assumptions concerning taxation to be used by proposers in their financial calculations (see Exhibit 3).

THE PHASE II SUBMISSIONS

Only two of the three invited developers were able to respond. The third dropped out after being unable to resolve a dispute between their architectural firm and the individual architect who had handled the original submissions.

Everyone concerned knew that financial feasibility was an essential issue. The property taxes from the proposed development had been estimated at as much as 5% of the entire Cambridge tax base. Each month of delay would mean lost revenue well in excess of $100,000 for the City. Because of the importance of this issue, the board had retained consultants experienced in real estate finance. The consultants reviewed the two proposals and prepared a comparison of the various programs and financial assumptions (see Exhibit 4).

The results of the second stage competition were now in front of Mr. O'Donnell. To reduce the amount of material he had to deal with, he extracted the critical parts of each developer's proposal, including site plans and financial summaries (see Exhibits 5 and 6). These materials were only part of the development teams' submissions.

As he looked over his materials, he appreciated the good job his consultants had done in summarizing the quantitative aspects. But was this the right approach to the decision? He knew that the issue was "hot," as the *Globe* editorial confirmed.

EXHIBITS

1. *Globe* editorial.

2. Site map.

3. Current tax policy.

4. Comparative financial summaries.

5. Carpenter/Cambridge proposal (excerpts).

6. Carbarn/Thompson proposal (excerpts).

QUESTIONS FOR DISCUSSION

1. As a responsible citizen, public official and member of the Review Board, which developer should Mr. O'Donnell vote to designate?

2. What are the strongest arguments for and against the decision?

3. How should Mr. O'Donnell go about comparing these proposals?

4. What level of financial analysis is appropriate for this stage?

5. Is a competition the best way to dispose of public land? What are the implication of alternative approaches?

Exhibit 1

18   The Boston Globe   Monday, February 13, 1978

The Boston Globe

WILLIAM O. TAYLOR, President and Publisher
THOMAS WINSHIP, Editor

JOHN P. GIUGGIO, Executive V.P. & Treasurer   ROBERT H. PHELPS, Managing Editor, AM
RICHARD C. OCKERBLOOM, V.P. Marketing & Sales   JOHN S. DRISCOLL, Managing Editor, P.M
DAVID STANGER, Business Manager   TIMOTHY LELAND, Managing Editor, Sunday

ROBERT L. HEALY, Executive Editor   ANNE C. WYMAN, Editor, Editorial Page

Globe Newspaper Company, 135 Morrissey Blvd., Boston, Mass. 02107 — 617-929-2000
A Wholly Owned Subsidiary of AFFILIATED PUBLICATIONS, INC.

DAVIS TAYLOR, Chairman of the Board   JOHN I. TAYLOR, President

Close call in Harvard Sq.

'A five-member review board will soon make its recommendations for developing four acres of land on the fringe of Harvard sq. The choice is between two estimable but radically different designs, both with ardent, politically sophisticated and determined supporters. But the time for partisan lobbying has passed, the public has been heard and the review board should be allowed breathing room for the close call it is competent to make for the future of Harvard sq.

Development of the parcel is of intense concern to local businessmen, neighboring residents and visitors to the square because of its inevitable effect on traffic congestion, pedestrian safety, air quality and business activity.

The proposals to develop a portion of the site once proposed for the Kennedy library and museum complex are the result of an open competition based on guidelines openly arrived at. Architect Benjamin Thompson, his wife Jane and entrepreneur K. Dunn Gifford are principals in one proposal. Carpenter & Co., in partnership with the architectural firm Cambridge Seven Associates, created the other. Both plans clearly seek to conform to the Harvard Square Policy Plan, but the degree to which they do is one of the many close judgments that must be made.

The Carpenter submission tends to emphasize office and retail development over new housing. It has solid financing, as might be expected, considering this approach, and it is architecturally adventurous.

The Thompson proposal tends to conform to physical characteristics of the surrounding academic-commercial environment, is less dramatic in scale, more modest in its commercial ambitions and oriented toward housing.

Thompson's centerpiece is a 200-unit luxury condominium complex with sale prices in the $80,000 to $150,000 range, plus a 150-room hotel. The financial feasibility of the Thompson plan has been questioned, partly because of uncertainty whether there is a market for the high-priced housing. Besides the retail and office space, Carpenter's focus is on a 210-room hotel and it envisions only 75 high-priced condominiums.

Some businessmen are anxious that a large-scale commercial development will bring too much competition to existing businesses in the square. Others doubt that a big commercial development built all at once can be sustained in the square. Still others argue that a high-toned commercial development will attract additional "carriage trade" clientele to Harvard sq. and benefit all businesses.

But no one doubts that whatever development is finally decided will generate more traffic on streets that are already supersaturated with cars. Both proposals before the review board contain parking facilities. Thompson plans 722 spaces compared to Carpenter's 856.

Cambridge is in need of tax revenue and it is this point, along with environmental and aesthetic concerns, on which the review board's recommendations must turn. No matter which side sentiments line up with, most people agree that the board is competent to weigh these considerations and decide fairly. Its decision should be awaited patiently and its recommendation should be respected.

Exhibit 2

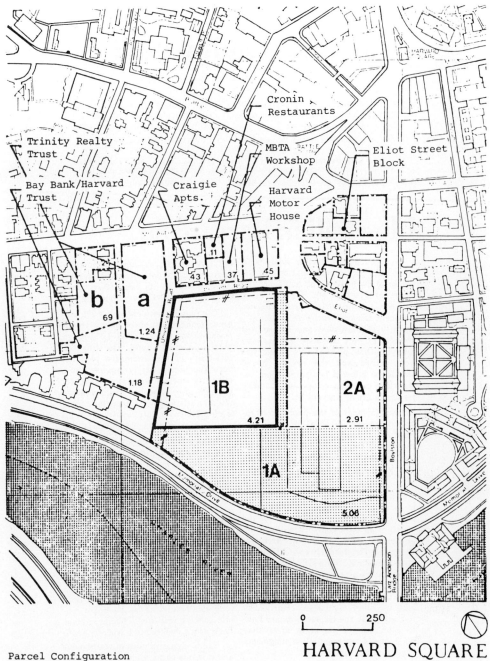

Parcel Configuration

The illustration above shows the
existing parcel configuration by
ownership. The size, shape and
location of each parcel is a major
factor in future development. The
sub-parcelization of the MBTA
yards is that recommended to the
legislature for approval.

Exhibit 3

CURRENT TAX POLICY:	(New Construction)
General Office:	5-year Phase-In beginning at 17% of gross rent in the first full operating year to an ultimate rate of 24% of gross rent by the fifth full operating year.
Retail:	20-25% of tenant rent on possible 5-year Phas-In schedule with long-term rise to a potential of 35% of tenant rent for older lower-rent space where sales volumes justify an abolute comparability with newer space.
Hotel:	3 year Phase-In beginning at $600/room in the first full operating year to $1,000/room in the third full operating year. At this point, taxes are levied on a long range basis at 4.25% of capitalized value.
Housing-Condominium:	Assessed at 27.5% of sales price = tax at 5% of sales price. Reassessed only after a majority of units in a building have been resold.
Housing-Rental:	30% of gross rent
Parking Garage:	30% of gross revenue
UNDER 100% VALUATION:	(Expected to be operational by 1981); (Does not include effect of any differential assessments which may be allowed under proposed legislation.
General Office:	27.33% of gross rent up to a limit of 6.287% of capitalized value. No Phase-In during operating years.
Retail:	22% of gross rent equivalent (tenant rent + operating expense - taxes) up to 6.287% of capitalized value. No Phase-Ins.
Hotel:	5% of first full operating year capitalized value, rising thereafter at a rate equal to inflation X year 1 tax to a limit of 6.287% of capitalized value.
Housing-Condominium:	6.287% of sales price
Housing-Rental:	30% of gross rent up to 6.287% of capitalized value.
Parking Garage:	6.287% of capitalized value.

Exhibit 4

Comparative Quantitative Summaries

Stage II Proposals	Carpenter/Cambridge	Carbarn/Thompson
Uses		
Hotel	210 Rooms 155,900 square feet	150 Rooms 144,725 square feet 45,863 sf Conf. Center
Retail	126,000 square feet incl. cinemas	20,000 square feet
Office	152,000 square feet	81,730 square feet
Residential	75 units 100,000 square feet	200 units 253,600 square feet 50 of these units are convertible to 100 Hotel units
Health Club		10,120 square feet
Public/Unassigned	24,000 square feet	
Subtotal	557,900 square feet	545,918 square feet
Parking	722 spaces 237,900 square feet	856 spaces 329,000 square feet
Maximum Height	119 feet	120 feet

Exhibit 4
continued

Capital Summary

	Carpenter/Cambridge		Carbarn/Thompson	
	gross ($000)	per unit ($)	gross ($000)	per unit ($)
Construction Cost:				
Hotel	8,158	38,850 /rm	6,803	45,350 /rm
Office	8,595	62.83 /sf	3,308.00	45.01 /sf
Retail	4,529	40.08 /sf	661.00	29.50 /sf
Parking	4,262	4,980 /space	5,624	10,770/522 spaces *
Total Construction Cost for Revenue Uses	$25,544		$16,396	
	=========		=========	
Non-Construction Costs:				
Land	4,163		4,163	
Fees	2,840		4,000	
Contingencies	738		2,000	
Financing	3,613		4,000	
Housing contrib.	(2,677)		(8,736)	
Marketing (excluding housing)	1,150		600	
Site Develop.	-		1,000	
Total Development Cost after Housing Sales	$35,371		$23,423	
	=========		=========	
Equity	4,226		3,897	
Mortgages	31,643		19,527	
Total Investment	$35,869		$23,424	
	=========		=========	

* 200 spaces sold with condominiums

Exhibit 4
continued

Hotel, Condominium, Office, Retail, and Parking Revenues

	Carpenter/Cambridge		Carbarn/Thompson	
	gross ($000)	per unit ($)	gross ($000)	per unit ($)
Hotel				
Quantity	210 rooms		150 rooms	
Room Rate	$51 /day		$40 /day	
Occupancy	75 %		75 %	
Room Revenue	2,932	13,962	1,643	10,953
Food & Beverage	1,173	5,586	2,209	14,727
Conference & Other	-	-	860	5,733
Gross Renue	4,105	19,548	4,712	31,413
Room Expenses	792	3,771	427	2,847
F&B Expenses	915	4,357	1,991	13,273
Other Expenses	944	4,495	1,149	7,660
Total Op. Expenses	2,651	12,624	3,567	23,780
Op. Cash Flow	1,454	6,924	1,145	7,633
Property Tax	210	1,000	175	1,167
NOI	$1,244	$5,924	$970	$6,467
Condominiums				
Quantity	75 Duplex		200 Duplex	
Sales Revenue	7,498	99,973 *	25,246	126,230 **
Construction	4,371	58,280	12,552	62,760
Gross Margin	3,127	41,693	12,694	63,470
Commissions, Fees, Carrying, etc.	450	6,000	2,525	12,625
Contrib. to Garage	-	-	1,433	7,165
Adjusted Contribution	$2,677	$35,693	$8,736	$43,680

* Exclude parking
** Include parking space

Exhibit 4
continued

	Carpenter/Cambridge		Carbarn/Thompson	
	gross ($000)	per unit ($)	gross ($000)	per unit ($)
Office				
Office NLA	136,800 square feet		73,500 square feet	
Rent/square foot		12.00		12.00
Gross Revenue	–		882	
Vacancy (2.5%)	–		22	
Rental Income	1,592		860	11.70
Operating Exp.	371	2.71	184	2.50
Operating C/R	1,221	8.93	676	9.20
RE Tax	328 *	$2.40	198	2.69
NOI	$893	$6.53	$478	$6.50
Retail				
Retail SFGLA	113,000 square feet		22,414 square feet	
Rent/sf gross	–	11.00		20.00
Rent sf/net net		10.67		8.75
Rental Inc. net net	1,206		448	20.00
Operating Exp.	5	0.04	252	11.25
NOI	$1,201	$10.63	$196	$8.75
Parking				
Revenue Producing	856 spaces		522 spaces	
Revenue	1,406	1,640	897	1,720
Operating Exp.	170	200	104	200
Operating Net	1,236	1,440	793	1,520
RE Tax	422	493	178	340
NOI	$814	$947.00	$615	$1,180

* Increases to 394 by 1985

Exhibit 5

Kennedy Square

**A Proposal for development of
Parcel 1B Southwest Sector
Harvard Square
Cambridge, Massachusetts**

December, 1977

**Carpenter/Cambridge Associates
A Joint Venture of
Carpenter & Company, Inc. and
Cambridge Seven Associates, Inc.**

Exhibit 5
continued

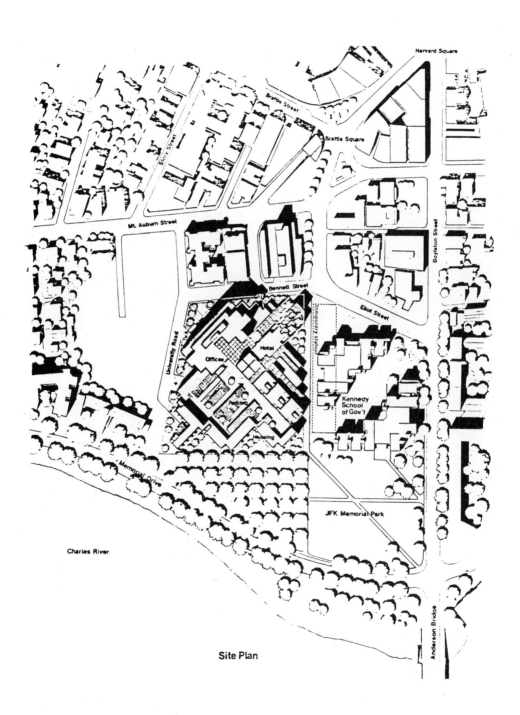

Site Plan

Kennedy Square A Joint Venture of Carpenter & Company, Inc., and Cambridge Seven Associates, Inc.

Exhibit 5
continued

General Financing Plan

The project's financial plan is strong and very straight-forward. We intend substantial ($4,250,000) equity funds to be invested in the project on a long term basis with the balance of funds coming from the State Street Bank and Trust Company of Boston during the construction phase and long term mortgage financing on a non-participating basis from New England Mutual Life Insurance Company. Each of these institutions has indicated its strong support of our project and interest in financing it. If for any reason we do not conclude our loan with them, we believe that with the substantial equity strength of our proposal other institutional lenders of similar quality will be receptive to our loan requests.

A summary of certain major aspects of our financial plan follows, plus letters from New England Life and State Street Bank.

Equity Partner

The equity partner is to receive a majority interest in the project's initial profits and losses until there has been an adequate cumulative return on invested capital plus full return of investment at which time the partner's interest will readjust to 50/50.

Debt

No debt is contemplated until construction commences; the entire investment until that point will be equity. The construction loan closing will have a first disbursement equal to 90% of the prior equity advanced and will continue in subsequent disbursements to be 90% of funds expended but not in excess of the amount of the permanent take out loan commitment. An average interest rate on the construction loan has been projected at 10%. The permanent loan is based upon capitalizing stabilized (1983) net income using a capitalization rate of 9.75% and a loan-to-value ratio of 75%. The loan is projected at 9.5% interest, 35-year term. The ability to achieve, or improve upon, the terms of the projected loan is somewhat associated with the creditworthy nature of the sponsor and the tenants. In that regard, obviously a Hillman entity is most acceptable and Conran's, Bonwit Teller, Sack Theatres, CP Hotels, Brookstone, Freedom Federal Savings, Charrette, Index Systems, Bay Bank Harvard Trust, Fitz-Inn and Synectics are financially strong entities. We intend to carefully balance the creditworthy nature of certain tenants with the fact that we do not want or intend the project to exclude individual entrepreneurs and small companies.

Kennedy Square A Joint Venture of Carpenter & Company, Inc., and Cambridge Seven Associates, Inc.

Exhibit 5
continued

Payment of Land Sale Price

We propose to pay the $4,162,500 land sale price as follows:

$100,000   deposited at the time of execution of the land disposition agreement (within 30 days after designation);

$1,900,000   by certified or bank check or checks to be delivered at the time of delivery of the deed to the site; and

$2,162,500   by a promissory note to be delivered at the time of delivery of the deed, which will call for the payments and be secured as outlined below

The promissory note will be guaranteed by the developer and will provide for the payment of interest on the unpaid balance at a rate equal to 1/2% over the then most recent borrowing rate paid by the State. The additional 1/2% is to cover any additional administrative expense incurred by the State in connection with the deferral of payment. In view of the fact that the delivery of the deed will convert this land into an income generating asset for the State, we believe that this below market rate of interest is justifiable. Furthermore, the deferral of payment at that rate will reduce the burden on the developer of carrying the relatively high cost of the land during the period that the project is not income-producing. We believe that it is in the best interests of insuring the ultimate success of the project.

The principal of the note will be payable as follows:

a)   if the project is developed in one phase, the entire principal will be payable in or within three years after delivery of the deed; or

b)   if the project is developed in two phases, approximately $1,322,500 of the principal will be paid in or within three years after delivery of the deed and the remaining $840,000 (or that portion attributable to the land on which the condominium phase is to be constructed at the rate of approximately $23.00 per square foot) will be payable on or before the later of (i) that date which is two years after substantial completion of the John F. Kennedy Park or (ii) five years after the date of delivery of the deed.

Kennedy Square   A Joint Venture of Carpenter & Company, Inc., and Cambridge Seven Associates, Inc.

Exhibit 5
continued

The promissory note will be secured by a purchase money mortgage of the entire site which will be subordinated to the institutional first mortgage financing for the project.

While it is not an essential element of our proposal we would appreciate your consideration of the subordination of the purchase money mortgage to the condominium master deed, with a provision for partial releases from your mortgage to be granted upon sale of individual condominium units. Such release would be predicated on a schedule of release prices to be agreed upon which would, in general, call for the pro rata reduction of the $840,000 portion of the land sale price attributable to the condominiums. We believe that such program of subordination and partial releases is consistent with conventional financing techniques and would minimize the developer's cost of carrying the land during the period of absorption of the condominium units.

Staying Power

In the preparation of our overall financial program, we have been highly sensitive to the Board's strong directive that the risk of an incomplete project or financial failure after completion be reduced to a minimum.

First of all, we have thoroughly analyzed each of our cost estimates, and where practicable tested them against actual comparables. We believe that this has resulted in conservative and reliable projections of cost of construction. We are confident that our rents and operating expenses are conservative.

Secondly, we have factored into our projections a generous provision for contingencies, which in a project of this complexity is sound fiscal planning.

Thirdly, we have agreed with our equity partner to defer $500,000 of our development fee until the project has been completed and fully paid for.

Lastly, and perhaps most importantly, Hillman has an impeccable reputation in financial circles and one can be sure they would be most jealous of protecting this position. Also, we have made provision in our agreement with our equity partner for the funding of capital cost overruns and operational deficits which exceed our provision for contingency and deferred fee. As indicated elsewhere in this proposal, the parent of our equity partner has a set worth in excess of $100,000,000. We firmly believe, therefore, that every reasonable precaution has been taken to insure the completion of the project and its successful operation.

Kennedy Square   A Joint Venture of Carpenter & Company, Inc., and Cambridge Seven Associates, Inc.

Exhibit 5
continued

Condominium Financing

If the project is built as a single phase, which we currently intend, the condominiums will be covered by the construction loan in our projections with takeout commitments provided by local Boston/Cambridge area institutional lenders who provide long term loans to the individual condominium purchasers. In the event that the condominiums are built as second phase, a separate construction loan will be made with takeout again provided by local institutions. We have discussed the condominium financing in some detail with our construction lender, and it is amenable to either approach provided we have reached an acceptable level of pre-sales (or make guarantees of same) which we are comfortable can be done given the relatively small number of units we plan.

Mr. Hillman and the Hillman Company

The Hillman Company, and investment holding company, based in Pittsburgh, had its beginnings in the late 1800's in the coal marketing business. The dynamic growth of the company occurred in the early 1900's, with diversification in coal land ownership and ancillary business related to coal and steel production. In the middle part of this decade, increasing investments in financial institutions, major corporations, and burgeoning smaller companies have marked considerable financial growth. Today, the Hillman Company is worth several hundred million dollars (financial reports are not available).

Heading the company today is Henry L. Hillman (late 50's), son of the major family entrepreneur during the major growth days, J.H. Hillman, Jr. Henry Hillman is a remarkable entrepreneur, especially as an investor, in his own right. He heads the company with professionalism and high standards and is highly regarded as a contributor and philanthropist in his native community of Pittsburgh. Mr. Hillman has been a member of the Pittsburgh Urban Redevelopment Authority and a director of Children's Hospital and a Trustee of the University of Pittsburgh as well as Pittsburgh Allegheny Conference on Community Development.

The company has invested in major corporations and burgeoning smaller companies. Recently, Hillman was a key investor in the acquisition of the famous J. Magnin retail chain on the West Coast. Some other of The Hillman Company's investment interests are the following companies:

> Pittsburgh National Bank
> Chemical Bank

Kennedy Square   A Joint Venture of Carpenter & Company, Inc., and Cambridge Seven Associates, Inc.

Exhibit 5
continued

> National Steel
> Copeland Corporation
> Cummins Engine
> The Shakespeare Company
> Marion Power Shovel (Note: Dresser Industries recently signed a Letter
>   of Intent to purchase the business and net operating assets for
> $125 million).

In recent years, The Hillman Company has increased its investment position in real estate and through various subsidiaries, now holds interest in over $100,000,000 of commercial and residential real estate. These projects (in California, Oregon, Arizona, Pennsylvania, Washington, D.C., Virginia, and Georgia) include housing developments, industrial parks, mixed-use projects, office buildings, and shopping centers. In 1977, Hillman entered into an agreement to be the joint venture financial partner with the Rouse Company for the development of a regional shopping center in Augusta, Georgia, and purchase 100% of the stock of Hayden Island, Inc. in Portland, Oregon. Hayden Island is a 375-acre development of residential and commerical real estate which presently contains a regional mall, two hotels, office buildings, and an industrial park. The project includes future development and a very successful venture.

Forbes Magazine (9/15/69) -- full article enclosed -- said:

> Henry Lea Hillman is only the second-richest man in Pittsburgh, and a poor
> second at that, but since Richard King Mellon ranks first, Hillman is
> nonetheless one of the riches# men in America. He is, in fact, worth
> something like $300 million, most of which is in solid value, rather than in
> inflated stock-market paper. Mr. Hillman is a member of the Board of
> Directors of the following companies:

> > General Electric Corporation
> > National Steel Corporation
> > Chemical Bank - New York
> > The Pittsburgh National Bank

Kennedy Square   A Joint Venture of Carpenter & Company, Inc., and Cambridge Seven Associates, Inc.

Exhibit 5
continued

D. G. SISTERSON & COMPANY

CERTIFIED PUBLIC ACCOUNTANTS
Pennsylvania

GRANT BUILDING

PITTSBURGH, P.A. 15219

Members of
American Institute of
Certified Public Accountants

55i Fifth Avenue, 10017
New York

December 14, 1977

Carpenter & Company, Inc.
59 Temple Place
Boston, Massachusetts 02111

Re: Kennedy Square, Parcel 1 B
     Southwest Sector Harvard Square, Cambridge, Massachusetts

Gentlemen:

At the request of Mr. Michael R. Chase, we wish to advise that we examined the balance sheet of Wilmington Securities, Inc at December 31, 1976 and submitted an "Accountants' Report" dated April 15, 1977. As set forth in such report, Wilmington Securities, Inc.'s stockholders equity at December 31, 1976 was in excess of $100,000,000.

Yours very truly,

D.G. Sisterson & Company

D. G. SISTERSON & COMPANY

ERS/deb

Exhibit 6

COMMONWEALTH OF MASSACHUSETTS
CAMBRIDGE MBTA YARDS
PROJECT REVIEW BOARD

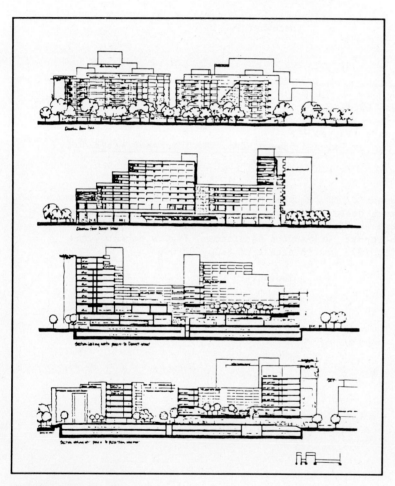

PARCEL 1B
DEVELOPMENT

PROPOSAL SUBMITTED BY:
CAMBRIDGE CARBARN COMPANY - DEVELOPER
BENJAMIN THOMPSON & ASSOCIATES - ARCHITECTS - PLANNERS

Exhibit 6
continued

SITE PLAN

COMMONWEALTH OF MASSACHUSETTS PROPOSAL FOR DEVELOPMENT OF PARCEL 1B

Exhibit 6
continued

PROJECT FINANCIAL INFORMATION

This section of the Proposal contains the information required by the Board for two of its three major evaluation categories: Financial Feasibility, and Evidence of Financial Commitment. The information is organized as suggested by the RFP.

Developer

The Cambridge Carbarn Company is the Developer of the project. The Company was formed during 1976 as a Massachusetts business trust for the purpose of participating in the development process for Parcel 1B, and its deed of trust was recorded in the Middlesex County Registry of Deeds on October 8, 1976. The principals of the Company are:

Benjamin C. Thompson, FAIA, Trustee and Chairman
K. Dun Gifford, J.D., Trustee and President
Jane McC. Thompson, Trustee and Vice President

The principals of the Company are identical to those who were principals for the Stage I Proposal. The Company has adopted a program of Development Affiliates to broaden the composition of its development team. Four principal development co-venturers have joined with the Company as Development Affiliates:

The Rouse Company, Retail Development
Intercontinental Hotels, Hotel Development
Dupree Associates, Residential and Office Development
George B. H. Macomber Company, Garage Development

The Company will work with each of these co-venturers on individual components of the Development as indicated. The Company will continue to act throughout as Developer of the project, in the context of these co-venture relationships.

In addition to these principal co-venture Affiliates, the Company has identified other organizations and individuals whose affiliations with the Company relate to financial, occupancy, management or consulting participation. These additional Affiliates are listed in the Letters of Association section of the Proposal.

The Company will elect a Board of Directors or Trustees to guide the development process, should the Company be designated. This Board will be drawn from among the Development Affiliates, from among those individuals who have signed Letters of Association, as well as from others experienced in the development process.

The Company intends, if designated as the Developer, to enter into a co-venture agreement with Waltch Associates pursuant to which Waltch Associates would become Development Manager for the project. Waltch Associates has an impressive record of involvement in successful and important mixed-use development projects in the Boston

CAMBRIDGE CARBARN COMPANY / BENJAMIN THOMPSON & ASSOCIATES

Exhibit 6
continued

area, and in addition has demonstrated its commitment to the Harvard Square area by locating its office there and investing there.

The Company plans, if designated as the Developer, to admit as a principal in the Company a Trust for the benefit of professional employees who have worked, and will work,. on the design and development of the project. This Employees' Trust will increase the sense of commitment and concern for the long-term goals of the project, and the Company believes that this will benefit the project and, consequently, the City.

Development Concept

Traditionally, large urban mixed-use projects -- a definition which applies to the Parcel 1B project -- are developed by a single development company which assumes responsibility for all aspects of design, financing, construction, leasing, and management. The results of this monolithic tradition are varied, by almost any review of mixed-use projects constructed around the country in the past ten years. As a process, it has never been an unqualified success in terms of the sensitivity of the projects to their surroundings.

The Company initially considered affiliating with an existing development company of the size and experience normally thought necessary to undertake a project of this scope, and has explored such an affiliation in detail with three different development companies. In each instance, it became apparent that the special characteristics of Parcel 1B, and the interests of the immediate neighbors, would have to be subordinated to a formalistic and standardized approach to urban mixed-use developments. This would require that substantial control over the design, leasing policies, and development sequencing would be removed from Cambridge and made subject to the exigencies of the controlling company.

Consequently, the Company adopted an alternative approach, building a team of affiliated development entities, each with specific experience in a given field and each with considerable experience in the Cambridge or Boston areas. Thus the Company has built an unusual team of Development Affiliates with rich specialized experience and independent financial strength, which are individually and jointly attractive to sources of equity and short- and long-term financing.

Negotiation and execution of individual co-venture or co-development agreements will take place after designation as Developer and before payment of the $100,000 deposit towards the land price. The Company does not desire to negotiate these agreements in advance of designation because of the Review Board's reserved authority to require changes in the Proposal, after its own review and after the results of the public hearing are known. The Company supports this policy of the Review Board to seek the views of the community upon the Proposal and to require changes after these views have been expressed.

CAMBRIDGE CARBARN COMPANY / BENJAMIN THOMPSON & ASSOCIATES

Exhibit 6
continued

Under the co-venture or co-development approach, a portion of the equity required for each element of the project would be provided by each participant. Similarly, the credit of each participant would be looked to by the short-and long-term lenders, as to that specific element. In other words, the strength and experience of each co-venturer would be separately measurable and would contribute to the strength of the whole.

Another way to view this development approach is that the Company has started with the Policy Plan and the PUD; built up a design from those parameters; and sought out partners whose experiences and successes verify that they can -- and will -- carry out the development program. This stands in contrast to identifying a balance sheet which can support the development, and then adjusting the design and leasing policies to the requirements of that balance sheet.

The Company also believes that owner-occupied development projects are intrinsically of higher quality than absentee development projects. The Company has sought to build up a team of affiliates who share the view that the project will be better if the participants have a stake in its development and management. For the sake of illustration. it takes one set of talents to design, finance, construct, and lease a project; but it takes other capabilities to then manage the development for 5, 10 or 30 years. The key difference is the element of continuity. This plan assures that the development is reared in the same spirit in which it was conceived.

Sources of Equity

The equity required for the project will be derived from four sources: from the principals of the Company; from an equity financing program to be prepared by a professional firm specializing in equity financing requirements; from co-venturers and co-developers; and, if necessary, from institutional lending sources.

The initial source of equity has been, and will be, the Cambridge Carbarn Company. The aggregate assets of the Company's principals are in excess of $ 4,500,000. In Stage I and Stage II of this competition, the principals have already made cash expenditures totalling more than $100,000, and are personally committed to procure or provide whatever equity is henceforth required to move the project forward until the construction financing is in. Equity will also be available from sources developed by the March-Eton Corporation and Waltch Associates, as is evident in the Letters of Association. Both March-Eton and Waltch Associates have in the past obtained the equity required for projects of this magnitude, and after review of the financial and development estimates, attest that they can do so for the Company.

As the Letters of Association also indicate, equity will be provided for specific elements of the project by the Company's co-venturers or co-developers. Reference is made, for illustration, to the letter from George B. H. Macomber, containing the statement of confidence about arranging the financing for one element of the project. Similar statements are contained in other of the Letters of Association. This

CAMBRIDGE CARBARN COMPANY / BENJAMIN THOMPSON & ASSOCIATES

Exhibit 6
continued

commitment of co-venturers and co-developers is one of the keystones in the Company's financial plan for this project.

The final source of equity could be institutional lenders. The Company does not believe that it will be necessary to co-venture a portion of the required equity with an institutional lender or lenders, but these sources remain open to the Company as an optional course.

Sources of Construction and Permanent Financing

The Company intends to utilize the traditional approach for real estate development financing: a short-term construction loan from a commercial bank, later "taken out" by a permanent loan from an institutional lender. Among the Letters of Association are letters from the New England Merchants National Bank and the Equitable Life Assurance Society of the United States, the former a source of short-term construction funds and the latter a source of permanent loan funds. The Company is confident of being able to obtain construction and permanent financing.

Financing Interrelationships

To attract and actually obtain each of the three necessary parts of the financing program requires the presence of two interrelated circumstances: a financially viable project, and a credible development team. Both must be present to attract and obtain the equity, the construction mortgage, and the permanent mortgage. The Company has assembled a highly capable development team, well suited to the design concept and the concept for financing it. It is the strength of this team approach which will assure the creation of a project of the highest possible standard of quality and sensitivity.

Financial Model

To gauge the financial feasibility of the Proposal, the Company has refined its financial model of the development program, and tested it against feasibility studies. This financial model has provided the information to complete the financial and development requirements of the Request. The Company understands that certain of the assumptions necessary to prepare this model, which gives assurance of the Proposal's financial feasibility, may change as the result of subsequent events. The Company believes this is proper and is prepared to address any of these subsequent changes should they occur.

Land Purchase

The Company has considered alternative methods of acquiring the site: purchasing in stages; purchasing the whole but paying over time; purchasing the whole and giving a purchase money mortgage for all or for a portion; and purchasing the whole, subsequently reselling it to an institutional purchaser which would then lease it back.

CAMBRIDGE CARBARN COMPANY / BENJAMIN THOMPSON & ASSOCIATES

Exhibit 6
continued

The Company is prepared to purchase the land in a mutually agreed upon manner; there are, however, certain specific elements of such an agreement integral to our proposal:

1.   A $100,000 deposit will be paid within 30 days of being named developer by the Secretary.

2.   An additional $1,900,000 -- to total $2,000,000 -- will be paid within an additional 18 months or when all land use approvals are obtained and the land is transferred. The Company will use its best efforts to reduce this period to less than 18 months.

3.   The remaining $2,162,500 is attributed to the residential uses and land adjacent to the Park. The Company proposes to make this payment when the Park is fully completed or when residential construction is begun, pursuant to the terms outlined in Review Board Memorandum #3.

The RFP and subsequent communications from the Review Board suggest the possibility of financing the acquisition of the land through the Commonwealth, which might be able to take a subordinated position. The Company would like to be authorized by the Review Board to meet with the Secretary of Administration and Finance, or his designated representative, to explore the specifics of this possibility. If such a financing arrangement would benefit the project, the Company would like to have the opportunity to have counsel for the Company and the Secretary reach agreement on its terms and conditions.

The Company has had discussions with an institutional banking house which has expressed interest in purchasing the land and leasing it back at very favorable rates, but the discussions were adjourned until after the proposals were submitted. The reason for the adjournment relates in part to the suggestions from the Review Board that the land could be taken down from the Commonwealth in stages. If the position of the Secretary on this matter can be made explicit, subsequent to authorization from the Review Board to meet with him, then the position of the Commonwealth on the land take-down can be related to the position of the banking house. Given the very high land price, utilization of land lease financing has a dramatic impact on equity requirements and return on investment, and consequently upon the ultimate quality of what can be built on the site.

Real Estate Taxes

The Company has adopted the guidelines for real estate taxes, as stated by the City of Cambridge and contained in the RFP, in preparing its financial plans. The Company intends to apply for Chapter 121A status during the course of the public approval process.

CAMBRIDGE CARBARN COMPANY / BENJAMIN THOMPSON & ASSOCIATES

Exhibit 6
continued

Height Limit

The PUD ordinance establishes a maximum allowable height of 60 feet for Parcel 1B, which may be increased to 80 feet if the Planning Board finds that the project provides certain amenities which benefit the public.

The Company seeks the guidance of the Review Board on this matter of height limit. The design contained in the Proposal contains a building element 110 feet high, which would require an amendment to the PUD ordinance if the Company elected to proceed under the terms of the ordinance instead of under the terms of the base zoning (see Sec. 3 of Article XI). In any case, a building above 80 feet in height would not be within the guidelines of the Policy Plan.

Given the high land price, it is desirable to utilize all the permitted F.A.R. in order to spread the cost of the land over the maximum number of built square feet. The Policy Plan suggests a preference for an urban form in the southwest area which avoids monolithic buildings of unvaried height. It also suggests repeatedly the critical importance of an open space network in the southwest area.

In response to these statements, the Company has designed a project which is, in a limited area, more than 80 feet in height. It is possible to redesign the project to keep within the 80 foot height limit, and in fact the Company has completed studies of a number of such designs. In the Company's judgement, such a project is financially feasible.

The real issue is whether it is desirable to trade away the open space for a more monolithic building complex which remains within the maximum allowable height limit.

The Company desires to discuss this matter with the Review Board and its consultants. If required to do so by the Review Board, the Company will adjust its design to meet the height limit. But in the Company's judgement, and that of its architect and planner, the Proposal as submitted is more suited to the spirit of the Policy Plan and its concerns for urban form than would otherwise be the case.

Consultations

The Company has prepared extensive cash flow and other financial materials not included in this Proposal. The Review Board has previously indicated its willingness to permit Stage II participants to meet with the Board's consultants. The Company requests the Board to authorize meetings among its consultants and the Stage II participants to examine these financial materials in detail. Financial presentations, at this stage, rest necessarily upon a large number of interrelated assumptions. These assumptions can be tested in meetings among technical specialists in a manner not well suited to meetings more attuned to policy issues. It is possible to state that a project is feasible, or not feasible, by varying room rates or rental rates a few percentage points one way or the other. The Company believes that meetings among the Board's consultants and the Stage

CAMBRIDGE CARBARN COMPANY / BENJAMIN THOMPSON & ASSOCIATES

Exhibit 6
continued

II participants can serve to eliminate unnecessary misunderstandings with regard to the critical assumptions upon which determinations of feasibility will be made.

An additional reason for this request for Review Board authorization to meet with the Board's consultants relates to the plans and sections prepared by Benjamin Thompson and Associates. Althouth the RFP requires that many be drawn to 1/16" scale, the RFP also requires that they may be bound into the Proposal Report at a size no larger than 81/2" x 17". Reducing the large drawings to this small size makes it very difficult to carry out area, circulation, and spatial relationship analyses.

For this reason, the Company desires the opportunity to discuss the full-size drawings with the Review Board's consultants.

CAMBRIDGE CARBARN COMPANY / BENJAMIN THOMPSON & ASSOCIATES

Case 12

Ken Stewart

Ken Stewart knew he had his work cut out for him. It was late on a Thursday evening in November 1983, and he had just gotten off the phone with Angus Cartwright, his senior partner in Skyline Development Associates of Boston. Angus had expressed delight that their negotiations to acquire 250 Portland Street seemed about to conclude -- one way or the other. Ken would be meeting his partner for breakfast, and a meeting with the owner's agent was set for shortly thereafter.

The outcome of the meeting would be extremely important to Skyline. If they succeeded in acquiring the property, a 100,000-square-foot historic structure in downtown Boston, they would proceed to rehabilitate and market it for office space. The development was large for Skyline and involved many risks. The company's first historic rehabilitation office development -- a joint venture -- recently had reached its breakeven point. That project had benefited from a very tight office leasing market and a relatively high rent location. The marketability of 250 Portland Street was considerably more uncertain.

Another source of risk related to the need for the acquisition to be completed within about 60 days time. This would be necessary if Skyline wanted to meet the occupancy schedule of a proposed tenant for 24,000 square feet of office space in the building. The project was located in an historic district and would benefit from the 25% Investment Tax Credit for certified rehabilitation costs. Although a tax-oriented equity syndication would very likely be undertaken, these funds would take several months to raise and could not be relied upon for the acquisition. Skyline would have to rely on debt financing for the acquisition and on its own limited resources.

For Ken Stewart personally, this project seemed to be a great opportunity. He would be project manager for Skyline -- responsible for all aspects of the project over its life. A graduate of a well-known eastern business school, Ken's initial experience in real estate had been as a location specialist for a major retail chain. On his own account, he had converted a Back Bay townhouse to condominiums. This experience had been educational, but the profits did not seem to justify the great amount of work which had gone into the project. Ken had joined Skyline a year ago for just the sort of larger scale opportunity that 250 Portland Street seemed to represent.

At the same time, Angus had reminded Ken in their conversation that any debt involved in the project would have to be personally guaranteed by each of them until breakeven occupancy could be reached. Their personal net worth totalled less than $1 million, and was substantially illiquid. With these facts in mind, Ken Stewart began a systematic review of the numerous materials he had collected in recent weeks.

LOCATION

The 250 Portland Street property was located on the northern edge of Boston's central business district in the North Station area (see Exhibits 1 and 2). This area was one of the last remaining underdeveloped districts in downtown Boston and was targeted by government agencies for considerable new investment in the mid-1980s. Key to this prospect was a major new Federal office building, which had recently begun construction directly across the street. Adjacent to this was the famed Boston Garden, home of the Boston Celtics and Boston Bruins professional sports teams, and the North Station transportation complex.

Immediately south of North Station was the Bulfinch Triangle Historic District. Charles Bulfinch in 1807 designed the triangular street pattern bounded by Causeway, North Washington and Merrimac Streets. This area contained numerous historic mercantile structures, typically 4 to 8 stories in height. The area developed as a center for manufacturers and wholesale dealers, particularly in the furniture trades. The architecture was diverse, with the most distinctive structures generally brick warehouses in the Richardsonian Romanesque and Victorian Commercial styles.

Situated within the historic district, 250 Portland Street was less than a ten minute walk from City Hall and the heart of Boston's financial district. The Faneuil Hall Marketplace, Massachusetts General Hospital, and the majority of Boston's government and financial institutions, restaurants and hotels were also within walking distance.

The area had excellent auto, commuter rail, and transit access to both inner city and suburban locations. Diagonally across the street was the North Station Terminal of the Boston and Maine Railroad, which operated commuter rail service to the western and northern suburbs. Less than one block away was an MBTA subway stop providing public transportation to all parts of the city. Nearby ramps offered direct access to Storrow Drive and the Central Artery, immediately connecting to the airport and to all the area's major regional highways. Within a three-block radius of 250 Portland Street, numerous garages and surface lots provided over 3,200 public and private parking spaces.

Several major public development efforts were in progress in the immediate vicinity of the building. Directly across the street, the new $100 million U. S. General Services Administration Building was under construction. Expected to be named for Congressman "Tip" O'Neil, this new office building was scheduled for completion in 1986 and would house about 4,000 Federal employees. A major recon-

struction of the MBTA Green Line was a long-range prospect, as was depression and reconstruction of the Central Artery, Boston's elevated inner belt highway. In addition, a nearby city-owned parcel had received tentative designation for the construction of a major hotel.

MARKET PERSPECTIVE

Economic conditions in Boston and New England were very strong. Related to strength in the high-technology industries and in services, Massachusetts unemployment had remained consistently the lowest of the major industrial states. As the national economy continued to rebound in 1983, prospects for economic growth in Boston seemed particularly bright.

The Boston Standard Metropolitan Statistical Area had a population of 2,760,000 in 1980. The City of Boston had a 1980 population of 563,000, ranking it 19th among U. S. cities. Although small relative to other center cities, Boston was the nation's 5th-largest office market. The city provided employment for one-third of the entire metropolitan area population and one-fifth of Massachusetts residents. Perhaps more important, most industry observers were optimistic about Boston's office market. It was one of only a few markets which had not become overbuilt during the 1982 recession.

Although the overall office market picture was bright, Ken knew it would be important to assess carefully the immediate market for 250 Portland Street. To begin this assessment, he assembled some market materials (Exhibit 3) for review. Part was an excerpt from a study prepared by Skyline for another project. To supplement this, he had surveyed all current competitive office projects. A number of these were found to be located in the Bulfinch Triangle area. Retail comparables in the district were all very low grade, with the best tenants being fast food franchises along Causeway Street. X-rated movies, bars and low-rent wholesale supply tenancies were most numerous of the existing uses.

THE BUILDING

Built in 1888, 250 Portland Street was a good example of Richardsonian Romanesque commercial architecture. It was designed by the 19th Century Boston firm of Hartwell and Richardson. The building was of heavy timber, wood frame construction with brick and brownstone exterior and was considered a contributing building to the Bulfinch Triangle National Register District in which it was located. Like many other buildings in the North Station area, the property was used primarily for furniture manufacturing and, in recent years, for low-grade office space. The building was in excellent structural condition.

The building contained six stories plus basement, with a total of 117,480 gross square feet. The architect's gross and net rentable areas were indicated on the plans prepared by the owner's architect (see Exhibit 4). The gross figures were accurate, but the rentable areas seemed to be lower than customary in the market. Ken expected that quoted rentable areas, including apportionment of common areas, would normally total between 90%-100% of gross building area, depending on the relative efficiency of a particular building. From a small tenant's point of view, net usable area was increased by a "load factor" of about 20% for common facilities. Smaller load factors were applied to large tenants, but corridor areas and bathrooms would often be included in usable areas.

In Ken's judgement, office use was clearly indicated for the upper floors, and retail could be housed at ground level. He was particularly uncertain as to the quality and rent level of retail use and the likely use of the basement. While he had seen examples of profitable uses for basements of rehabilitated buildings, the costs of dealing with ground water and headroom problems and of providing vertical access could be high.

Significant construction work had already been completed by the present owner, based on plans prepared by an experienced architectural firm. Ken and his construction management consultant had toured the building twice with the architect and found the completed work to be of good quality. As illustrated in the plans, the design included new bathrooms, restored storefronts, a new office lobby, and increased air conditioning capacity, all of which were completed during 1983.

Skyline would complete any other construction work and tenant finishes during 1984 on an historically certified basis. This would result in an Investment Tax Credit of 25% of the cost of qualified capital improvements. The tax credits would be earned by the property owner at the time the building was placed in service, that is, ready for initial occupancy.

THE PROPOSED SALE

The present owners were a European family, who bought the property on impulse in 1980 and began to rehabilitate it for office space in 1982. Their local representative, Mr. Goode, was a lawyer with substantial real estate experience. As trustee for the owners, he negotiated contracts with the architect and with a construction management firm with whom he had worked in the past. Approximately $1.6 million in hard construction had been invested during 1982-3, bringing the property to a point where it could be leased and finished to suit specific tenants. The property had not yet been put into service, and hence the investment tax credits provided by the 1981 Tax Act would be available to the buyer.

One particular tenant -- a non-profit organization -- wanted fast action. They would take 24,000 rentable square feet at a rent of $14.50 per square foot plus tenant electricity for the first five years, with renewal options at somewhat higher rents. The landlord would be responsible for base year operating expenses (about $3.00/SF) and real estate taxes (about $2.00/SF). The tenant had prepared a space plan which required a large number of private offices. The tenant's existing lease would expire on February 29, 1984, although they could likely hold over in their present space for a month or two. After that, they were sure to be evicted, as the owner of that property was planning a major rehabilitation project.

As this situation unfolded during late summer, Mr. Goode realized he was being drawn increasingly into day-to-day management of a real estate development venture, something he no longer wished to do. He therefore obtained permission from the owners to offer the property for sale. The price would be $4 million, all cash, with buyers being responsible for any brokerage commission involved.

Skyline's principals and their construction management consultant had done considerable homework prior to submitting their initial offer (see Exhibit 5). As they continued to talk with the various parties, it became clear that many bidders were actively considering this acquisition. In declining this offer, Mr. Goode, the owner's representative, said he believed he would get his asking price within the next few days and agreed to meet promptly with Skyline.

COSTS AND FINANCING

Skyline's initial review of the tenant's proposed space plan indicated a probable cost of direct subcontract construction for tenant work in the range of $20 to $24 per rentable square foot. Other tenants space plans would normally average about $15.

In addition to the tenant finish work, at least $1 million in additional hard construction costs would be required. This would allow them to complete rehabilitation of the existing elevators, replace the windows, repoint the exterior, and build new bathrooms on floors 4, 5 and 6, where these had not yet been completed. It would not provide for any major changes to the structure or services. Skyline would have to make do with all other core and shell building systems in their present state, including the lobby, boiler, air conditioning, sprinklers, stairwells and roof. Other direct and indirect development costs would certainly be incurred, and many optional costs could be envisioned.

As he worked on a cost budget, Ken wanted to bear in mind the cost of Skyline's recently completed project. This was a 6-story building of about 14,000 square feet per floor and total project cost had been nearly $120 per rentable square foot. This total included $15 for shell acquisition and about $70 for construction, including a tenant standard allowance of $17 for office space. A substantial cost of that project had been incurred for carrying costs during the rent up period. This project had been physically more difficult to rehabilitate than 250 Portland Street, and had been designed to a higher standard of finish than would seem to be necessary. On the other hand, if the North Station area improved rapidly, which seemed likely, Skyline's principals would want the flexibility to meet the requirements of Class A tenants as they materialized.

Financing was also an area of great uncertainty. With the experience of high inflation fresh in the minds of lenders, most real estate loans were at floating interest rates or were fixed rate loans for short terms of 5 to 10 years. Ken did not believe a fixed rate would be available, but knew of recent loans on existing income properties in the 13% to 14% range. Lenders normally required a coverage ratio of 1.2 to 1.3 (free and clear income as a ratio to debt service constant). Floating rates would likely be at 1% to 2% over the prime rate, which was currently at 11%. Some lenders would agree to accrue any interest above 13% to 14%, adding this to the principal due at maturity.

Equity financing was also uncertain at this point. Skyline would work closely with its syndicator to structure an optimum package. Without going into a detailed financial projection, Ken knew of comparable projects in which total equity dollars were approximately 70% of the mortgage debt, where the debt was underwritten with conventional coverage ratios. Some syndicators used a rule of thumb of 2.5 times the Investment Tax Credit amount as a starting point. Investors generally were looking for a 25% to 30% internal rate of return, including tax effects.

Equity syndication proceeds would be available approximately 90 days after the debt structure was determined. This allowed adequate time for clearance of offering documents with state "Blue Sky" regulators and marketing the investment units to qualified investors. In any event, to prevent loss of tax credits, investor limited partners would have to be admitted before the building were placed in service. Equity funds would normally be paid in over approximately a three-year period, although it was sometimes arranged for a developer to borrow against the deferred investor contributions. Mortgage financing would have to be committed for a minimum of five years for a syndication to be accomplished. This assured investors that a forced sale would not be likely to occur during the five-year period in which the tax credit would be recaptured by the Internal Revenue Service.

Skyline could not plan on using the equity syndication proceeds to purchase 250 Portland Street if the tenant's schedule were to be honored. They would instead have to purchase the building and complete tenant improvements in parallel with the process of raising the equity. The only other source of cash available to Skyline was its recently formed venture capital partnership, Historic Ventures, Limited. Historic Ventures could commit as much as $300,000 for a short period of time without adversely affecting a suburban mill rehabilitation Skyline was planning for later in 1984. Investors in Historic Ventures would share in Skyline's profits from development fees and in residual ownership of each property.

NEXT STEPS

Having rushed through the available materials, Ken Stewart reflected on the task at hand. Angus Cartwright was a stickler for fundamentals. Ken knew he would have to be prepared at breakfast to deal with several basic questions:

1. What leasing and construction program would be best for this property?

2. What would be the capital cost budget? How much uncertainty would there be as to the eventual totals?

3. How much annual income could potentially be generated? How long would it take to achieve it?

4. What financing could be obtained at the time of acquisition and thereafter? How would a potential acquisition and construction lender look at it?

5. How might Skyline's previous offer be modified during the meeting tomorrow? Should they go ahead and offer the asking price, or risk losing the deal?

Finally, Ken was concerned that they not get caught up in the competitive bidding process and lose sight of their objectives. They very much wanted to develop the project, but a profit would be necessary for their investors and themselves. If the project were infeasible or unduly risky at a higher purchase price than their earlier offer, he wanted to warn his partner promptly.

EXHIBITS

1. Aerial photograph.

2. Site plan.

3. Market materials.

4. Architectural drawings.

5. Letter from Angus Cartwright to Bill Goode.

QUESTIONS FOR DISCUSSION

1. Should Skyline buy the property?

2. If so, what points should they seek to negotiate with the seller?

3. What schedule should Skyline anticipate for the project?

4. What priorities should they establish for their near-term objectives?

Exhibit 1

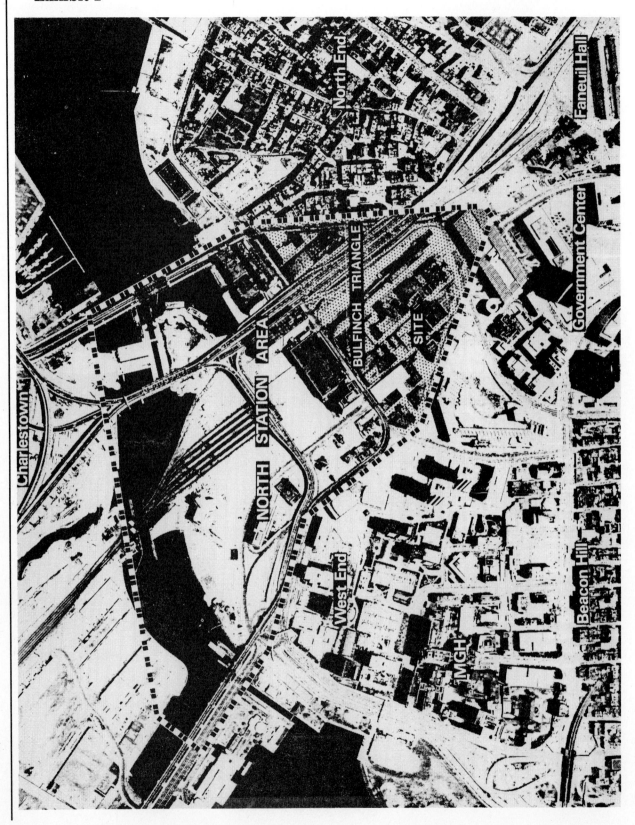

Exhibit 2

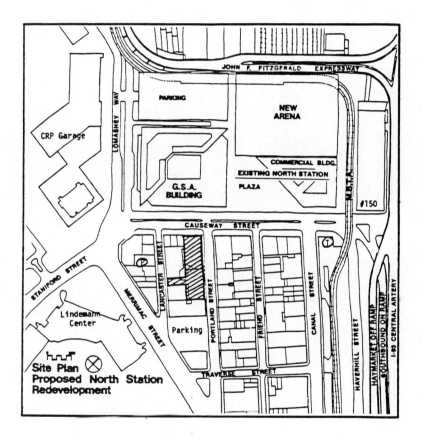

Site Plan ⊗
Proposed North Station
Redevelopment

Exhibit 3

Boston Office Market Overview

The Metropolitan Boston office market can be divided into four sectors which total 38.4 million square feet (MSF) of Class A office space available as of October 1983. Unless otherwise noted, data in this section are derived from the Spaulding and Slye Office Report. The four market areas can be described as follows:

o   Downtown -- serves as the headquarters for New England's major banks, venture capital firms and mutual funds, as well as many legal and accounting firms and government offices. Nearly all the office space is located in the central business district, which is bounded on the west by Tremont Street and Essex Street, on the north by Storrow Drive and Charles Street, and on the east and south by the Central Artery and the Boston Harbor. Downtown contains 15.4 MSF, of which 10.2 MSF represents the 11 existing tower buildings.

o   Back Bay -- is a primarily residential area centered around Beacon Street, Commonwealth Avenue and the Newbury Street retail district. Back Bay contains 5.4 MSF of Class A space, of which 3.4 MSF are in the Prudential Center and the John Hancock Tower. The major Back Bay tenancies are insurance and advertising companies, with IBM a recent major arrival. Back Bay's remaining office space is scattered in small blocks and serves smaller professional tenancies and secondary office functions.

o   Cambridge -- is a major near-downtown market area, which competes with both the downtown and the western suburbs. Cambridge has excellent highway access to the west, as well as public transportation access to downtown. It presently has 3.1 MSF of competitive space available, in addition to a substantial quantity of owner-occupied facilities. Cambridge serves a market of engineering, consulting and high technology firms.

o   The Suburbs - of Boston have become substantial office and industrial real estate markets. High technology growth has made this area the "Silicon Valley" of New England. The suburban markets include three sectors of suburban Route 128--the northern, western, and southern areas.

Exhibit 3
continued

The dimensions of the market and current occupancy conditions as of October 1983 are summarized as follows:

Market Area	Rentable Area	% of Total	Sq. Ft. Available	% Occupancy
Downtown	15,366,173	40%	275,985	98%
Back Bay	5,379,000	14%	52,704	99%
Cambridge	3,101,933	8%	524,950	83%
Suburbs	14,592,785	38%	1,762,084	88%
Total	38,439,891	100%	2,615,723	93%

In recent years, the rehabilitation market has become quite
significant. In both downtown Boston and the suburbs, considerable high quality office and industrial rehabilitation
and historic preservation developments have occurred. According to a recent survey by a major brokerage firm, 4.5 MSF
of office building rehabilitations have been completed in
Downtown and Back Bay. Other small buildings not surveyed
there bring the total to 5.0 MSF, including owner-rehabil-
itated offices, as well as speculative space. Of this,
about 2.0 MSF is in small buildings not included in the
above market totals. A considerable quantity of secondary
space has been upgraded in the recent past as well.

The following sections will examine closely the regional
office market and the downtown area in particular.

Office Production and Absorption

The majority of Greater Boston's first class office space
was built during the past decade. Table 1 shows Boston and
suburban production figures. The Boston figures include the
Downtown and Back Bay markets. The suburban figures include
the City of Cambridge and all sectors of Route 128.

These data indicate that the suburbs have accounted for an
increasing share of the regional office space production in
the recent past. This experience coincides with the period
during which the Downtown and Back Bay markets have been
stabilized by the actions of the Boston Redevelopment Authority (BRA). Through its zoning and permitting powers, the
BRA controls the level of development activity in the city.

Exhibit 3
continued

Table 1:   Class A Office Production (000 SF/YR)

Year	Metro Area	Boston & Back Bay	Suburbs
pre-1973	13,202	8,918	4,284
1973	2,388	1,295	1,093
1974	3,694	3,125	569
1975	606	182	424
1976	2,981	2,404	577
1977	1,750	1,114	636
1978	493	95	398
1979	1,053	264	789
1980	2,731	634	2,097
1981	4,118	1,935	2,183
1982	4,054	763	3,291
1983 (est.)	2,279	272	2,007
	39,349	21,001	18,348
Average 1974-1978:	1,905	1,384	521
Average 1979-1983:	2,847	774	2,073

Table 2:   Metro Area Office Absorption (000 SF/YR)

Year	Cumulative Production	Year End Vacancy	Net Occupied	Absorption
pre-1973	13,202	5.2%	12,516	--
1973	15,590	10.7%	13,922	1,406
1974	19,284	7.8%	17,780	3,858
1975	19,890	7.5%	18,398	618
1976	22,871	12.1%	20,104	1,706
1977	24,621	13.6%	21,273	1,169
1978	25,114	7.0%	23,356	2,083
1979	26,167	1.6%	25,748	2,392
1980	28,898	2.9%	28,060	2,312
1981	33,016	4.7%	31,464	3,404
1982	37,070	9.5%	33,548	2,084
1983 (est.)	39,349	6.8%	36,673	3,125
Average 1974-1978:				1,887
Average 1979-1983:				2,663

Exhibit 3
continued

The city policy--likely to continue under the new administ-
ration--is to limit new downtown development to keep pace
with the historical annual absorption rate. As a result of
this intervention, Boston is probably the only major city in
the U.S. that is not overbuilt in 1983. As a result also,
rehabilitation projects have flourished, and the suburbs are
booming.

Overall, the market has been very active, with production
averaging 3.5 MSF per year since 1980. This level of production is considerably above the long term average, but
appears to be continuing. Nearly 8 million square feet of
projects are planned or under construction for 1984 and
1985.

Table 2 computes the absorption experience in the metropolitan market. Overall year end vacancy rates are derived
from Spaulding and Slye and Building Owners and Managers
Association (BOMA) data. From these figures and the
previous production data, the absorption has been estimated
on a year-by-year basis.

As expected, Boston's overall vacancy rates have increased
with the surge in production and the national recession.
Perhaps surprising, however, is the sustained higher levels
of absorption, evidence of the strength of the market. Average market absorption since 1973 has been 2.2 million square
feet. For the most recent five years, however, the average
has been over 2.6 MSF. Even in 1982, the year of the national recession, absorption was at the 2.1 MSF level.

It seems clear that 1983 has been a good year in the Greater
Boston office market. Overall absorption will be over 3 MSF
and would undoubtedly have been greater except for the shortage of downtown space. As will be detailed below, considerable pentup downtown demand is in evidence. With the national economy continuing to improve in 1984, overall absorption is likely to reach or exceed the 4 MSF level. Suburban
absorption has not been constrained, however, so no dramatic
increase in suburban absorption over 1983 levels is to be
expected.

Downtown Market Conditions

Due to the previously noted supply restrictions and construction delays experienced by major projects, the vacancy rate
in the Downtown and Back Bay market area is presently only
2%. Developers have naturally responded to this tight market situation, and there are ten new office developments now
under construction in these locations.

Exhibit 3
continued

Table 3: City of Boston New Office Construction (000 SF)

	Pre-leased	Schedule/Completion 1983	1984	1985	Rent/SF
Towers:					
Copley Place	225		845		$32-38
53 State Street	250		1095		$29-45
Dewey Square	175		1250		$29-45
Subtotal:	650		3190		
Other New Construction:					
155 Federal	120	200			$28-30.50
303 Congress	29	60			$25-27.50
265 Franklin	62		322		$28-32
Boylston Place	221		221		$30-32
1 Exeter	--		207		$28-32
260 Franklin	62			348	$30-35
200 State	--			385	$35-45
Total:	1144	260	3940	733	

Table 3 summarizes the projected space and completion dates.
With the current scarcity of available space, over 1.1 million square feet in the projects now under construction have
already been pre-leased. This fact will substantially miti-
gate the impact of 1984 completions on the market, although
some increase in the downtown vacancy rate is reasonably to
be expected.

Rent levels will be extremely important in determining the
future course of events. As can be seen in Table 3, asking
rents for space in new downtown buildings are from $28 to
$45 per square foot for occupancy in 1984 and 1985. Subur-
ban rental rates are significantly lower, in the $14-24/SF
range, depending on location and physical quality. The dis-
parity between downtown and suburban rental rates has
increased sharply in recent years. As a consequence, much
downtown expansion has been postponed, and suburban absorption has been at historically high levels. Cambridge has
also benefited from this spill-over demand.

The office rehabilitation market has also expanded sharply
throughout the city. During the period 1979-1983, 4.0 MSF of
rehabilitation space was completed and absorbed, an average

Exhibit 3
continued

of 800,000 square feet per year in Downtown and Back Bay combined. Rehabilitation developments also have a major rent advantage over new construction, and rehabilitation projects should continue to be a substantial force in the market.

Overall, Downtown/Back Bay absorption will exceed 2 MSF per year in 1984 and 1985. This will mean an orderly absorption of the forthcoming new construction space. Some increase in vacancy will undoubtedly occur--both in new space and in turnover rentals of older towers--but no significant declines in rent levels can be expected.

Exhibit 3
continued

Boston Rehabilitation Space Available

Location/ Project	Compl. Rehab.	Total Area	Sq.Ft. Avail.	Ave. Floor	Rent /SF
Financial District					
1. 45 Milk St.	1982	66,000	18,500	7,300	$27-30
2. 10 P.O. Sq.	1983	240,000	7,900	17,600	$28
3. 2 Oliver St.	1981	183,400	64,400	16,700	$18-20
4. One Liberty Sq.	1981	161,000	5,600	11,800	$28
5. 470 Atlantic	1981	312,000	27,000	25,400	$25
6. 1 Winthrop Sq.	1974	105,000	4,300	21,000	$20
7. 20 Winthrop Sq.	1983	30,000	18,000	6,000	$25-27
North Station Area					
8. 85 Merrimac St.	1983	30,000	4,500	5,500	$16
9. 66 Canal Street	1981	45,000	3,500	7,500	$15
Fort Point Channel					
10. 268 Summer St.	1983	68,000	15,800	7,900	$15-20
11. 330 Congress St.	1982	31,000	12,400	6,200	$15
12. 332 Congress St.	1982	27,500	20,000	5,500	$15
Downtown Crossing					
13. 99 Bedford St.	1983	83,000	4,000	13,800	$25
14. 38 Chauncey St.	1981	120,000	21,000	8,700	$16
Back Bay					
15. 120 Boylston St.	1982	156,000	43,000	18,500	$16-19
16. 330 Stuart St.	1981	103,000	4,400	10,700	$21
17. 142 Berkeley St.	1983	74,400	65,400	20,000	$18-20
18. 575 Bolyston St.	1982	32,000	16,000	4,000	$19-23
19. Two Newbury St.	1983	12,500	3,300	1,600	$30-32
20. 181 Newbury St.	1975	25,000	5,000	8,300	$15
21. 355 Commonwealth	1982	30,000	10,800	6,000	$14-18
Total		1,934,800	374,800		

Exhibit 3
continued

Current Rehabilitation Developments

Location/ Project	Date Avail.	Total Area	Sq.Ft. Avail.	Ave. Floor	Rent /SF
Under Construction:					
Financial District					
22. 400 Atlantic	1984	100,000	100,000	17,000	$30
North Station					
23. 217 Friend St.	1984	56,000	44,000	8,100	$16-17
Fort Point Channel					
24. 274 Summer St.	1984	72,000	72,000	8,000	$17-19
25. 347 Congress St.	1984	65,000	65,000	12,500	$15-16
Downtown Crossing					
26. 110 Chauncey St.	1984	75,000	75,000	8,800	$16-18
Back Bay					
27. 410 Boylston St.	1984	12,000	8,000	2,000	$19-20
28. 419 Boylston St.	1984	45,600	45,600	5,700	$25
Planned:					
North Station					
29. 250 Portland St.					
Fort Point Channel					
30. 313 Congress St.	1984	72,000	36,000	19,000	$17-18
Downtown Crossing					
31. 77 Summer St.	1984	42,900	42,900	4,700	$22-24
Total		612,700	536,700		

Exhibit 3
continued

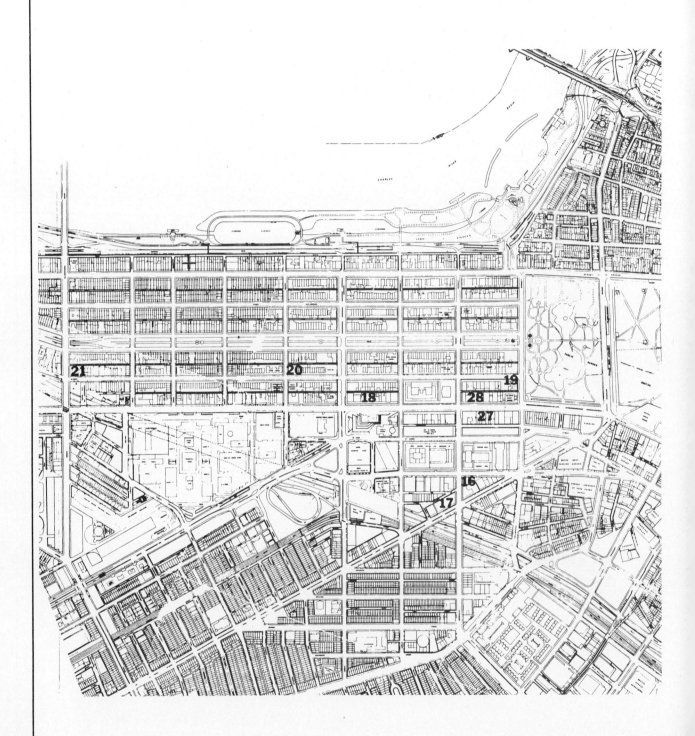

Exhibit 4

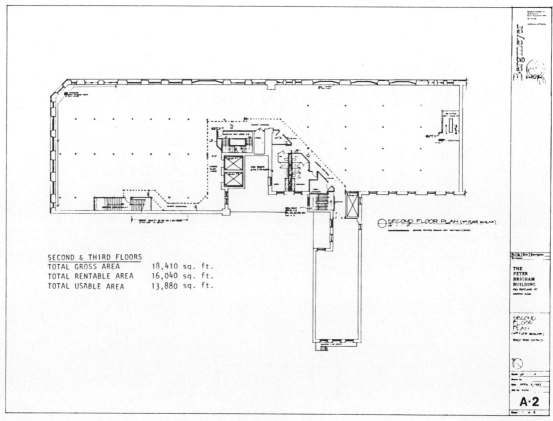

SECOND & THIRD FLOORS
TOTAL GROSS AREA   18,410 sq. ft.
TOTAL RENTABLE AREA 16,040 sq. ft.
TOTAL USABLE AREA   13,880 sq. ft.

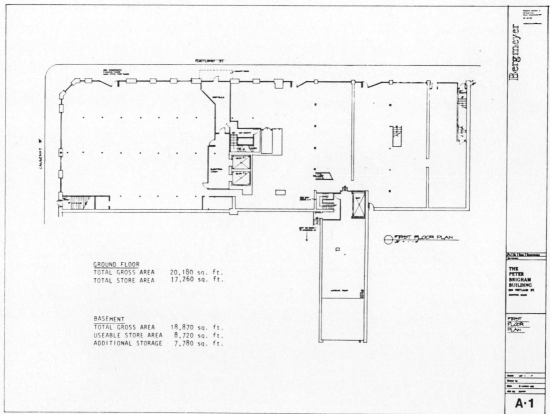

GROUND FLOOR
TOTAL GROSS AREA   20,180 sq. ft.
TOTAL STORE AREA   17,260 sq. ft.

BASEMENT
TOTAL GROSS AREA   18,870 sq. ft.
USEABLE STORE AREA   8,720 sq. ft.
ADDITIONAL STORAGE   7,780 sq. ft.

Exhibit 4
continued

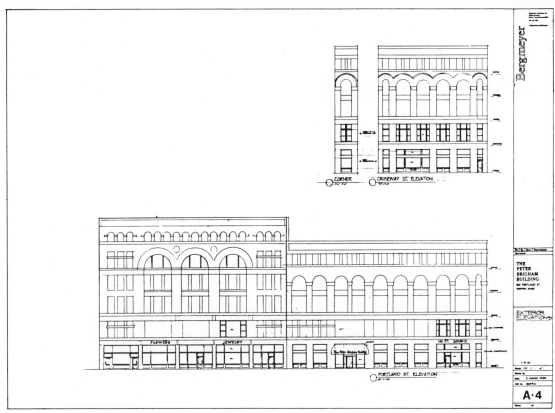

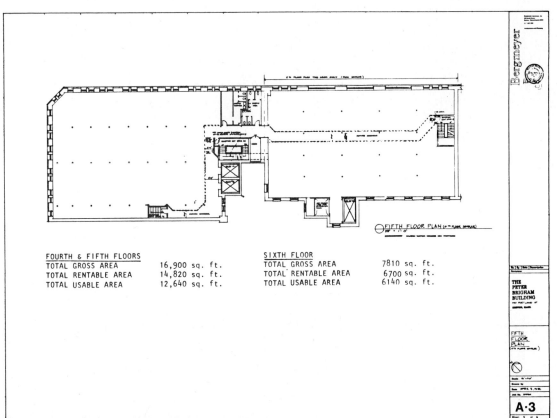

FOURTH & FIFTH FLOORS
TOTAL GROSS AREA   16,900 sq. ft.
TOTAL RENTABLE AREA   14,820 sq. ft.
TOTAL USABLE AREA   12,640 sq. ft.

SIXTH FLOOR
TOTAL GROSS AREA   7810 sq. ft.
TOTAL RENTABLE AREA   6700 sq. ft.
TOTAL USABLE AREA   6140 sq. ft.

Exhibit 5

SKYLINE DEVELOPMENT CORPORATION
88 Broad Street
Boston, MA 02109

October 4, 1983

Mr. Bill Goode
Portland Realty Trust
275 Franklin Street
Boston, MA 02110

Re: 250 Portland Street, Boston

Dear Mr. Goode:

I am pleased to submit the following offer to purchase your client's property located at 250 Portland Street, Boston. This offer is conditioned only on our execution of a purchase and sale agreement not later than November 4, 1983:

Price:	$3,500,000
Terms:	$2,000,000 cash at closing (approximately 60 days) with the balance in the form of a purchase money mortgage.
Purchase Money Mortgage:	Seller's mortgage loan will carry interest only at 13% with a 10 year maturity and will be subordinate to not more than $6,000,000 in first mortgage financing.
Buyer's Equity:	Prior to closing, Buyer will subscribe not less than $4,000,000 in equity to be fully invested in the project prior to drawing down any first mortgage financing.
Broker:	Seller will be responsible for paying any commissions associated with this transaction.

Mr. Stewart and I are very excited about the prospects for 250 Portland Street. If this offer is of interest, let us get together promptly to work out the details.

Sincerely yours,

Angus P. Cartwright
President

The Warner Theatre Project

Byrne Murphy felt that 1988 was going to be a big year for both himself and his company. It was now late December 1987, and since April, Byrne had been working as Project Manager for The Kaempfer Company on the Warner Theatre project, a proposed office development in Washington, D.C.'s East End. The project was a complicated one involving the restoration of the 65-year-old Warner Theatre and, as originally conceived, the addition of about 200,000 square feet of office space. With the acquisition of several small parcels on "E" Street and the hope of getting city approval to move an alley, the project had grown and now involved at least 350,000 square feet.

Several prominent developers had tried their hands at this difficult parcel and lost (see Exhibit 1). But at this moment, success was near. The company's founder, J.W. Kaempfer, Jr., was touching down at Washington's Dulles International Airport, having concluded a $25 million equity investment in the project with a prestigious European investment fund. It had not been easy; the partner was conservative and had never before invested this much this early in a development across the Atlantic. Now, however, the deal was closed.

Byrne had been with this project from the start and had watched it grow. Recently, the possibility had arisen to acquire one final parcel and thus control an entire half-city block. This would make the development well over 500,000 square feet, The Kaempfer Company's biggest project ever and a "trophy" project like a number of others along Pennsylvania Avenue, all designed by prominent architects and built by major developers. But to make this larger development happen, Byrne would need a new set of approvals from the city, Federal and historic preservation review boards, and the cooperation of several interest groups involved. Moreover, he would need a new and much larger commitment from the equity partner. When Mr. Kaempfer returned, Byrne

wanted to be able to suggest the right strategy for the new year.

ORGANIZATION

From its founding in 1977 as a small residential builder, The Kaempfer Company : Investment Builders had grown to become one of the largest commercial developers in Washington. Their first office project, Park Place, opened its doors in 1983 with no space yet leased. Mr. Kaempfer managed to replace his committed participating lender, who wanted out, with a new loan for the same dollars, but with no equity participation. He then brought in $2.75 million in an equity syndication facilitated by a tax law change. The building eventually leased well, and Mr. Kaempfer's firm went on to build a number of other office buildings and a hotel (see Exhibit 2).

His organization grew as well and now included 43 head office staff and 31 management employees (see Exhibit 3). John Nichols, the construction supervisor in 1977, was now the Senior Vice President for Construction. John Graybar, Mr. Kaempfer's second in command in 1982, left. Mr. Kaempfer explained in a 1986 interview, "He was a key player and an extremely close friend. He now has his own company, which I encouraged him to do. He oversees a fund of money for three families from Europe. . . . We talk on and off about doing deals together with the hope that we may do some, although my risk profile is a lot more than his."

When asked what he meant by "risk profile," Mr. Kaempfer explained: "You know, I see a piece of property, and I want to buy it, I want to control it, I want to get involved in the excitement of designing it, building it, holding it, managing it. And that's wonderful: I want, I want, I want. But to do that, you have to take some pretty spectacular risks along the way. . . .I am prepared to have an occasional disaster, although nobody wants it, or looks for it. I am prepared to have that in return for some real hot killers."

Following Mr. Graybar's departure, a great deal of responsibility was shifted to Mary Motherwell, Vice President and Director of Development. She had an MBA from Michigan and later worked for Continental Illinois National Bank, where she became a second vice president in the real estate department and originated more than $600 million of development loans. From Continental Illinois, she joined Intercorp, Inc., a Chicago-based residential developer where she was Chief Financial Officer and Director of Project Managers. There she oversaw the development of $100 million of condominiums and Planned Unit Developments. She came to Kaempfer in 1983 and became the Project Manager for 1250 24th Street and the St. Matthew's project. Since then she has had a hand in every development project that has come through the office.

Two years ago, Mr. Kaempfer hired Byrne Murphy, an MBA graduate from the Darden School of Management. He was 27 at the time, but had an adventurous past, having sailed around the world. While at Darden, he had cross-registered for several courses in the Urban Planning Department. He was hired as an assistant project manager and so spent his time on several projects. At one point he was assigned to market and lease 1525 Wilson Boulevard, a 300,000 square foot office building nearing completion. He helped land the lead tenant. As a new assistant project manager, Byrne worked closely with Mary Motherwell.

Along with Mary and John Nichols, Mr. Kaempfer had a core group of employees he considered "family" -- all equity participants in the company's deals. They were all vice presidents, including Mark Portnoy, Vice President of Finance. After a long search, Mr. Kaempfer hired him in 1984 as a personal assistant, but his role expanded. "Mark was almost Chief Finan-cial Officer. He's a CPA and a Harvard MBA, a Brown graduate, and he's very smart. . . . Saturday is a normal work day for him."

Mr. Kaempfer ran the company on a break-even basis; that is, any cash profits were reinvested in expanding the company's portfolio of real estate. Typically, The Kaempfer Company retained 50% ownership in its deals, giving the other 50% to equity partners. Mr. Kaempfer would then distribute ownership shares to individuals within the company.

The Kaempfer Company had plans to expand into new markets. In 1986, the company had joint venture projects in Los Angeles, but now looked closer to home. New York, Boston and Baltimore were targets, and the formation of an industrial division was a possibility. The company's venture into hotel development and, later, operations was less successful than they would have liked. The Company now tried to avoid products with which it had no experience.

THE WARNER THEATRE PROJECT

Because of its location, the Warner Theatre was for years the object of affection for several major developers. Yet it had remained undeveloped. One night in late January 1987, Mr. Kaempfer was returning from a business meeting when his taxi driver took an unexpected route from the airport, going up Pennsylvania Avenue and passing by the property (see Exhibit 4). Mr. Kaempfer realized immediately how great the location was and understood the potential for its development.

A regular acquisitions meeting was scheduled the next day with a local brokerage firm, and Mr. Kaempfer asked about the Warner's availability. By coincidence, the week before the broker had been in contact with the owners of the Theatre Building. Mr. Kaempfer expressed an interest and asked the brokers to research it further. He realized that the site improved dramatically if it were combined with the three smaller parcels adjacent to it. Moreover, there were two more small parcels across from the existing alley which would make the site even more worthwhile if they were included. These six parcels totalled 32,560 square feet of land in all.

Mary studied the site and ran some numbers for discussion. With the Warner Theatre property and the three smaller adjacent parcels, she calculated, they would be able to build 220,000 square feet of commercial space. The project was proposed to the senior management, and Mary remembered the consensus, "We were willing to do it, but it was still very tight." With the decision to go ahead on this first assemblage, Mr. Kaempfer began to place the parcels under contract, putting down substantial deposits on the Warner Theatre and on Lot 803 (see Exhibit 5).

Mr. Kaempfer set up the development team, picking Byrne Murphy as the Project Manager, working with Mary. She described their roles: "I'm the Vice President and Director of Development who works with the project managers on the different projects. I am helpful from the process standpoint, the approvals standpoint and the schematic standpoint. At this point, Byrne is the one who has every detail in his head and runs the project day to day. . . . He lives and breathes the Warner Theatre."

ACQUISITION

By May, the complicated land assembly for the project was well-documented in the Washington press (see Exhibit 1). Mr. Kaempfer had already decided to jump the alley, acquire the two next parcels on the other side of it, and work with the city to relocate the alley adjacent to the last large parcel on the block, Lot 843 (see Exhibit

5). Alley closings in Washington, if they happen at all, typically take 12 to 18 months. But by acquiring the two extra parcels and using the 10 FAR allowed because of the project's 13th Street frontage, and including the land formerly taken up by the alley, the development had the potential of increasing from the 220,000 square feet allowed by the first assemblage to 350,000 square feet. There was one remaining large site on the south side of the block, Lot 843 (16,072 square feet), but it had a 1960s office building on it with an FAR of 8. The entire other half of the city block was occupied by Gerald Hines' new Columbia Square development, designed by I.M. Pei & Partners. Neither of these properties was for sale.

DESIGN

The design of the project was very sensitive because of the need for multiple approvals. These included four from city agencies, one from the City Council, one from the Historic Preservation Review Board, and one from the Federal Commission of Fine Arts. In addition, there were several civic, preservationist, and arts groups who had the ability to oppose and prevent the project during the approvals hearings or by bringing suit, as one preservationist group had done in the recent past. The choice of Shalom Baranes Associates as architect was based on their previous involvement with the project, their good relationship with the preservation groups and their very successful record of restoration and adaptive re-use in Washington.

Meanwhile, the size of the project kept expanding, and the architect had to keep pace with his drawings. By mid-June, with the two parcels across the alley included in the assemblage, the project settled down to about 350,000 square feet, the size that would be proposed to the Design Review Boards. There were many constituents whose needs would influence the outcome of the review hearings. These included the theater users, the theater preservationists and the city agencies, as well as potential commercial tenants. Because the theater was a landmark, The Kaempfer Company was trying to strike a delicate balance between these sometimes competing interests. Mary recalled, "Really what everybody would have liked to have seen was for the theater to be preserved exactly as it was, and a new project to be next door." However, the office building clearly needed a corner entrance, and this meant altering the theater slightly by raising the stage. In order to arrive at a satisfactory solution, Mr. Kaempfer, Mary and Byrne had to work closely with all these groups.

FINANCING

Early on in the project, Mr. Kaempfer had made the decision to go after an equity partner first, before going after debt financing. A financing package had been prepared in March, and the company engaged an international, full-service real estate company to try to identify a partner. Byrne spent a good part of his time explaining the project and giving tours to prospective partners.

In July, the search netted a European investment group who agreed to fund the 350,000 square foot project. The year before, the same group had been interested in funding the 1525 Wilson Boulevard project and had begun negotiations with Kaempfer. However, their due diligence inquiry into the company, the local real estate market and the local economy took so long that Kaempfer found and closed with another partner.

For the Warner project, a complicated investment structure was proposed, and Mark Portnoy remembered that the terms "drove the lawyers crazy." A participating loan of $25 million was proposed with the investment group entitled to earn 8% on their money from day one. However, until the project was well into the black, they

were guaranteed only a 6% current return, paid quarterly. The rest accrued until cash flow after first mortgage financing was sufficient to let them "catch up" to the 8% rate on their equity funds. They also shared in any refinancing and sales proceeds and in any operating income above pro forma levels.

Closing was set for September 1. Up to then, The Kaempfer Company had been operating on Mr. Kaempfer's personal funds and had scheduled several closings on the assemblage parcels for September. In late August, though, the deal with the equity partner still hadn't closed, and Byrne remembered the scene: "We were going to close on the loan and take down the Warner parcel, and we had already entered into binding purchase agreements on the other parcels. Mr. Kaempfer walked into a big conference room full of lawyers and myself and a few others, and one of our attorneys said, 'We can't get there from here. It's more complex than anyone thought. We're all discovering the issues, ourselves as well as our partner's counsel.'" Eventually it was decided that instead of rushing through all the complex issues of an international participating loan and trying to force a closing, the partners would agree to negotiate the final joint venture terms during the fall. The European partner would provide an interim loan to the project until December, when the final closing would take place.

APPROVALS

The approvals process was crucial to the project, and Mr. Kaempfer, Mary and Byrne had organized earlier that summer to work with the various preservationist, arts, and public sector groups involved. Mary had previous experience with the process: "It was my role to steer that. Mr. Kaempfer would attend the meetings where his presence was important. I worked primarily with the zoning attorneys, and Byrne was the coordinator, working with all the groups." Byrne recalled his initiation: "In July, I said, 'Mary, I don't know enough about this; let's go to breakfast.' And at one breakfast over at the Grand Hotel, she listed all these different groups, and the next week I got together with the zoning attorneys. . . By the end of August, I was up to speed. By the end of September, I was up to my eyeballs."

By October, Byrne and Mary felt that they had addressed the needs of the different groups. The preservationists, theater operators, citizens groups and arts groups were behind them. The city had agreed to investigate the possibility of a Pennsylvania Avenue address and the potential for public financial support to help restore the theater. On October 22, the project was scheduled to come before the Historic Preservation Review Board (H.P.R.B.), and on the 23rd, before the Commission of Fine Arts.

With the approvals meetings approaching, the development team worked feverishly right up to the company's scheduled management retreat on October 17. Byrne remembered the last minute consultations: "In an evening meeting at Mr. Kaempfer's house, we had speakerphones on, we had architects, lawyers, architectural historians, everyone around the table, and we were deciding what to do." The scheme that was developed involved raising the stage only a few feet, less than originally thought feasible. The team was convinced that all the interest groups would be satisfied.

"We got down to the retreat, and a couple of things happened: first, October 19 came around, and the stock market crashed. When they finally got through by phone to Washington, they found out that one of the parties had backed off in its support. We were on the phone with our lawyers and consultants saying, 'Check with this person! Check with that person!' In the end, Mary flew back early to ensure that everything was in line." The Historic Preservation Review Board did, in fact,

approve the proposal on schedule (see Exhibit 6), and the next day, the Commission of Fine Arts approved the exterior.

RECENT DEVELOPMENTS

With the approvals in hand, Byrne turned his attention to refining the design and marketing concept. Byrne estimated that the project could have 294 parking spaces, 16,000 square feet of retail, and about 304,000 square feet of rentable office space. The theater would not produce a significant profit. He thought the pro forma rent level would be in the low $40's and expenses would be $9.50 per square foot. The parking spaces would net $1,600 each per year. The total project cost presented to the partner was $113 million for 350,000 gross square feet.

The current design by Shalom Baranes gave 33,000 square foot floor plates on the floors above the theater. Byrne was having worries about the efficiency of the design, particularly since the projected rents were among the highest in the city. To succeed, the project needed to highlight its hoped-for Pennsylvania Avenue address with emphasis on its corner office entrance. Byrne also believed that competing with other high-quality Washington office buildings called for spectacular atria and lobby spaces.

December was a crucial month. Byrne faced closings on three of the pieces of the assemblage with a total commitment of several million dollars, and the interim loan from the partner was due on December 15: "We were still having problems documenting the equity investment and the partnership. They were foreign and institutional, and this project was still in the early phases. There was no final design, there was no pre-leasing, there were still more approvals to get. The project was moving across the map, and they were, understandably, skittish."

THE LAST PARCEL

In early December, Mr. Kaempfer began to wonder if he might be able to acquire the last parcel on the block. The owner of the land was one of the largest developers in the Washington area and had an iron-clad reputation for not selling his property. Notwithstanding this, Mr. Kaempfer expressed an interest in the parcel. Instead of what he expected -- a flat "no," Mr. Kaempfer was told to make an offer.

Byrne described the equity partner's reaction to this: "We turned to our investment partner and said, 'We may be able to expand the site. We could now have a world-class building in the best location in the strongest market in the United States.' And they said, 'We're not sure we want to expand the site. We think we should do one thing at a time.'"

Negotiations continued therefore on the basis of the existing land assembly. However, even in December there were difficulties in resolving the complex issues. By December 15, the deal still hadn't closed. This presented a substantial risk because there was nothing legally binding that committed the investment partner to funding after that date. Only a few days ago, Mr. Kaempfer had returned to Europe to attempt to complete the deal.

Byrne was relieved to hear that it had finally closed, and Mr. Kaempfer would be back shortly. He knew, however, that the agreement still left the responsibility for the possible acquisition of the last parcel with The Kaempfer Company: "We had one short paragraph in the original agreement that said we both recognized the possibility of Lot 843's acquisition, but that Kaempfer would handle that. We would take the risk in putting up the deposit. We thought that it would be maybe $1 million with a 90-day closing."

Acquiring the last parcel would have a major impact on the project. Byrne esti-mated it would mean a program of approximately 350 parking spaces, at least 42,000 square feet of retail and 420,000 square feet of rentable office space. The theater dimensions would remain the same. He thought the pro forma rent level would remain in the low $40's and expenses at $9.50 per square foot. He estimated that the new total project cost for 550,000 gross square feet would be about $185 million. From a marketing standpoint, he would have a 46,000 square foot floor plate, uncommon in Washington and, in his opinion, a competitive advantage in attracting the rapidly growing law and accounting firms that were the most likely tenants for the building.

THE OWNER'S TERMS

Before leaving for Europe, Mr. Kaempfer had submitted his offer to purchase the last parcel for $20 million with a $1 million deposit. The building contained 116,000 rentable square feet and was leased almost in its entirety to the Government, whose lease would expire on May 31, 1988.

Earlier in the day, Byrne received the owner's response: he asked for a $10 million deposit on a $20 million purchase price with 90 days for The Kaempfer Company to close! Byrne believed the owner was concerned not to be left with an empty building, should the deal fall through. If the owner renewed the Government's lease, he was likely to receive a rent in the low $20's. Therefore, he wanted to structure the purchase agreement with Kaempfer so that he would be protected in a situation where he did not renew the Government's lease.

Regardless of the terms, Byrne was unsure if they should go ahead with the acquisition: "First of all, it's a 1960s building replete with asbestos. Asbestos can be a big deal with bankers nowadays, and it is *very* expensive to clean it up. Also, when the Government is a tenant, they can holdover past the termination date of their lease. On any normal tenant you file a suit, you get them out of there because they are a tenant at sufferance, and they have no tenancy rights. But the Government, unlike a private sector tenant, just says, 'We're not ready to leave. We're going to invoke eminent domain, and we're staying here.'   And there's no getting them out until they want to get out be-

cause who are you going to call? You're going to call the Government to get the Government out? That's a risk."

Byrne saw the light come on in Mr. Kaempfer's office. He turned off his overheated computer and headed over to talk strategy.

EXHIBITS

1. *Washington Business Journal* article.

2. The Kaempfer Company portfolio (excerpts).

3. The Kaempfer Company organizational chart.

4. Aerial view and city map.

5. Plat map.

6. Approved plans and elevation.

QUESTIONS FOR DISCUSSION

1. Should The Kaempfer Company acquire the last parcel?

2. What sort of counter-offer would the owner of the last parcel find acceptable?

3. Will the investment partner go for an expanded deal? What if they don't?

4. What other steps should The Kaempfer Company take?

Exhibit 1

WASHINGTON BUSINESS JOURNAL

WEEK OF MAY 18, 1987 • VOLUME 5, NUMBER 51

Kaempfer gets Warner Theater

Last parcel is sold in Penn. Ave. corridor

By Heidi C. Daniel

The Kaempfer Co. has agreed to buy the Warner Theater on the corner of 13th and E streets and three other adjacent lots totaling some 130,000 square feet for $22 million.

Company president J.W. Kaempfer Jr. said he plans to restore the 65-year-old theater and build a 12-story building with 207,000 square feet of office and 10,726 square feet of retail space.

None too soon: The Warner has suffered the degradation of time. The once-plush theater has grown shabby. The springs are popping out of the seats and the red velvet curtains are fraying. Instead of the jugglers, acrobats, animal acts, concerts and films of the past, it's been hosting a string of hopeful buyers. At least three groups tried to purchase the building and lost an estimated total of $750,000 in deposits, sources familiar with the project say.

"Nobody could get it together in a creative fashion," said Robert Cohen, president of Barnes, Morris & Pardoe Inc., who assembled the four parcels for The Kaempfer Co.

"The other people really didn't want to go to the trouble," said J. Fernando Barrueta of Barrueta & Associates. "Joey had the vision to go after (the other lots) and was willing to take the risk."

But to Kaempfer, 40, it was obvious. "How could anyone pass it up? It's one of the last great sites downtown."

"It was a heroic effort on (Kaempfer's) part," said Shalom Baranes, the architect who is designing the new building and overseeing the renovation of the theater. "It's a very complex, very difficult project. What we learned from other people's problems is that the Warner can't support itself."

Alone, the site is too small and expensive to be economically feasible, Cohen said. Kaempfer needed the additional 6,792 square feet to make the numbers work, he said.

With the added ground, he can build an office to carry the extra expense of operating the theater. The six-story theater building does

continued on page 29

The last picture show: Warner's grand interior.

Exhibit 1
continued

Kaempfer buys Warner Theater
continued from page 1

not use all the FAR (floor to area ratio) allowed in that district. The unused balance can be transferred to the new building, which will permit 12 floors.

The land will cost about $80 an FAR foot. Sites in the prime area of the East End are commanding prices well in excess of $100 per FAR foot, while sites on Pennsylvania Avenue, if available, would sell for more than $125 per FAR foot, according to Jones Lang Wootton, real estate counselors.

Technically, none of the four sites Kaempfer bought lie on Pennsylvania Avenue, but because the new building is catty corner from Western Plaza brokers say Kaempfer will be able to charge Pennsylvania Avenue-style rents.

Currently, the Willard's office building is asking $38 a square foot, the highest in the city. With the 4 percent annual increase in rents, by the time the Warner building is ready for occupancy in three years, the going rate will easily have climbed into the low $40s. Kaempfer is confident he'll be able to lease the building for unprecedented rates of $43 to $45 a square foot, despite predictions of continued overbuilding.

Cohen said those figures are not out of line. If the site had been developed at the same time as Oliver Carr was renovating the Willard, Cadillac Fairview was building 1001 Pennsylvania or Gerald Hines was building Columbia Square directly behind the Warner, "it wouldn't have been so desirable." But now leasing of those projects is winding down, turning the Warner into "the prime site on Pennsylvania," he says.

In initial discussions, "the city has been very receptive to helping us because of our commitment to maintaining the theater as a viable operation," Kaempfer said.

It took Cohen five months to put the deal together, starting with the three small pieces: a Chinese restaurant, a shoe store, and an 800-square-foot strip belonging to Gerald Hines. "Each was negotiated independently, but the timing was coordinated. We wouldn't buy one without knowing the second and third were coming too," he says.

The owners of Storm's Shoes at 1219 E St. and Ding How restaurant at 1221 E St. weren't tough to convince because "they'd been preconditioned to selling," Cohen said, by the previous groups that had approached them. The shoe store was just as happy to relocate to a newer retail area, and the Chinese restaurant liked the price offered, Cohen said.

Gerald Hines was a harder sell. The small plot, critical to Kaempfer's assemblage, was a remnant from Hines' Columbia Square project on F Street. The developer wanted a guarantee that the views from the back of the building would not be ruined by the new structure. Kaempfer had to agree not to substitute poorer quality brick on the rear of the building and to "coordinate the loading dock and dumpsters with the existing alley configuration," said Bill Alsup, vice president of Gerald Hines Interests. "We wanted to make sure it's a quality development which (Kaempfer) generally does anyway."

After Cohen secured the three lots, he approached J.A. Weinberg, one of the four businessmen who bought the Warner Theater in 1971. Weinberg, who could not be reached for comment, is in his 90s. "The partners were of an age that they weren't interested in redeveloping the property themselves," Cohen said.

When he started negotiating, an uniden-

tified group from New York was bidding on the building simultaneously. "The reason (Weinberg) was interested in The Kaempfer Co. was because it already owned the parcels next door." He closed the deal two and a half months later.

In 1980 Gerald Hines tried to buy the theater when it was assembling the site for Columbia Square. The company planned to tear down the building. Hines signed a contract. Then the Warner theater, both inside and out, was nominated for historic landmark status. The Houston-based company didn't want to get embroiled in a squabble with the preservationists on its first project in town, sources say. Some estimate the company lost a $250,000 deposit when it backed away from the deal; others say a clause in the contract stipulated the money would be refunded if the theater became an historic landmark.

About six months ago Sigal/Zuckerman attempted to pull off the same deal as Kaempfer. The company claims it contracted to buy the theater, the Chinese restaurant, the shoe store and Hines' piece. But, "it didn't pencil out for us from a feasibility point of view. It was a question of losing a tremendous amount of money," said Neal Bien, vice president of Sigal/Zuckerman. As it was, the company had to forfeit $500,000 worth of deposits, sources said. Bien wouldn't

comment.

Kaempfer may have succeeded where others failed, but the test is just beginning. Both the Beaux Arts facade and the ornate lobby are historic landmarks, the only interior in Washington to have such a designation. They must be preserved, according to Mike Quinn, executive director of the D.C. Preservation League.

Barnes estimated it will cost millions of dollars to bring the theater up to the latest revisions of the code. Any proposal to alter the interior, from new wiring to major refurbishing, has to be approved by the D.C. Historic Preservation Review Board. Quinn was relieved to hear of Kaempfer's commitment to preserving the interior because often such landmarks are the center of protracted battles between preservationists and developers. "We can feel good about one for a change," he said.

Kaempfer has hired a special theater consultant to help restore the vaulted gold-leaf ceiling, the grand marble staircase and large Palladian windows. Barnes plans to move the elevator from the corner of the building, where it blocks views down Pennsylvania Avenue, into the center. The theater entrance at 13th and E streets will be enlarged to accommodate tenants as well as theater goers. A series of penthouses that detract from the "bold, muscular look" of the exterior will be refaced and an outside stairway that led from the sidewalk to the lower level will be restored to add the retail space.

The new building will contain additional parking for the theater crowd as well as complement the Warner's architecture. Barnes, who has such renovations as The Bond Building, the Southern Building and the Army/Navy Club to his credit, says this is one of the two most difficult and complex projects he's ever undertaken.

The Warner Theater has special significance for the rebirth of Pennsylvania Avenue. "It's been a part of the cultural heritage of Washington from the day it opened. There were a dozen theaters in downtown then, now it's one of only three," Quinn says. "Theater is part of what makes a viable downtown and an attractive place to stay after work. The Warner and the National are our theater district."

F STREET, N.W.

COLUMBIA SQUARE

(SQUARE 290)

PLAZA ONE & WARNER THEATRE

13TH STREET, N.W.

12TH STREET, N.W.

E STREET, N.W.

1275 PENNSYLVANIA AVENUE

1201 PENNSYLVANIA AVENUE

PENNSYLVANIA AVENUE

Exhibit 2

1525 Wilson Boulevard combines a unique building design by Keyes Condon Florence with an open plaza to create an exciting urban space that is destined to become a landmark location. The 300,000 square foot building will be ready for occupancy in July 1987.

Designed by Skidmore, Owings & Merrill, 2300 M Street is a 9-story, 120,000 square foot office building in the heart of Washington's West End. The building has been fully occupied since early 1984.

Exhibit 2
continued

Park Place is a 190,000 square foot office building in Arlington County, Virginia, directly across the Potomac River from Washington, D.C. The 12-story building, completed in 1983, offers expansive views of the Nation's Capital.

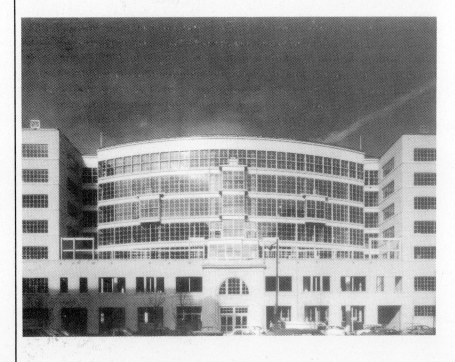

Designed by Don M. Hisaka and Associates, 1250 24th Street integrates an historically significant facade into a contemporary design featuring an eight story skylit atrium. With a total leasable area of 227,000 square feet, the building was completed in May, 1987.

Exhibit 2
continued

Designed by Clark Tribble Harris & Li, 1201 New York Avenue is a 315,000 square foot office building situated in Washington's rapidly developing East End business district. Scheduled for completion in late 1987, the building offers 12 stories plus a penthouse floor of prime office space.

The Grand Hotel is a European-style, five-star luxury hotel on the corner of 24th & M Streets in Washington, D.C. Designed by Skidmore, Owings & Merrill, the 263-room Grand is recognized by many as on of the most elegant luxury hotels in the country.

Exhibit 2
continued

Designed by I.M. Pei & Partners, 1001 19th Street North will add a dramatic presence to the Rosslyn skyline directly across the Potomac River from Washington, D.C. The 19-story, 252,000 square foot building will feature spectacular views for all offices. The building is being developed jointly with Park Tower Realty Corp. of New York, and will be available for occupancy in late 1988.

At 1717 Rhode Island Avenue, N.W., Skidmore, Owings & Merrill has designed a 10-story, 165,000 square foot building that combines new construction with the historic restoration of several townhouses adjacent to St. Matthew's Cathedral. The building will be available for occupancy in late 1988.

Exhibit 3

THE KAEMPFER COMPANY
PERSONNEL

J.W. Kaempfer, Jr. Staff
4 People   Assistant to the President
                                  Assistant to the President (Part-time)
                                  Executive Secretary to the President
                                  Intern

Finance
2 People   Vice President of Finance
                                  Departmental Secretary

Accounting
8 People   Controller
                                  Management Division Controller
                                  Assistant Controller/Development
                                  Accounting Assistant/Development
                                  Accounts Payable
                                  Accounting Assistant/Management Division
                                  Staff Accountant
                                  Departmental Secretary

Construction
4 People   Senior Vice President
                                  Vice President
                                  Assistant Construction Manager
                                  Departmental Secretary

Legal
3 People   General Counsel
                                  Associate General Counsel
                                  Departmental Secretary

Kaempfer Management Services, Inc.
8 People   Vice President, Management Division
                                      and Marketing
                                  Director of Property Management
                                  Property Manager
                                  Property Manager
                                  Leasing Administrator
                                  Departmental Secretary
                                  Departmental Secretary
                                  Marketing Coordinator

Project Development
10 People   MBA   Vice President/Director of Development
               MBA   Vice President/Project Manager
               MBA   Project Manager
               MBA   Project Manager

Exhibit 3
continued

The Kaempfer Company Personnel
Page Two

<u>Project Development</u> (continued)
```
            MBA         Assistant Project Manager
            MBA         Assistant Project Manager
                        Marketing Center Assistant
                        Departmental Secretary
                        Departmental Secretary
                        Departmental Secretary
```

<u>Office Management</u>
```
4 People                Office Manager
                        Receptionist
                        Receptionist
                        Company Maid
```

TOTAL: 43

KAEMPFER MANAGEMENT SERVICES, INC.

<u>2300 M Street</u>
Winston
John
William
Renee

<u>Warner Theater</u>
Rob
Herman

<u>1250 24th Street</u>
Steve
George
Michael
John
Khosrow

<u>1525 Wilson Boulevard</u>
Ralph
Mike
Jose
Josh

<u>Investment Building</u>
Arnie
John
Robin
Patrick
David
Stuart
Linwood
Ben
Sharnita

<u>Park Place</u>
Jerry
Carlos
Manuel

<u>Plaza East</u>
Tariq
Mark
Gary

<u>1201 New York Avenue</u>
Edward

Exhibit 4

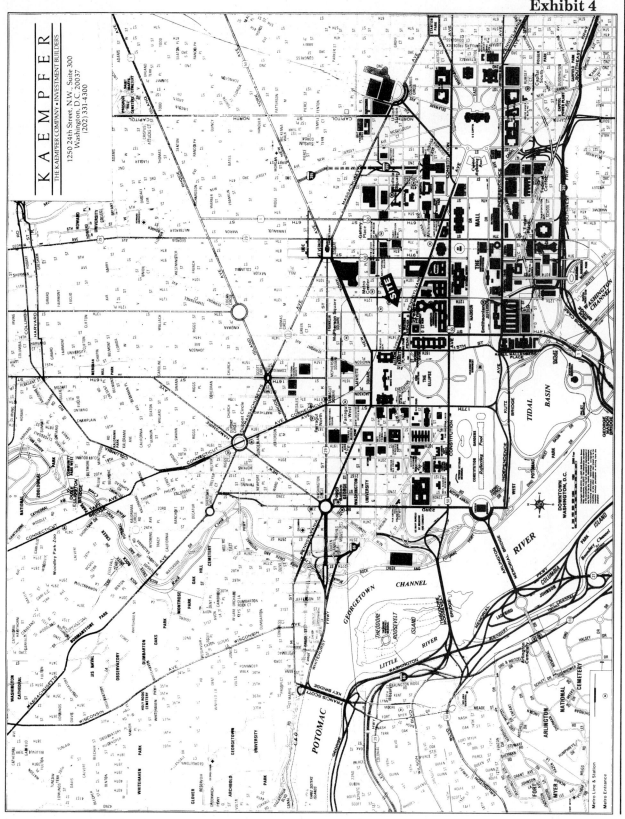

Exhibit 4
continued

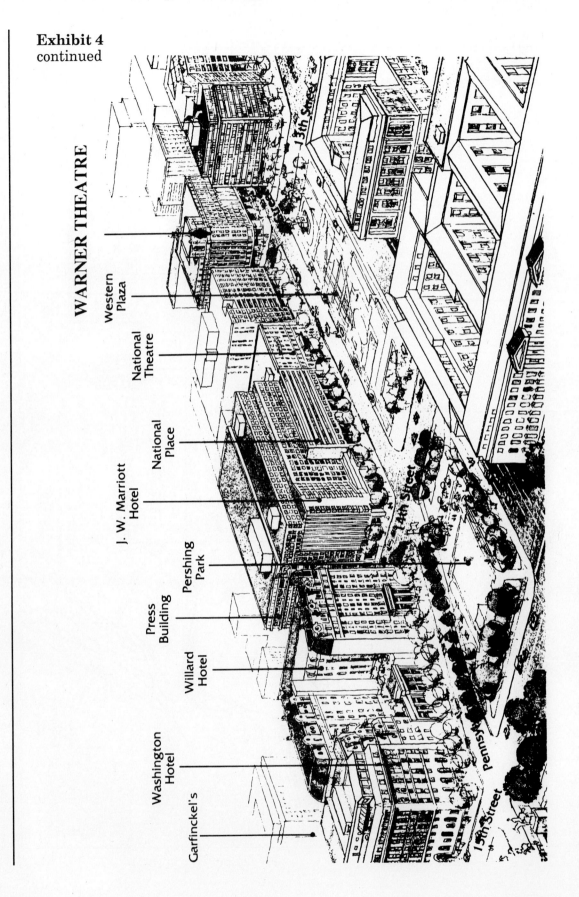

WARNER THEATRE

Western Plaza

National Theatre

National Place

J. W. Marriott Hotel

Pershing Park

Press Building

Willard Hotel

Washington Hotel

Garfinckel's

13th Street

14th Street

15th Street

Pennsy

Exhibit 5

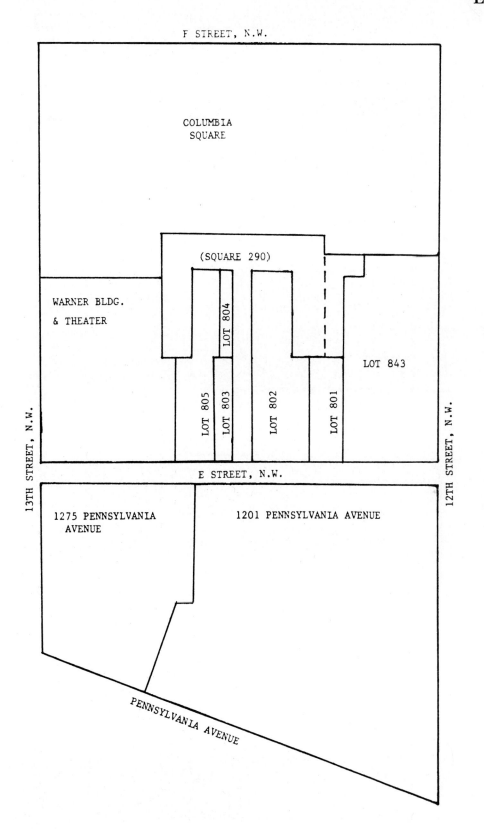

Exhibit 6

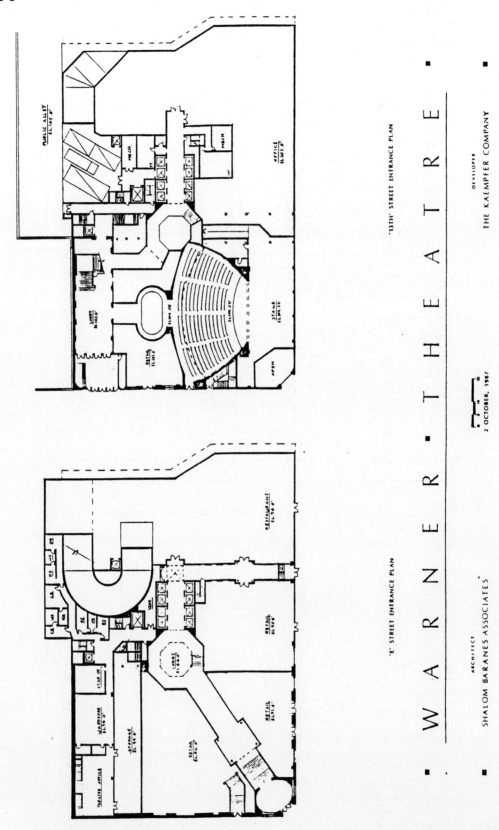

WARNER · THEATRE

'E' STREET ENTRANCE PLAN

'13TH' STREET ENTRANCE PLAN

ARCHITECT
SHALOM BARANES ASSOCIATES

DEVELOPER
THE KAEMPFER COMPANY

2 OCTOBER, 1987

Exhibit 6
continued

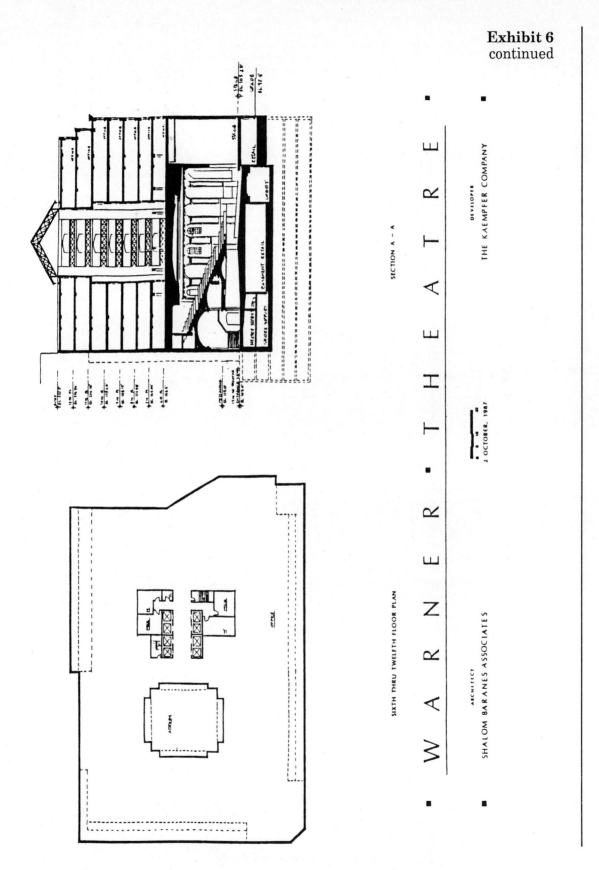

SECTION A – A

SIXTH THRU TWELFTH FLOOR PLAN

· W A R N E R · T H E A T R E ·

■ ARCHITECT
SHALOM BARANES ASSOCIATES

■ DEVELOPER
THE KAEMPFER COMPANY

2 OCTOBER, 1987

Exhibit 6
continued

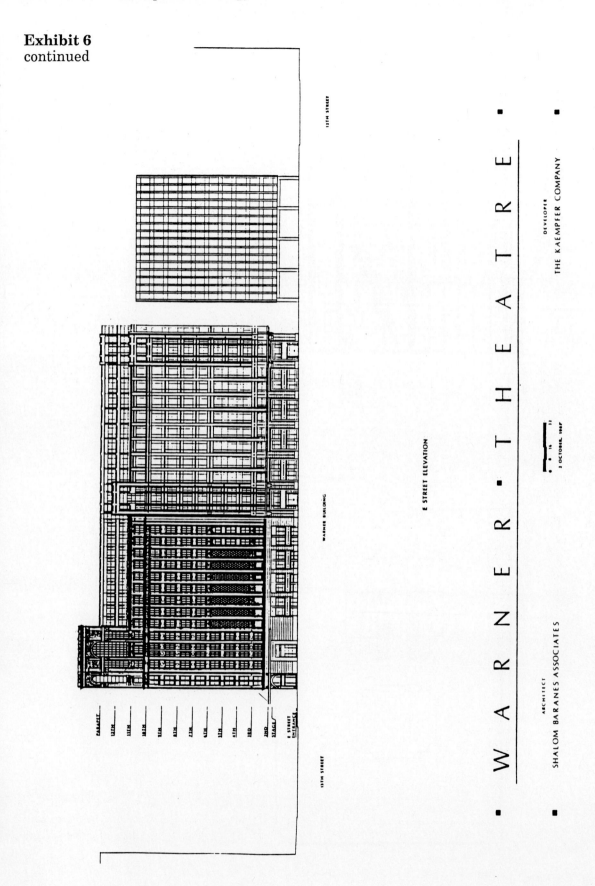

Case 14

Lumber Mutual

In December 1979, Dick Reynolds and Jack Griefen of the Boston office of Gerald D. Hines Interests were considering prospects for a Phase 2 building at their Point West Office Center (see Exhibit 1). They had succeeded in putting a development together for the Zayre Headquarters Tract, and Phase 1 construction was underway. The development would consist of 225,000 square feet of first-class office space in three buildings. The first, a triangular three-story structure, would provide 66,000 square feet at a total project cost of $3,597,500. A prime tenant, the Lumber Mutual Insurance Company, had been secured and would occupy the entire third floor. A marketing program was underway for the remaining space. Permanent financing at 10.25% and a construction loan with a 13% maximum were in hand. Planning for the second phase was underway, but the October 5 increase in the prime interest rate suggested a drastic change in financing costs and a reassessment of the economics of the final two buildings.

As project manager for Hines/Boston, Dick Reynolds reflected on the events of the six months since the June 1st meeting with Stanley Feldberg of Zayre. It was in preparation for that discussion that he had initially sketched out what was to become the ground lease agreement between Hines and Zayre. Going into the meeting, he had fully expected that some kind of phased sale of land would have to be arranged. However, in the course of the discussion, Stanley Feldberg made it known that Zayre would consider participating in the development on the basis of a ground lease. Having done his homework, Mr. Reynolds was able to suggest a deal structure that was acceptable to both Hines and Zayre. A tentative agreement was reached that day (see Exhibit 2). The details were to be specified in further negotiations and eventually translated into legal documents, which were concluded in October (see Exhibit 3). Dick thought it was essential that the development get underway as soon as possible to take advantage of favorable market conditions. Design, financing, marketing, and securing the necessary town approvals all lay ahead.

A master plan to accommodate the 225,000 square feet in three buildings on the site was prepared by the SWA Group, a Boston landscape architecture firm. In order to expedite the approval process, it was decided to seek town approval for only the first phase, which did not involve any of the major site constraints. Dick had been confident that this part of the development would be quickly approved by the Town of Framingham, and that ultimately the development plan for the entire site would be accepted.

By the second week of June 1979, a potential prime tenant, the Lumber Mutual Insurance Company, had expressed interest in 22,000 square feet of space in the first building. Following some general discussions, a lease proposal was outlined by Dick Reynolds on July 2 (see Exhibit 4). The proposal was accepted by Lumber Mutual by the end of the summer.

The Hines organization typically forms a project team including the architect and contractor early in the process. For the Point West development, Keyes Associates, architects and engineers, and the Macomber Construction Company were selected to work together with John Kastler, the construction manager in the Hines/Boston office. The design and construction documents progressed rapidly over the summer. By October, the major pieces of the development were set. An agreement was reached with Macomber for a cost-plus-fixed-fee contract with a guaranteed maximum price of $2,867,500. Groundbreaking occurred November 1st, 1979 with substantial completion scheduled for August 1980.

During the same time, Dick had been working on the financing. He had secured a construction loan from State Street Bank and Trust Company at one point over the prime rate with a 13% maximum. Because it was the first speculative deal for the Hines/Boston office, the lender requested a guarantee from Gerald Hines for the construction loan. Permanent financing at 10.25% with a 32-year term was arranged with Union Mutual Insurance. Based on early cost and rent projections, the loan amount was negotiated at $3,475,000. This proved to be about $125,000 short of the revised estimate of total development costs of $3,597,500. Given the present interest rate situation, however, Dick thought it better to delay seeking an increase in the loan amount until the rates eased and higher project rents were proven. Until then, the difference would have to come out of Hines/Boston funds.

The marketing program for the remaining space on the first and second floors was underway, and a brochure describing Point West was ready for distribution (see Exhibit 1). Mr. Reynolds believed that the $12.75 per square foot rent used in his most recent pro forma (see Exhibit 5) was conservative, and rents of at least $13.00 per square foot could probably be achieved upon completion.

The Town of Framingham had been very cooperative, and all of the approvals for Phase 2 were quickly granted. There was support for the project from abutting property owners and the town planning staff, so Mr. Reynolds was encouraged that the more difficult issues like the parking

variance could be resolved for the final two buildings. The variance was required because the zoning ordinance had not been revised as planned.

An important factor in Hines/Boston's enthusiasm for the Point West Office Center was the quality of the product that they had been able to achieve. The distinguishing mark of developments by the Hines organization nationally was its ability to produce a good design as part of a profitable development venture. Hines/Boston saw the final design for the first building, with its triangular shape and three-story atrium, as consistent with that tradition and an important step in establishing its track record in the Boston office market.

Looking ahead, Dick expected the "fast-track" development process he had managed so far could potentially be repeated in the final phases. There already was interest from a potential prime tenant for the second building, but the financing outlook was very uncertain. It would be impossible to secure the same interest rates as the first phase, but the office market remained strong, and rents continued to rise. With the foundations in place for Phase 1, the Hines/Boston office looked forward to completing the remaining two buildings, if possible.

EXHIBITS

1. Marketing brochure, Point West Office Center.

2. Letter from Dick Reynolds to Stanley Feldberg.

3. *New England Real Estate Journal* article.

4. Letter from Dick Reynolds to Jack Holmes.

5. Revised pro forma.

QUESTIONS FOR DISCUSSION

1. What should Dick Reynolds do now?

2. What priorities did Mr. Reynolds establish once the agreement had been reached? Why did he not wait for binding agreements?

3. Should he have done anything differently?

Exhibit 1

Point West Office Center Building One

READY FOR OCCUPANCY FALL 1980

66,150 Rentable Square Feet

First Floor: 19,140 Square Feet
Second Floor: 22,250 Square Feet
Third Floor: Leased

SPECIFICATIONS

Construction: Steel frame with brick facade.

Windows: Dual pane, Solar Cool bronze reflective glass for reduced solar load and increased privacy

Heating/Ventilating/Air Conditioning: Variable volume air handling system with full economizer cycle. This feature introduces outside air to achieve a predetermined mixed air temperature, thereby reducing heating/cooling energy requirements. Return air vents through the lighting system. 25 zones per floor

Lighting: Miller fixtures with General Electric Watt Miser ballast and lamps and Carroll's Radial Lense II, a combination designed to significantly reduce annual lighting costs

Ceilings: 8'6", 2'x2' Tegular Acoustical Tile with recessed grid

Walls: gypsum applied to both sides of 2 x 4 metal studs. Two coats of eggshell finish latex paint. Accent colors available

Flooring: Fully carpeted corridors and tenant areas. Color selection available.

Doors: Full height, solid core, stain grade wood in metal frame. Lever handle hardware. In addition, tenant entry features floor to ceiling side light.

Elevators: Two hydraulic passenger elevators for tenant convenience

Fire Protection: Fire alarm and sprinkler system throughout

Visitors to Building One enter a spacious lobby with its dramatic stairway rising against a two-story wall of glass. The triangular shape of the building permits numerous corner offices and encourages interesting floor plan arrangements, both for individual offices and efficient open space. A high ratio of window to floor area provides abundant outside light as well as attractive views across the wooded site.

GERALD D. HINES INTERESTS

Exhibit 1
continued

An Exceptional Business Environment.

Three handsome, new office buildings ... architecturally appealing and sited with care on 21 acres of stately oaks and white pines. 225,000 square feet of impressive office space ... energy efficient and readily adaptable to your specialized needs. A distinguished business address, conveniently located between Boston and Worcester.

Point West Office Center is ideally situated, overlooking Exit 13 of the Massachusetts Turnpike in Framingham. Downtown Boston is only 20 minutes away ... Worcester is 25 minutes. The site offers convenient access to Routes 30, 9, 128 and 495. From Point West you're on your way quickly, for business appointments anywhere in New England. Boston's Logan International Airport is 30 minutes away for business trips outside of the driving area.

Major shopping centers, hotel accommodations, entertainment and fine restaurants are all just moments away. Point West is a quick, fuel-efficient commute from a wide range of attractive residential areas west of Boston, and is equally accessible to the rapidly expanding communities outside of Route 495.

Point West Office Center is being developed by the Boston office of Gerald D. Hines Interests, a national development and investment building firm, headquartered in Houston. The company has constructed more than 210 projects totaling nearly 30 million square feet in 30 cities throughout the United States, Canada and Mexico. Typical of these Hines' projects are Pennzoil Place in Houston, The First National Bank of Chicago and Pillsbury Center in Minneapolis. Current Hines' projects under construction will add about 15 million square feet of space.

The site plan for Point West Office Center includes three buildings set into the gentle, south-facing grade. Amply screened, paved parking areas are convenient to each building and extensive border planting blends comfortably with the natural tree cover of the site.

Visually exciting common areas in each building welcome visitors to Point West and reflect the attention to detail and high level of excellence to be found throughout all Gerald D. Hines' projects ... The tasteful selection of colors and textures, hardware and surface finishes. Effective noise reduction techniques. Energy saving climate control and lighting. Fire protection. All contribute to make Point West Office Center one of the finest business locations anywhere.

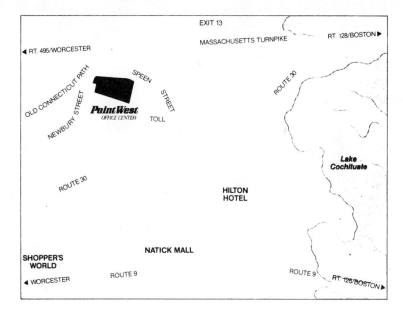

Exhibit 1
continued

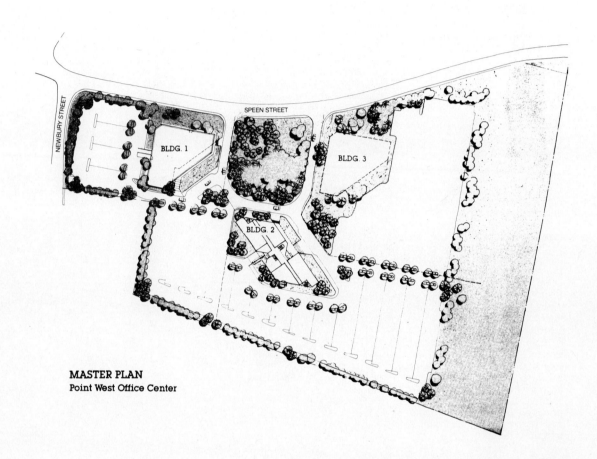

MASTER PLAN
Point West Office Center

Exhibit 1
continued

FIRST FLOOR

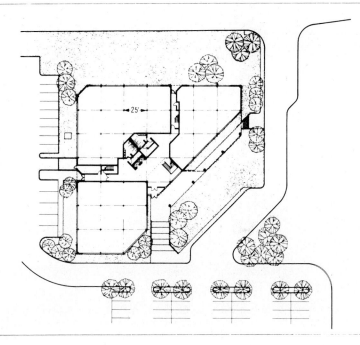

SECOND FLOOR

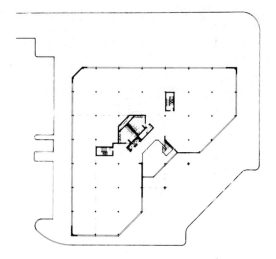

Exclusive Leasing Agent

LEGGAT McCALL & WERNER INC.
COMMERCIAL AND INDUSTRIAL REAL ESTATE

60 State Street, Boston, Massachusetts 02109/(617) 367-1177

Exhibit 2

Gerald D. Hines Interests   Two Faneuil Hall Marketplace   Boston, Mass. 02109   617-723 3055

June 4, 1979

Mr. Stanley H. Feldberg
Chairman of the Executive Committee
Zayre Corporation
270 Cochituate Road
Framingham

RE: The Site
    Speen Street
    Framingham

Dear Mr. Feldberg:

Pursuant to our meeting of June 1, the following outlines the revised ground
lease program which we have discussed:

1. A ground lease between the Zayre Corporation and Gerald Hines Development
    Boston, Ltd. (the operating partnership of the Boston office, of which
    Gerald D. Hines is the general partner and majority owner) will be
    established for the entire parcel of approximately 20 acres with an
    intial term of 50 years, plus options which shall extend to a total term
    of 99 years.

2. The ground rent payable under this lease shall be made up of two
    elements: a base rent and an escalation rent based on the operating cash
    flow of the buildings which we will develop on the site. The imputed
    value of the overall site shall be set as $2,250,000, which is based on a
    land component value of $10/square foot for the 225,000 square feet of
    building area which we believe is feasible in three building phases. The
    land value for each phase, therefore, shall be set at $10 per square foot
    of that phase's building area; however, we recognize that the overall
    value must total $2,250,000 and should the later phases result in less
    than 225,000 square feet overall, the per square foot land value shall be
    increased proportionately. The base ground rent shall then be 10% per
    year on the land value of each phase.

    Additional rental shall be paid based on the net cash flow of completed
    buildings after all operating expenses, real estate taxes, first mortgage
    debt service, base ground rent, and a return to Hines of $1 per square
    foot of building according to the formula:

    a. of the first $1 per square foot of net cah flow in excess of the
        items listed above, Zayre shall receive 30% and Hines 70%.

    b. of the second $1 per square foot, Zayre shall receive 30% and
        Hines 60%.

    c. of all additional dollars thereafter, Zayre shall receive 45% and
        Hines 55%.

Exhibit 2
continued

Mr. Stanley H. Feldberg
June 4, 1979
Page two

3.   It is understood that the overall site shall be developed in phases and
      that ground rent shall become payable on each phase at such time as
      construction commences on that phase. A schedule would be established
      for a program of development based on the initiation of construction of
      phase 1 in September 1979 and the initiation of construction of
      succeeding phases within one year of completion of the preceeding phase
      so long as that preceeding phase is producing income from at least 75%
      of the space. The intended maximum schedule would therefore be:

      phase 1 land takedown September 1979

      phase 2 land takedown June 1981

      phase 3 land takedown March 1983

      While we believe that the actual development program will proceed more
      rapidly than this, initiation of the schedule is subject to receipt of
      the necessary approvals and permits for construction of phase 1. We ask
      that the schedule be extended for any delay in the initiation of phase 1
      construction caused by elements beyond our control, but, in any event,
      Zayre shall retain the right to terminate this agreement if phase 1 has
      not begun by May 1980. Should we not proceed in accordance with this
      schedule for future phases, the lease would be terminated for all
      undeveloped phases.

4.   This ground lease shall be subordinated to mortgage financing at market
      rate and term in an amount necessary to cover the development and
      construction costs over and above the land according to the pro forma
      budget Hines shall establish prior to construction of each phase. Once
      the mortgage debt service has been established, Hines will be able to
      refinance such debt during the life of the ground lease so long as the
      debt service does not exceed the original amount.

5.   At the conclusion of the original lease term, each party shall have the
      option to purchase the interest of the other at the then fair market
      value. If the offeree does not wish to sell, he has the right to
      purchase the interest of the original offeror.

      While we did not dicuss this previously, we also ask that you consider
      providing Hines with the option to purchase the ground after the 10th
      lease year at the then fair market value of the leased fee interest.

6.   We need to discuss further the handling of site development costs which
      are necessary or appropriate during phase 1, but which are applicable to
      later phases.

Exhibit 2
continued

Mr. Stanley H. Feldberg
June 4, 1979
Page three

If these outline terms are acceptable, we would like to proceed to
documentation of the ground lease with this serving as a letter of intent. As
you know, we are in negotiation with a lead tenant for the initial phase and
would like to proceed immediately with project design and the necessary legal
work on the site.

We are most enthused about this project and look forward to a long and
satisfying relationship.

Yours truly,

Richard W. Reynolds

RWR/tt

cc: R.J. Griefen
    J. Brad Griffith
    John J. Griffin, Jr.

Griffith of Leggat McCall & Werner broker

Hines signs ground lease with Zayre for office site

FRAMINGHAM, MA. — Point West Office Center, this town's newest office park, was announced recently by the Boston office of Gerald Hines Interests.

According to John Griefen, Hines has signed a 50 year ground lease agreement with Zayre Corp. for a 20 acre site on Speen st., adjacent to exit 13 on the Massachusetts Turnpike.

Griefen said the master plan for Point West Office Center calls for a total of 225,000 s/f in three buildings, plans for the first of which will be announced shortly.

"We believe the westward corridor of the pike offers a superb environment for premium quality office development, and we're pleased that Zayre and the town of Framingham share our enthusiasm," he said.

Gerald Hines Interests recently completed more than 300,000 s f of manufacturing and research space for Prime Computer here.

Brad Griffith of Leggatt McCall & Werner was the broker in the transaction.

Shown at lease signing are (standing, from left) Mr. Griefen; Atty. Donald Bloch of Lane & Altman, representing Zayre; and Atty. John Griffin Jr. of Rackemann, Sawyer & Brewster, representing Hines. Seated are Richard Reynolds of Hines; Stanley Feldberg, chairman, Zayre; and Mr. Griffith.

Exhibit 4

Gerald D. Hines Interests   Two Faneuil Hall Marketplace   Boston, Mass. 02109   617-723 3055

July 2, 1979

Mr. Jack E. Holmes
President
Lumber Mutual Insurance Co.
45 Williams Street
Wellesley, MA 02181

RE: Speen Street
    Framingham, MA

Dear Mr. Holmes:

In keeping with our discussions since our letter of June 8th, the following
sets forth what we understand to be the agreement between us for your
occupancy of the initial building in our 20 acre office park on Speen Street
at Exit 13 of the Massachusetts Turnpike.

<u>1. General Terms:</u>
You will occupy the entire third floor of the building with a total rentable
square footage of 22,000 square feet (subject to final design adjustments).
The lease shall have an initial term of fifteen (15) years with rents of:
   a. $11.75 per square foot for the first five lease years.
   b. $12.00 per square foot for lease years six through ten and
   c. for lease years 11 through 15 a rent of $12.00 plus 25% of the increase
       in the consumer price index between the date of initial occupancy and
       the end of the tenth lease year, but in no event more than $13.00 per
       square foot.

As to b. and c., any operating expense or real estate tax escalations then in
effect in accordance with paragraph 5 shall continue in addition to these
adjustments in base rent.

<u>2. Expansion Options:</u>
You shall have the option after five lease years to add an additional 5,000
square feet of rentable area on the second floor at a rental for lease years
six through ten of $13.50 per square foot plus all operating expense and real
estate tax escalations which then may be in effect.

You shall have a further option after seven lease years to add an additional
amount of space on the second floor of approximately 2,500 square feet, the
final amount to be adjusted depending on then existing other leases, at a
rental rate of $13.75 per square foot plus any operating expense and real
estate tax escalations then in effect.

Exhibit 4
continued

Mr. Jack E. Holmes
July 2, 1979
Page Two

At the end of ten lease years, you shall have the option to add such
additional space as would provide a total of 11,000 square feet on the second
floor with the rent for lease years eleven through fifteen on this total
expansion area equal to $12.00 plus 33% of the increase in the consumer price
index between date of occupancy and the end of the tenth year.

If you elect to exercise your initial renewal option after the original
fifteen year term and you then occupy the 11,000 square feet expansion on the
second floor, you shall have the right to add the remainder of the second
floor as it becomes available, but in no event later than the 19th lease year,
with rent in accordance with that set for the renewal options.

3. Cancellation Option:
At the end of the tenth lease year, you shall have the option to cancel the
lease on either the second floor expansion area or your entire tenancy
subject to receipt of notice eighteen months in advance and payment of
six months rent, such payment to be reduced by any rental received from releasing of the space within six months. In addition to the above, should you
exercise this cancellation option, you will refund one-third of the move-in
allowance described in the next paragraph.

4. Occupancy Schedule and Moving Allowance:
Subject to receipt of all necessary permits and approvals, we expect to begin
construction in October of 1979 and provide initial occupancy in August of
1980. In order to assist you in the expense of moving, we shall allow a three
month period without rental payments, such period to begin at such time as the
building has received its certificate of occupancy.

5. Operating Expense and Real Estate Taxes:
The rent quoted in paragraph 1 is full service except for tenant electricity
which shall be seperately metered and billed to tenant. This rent includes an
operating expense base of $2.50 per rentable square foot. All actual
operating expenses of the building in excess of that amount shall be paid by
the tenant in the proportion of your rentable area to the total rentable area
of the building.

The rent also included a real estate tax base of $1.40 per rentable square
foot. All actual real estate taxes in excess of that amount shall be paid by
the tenant in the proportion of your rentable area to the total rentable area
of the building.

In order to assist in your initial relocation, we shall guarantee that there
be no escalation payable during the first lease year.

Exhibit 4
continued

Mr. Jack E. Holmes
July 2, 1979
Page three

6. Tenant Finish:
Your occupied area shall be finished in accordance with the attached schedule
except: a. We are willing to discuss the concealed spline ceiling although we
          believe that our specified alternative is superior for tenant and
          landlord.
       b. We shall provide three 208 volt outlets.
       c. We are willing to consider a Zola tone type wall finish subject to
          final pricing of your partition requirements.

7. Renewal Options:
After the initial fifteen year lease term, you shall have the option to renew
either the third floor or your then overall tenancy for two terms of 5 years
each upon one year's written notice. The rent for the first option shall be
$12.00 plus 50% of the increase in the consumer price index between the date
of initial occupancy and the end of year fifteen and for the second option,
the rent of the first option plus 50% of the increase in the consumer price
index between the end of year fifteen and the end of year twenty. For each
option, all operating expense and real estate tax escalations then in effect
shall be continued in addition to the rents determined by the above formula.

Other Conditions:
We shall provide 10 reserved parking spaces with such restriction as may be
necessary to assure your exclusive use.

It is our intention to provide, in the second building to be built in this
park, an eating area for tenant use which will provide tables and a reasonable
lunch food service beyond vending machines.

As final plans proceed for the building, we will be working with you in the
layout of your space in order to prepare working drawings for tenant finish
construction.

If the above is in accordance with your understanding, we would appreciate
your executing the enclosed copy whereupon our counsel will prepare a lease in
accordance with this letter of intent. We look forward to a successful
conclusion of these discussions and a long relationship in what we believe
will be an outstanding office building.

Yours truly

Richard W. Reynolds

RWR/tt
Enclosures
cc: Mark Kisiel
    R.J. Griefen
    J.J. Griffin, Jr.

Exhibit 5

```
REVISED PRO FORMA
POINT WEST OFFICE CENTER, PHASE 1
DECEMBER 21, 1979
```

```
COST:  Land:      under subordinated ground lease
       Building:  66,150 @ $43.35
                  (guaranteed G.C. maximum price)            $2,867,500
       Indirect:  A/E                        $155,000
                  Constr. Interest            220,000
                  Leasing                     175,000
                  Fees                         80,000
                  Lease up deficit            100,000           730,000
                                                             $3,597,500


INCOME:  Lumber Mutual  24,800 @ $12.00 average                 297,600
         To be leased   41,350 @ $12.75 average                 527,200
                                                               $824,800
         Less 5% vacancy                                         41,240
                                                               $783,500
         Operating expenses and taxes @ $3.90 (stopped)         258,000
                                                               $525,560
         First mortgage debt service 10.66k on $3,600,000       383,750

         NET CASH FLOW                                         $141,810

Zayre Ground rent                                              $66,150
Hines Cash flow (base)                                          66,150

Excess cash flow @ 70 Hines/30 Zayre                            $6,650
                                                                $2,850
```